STUDENTS MARATHI GRAMMAR

STUDENTS MARATHI GRAMMAR

GANPATRAO R. NAVALKAR

GYAN

Published by

GYAN

Gyan Publishing House
5, Ansari Road
Daryaganj, New Delhi-110002
Phone: 011-47034999, 9811692060
E-mail: books@gyanbooks.com

Distribution Network
gyanbooks.com
India, USA, Canada, UK, Australia, France

ISBN : 978-81-212-3055-1 (PB)
First Published, Original Published 1894

2nd Impression 2020

Printed at: Gyan Press, Delhi.

Students Marathi Grammar
Author: GanpatRao R. Navalkar

THE

STUDENT'S MARATHI GRAMMAR.

BY THE

REV. GANPATRAO R. NAVALKAR,

FELLOW OF THE BOMBAY UNIVERSITY.

"Though it would be a mistake to attempt in our elementary schools to replace an empirical by a scientific knowledge of Grammar, that empirical knowledge of Grammar ought in time to be raised to a real, rational, and satisfying knowledge,—a knowledge not only of facts, but of reasons; a knowledge that teaches us not only what Grammar is, but how it came to be what it is."—*Max Müller.*

THIRD EDITION (REVISED AND ENLARGED).

Bombay:

PRINTED AT THE

EDUCATION SOCIETY'S PRESS, BYCULLA.

1894.

PREFACE TO THE SECOND EDITION.

THIS is a new and enlarged edition of the "STUDENT'S MANUAL OF MARÁṬHÍ GRAMMAR," designed equally for beginners and advanced students. The former are advised to pass over the *Notes,* printed in small type, as well as the portions in the text which are specified as useful at an advanced stage of study. I have given copious explanations, not seldom venturing to offer a rationale of the facts or forms discussed, as intelligent students, in these days, are expected to know more than what is merely elementary and practical. I have also endeavoured to determine the exact form and sense of every grammatical word and inflection; and the value of definite opinions on these points can be truly estimated only by those who are acquainted with the present painful state of uncertainty and doubt that generally prevails. I have, moreover, attempted to simplify and systematise several difficult departments of Maráṭhí grammar. I would specially cite, by way of example, the *Declension of Nouns.* The number of the Declensions has been reduced from six or seven to three, if not absolutely to one, while a most simple method of deriving the crude-form has been suggested. By the aid of two pronominal letters any Maráṭhí noun could be declined with absolute certainty. For this and other important changes in my book, I am indebted chiefly to the *Comparative Grammar* of BOPP, a work which is not more valuable for what it explicitly teaches than for what it obscurely suggests. It is by a study of this wonderful work that I have been led to look for something deeper, truer, and more spiritual in words than what their external form reveals, and it is under its guidance that, I believe, I have attained, though but imperfectly, to the hidden life of some of the Maráṭhí words and inflections. Indeed, there is nothing arbitrary and conventional in language: every form of it is instinct with life and reason. Páṇini may be said to have given it a body of perfect beauty and symmetry, but Bopp has the honour of having communicated to it the breath of life.*

The sections on the Inherent अ, the Accent, the Compound Verbs, &c., may be regarded as quite new and original, while the chapters on Etymology, though they cannot claim much originality, will not fail to prove interesting. They have been written chiefly with the aid of Dr. MUIR's *Sanskrit Texts*, Professor COWEL's *Prákṛit Prakása*, and Mr. BEAME's *Comparative Grammar of the Indo-Aryan Vernaculars*. Very valuable information on the Maráṭhí idioms has been derived from the works of MOLESWORTH, CANDY and STEVENSON.

Besides the works cited above, I have profitably consulted many others, among which I would mention with prominence the miscellaneous writings of Profs. MAX MÜLLER and WHITNEY, presenting, as they do, the results of the modern philological investigations, in a simple and attractive form, lit up with original observations of great beauty and force, as well as the Maráṭhí Grammars of my personal friends, Messrs. DADOBA and GODBOLE, together with the Hindi and Urdú Grammars of the Rev. W. ETHERINGTON and Prof. DOWSON.

I pray that the Divine blessing may rest upon this humble effort to benefit students.

PREFACE TO THE THIRD EDITION.

Some portions of this book have been re-written and a great deal of new matter has been added, which, I trust, will enhance its utility and importance.

---

* "Every form of declension and conjugation, every genitive, and every so-called infinitive and gerund is the result of a long succession of efforts and of intelligent efforts. There is nothing accidental, nothing irregular, nothing without a purpose and meaning in any part of Greek or Latin grammar. No one who has once discovered this hidden life of language, no one who has once found out that what seemed to be merely anomalous and whimsical in language is but, as it were, a petrifaction of thought, of deep, curious, poetical, philosophical thought, will ever rest again till he has descended as far as he can descend into the ancient shafts of human speech, exploring level after level, and testing every successive foundation which supports the surface of each spoken language."—*Max Müller*.

TABLE OF CONTENTS.

PART I.

Orthography.

Etymology.

PART II.

Derivation.

PART III.

Syntax.

PART IV.

Prosody.

APPENDIX.

THE

STUDENT'S MARÁTHÍ GRAMMAR.

CHAPTER I.

Orthography. (वर्णविचार.)

LETTERS: THEIR FORMS AND SOUNDS.

§ 1—§ 14.

1. The Marathi alphabet, as popularly given, consists of fifty-two letters, only fifty of which represent distinct original sounds.

2. The letters are methodically enumerated in the alphabet, the Vowels (स्वर) being given first, and next the Consonants (व्यंजनें).

THE VOWELS.

अ *a*, आ *á*, इ *i*, ई *í*, उ *u*, ऊ *ú*, ऋ *ṛi*, ॠ *ṛí*, ऌ *ḷi*, ॡ *ḷí*, ए *e* ऐ *ai*, ओ *o*, औ *au*, अं *aṁ*, अ: *ah*.

Note.—The sounds represented by अं *aṁ* and अ : *ah* are consonants, but are given along with the vowels as they are always used with them. (Sect. 9.)

THE CONSONANTS.

क *ka*, ख *kha*, ग *ga*, घ *gha*, ङ *ṅa*, च *cha*, छ *chha*, ज *ja*, झ *jha*, ञ *ña*, ट *ṭa*, ठ *ṭha*, ड *ḍa*, ढ *ḍha*, ण *ṇa*, त *ta*, थ *tha*, द *da*, ध *dha*, न *na*, प *pa*, फ *pha*, ब *ba*, भ *bha*, म *ma*, य *ya*, र *ra*, ल *la*, व *va*, श *śa*, ष *sha*, स *sa*, ह *ha*, ळ *ḷa*, क्ष *ksha*, ज्ञ *dnya*.

Note.—क्ष *ksha* and ज्ञ *dnya* are compound consonants and do not represent original simple sounds ; but they are assigned a place in the alphabet only as they are represented by peculiar forms.

3. The Vowels are pronounced freely, the breath being unimpeded by the parts of the mouth, but the breath does not pass so freely when the Consonants are uttered. Hence the distinction between the Vowels and the Consonants.

Note.—" In forming consonants, the breath or voice is stopped or squeezed, with an effect of percussion, sibilation, buzzing, or vibration, in some part of the guttural or oral passage ; and in forming vowels, the breath or voice flows through similar but more open and 'fixed' configurations, which merely shape or mould the breath, without impeding its emission "— A. M. BELL.

4. Besides the general division of the letters of the Marathi alphabet into the Vowels and the Consonants, there are other points of distinction noticeable in the classification of the letters, which are specified below.

Note.—The Marathi alphabet is most perfect, every letter being assigned in it the exact place it is entitled to, in harmony with the scientific laws of utterance.

5. The Vowels are called विवृत or open letters as the larynx is quite open when they are uttered, and the breath passes freely through it (Sect. 3); but in uttering the Consonants, the breath is impeded by the *complete* or *partial* closure of the organs of the month (Sect. 7). When the closure is complete, they are called स्पर्श or contact, and when it is imperfect, they are called either ईषद् विवृत (partially open), or ईषद् स्पृष्ट (partially closed).

6. The open letters may be called *Vocals,* the completely closed, *Mutes,* and the partially open or closed, *Semi-vocals.* Thus—

THE VOCALS.

अ *a*, आ *á*, इ *i*, ई *í*, उ *u*, ऊ *ú*, ऋ *ṛi*, ॠ *ṛí*, ऌ *ḷi*, ॡ *ḷí*, ए *e*, ऐ *ai*, ओ *o*, औ *au*.

THE MUTES.

क *ka*, ख *kha*, ग *ga*, घ *gha*, ङ *ṅa* ; च *cha*, छ *chha*, ज *ja*, झ *jha*, ञ *ña* ; ट *ṭa*, ठ *ṭha*, ड *ḍa*, ढ *ḍha*, ण *ṇa* ; त *ta*, थ *tha*, द *da*, ध *dha*, न *na* ; प *pa*, फ *pha*, ब *ba*, भ *bha*, म *ma*.

THE SEMI-VOCALS.

(1) *Partially Open*, or Liquids.—य *ya*, र *ra*, ल *la*, व *va*.

Note.—These semi-vocals are called अंतःस्थ (or those holding a middle place) by the Sanskrit Grammarians as they stand between the Mutes and the Partially Closed consonants. They are, also, denominated Liquids, as they have a smooth and flowing sound, and easily unite with the other letters.

(2) *Partially Closed*, or Sibilants.—श *śa*, ष *sha*, स *sa*, ह *ha*.

Note.—These are called ऊष्म or sibilants—being uttered with a hissing sound.

7. The mutes are further arranged in the alphabet into five classes according to the *organs* or parts of the mouth which affect their utterance. The organs or parts of the mouth (स्थानें) are five, and they are *the throat, the palate, the roof of the palate, the teeth* and *the lips*. We give below the five organic classes of the Mutes:—

1. *Gutturals* or कंठ्य (throat sounds): क *ka*, ख *kha*, ग *ga*, घ *gha*, ङ *ṅa*.
2. *Palatals* or तालव्य (palate sounds): च *cha*, छ *chha*, ज *ja*, झ *jha*, ञ *ña*.
3. *Linguals* or मूर्धन्य (top-palate sounds): ट *ṭa*, ठ *ṭha*, ड *ḍa*, ढ *ḍha*, ण *ṇa*.
4. *Dentals* or दंत्य (teeth sounds): त *ta*, थ *tha*, द *da*, ध *dha*, न *na*.
5. *Labials* ओष्ठ्य (lip sounds): प *pa*, फ *pha*, ब *ba*, भ *bha*, म *ma*.

8. In each of the above five classes of the mutes the letters are distinguished as *Surds* (अघोष), *Sonants* (घोषवत्), *Aspirates* (महाप्राण), *Non-aspirates* (अल्पप्राण), and *Nasals* अनुनासिक. The first two letters are surds, and the last three sonants. The first surd and the first sonant are unaspirated; the second surd and the second sonant are aspirated; and the last sonant is a nasal. Thus—

Organic Classes.	Mutes (स्पर्श).				
	Surd.		Sonant.		
	Unaspirate.	Aspirate.	Unaspirate.	Aspirate.	Nasal.
Gutturals	क *ka*	ख *kha*	ग *ga*	घ *gha*	ङ *ṅa*
Palatals...	च *cha*	छ *chha*	ज *ja*	झ *jha*	ञ *ña*
Linguals..	ट *ṭa*	ठ *ṭha*	ड *ḍa*	ढ *ḍha*	ण *ṇa*
Dentals..	त *ta*	थ *tha*	द *da*	ध *dha*	न *na*
Labials..	प *pa*	फ *pha*	ब *ba*	भ *bha*	म *ma*

Note.—In pronouncing the surds (अघोष voiceless), the breath is simply used, but not the voice, but in uttering the sonants (घोषवत् voiced) the voice is used. The aspirates (महाप्राण strong breaths) are pronounced with an audible breath as *h*. The nasals (अनुनासिक co-nasal or nasalised) are uttered through both the nose and the mouth simultaneously. The unaspirated letters are अल्पप्राण (weak breaths).

9. Of the letters of the alphabet which are not included in the above details of classification are the अं, अः, ळ, क्ष and ज्ञ.

(*a*) The dot over अं is called the *Anusvár*, and it marks a purely nasal sound uttered exclusively through the nose like the *n* in the French word *bon*, *unmodified by the organs of the mouth.* It is put on a vowel, and uttered after it. The purely nasal sound of the Anusvár is called नासिक्य or nasal, and the modified nasal sound is called अनुनासिक (Sect. 8).

(*b*) The two dots by the side of अः are called the *Visarga*, and they are put by the side of a vowel to express a strong aspirate. The Visarga is said to be produced entirely in the chest, unmodified by the organs of the mouth. It belongs to the class of the sibilants.

(*c*) The ळ *ḷa*, is a modification of ल *la*, and does not occur in Sanskrit, except in some passages of the Vedas, where it is used for ड *ḍa*. It belongs to the class of the linguals.

(*d*) The क्ष *ksha* and ज्ञ *dnya* are compound consonants, for which see Section 14.

10. The above details in regard to the classification of the letters of the Alphabet, including the vowels, are put together in the following table:—

Organic Classes. (स्थानवर्ग)	Mutes. (स्पर्श)					Semi-Vocals. ईषद्वि॰or स्पृ॰		Vocals. (विवृत)
	Surds.		Sonants.			Sonants.	Surds	Sonants.
	Uuaspirated. (अल्पप्राण)	Aspirated. (महाप्राण)	Unaspirated.	Aspirated.	Nasals. (अनुनासिक)	Liquids. (अंतःस्थ)	Sibilants. (ऊष्म)	
Gutturals (कंठ्य) ..	क	ख	ग	घ	ङ	...	ह	अ, आ, ए, ऐ.
Palatals (तालव्य)..	च	छ	ज	झ	ञ	य	श	इ, ई.
Linguals (मूर्धन्य)...	ट	ठ	ड	ढ	ण	र	ष	ऋ, ॠ.
Dentals (दंत्य) ..	त	थ	द	ध	न	ल	स	ऌ, ॡ.
Labials (ओष्ठ्य) ...	प	फ	ब	भ	म	व	...	उ, ऊ, ओ, औ.

11. There are two modes of writing Marathi, the *Bálbodh*, and *Moḍí*, the former being employed in printed books, and the latter in epistolary and business transactions. The alphabet given above in the second Section is in the Bálbodh character.

Note.—Balbodha literally means "teachable to children," and Moḍí, "broken or crooked." The Bálbodha character is classically called *Devanágarí* or relating to the city of the gods, and is exclusively employed in writing Sanskrit, the language of the gods, from which Marathi is derived. The Moḍí letters are given in the Appendix.

Note.—The Balbodha character is said to be of Semitic origin, but the point has not yet been conclusively established.

12. Marathi is written from left to right; and in forming the letters, the principal portion is written first, then the perpendicular line, and the transverse line last of all. Thus, ० then व, and then व *va*; so ग, ग, ग *ga*; ८, ख, ख, ख *kha*.

13. The letters are thus pronounced :—

The Vowels.

अ	*a*	corresponds	in sound	to	*a*	in "Roman"
आ	*á*	„	„	„	*a*	in "*far*"
इ	*i*	„	„	„	*i*	in "pin"
ई	*í*	„	„	„	*i*	in "police"
उ	*u*	„	„	„	*u*	in "put"
ऊ	*ú*	„	„	„	*u*	in "rude"
ऋ	*ṛi*	„	„	„	*ri*	in "*rid*"
ॠ	*ṛí*	„	„	„	*ri*	in "*read*"
ऌ	*ḷi*	„	„	„	*li*	in "*lid*"
ॡ	*ḷí*	„	„	„	*lea*	in "*lead*"
ए	*e*	„	„	„	*e*	in "there"
ऐ	*ai*	„	„	„	*ai*	in "*ai*sle" or "Mai" (Italian)
ओ	*o*	„	„	„	*o*	in "so"
औ	*ou*	„	„	„	*ow*	in "now"

The Consonants.

क	*ka*	corresponds	to *k*	in "*k*ing"
ख	*kha*	„	„ *kh*	in "*kh*an"
ग	*ga*	„	„ *g*	in "*g*ive"
घ	*gha*	„	„ *gh*	in "lo*g*—*h*ut"
ङ	*ṅa*	„	„ *n*	in "si*n*g"
च	*cha*	„	„ *ch*	in "*ch*urch"
छ	*chha*	„	„ *ch* + *h*	
ज	*ja*	„	„ *j*	in "*j*et"
झ	*jha*	„	„ *s*	in "plea*s*ure"
ञ	*ña*	„	„ *n*	in "si*n*ge"
ट	*ṭa*	„	„ *t*	in "*t*rumpet"
ठ	*ṭha*	„	„ *t* + *h*	
ड	*ḍa*	„	„ *d*	in "*drain*"
ढ	*ḍha*	„	„ *d* + *h*	
ण	*ṇa*	„	„ *n*	in "di*n*t"
त	*ta*	„	„ *t*	in "*t*ube"

थ *tha*	corresponds to	*th*		in "*th*in"
द *da*	,,	,, *d*		in "*d*ue"
ध *dha*	,,	,, *d*	+	*h*
न *na*	,,	,, *n*		in "the*n*"
प *pa*	,,	,, *p*		in "*p*ush"
फ *pha*	,,	,, *ph*		in "u*ph*ill"
ब *ba*	,,	,, *b*		in "*b*ag"
भ *bha*	,,	,, *b*	+	*h*
म *ma*	,,	,, *m*		in "*m*an"
य *ya*	,,	,, *y*		in "*y*ou"
र *ra*	,,	,, *r*		in "*R*ome"
ल *la*	,,	,, *l*		in "*l*ive"
व *va*	,,	,, *v*		in "*v*ein"
श *śa*	,,	,, *ss*		in "se*ss*ion"
ष *sha*	,,	,, *sh*		in "*sh*ew"
स *sa*	,,	,, *s*		in "*s*on"
ह *ha*	,,	,, *h*		in "*h*and"

ळ *ḷa* has no exact equivalent.

14. The following particulars regarding the pronunciation of the Marathi letters may be carefully noted :—

(1) The letters ङ *ṅa* and ञ *ña* are never used in Marathi.

(2) The letters च *cha*, छ *chha*, ज *ja*, and झ *jha* are given in the alphabet with their classical sounds, but they are usually pronounced in Marathi as *tsa*, *tsha*, *dza*, and *dzha*. The letters assume their classical or fully palatal sound in words of Sanskrit origin as well as when they are combined with इ, ई and ए, otherwise they invariably have the dento-palatal sound; thus, विचार *vichár* a thought, Sk.; चाकर *tsákar*, a servant, चौरंग *tsaurang*, a stool, a seat; चिमटा *chimtá*, a pinch; चेंगट *chengat*, slow. The Marathi word चार four, is always pronounced as *chár*.

Note.—The genitive termination assuming ई or ए may optionally be uttered with the dento-palatal sound, in harmony with its origin; as, त्याचे आईबाप, *tyátse ái báp*, his parents; त्याची चाकरी, *tyátsí tsákarí*, his employment.

(3) The linguals ट *ṭa*, ठ *ṭha*, ड *ḍa*, ढ *ḍha*, and ण *ṇa*, are somewhat differently pronounced from the English "t," "d," &c. In pronouncing the Marathi linguals the tip of the tongue is turned round, and forcibly struck against the palate.

(4) The letter ड *ḍa* is pronounced in two ways: when it commences a word, it has its usual sound; but when it comes in any other position, in the middle or at the end of a word, it is pronounced as *rḍ*; डफ *daph*, a drum; बडबड *barḍbarḍ*, a confused noise: पडत *parḍat*, falling. It, however, assumes its initial sound, both medially and finally, when it is preceded by the *anusvár*, or makes up a double letter; thus, बंड, a rebellion, is *band*, not *banrd*; अड्डा, a stand for vehicles, &c., is *aḍḍá*.

Note.—In the Dakhan, the lingual ण *ṇa* is often erroneously pronounced as the dental न *na*; कन *kan* for कण an atom.

(5) The dental letters त *ta*, थ *tha*, द *da*, and ध *dha*, have, strictly speaking, no corresponding sounds in English. The Marathi letters are pronounced by making the upper surface of the tongue touch the gums, while in uttering the English "t," and "d," the tip of the tongue is raised a little higher up.

(6) The letter फ *pha* is a pure labial, and not dento-palatal like the English "f," the latter being uttered by pressing the upper front teeth against the lower lip, and trying to emit an aspirated sound. The Marathi फ *pha* is pronounced, on the other hand, by pressing the upper and lower lips against each other, and attempting to emit forcibly a rough aspirated sound.

(7) The Marathi व *va* cannot be accurately represented in English; it is a dento-palatal sound like "*v*" without its aspirate, *i. e.*, its *h* sound. The English "w" is purely labial produced by compressing and elongating the lips, as in uttering *oo* in "cool." The Marathi वाल, a kind of seed, is *vál*, not "wall."

(8) The letter श *śa* is a palatal, and belongs to the class of च *cha*, छ *chha*, &c.; ष *sha*, a lingual, belonging to the class of ट *ṭa*, ठ *ṭha*, &c.; and स *sa* a dental, agreeing with the class of त *ta*, थ *tha*, &c. The full sound of each of these sibilants could be mastered by attempting to utter them along with the class of letters to which they belong; thus,

च *cha*, छ *chha*, ज *ja*, झ *jha*, श *śa*.
ट *ṭa*, ठ *ṭha*, ड *ḍa*. ढ *ḍha*, ष *sha*,
त *ta*, थ *tha*, द *da*, ध *dha*, स *sa*.

(9) The letter ळ *ḷa*, which belongs to the class of the linguals, has no corresponding sound in English. It never begins a word in Marathi and is usually substituted for the ल *la* of Sanskrit words. In Canarese and the other Dravidian languages, it is freely interchanged with द *da* and ड *ḍa*.

(10) The क्ष *ksha* and ज्ञ *dnya* are not written as other compound consonants are, but have each a peculiar form, on which account they are assigned a place in the Alphabet, and given in the dictionaries as independent letters. The क्ष is composed of क *ka* and ष *sha*, and may be written as क्‌ष *ksha* and also pronounced as such; but ज्ञ *dnya*, which is composed of ज *ja* and ञ *ña*, may be written as ज्‌ञ, but not pronounced as such in Marathi, though it assumes the sound in Sanskrit. In Marathi it is pronounced as *dnya*, as if it was composed of द *da* न *na* and य *ya*. In Gujarati it has the sound of *gnya*, and in Hindi of *gya*; as ज्ञानोबा, *jñánobá*—M. *Dnyánobá* G. *Gnyánobá*, and *H. Gyánobá*.

CHAPTER II.

On the Nature of the Letters.

1. THE VOWELS.

§ 15—§ 28.

§ 15. The vowels are simple sounds, which can be uttered by themselves without the aid of other letters. They are in all fourteen in number.

§ 16. The vowels are either *similar* समान or *dissimilar* असमान; thus, अ is similar to अ or आ, but dissimilar to every other; so इ is similar to इ or ई, but dissimilar to अ, उ, ओ, &c.

§ 17. The vowels are further considered as *short* (ह्रस्व), or *long* (दीर्घ,) according to the *time* they take in utterance. The short vowels are uttered in half of the time that the long are, and are said to be equal to one मात्रा or moment. अ, इ, उ, ऋ, and ऌ are short, and the remaining nine vowels आ, ई, ऊ, ॠ, ॡ, ए, ऐ, ओ, औ, are long.

§ 18. The long vowels are produced either by the union of two *similar* vowels, or by the coalition of two *dissimilar* vowels. The former, by way of distinction, are simply denominated *long vowels* (दीर्घस्वर), and the latter, *diphthongs* (संयुक्तस्वर). When both the uniting vowels in the diphthong are fully sounded, it is said to be a *proper diphthong* or वृद्धि (augmentation), and when neither of the vowels is heard, but both melt into a third sound, it is said to be an *improper diphthong* or गुण (virtue).

The Long Vowels.

अ *a* + अ *a* = आ *á*	ऋ *ṛi* + ऋ *ṛi* = ॠ *ṛí*
इ *i* + इ *i* = ई *í*	ऌ *ḷi* + ऌ *ḷi* = ॡ *ḷí*
उ *u* + उ *u* = ऊ *ú*	

The Diphthongs.

Imp. Diph.	*Prop. Diph.*
अ *a* + इ *i* or ई *í* = ए *e*.	आ *á* + इ *i* or ई *í* = ऐ *ai*
अ *a* + उ *u* or ऊ *ú* = ओ *o*	आ *á* + उ *u* or ऊ *ú* = औ *aú*

Note.—आ is considered a Vriddhi vowel, and is equivalent to आ + अ.

Note.—"That in ए *e* and ओ *o* a short, in ऐ *ai* and औ *au*, a long *a* is bound up, I infer from this, that where, in order to avoid a hiatus, the last element of a diphthong merges into its corresponding semi-vowel, out of ए and ओ proceed the sounds अय् and अव् (with short *a*), but out of ऐ and औ proceed *ái* and *áu*. In Zend आइ always stands in the place of ऐ and आऊ or आओ in that of औ. In combination (संधि) आ + ई does not make ऐ but only ए; for in combination आ is shortened to अ, as in infletcional changes आ before a dissimilar vowel entirely disappears; दा + उस् = दुस्."—*Bopp*.

§ 19. The vowels are, also, viewed as *strong* or *weak*, *grave* (गुरु) or *light* (लघु), in regard to the *manner* in which they affect each other, in *inflection* and *composition*. Thus "अ and आ are graver than the corresponding quantity of the vowel इ" or ई; while ऊ and the diphthongs are most strong and obstinate. (*See Declensions*.)

Note.—In Latin, also, *i* may be considered as lighter than *a*, and takes the place of *a*, "when a root with an original *a* would be burthened with a duplication of sound. Hence, for example, *abjicio* for *abjacio*, *tetigi* for *tetagi*."

"The *u* is a vowel too decided and full of character to allow of its being exchanged in this language (Sanskrit), in relief of its weight, for any other. It is the most obstinate of all, and admits of no exclusion from a terminating syllable, in cases where *a* and *i* admit of suppression. Nor will it retire from a reduplicated syllable in cases where *a* allows to be weakened down to *i*.

"In the Gothic, also, the *u* may boast of its pertinacity: it remains firm as the terminating vowel of classes of nouns where *a* and *i* have undergone suppression, and in no single case has it been extinguished or transmuted." "In Arabic the *u* takes precedence in nobility, as having its place in the nominative, while the declension is governed by the change of the terminating vowel."—*Bopp*.

Obs.—The Maráthí strong vowels can be *weakened*; and there are three ways of weakening them—1st, by putting the Anusvár over them; as तळें a tank, तळ्याला to a tank, the diphthong being displaced in declension; 2nd, by making them terminate feminine and neuter nouns; as बायको a woman, बायका women; जाळें a net, जाळीं nets: and 3rdly, by their being uttered by people of a soft and feeble *physique*. Now most of the words in ऊ, which, strictly speaking, should not change in declension, are inflected in the Konkan, but they pertinaciously retain their forms in the Dakhan. Thus, an inhabitant of the latter province will never say जळवेला, but जळूला (to a leech), or बाजवेला, but बाजूला to a side; while the native of the Konkan will mutilate one and all such forms. But when the vowels, though weakened by being affixed to feminine nouns, terminate nouns which designate *persons*, they are raised to a position of honour and dignity, and then they reject all mutilation, whether as regards their inflection in the crude form, or in the plural form.

§ 20. The vowels इ, ई, उ, ऊ, ऋ, ॠ, ऌ, ॡ, and the diphthongs are sometimes changed to the liquids (§ 6) in *inflection* and *composition*, and the liquids in reference to these vowels, are denominated *semi-vowels*. Thus—

The Liquids.		
य *ya*	corresponds to	इ *i*, ई *í*, ए *e*, and ऐ *ai*.
व *va*	,,	,, उ *u*, ऊ *ú*, ओ *o*, and औ *au*.
र *ra*	,,	,, ऋ *ṛi* and ॠ *ṛí*.
ल *la*	,,	,, ऌ *ḷi* and ॡ *ḷí*.

Note.—In Maráthi, the strong vowels, if forced to a displacement by a semi-vowel, not corresponding to their class, drop the distinguishing element of the obnoxious semi-vowel and substitute a semi-vowel corresponding to their own class; thus गहूं wheat + याला = गव्हाला to wheat, and not गह्याला.

2. THE CONSONANTS.

§ 21. A consonant is a letter which cannot be sounded by itself, without the aid of a vowel. When the consonant is written without the union of a vowel, the mark, called *viráma* or stoppage, is put below it; as क् *k*. A consonant by itself is equal to half a moment. (§ 17.)

§ 22. The consonants are given in the alphabet combined with the vowel अ *a*, and its presence is indicated by the omission of the *viráma* or stoppage. The अ is said to be *inherent* in the consonants; thus क् *k*, + अ *a* = क *ka*.

§ 23. In reference to *pronunciation* and *versification*, the consonants are considered as *strong*, or *weak*. Those consonants are strong which require a *strong effort* to utter them, and those are weak which are easily uttered. The following is a table of strong and weak consonants :—

I.—*Strong consonants :*	क	ख	ग	घ	
	च	छ	ज	झ	
	ट	ठ	ड	ढ	
	त	थ	द	ध	
	प	फ	ब	भ	
II.—*Weak consonants :*	ङ	ञ	ण	न	म
	य	र	ल	व	
	श	ष	स	ह	ळ

§ 24. A consonant may combine with one or more consonants, and produce a *compound consonant ;* as क् *k* + न *na* = क्न *kna ;* स् *s* + थ *tha* = स्थ *stha ;* क् *k* + म् *m* + य *ya* = क्म्य *kmya.* The compound consonant is called in Maráṭhí जोडाक्षर a compound letter.

§ 25. In the combination of the consonants, the last letter usually retains its full form. The changes which the initial consonants undergo are confined to their perpendicular line, which is dropped. Thus, in the compound letter प्य, the प *pa*, which is the first member, drops its perpendicular stroke, while य retains its full form.

§ 26. Some consonants assume peculiar forms in combination, the principal of which are the following :—

(*a*) When र *ra* forms the first member, it is written as ᐟ at the top of the letter with which it unites; thus in the word धर्म *dharma,* duty, र *ra* is combined with म *ma.* This form of र *ra* is called रेफ *reph.* Any mark over a letter, besides the *reph,* is put on the left of the *reph* ; धार्मिक *dhármik,* religious ; पर्यंत *paryant,* until. When the र *ra* forms the last member, it is changed to a transverse stroke put at the foot of the letter with which it unites; as क्र *kra* = क् *k* + र *ra.* The final र *ra,* in combination with the cerebrals ट *ṭa,* ठ *ṭha,* ड *ḍa,* and ढ *ḍha,* assumes two strokes ; as ट्र *ṭra* = ट् *ṭ* + र *ra ;* ड्र *ḍra* = ड् *ḍ* + र *ra.*

(*b*) श *śa* optionally assumes the form of श्‍ in combination with a consonant ; श् *ś* + न *na* = श्न *śna.*

(*c*) The combinations of क् *k* + ष *sha,* and ज् *j* + ञ *ña,* are क्ष *ksha* and ज्ञ *jña.* (§ 9.)

(*d*) Some compounds assume two forms; क्र or क्र *kra*; त्र or त्र *tra*; स्थ or स्थ *stha*.

§27. The following is a list of the principal compound letters:—

क्क *k-ka*	ट्ट *ṭ-ṭa*	द्म *d-ma*	व्र *v-ra*
क्त *k-ta*	ट्य *ṭ-ya*	द्ब *d-ba*	श्च *s'-cha*
क्त्व *k-tva*	ठ्र *ṭh-ra*	ध्ध *dh-dha*	श्र *s'-ra*
क्न *k-na*	ठ्य *ṭh-ya*	ध्न *dh-na*	श्न *s'-na*
क्म *k-ma*	ड्ग *ḍ-ga*	ध्र *dh-ra*	श्य *s'-ya*
क्र *k-ra*	ड्य *ḍ-ya*	ध्य *dh-ya*	श्ल *s'-la*
क्य *k-ya*	ड्व *ḍ-va*	र्ध्व *r-dh-va*	श्व *s'-va*
क्ल *k-la*	ड्म *ḍ-ma*	न्न *n-na*	ष्क *sh-ka*
क्व *k-va*	ढ्य *ḍh-ya*	न्ह *n-ha*	ष्क्र *sh-k-ra*
क्ष *k-sha*	ण्ण *ṇ-ṇa*	प्त *p-ta*	ष्ट *sh-ṭa*
क्ष्य *k-shya*	ण्म *ṇ-ma*	प्स *p-sa*	ष्ट्र *sh-ṭ-ra*
क्ष्व *k-shva*	र्ण्य *r-ṇ-ya*	प्न *p-na*	ष्ट्व *sh-ṭ-va*
ख्य *kh-ya*	ण्ह *ṇ-ha*	प्य *p-ya*	ष्ट्य *sh-ṭ-ya*
ग्ध *g-dha*	त्त *t-ta*	प्म *p-ma*	ष्ठ *sh-ṭha*
ग्न *g-na*	त्य *t-ya*	प्ल *p-la*	ष्ठ्य *sh-ṭh-ya*
ग्र *g-ra*	त्र *t-ra*	प्र *p-ra*	ष्प *sh-pa*
ग्र्य *g-r-ya*	त्प्र *t-p-ra*	ब्ध *b-dha*	ष्ण *sh-ṇa*
ग्ल *g-la*	त्स *t-sa*	ब्र *b-ra*	ष्य *sh-ya*
घ्य *gh-ya*	त्र्य *t-r-ya*	भ्य *bh-ya*	स्क *s-ka*
घ्र *gh-ra*	त्स्य *t-s-ya*	भ्र *bh-ra*	स्ख *s-kha*
घ्व *gh-va*	त्थ *t-tha*	भ्ण *bh-ṇa*	स्त *s-ta*
घ्न *gh-na*	त्स्न *t-s-na*	भ्व *bh-va*	स्र *s-ra*
ङ्क *ṅ-ka*	त्त्र *t-t-ra*	भ्न *bh-na*	स्फ *s-pha*
ङ्क्त *ṅ-k-ta*	थ्य *th-ya*	म्र *m-ra*	स्य *s-ya*
च्य *ch-ya*	द्ग *d-ga*	म्व *m-va*	ह्न *h-na*
च्च *ch-cha*	द्व *d-va*	म्म *m-ma*	ह्म *h-ma*
च्छ *ch-chha*	द्य *d-ya*	य्व *y-va*	ह्य *h-ya*
च्छ्व *ch-chhva*	द्द *d-da*	ल्क *l-ka*	ह्र *h-ra*
च्म *ch-ma*	द्र्य *d-r-ya*	ल्य *l-ya*	ह्व *h-va*
च्छ्र *ch-chhra*	द्ब *d-ba*	ल्प *l-pa*	ह्ल *h-la*
ज्ज *j-ja*	द्ब्र *d-b-ra*	ल्म *l-ma*	
ज्र *j-ra*	द्व्य *d-v-ya*	ल्ल *l-la*	
ज्व *j-va*	द्र *d-ra*	व्य *v-ya*	

Note.—This list is given only for reference, and not for study. The student can, after he has mastered the alphabet, easily decipher the compound letters in the reading lesson as well as form them in the writing exercise.

§ 28. The compound consonants are divided into three classes, according to their *composition*, viz., the *strong*, the *weak*, and the *mixed*. (See § 23.)

I.—The *strong* are wholly composed of strong letters : as क्त *kta*, प्त *pta*, ब्ज *bja*, ग्द *gda*, &c.

II.—The *mixed* are composed partly of strong and partly of weak letters : as त्र *tra*, न्द *nda*, ध्य *dhya*, &c.

III.—The *weak* are composed wholly of weak letters : as श्य *śya*, र्म *rma*, ल्व *lva*, &c.

CHAPTER III.

On the Powers of the Letters.

SYLLABIFICATION.

§ 29—§ 39.

§ 29. A vowel by itself, or in union with a consonant, forms a syllable; and a syllable is as much of a word as can be uttered at once. Thus, आई *ái*, a mother, is a word of two syllables, आ *á* + ई *í*; आपण *ápaṇ* is composed of three syllables, आ *á* + प *pa* + ण *ṇa*. (See § 33, 1.)

§ 30. When a vowel combines with the consonants, it assumes a modified form; thus क् *k* + आ *á* = का *ká*: the perpendicular stroke by the side of का *ká* represents the आ.

आ *á*, इ *i*, ई *í*, उ *u*, ऊ *ú*, ए *e*, ऐ *ai*, ओ *o*, औ *au*.
ा ि ी ु ू े ै ो ौ

§ 31. We give below क *ka* and ट *ṭa* in combination with the vowels:—

क *ka*, का *ká*, कि *ki*, की *kí*, कु *ku*, कू *kú*, के *ke*, कै *kai*, को *ko*, कौ *kau*.

ट *ṭa*, टा *ṭá*, टि *ṭi*, टी *ṭí*, टु *ṭu*, टू *ṭú*, टे *ṭe*, टै *ṭai*, टो *ṭo*, टौ *ṭau*.

Note.—The vowels ऋ, *ri* ॠ *rí*, ऌ *ḷi*, and ॡ *ḷí*, assume these modified forms respectively:—

ृ, ॄ, ॢ, ॣ.

Note.—The following is an example of क *ka* in combination with ऋ, ॠ, ऌ and ॡ:—

कृ *kri*, कॄ *krí*, कॢ *kḷi*, कॣ *kḷí*.

Note.—श *ś* is optionally changed to श्‍ combination with the vowels; as शु or श्‍ु *śu*.

§ 32. The Maráṭhís denominate the tables of syllabification बाराखड्या *Bárákhaḍyá* (= बारा + अक्षऱ्या "twelve-lettered" rows), and to make up the number "twelve in each row," the *Anusvára* and the *Visarga* are added; as कं *kam* and कः *kah*; टं *tam* and टः *tah*. Here is a *Bárákhaḍi* with its complete number of twelve syllables:—

ग *ga*, गा *gá*, गि *gi*, गी *gí*, गु *gu*, गू *gú*, गे *ge*, गै *gai*, गो *go*, गौ *gau*, गं *gam*, गः *gah*.

SYLLABIC PRONUNCIATION.

§ 33. The letters or syllables which compose a Maráṭhí word are not all pronounced in a uniform way. Some are *fully* sounded, some *imperfectly*, and some others *forcibly*.

1. A syllable, *composed of* अ *a*, may, or may not, be fully sounded; thus, कळप a flock = *ka-ḷap:* the last letter प is imperfectly uttered, making as it were a dissyllabic word, while क and ळ are fully sounded.

2. When a syllable is *nasalised*, or is *followed* by a *Visarga*, or by a *compound letter*, it is forcibly pronounced, or, in other words, *accented*: as अंग a body = *ang*: धिःकार contempt = *dhih-kár*; घट्ट firm = *ghaṭṭ*.

§ 34. Hence the laws of Maráṭhí syllabic pronunciation apply to—(1) the Inherent अ, (2) the Anusvára, (3) the Visarga, and (4) the Compound letters.

Obs.—Most of these laws of syllabic pronunciation have been announced for the first time, but they are most useful, and apply to all the Indian vernaculars derived from Sanskrit. They are treated in a detailed form below, to which the student is advised to direct his attention after he has made some advance in Maráthí reading and grammar.

(1) *The Inherent* अ.

§ 35. The following rules apply to the pronunciation of the *inherent* अ:—

1. The final अ is always silent, and the initial fully sounded; घर *ghar*, a house.

2. In a word of *three* letters or syllables, the inherent अ, immediately preceding the final silent अ, is always sounded; कापड *ká-pa-ḍ*, cloth; वळण *va-ḷa-ṇ*, inclination. If the final be any other vowel, the preceding अ becomes silent; कापडें *ká-p-den*, clothes; चाळणी *tsá-l-ṇí*, a sieve.

When a word of three syllables is inflected by a syllable composed of any other vowel than अ, (as, for instance the inflection ला or तो) the third syllable in the inherent अ is silent, and not fully sounded as in a radical word of four syllables like उलगडा (*ul-ga-dá*); as विसर forget thou, + ला= विसरला he forgot=*vi-sar-lá*, and not *vis-ra-lá*.

3. In a word of *four* syllables, the first and the third inherent अ are always sounded, and the second and the fourth are silent; as करवत *ka-r-va-t* or करवती *ka-r-va-tí*, a saw; उलगडा *u-l-ga-dá*, an explanation; मेहनत *me-h-nat*, labour.

Note.—Persons often infringe this rule when two *similar* consonants with the inherent अ come together in a word: they erroneously pronounce both the letters fully. For instance, येववत being able to come =*yev-vat*, is pronounced as *ye-va-vat*. The existence of two similar consonants is indicated by the *accent*, as in the case of the compound letters.

4. In a word of *five* syllables, the first, the third, and the fourth अ are fully sounded, if the final is अ, otherwise, only the first and the third, as in a word of four syllables; (1) कळमळत *ka-ḷ-ma-ḷa-t*; सारखपद resemblance. (2) कळमळतें *ka-ḷ-ma-ḷ-ten*; वरसवळा *va-r-tu-v-ḷá*, an extra payment.

Note.—These rules, so important in reference to Maráthí and the other Indian vernaculars, do not apply to Sanskṛit, in which every letter is fully uttered unless a *viráma* be subscribed at the foot of it; as देव a god=Sk. *de-va* (but in Maráthí=*de-v*).

Obs.—In the Dakhan, every inherent अ is fully sounded, and even the educated classes, unless they have long resided in Poona and its vicinity, are prone to do the same; thus, गोधडी, a coverlet=*god-ḍi* (but in the Dakhan—*go-da-ḍi*).

(2) *The Anusvára.*

§ 36. The Anusvára, in regard to its pronunciation, has other peculiarities besides those of the accent, and we shall treat of the former, before we consider the latter characteristics.

§ 37. The Anusvára is a convenient sign for the nasal sounds in the language, which are of four kinds. They are the *Organic*, the *Násikya*, the *Provincial*, and the *Classical.*

1. When the Anusvára is pronounced like any of the nasals ङ, ञ, ण, न, and म, representing the five *organs* of speech (§ 7), it is said to have an *Organic* sound; कंठ the throat=कण्ठ *kaṇṭh*; अंक a figure=अङ्क *aṅk.*

2. When the Anusvára is simply pronounced through the nose, without giving it any organic sound, as in the French word *bon*, it is said to be a *Násikya* (नासिक्य), or a pure nasal. This is the original and principal sound of the Anusvára, and may be optionally represented by this mark; as अँ *ă*; जँव *dzăv*, barley.

Note.—The Násikya is usually omitted in the Dakhan, and when it is considered necessary to pronounce it distinctly, chiefly in honorific forms, it is changed, even by the higher classes, to the dental न; त्यांला *tyă'la* to them, erroneously त्यानला *tyá-n-lá.*

3. When the Anusvára assumes the sound of *nv*, a Maráthi substitution for the Sanskrit म्, it is said to be *provincial*; as संरक्षण protection, is *sanvrakshaṇa.*

4. When the Anusvára, as in purely Sanskrit words, doubles the letter which follows it, assuming, at the same time, a weakened nasalised sound, it is said to be *classical*; as संयोग junction = सँय्योग *saỹyoga.*

§ 38. The Anusvára assumes the above four sounds in the following positions :—

1. When the Anusvára is followed by a *sonant mute* (§ 8, it assumes the *organic* sound, *i.e.*, the sound of the nasal corresponding to the class of that mute ;

Sk. दंभ hypocrisy = दम्भ *dambha* (म् *m.*)
M. मांडी a thigh = माण्डी *mándí* (ण् *n.*)

2. But when the Anusvàra is followed by a *surd mute*, it may assume either (*a*) the *organic* sound, or (*b*) the *násikya* sound.

(*a*) It assumes the *organic* sound if it is placed over a *short* letter; as सुंठ dry ginger = सुण्ठ *sunṭh ;* डंका a drum = डङ्का *ḍaṅká*.

(*b*) It takes the *násikya* sound, if it is placed over a long vowel ; कांटा a thorn = *kåṭá ;* आंत in = *å't*. This rule does not apply to Sanskṛit words occurring in Maráthi ; as, कांता a wife = कान्ता *kántá*.

Note.—In Sanskrit words, the Anusvára always assumes the sound of the nasal corresponding to the class of the mute that follows it ; as अंत = अन्त *anta*, an end ; शंख = शङ्ख *śankha*, a shell. In Sanskṛit, moreover, the Anusvára might be optionally substituted, in writing, by its corresponding nasal letter, as in the above examples, अंत or अन्त, शंख or शङ्ख. In Maráthí this mode of writing may not be followed even in regard to Sanskṛit words:

3. When the Anusvára is followed by the semi-vocals (§ 6), it assumes *three* kinds of sounds, viz. (*a*) the *násikya*, (*b*) the *provincial*, and (*c*) the *classical*.

(*a*) In all pure Maráthi words, the Anusvára assumes the *násikya* sound; as दंव dew = *dåv* ; भोंसकणें to pierce = *bhôsakṇe* ; सांई a religious mendicant = *så'i*.

It assumes the *násikya* sound, also when it is placed over the final letter of a Maráthi word; कं *kå*, a musical note. In Sanskṛit कं would be pronounced as कम् *kam*.

(*b*) In all Sanskṛit words, the Anusvára assumes either the *provincial*, or the *classical* sound.

(1) The Anusvára followed by र *ra*, श *śa*, ष *sha* स *sa*, and ह *ha*, assumes the *provincial* sound, *i.e.*, the sound of *nv*. Thus,

संरक्षण protection = *sanvrakshaṇa.*
संशय a doubt = *sanisaya.*
संसार the world = *sanvsára.*
संहार massacre = *sanvhára.*

(2) The Anusvára followed by य *ya,* ल *la,* व *va,* take the classical sound, *i.e.*, it doubles the letters, य, ल, and व, giving them a slightly nasalised sound (§ 30, 4):—

संयोग junction = सय्ँयोग *sayyoga.*
संलग्न connection = सल्ँलग्न *sallagna.*
संवाद conversation = सव्ँवाद *savváda.*

Note.—"Besides the five nasal letters, there are still three nasalised letters, the य्, ल् and व्, or यँ, लँ, and वँ, *y, l, v,* which are used to represent a final म् *m,* if followed by an intial य् *y,* ल् *l,* व् *v,* and modified by the pronunciation of these three semi-vowels."—*Max Müller.*

Note.—"The only consonants which have no corresponding nasals are र् *r,* श् *ś,* ष् *sh,* स् *s,* ह् *h.*"—*Max Müller.*

The Accent.

§ 39. In Maráṭhi every word is uttered in an even tone, the initial syllable being alone, in the effort of utterance, slightly raised above the others; but accent, in the sense of *increased force,* as in English, is foreign to Maráṭhi, except in the three following instances:—

1. When a letter is followed by a compound letter, it is accented; as घट्ट *ghaṭṭ,* forcibly; पक्का *pakka,* complete. But the accent may be either *weak,* or *strong.* If the compound letter is composed of strong letters (§ 23), the accent is strong, but if of weak letters, it is weak. Thus,

I.—*Strong:* खड्ग a sword; शब्द a word; भक्त a devotee; मुक्ति salvation.

II.—*Mixed:* कङ्कण a bracelet; चञ्चु, a beak; चंद्र the moon; लग्न a marriage; शुष्क dry; पुस्तक a book; मार्ग a road; सर्प a serpent; सत्य truth; मद्य wine.

III.—*Weak:* अन्य other; अरण्य a desert; कर्ण an ear; कृष्ण Krishṇa; चौर्य theft; मौल्य price.

Note.—In English the double letters are pronounced as single letters, but not so in Maráṭhi. In English the adjective "better" is pronounced as बॅटर, not बॅट्टर, and consequently Englishmen are apt to pronounce words like उद्देश *uddeś* an aim as *udeś, without a strong force.*

2. When a letter has the Anusvára over it, it is usually accented; बंड *band*, a rebellion. If the Anusvára is *násikya* (§ 30, 2), it is not accented; कांटा *kā̃ṭá*, a thorn; दंव *dā̃v*, dew.

3. When a letter is followed by a Visarga, it is fully accented; दुःख *duḥkha*, grief.

Note.—In versification, the accented letters, though short, are reckoned as long, and equal to two *mátrás* or moments.

Note.—In Latin, Greek, and Sanskṛit, "the ordinary accented syllable is described as one uttered in a higher tone than the rest. In each one, moreover, is recognised a second accent, a 'Circumflex,' which is defined as a combination of a higher and a lower tone within the limits of the same syllable, a downward leap or shot of the voice. A syllable is, according to Sanskṛit grammarians, उदात्त ('taken up, varied, elevated') or acute अनुदात्त ('not raised, elevated'), or grave, and स्वरित ('toned') or circumflex."—*Whitney.*

RULES ON SPELLING.

§ 40. The following rules on spelling apply to Maráthí words only. The Sanskṛit words occurring in the language cannot be reduced to any fixed rules of orthography.

1. All words ending in इ and उ take the long vowels; गढी a fortress; बाई a lady; लाडू a sweet cake; ऊ a louse.

2. When a word ends in the inherent अ, the preceding इ or उ is always long; पीठ flour; लाकूड wood. But if the इ or उ has an Anusvára over it, the vowels are short; चिंच tamarind उंट a camel. *Exc.* The unaccented Anusvár does not shorten the ई or ऊ; as ऊंस *ū́ns*, sugarcane.

3. The short इ or उ in any other position is always short; शिवण sewing; फुकट gratis; भुसकट chaff; भुगा powder.

4. None but Sanskṛit words may end in a short इ or उ; मति intelligence; भानु the sun.

6. In inflection, the termination beginning with a vowel usually displaces the final vowel of the word to which it is joined; as परभू a Prabhu, परभीण a Prabhu woman; कर do thou + ईन = करीन I shall do; राह live thou + ऊं = राहूं to live; घर a house + ईं = घरीं in a house; घोडा + ई = घोडी a mare. But if the root is a monosyllable, both the vowel of the termination and of the root retain their places; ने take thou + ईल = नेईल he will take. आ in combination with the ई or ए of the root is changed to या, and ओ is changed to यो; ने + आ = न्या take ye; पी + आ = प्या drink ye; घे take thou + ओ = घेवो may he take; पी + ओ = पिवो may he drink. ओ before आ is also changed to वो; जा go thou + ओ = जावो may he go.

7. All neuter words, not ending in अ, take an *Anusvára* over the final letter; मोतीं a pearl; लेंकरूं a child. Exc. लोणी butter, पाणी water.

8. Finally ई is preferable to यी; बाई a lady, not बायी. The ई may be changed to य; as आई or आय a mother.

9. When a word is inflected, the penultimate or the last but one syllable, if composed of ई or ऊ, is either shortened, or changed to अ; as, बटीक, a female slave, बटिकी, or बटकी female slaves; बकूळ a kind of a plant, बकुळी plu.

(1) In a word of two syllables, the ई or ऊ is always shortened; दूध milk, दुधास to milk; मीठ salt, मिठानें by salt.

(2) In a word of three or more syllables the ई or ऊ may, either be shortened, or changed to अ; बटीक a female slave बटकी or बटिकी female slaves.

(*a*) If the syllable immediately preceding the penultimate is made up of a *long* or *nasalised* vowel, the penulimate is usually changed to अ; as रेशीम silk, रेशमास to silk; वाघूळ a flying fox, वाघळें plu; निंबूण the lime-tree, निंबणी plu; शेंदूर red lead, शेंदरास to red lead; बेडूक a frog, बेडकीण *f.*

Note.—The words in ईण only shorten the penultimate; पापीण a sinner, and पापिणी plu., कुणबीण a peasant woman, कुणबिणीस to a peasant woman.

(*b*) If the syllable preceding the penultimate is composed of a *short* or *unnasalised* syllable, the penultimate is usually shortened as, विहीर a well, विहिरी plu; आंबसूल dried peelings of a fruit, आंबसुलें plu; परीट a washerman, परिटीण a washerwoman.

(*c*) When the penultimate is a pure ई or ऊ, it may be shortened or changed to its corresponding semi-vowel, subject to the above two rules (*a* and *c*); सुईण a midwife, सुइणीस to a midwife; कवाईत military exercises, कवायतीस to m. exercises; दऊत, an inkstand, दउती or दवती inkstands; पाऊस rain पावसास to rain; पाऊल a step, पावलास to a step.

(3) The penultimate ई or ऊ in Sanskrit words may or may not be shortened; नीति virtue, नीतीस or नितीस to virtue; पूजा worship, पूजेस or पुजेस to worship.

CHAPTER IV.

Etymology.

GENERAL OBSERVATIONS ON THE CLASSIFICATION AND INFLECTION OF WORDS.

§ 41—§ 53.

§ 41. Etymology treats of the *Classification* (जाति), *Inflection* (प्रत्यय), and *Derivation* (व्युत्पत्ति) of words.

§ 42. Words are divided into three principal classes, viz., *Nouns* (संज्ञा), *Verbs* (क्रियापदें), and *Particles* (अव्ययें).

§ 43. Under Nouns or names are comprehended *Substantives*, or names of things (नाम); *Adjectives*, or names of qualities (विशेषण); and *Pronouns*, or substitutes for nouns (सर्वनाम).

§ 44. Under Verbs are included such words as directly or indirectly affirm an action of a noun; those which affirm action directly are strictly verbs, and those which predicate action indirectly, are called *participles* (धातुसाधितें), or words derived from verbs.

§ 45. Under Particles are included *Adverbs* (क्रियाविशेषण,) or words describing actions; *Postpositions* (शब्दयोगी), or words connecting words; *Conjunctions* (उभयान्वयी), or words connecting clauses; and *Interjections* (उद्गारवाचक), or words denoting a sudden emotion.

Note.—Adverbs "are claimed by some to be properly case-forms of pronouns," originally denoting place and direction, and latterly converted into words of time.

Postpositions are of more recent origin, being "created a separate part of speech by the swinging away of certain adverbs from apprehended relation to the verb, and their connection in idea with the noun-cases which their addition to the verb had caused to be construed with it."

"Conjunctions . . . are of secondary origin, being among the most characteristic products of the historical development of speech. To be able to part clauses together into periods, with due determination of their relation to one another, is a step beyond the power to put words alike determinately together into clauses."—*Whitney.*

§ 46. Words of the first two classes, viz., the Nouns and Verbs, are *inflected, i.e.*, modified by means of terminations to express their relation to other words in the sentence; those of the last class, viz., the Particles (अव्ययें), are uninflected.

Note.—Adverbs and postpositions, ending in an unnasalised आ, are inflected (§ 47); तो घरा भोंवताला फिरला, He walked round the house; ती त्या झाडाच्या भोंवताली चांगली नाचली, She danced well round the tree. In both of the above sentences the postposition भोंवताला around, is changed to agree with the agents तो he and ती she, while in the last, the adverb चांगला is modified to agree with the agent ती she. The आ, if nasalised, is not modified; as भोंवतां, around, जेव्हां when, केव्हां, when? etc.

§ 47. The inflectional terminations of a noun, called the *case-endings,* indicate its *case* (विभक्ति), *number* (वचन), and *gender* (लिंग). Those of a verb, denominated the *personal-endings,* denote its *gender, number, person* (पुरुष), *tense* (काळ), *mood* (अर्थ), and *participles* कृदंतें. The distinctions of gender and number are common to both classes of words.

Note.—"The characteristic of the noun is the case-ending, as that of the verb is the personal-ending. Case and number are to the noun what person and number are to the verb, fitting it to enter into definite relation with anything, &c."—*Whitney.*

§ 48. I.—Gender is a difference in words, or their inflections, indicating the distinction of sex लिंग, whether really existing or imagined to exist in objects; पुरुष a man, स्त्री a woman; घोडा a horse; घोडी a mare; दिवा a lamp, *m.*; भिंत a wall, *f.*

§ 49. II. Number is a difference in the inflection of words, denoting whether the object is one, or many; लेंकरूं a child, लेंकरें children; बायको a woman, बायका women.

§ 50. There are three genders in Maráthi, viz., the *Masculine* पुल्लिंग, the *Feminine* स्त्रीलिंग, and the *Neuter* नपुंसकलिंग.

§ 51. The Masculine gender denotes objects of the male kind; the Feminine, objects of the female kind; and the Neuter, objects which are neither male nor female. Thus, masculine बाप a father, feminine आई a mother, neuter घर a house.

Note.—It is but natural that living beings should be considered as male or female, but in Maráthi, as in Sanskṛit and all its offshoots, this distinction of sex belongs even to inanimate objects. Originally in Sanskṛit, however, all lifeless objects were arranged under a separate class, called क्लीब *klíb*, *i.e.*, eunuch, but, gradually, the old limits were disregarded. For "language imparts life to what is inanimate, and, on the other hand, impairs the personality of what is by nature animate."—*Bopp.*

Note.—"Great classes of names are masculine or feminine partly by poetical analogy, by an imaginary estimate of their distinctive qualities, as like those of the one or the other sex in the higher animals, especially man; partly by grammatical analogy, by resemblance in formation to words of gender already established."—*Whitney.*

Note.—In English the natural distinction of genders is maintained, all inanimate objects being considered as neuter, *i.e.*, of neither sex.

§ 52. There are two numbers in Maráṭhi, the *Singular* (एकवचन) and the *Plural* (बहुवचन). The *Singular* number denotes one object, and the *Plural*, more than one.

Note.—In some languages, such as Sanskṛit, Greek, Hebrew, Arabic, &c., there are three numbers, the singular, dual (द्विवचन), and plural; as रामः Ráma, रामौ two Rámas, and रामाः Rámas.

§ 53. The following terminations are usually employed to modify nouns, verbs, and even some particles, to indicate their *gender* and *number*; and they have been denominated in this book the *Principal Gender Terminations* :—

Singular.			*Plural.*		
M.	*F.*	*N.*	*M.*	*F.*	*N.*
आ	ई	एं	ए	आ	ईं

EXAMPLES.

Masculine.

		Pron.	*Noun.*	*Adj.*	*Verb.*	
Singular	आ	माझा	घोडा	काळा	होता	My horse was black.
Plural	ए	माझे	घोडे	काळे	होते	My horses were black.

Feminine.

Singular	ई	माझी	घोडी	काळी	होती	My mare was black.
Plural	आ	माझ्या	घोड्या	काळ्या	होत्या	My mares were black.

Neuter.

Singular	एं	माझें	तळें	मोठें	होतें	My tank was large.
Plural	ईं	माझीं	तळीं	मोठीं	होतीं	My tanks were large.

Note.—These terminations are derived from Sanskṛit. The masculine singular आ, which, along with the feminine ई, is common to most of the Indian Sanskṛitic vernaculars, is derived from the Sanskṛit visarga (ः) changed to ओ in Prákṛit; thus, Sk. घोटकः a horse, Prák. घोडो, M. घोडा. In Gujarati, the Prákṛit ओ is often retained, but in Maráṭhi it occurs only in one or two pronominal forms; Sk. यः who, Prák. जो, M. जो. The feminine singular, ई is generally employed even in Sanskṛit "as a characteristic addition in the formation of the feminine bases; the feminine base महती great, springs from महत्. This holds good in Zend."—*Bopp.* The neuter singular एं is the modification of the Sanskṛit anusvár: Sk. अंडं an egg, M. अंडें; Sk. तं, it Prák. तं, M. तें. In Gujarati it is changed to उं, and occasionally as well in Maráṭhí. When the Maráṭhí neuter forms indicate "a young one," they assume रूं एं; बकरूं a kid, लेंकरूं a child. Some Maráṭhí forms drop the Prákṛit anusvár; Sk. गृहं a house, Prák. गेहं, M. घर. The anusvár is an appropriate expression of the neuter gender, "as it is less personal, less animated, and hence appropriated to the accusative as well as the nominative in the neuter."—*Bopp*.

Note.—The Maráthí plural terminations could be easily traced to their Sanskṛit originals in the following forms:—

Plu. M. Sk. सर्वे all, Prák. सव्वे, M. ए. (घोडे horses).
„ *F.* Sk. सर्वाः all, Prák. सव्वाओ or सव्वा, M. आ (घोड्या).
„ *N.* Sk. सर्वाणि all, Prák. सव्वाणि or सव्वाइं M. इं (घोडीं).

Note.—The feminine plural आ is changed to या or वा when the singular ends in ई or ऊ, in harmony with the Sanskṛit rules of the Permutation of Letters; नदी a river + आ = नद्या rivers; जळू a leech + आ = जळवा leeches. In Hindi the presence of ई always changes the आ or ओं to या or यो; माली a gardener + ओंनें = मालीयोंनें by gardeners; बुद्धि intellect + आं = बुद्धियां intellects.

CHAPTER V.

The Substantive (नाम).

DIVISION OF SUBSTANTIVES.

§ 54—§ 69.

§ 54. A substantive is the name of a being or thing, whether material or immaterial, or the name of its attribute, viewed as a distinct object; घर a house, देव God, मन mind, शहाणपण wisdom.

§ 55. The substantives are *proper* (विशेष) and *common* (सामान्य).

§ 56. The proper noun is a name pertaining to a particular object; as रामा Rámá, पुणें Puṇa.

§ 57. The common noun is a name common to every one of a class of objects; माणूस a man, गांव a village, पुस्तक a book.

Note.—A common noun has sometimes the force of a proper noun and *vice versá*; रामीचा जाहीरनामा तुम्हीं पाहिला काय? Have you seen the proclamation of the Queen? In this sentence राणी denotes the Queen Victoria; तो केवळ राम होता, वचनाला फिरत नसे He was quite a Ráma; he never swerved from his promise.

§ 58. Common nouns are of three kinds, Collective Nouns, Noun of materials, and Abstract Nouns.

1. A common noun of the singular number expressing a collection or multitude of objects is called a *collective noun* (समुच्चयवाचक नाम); as सैन्य an army; कळप a flock; मंडळी an assembly.

2. A common noun which denotes the matter or substance of which an object is composed, and not its form or number, is called a *noun of materials* (पदार्थवाचक नाम); as सोनें gold साखर sugar, रेशिम silk.

3. The name of a property or quality of an object, viewed as a separate entity, is called an *abstract noun* (भाववाचक नाम); as नम्रता humility, चांगुलपणा goodness.

Note.—A word designating both a quality and the subject in whicl. it exists is called a *concrete noun*, it being opposed to an abstract noun. T us, प्रामाणिकपणा honesty is an abstract noun, and प्रामाणिक मनुष्य an honest man is the concrete noun corresponding to it.

§ 59. A substantive is inflected (विकार पावतें) to indicate its gender, number, and case.

THE GENDER OF SUBSTANTIVES.

§ 60. The gender of Maràṭhí nouns can be determined neither by their *form* nor *signification*, and it is, consequently, impossible to give any precise rules on the subject. The following obesrvations may, however, prove of some utility to the Maráṭhí student.

§ 61. *Rules for Determining the Gender of Substantives by their Forms.*

1. The Maráṭhí nouns ending in अ are of all the three genders.

2. The pure Maráṭhí substantives in आ are always masculine; but Sanskrit nouns ending in आ are either masculine or feminine; M. आंबा a mango, *m.*; M. दोरा a thread, *m.*; Sk. कथा a tale, *f.*; Sk. आत्मा spirit, *m.*

Note.—The following Sanskṛit feminine words ending in आ are of common use in the language.

आज्ञा an order; कथा a tale; परीक्षा a trial; विद्या science; घटिका twenty four minutes; छाया a shade; पूजा worship; वेदना agony; तारा a star, *m.*, *f.*; प्रजा the subject of a king; भाषा a language; व्यथा pain; दशा state; यात्रा a pilgrimage; शिक्षा instruction; सत्ता authority; निंदा a reproach; वार्ता news; सभा an assembly; सूचना a suggestion; हत्या murder.

Note.—Maráṭhí derivatives from Sanskṛit words in आ sometimes retain the classical आ; as M. जत्रा, Sk. यात्रा pilgrimage.

Note.—The names of women and rivers usually end in आ:—

Names of women: चंद्रा, चांगुणा, चिमणा, मैना, रमा, सीता.

Names of rivers: कृष्णा, गंगा, नर्मदा, भीमा, यमुना.

Obs.—The names of women are courteously written with the final आ, and familiarly or contemptuously with ई; as यमुना and यमुनी; रमा and रमी. The vulgar change even the radical ई to आ to give the word a respectful form; thus, भागीरथीबाई is changed to भागीरथाबाई; आनंदीबाई to आनंदाबाई. The lawgiver Manu thus observes on the dignity of the open vowel आ, and its fitness, in consequence, to make up feminine names:—"The names of women should be agreeable, soft, clear, captivating the fancy, auspicious, *ending in long vowels*, resembling words of benediction."—*Manu* I., 30.

Note.—"The feminine in Sanskṛit, both in the base and the case-terminations, loves a luxurious fulness of form; and when it is distinguished from the other genders, in the base or the termination, it marks the distinction by broader and more sonant vowels."—*Bopp.*

Obs.—It is vulgar to address females above the rank of a menial without the honorific word बाई a lady, attached to the radical form, as यमुनाबाई, राधाबाई, आनंदीबाई; and foreigners should take special note of this. The modified form in ई instead of आ, should never be attempted to be used by foreigners, and they would be always on the safer side by habitually employing the full form in बाई.

Note.—The following Hindustani feminine words ending in आ are of common use in Maráthi:—इजा vexation; परवा care; मुभा full permission; जमा a collected sum; पागा a stable; रजा leave; सजा punishment; जागा a place, *m.*, *f.*; मजा flavour, taste; साय cream; जिम्मा

charge, trust, *m.*, *f.* ; तऱ्हा a kind or sort ; बोलवा rumour, *f.*, *m.* ; सुंता circumcision ; थट्टा jesting ; मका Indian corn, *m.*, *f.* ; हवा air ; दवा medicine ; मनुका raisins.

3. Maráthi nouns in ई are usually feminine, as गाडी a carriage. The following words are exceptions :—

(*a*) पक्षी a bird, *m.* ; मणी a jewel, *m.* ; हत्ती an elephant, *m.* ; लोणी butter, *n.* ; पाणी water, *n.*

(*b*) All words denoting *profession, character, office*, &c., are masculine ; as धोबी a washerman ; माळी a gardener ; वाटाडी a guide ; कारभारी a manager ; पापी a sinner, &c.

(*c*) All words ending in ई, having an anusvár on them, are neuter ; मोतीं a pearl. (See Sect. 39.)

4. The nouns ending in short इ and उ are pure Sanskrit words, and belong to all the three genders ; कवि a poet, *m.* ; मति intelligence, *f.* ; अस्थि bone, *n.* ; भानु the sun, *m.* ; धेनु a cow, *f.* ; अंबु water, *n.*

5. The nouns in ऊ, which are very few, belong to all the three genders.

6. The nouns in ए and ऐ are feminine, but those in the nasalised एं, are neuter. The feminine nouns in ए and ऐ are but two or three, and are usually written with य or ई ; as तिवै a tripod, being written as तिवय or तिवई ; सवै a habit, as सवय or सवई.

7. There are some seven or eight words in the language which end in ओ and औ, and which, except बायको a woman, *f.*, are masculine ; as लाहो covetousness, *m.* ; औ a mark on a die, *m.* The final औ is often changed to अऊ or अव, as पौ, or पऊ or पव. The word मोहो bees' nest, written also as मोहळ, is either masculine or neuter.

Note.—The solitary feminine word in ओ, is thus formed ; Sk. मातृ a mother, Prak. माई or माय, M. माय or बाय ; and the बाय with the diminutive suffix कू or को makes बायकू, or बायको a little mother or a wife. Similar forms exist in Gujarati ; बायडी.

Note.—"Few monosyllabic primary forms end in Sanskrit in the diphthongs, not any at all in ए ; in ऐ only रै *m.*, ऐ being changed in many languages to आ." Primary forms in आ are rare in Sanskrit ;

the only ones known to me are द्यो heaven, and गो cow." "I know only two words in Sanskṛit which end in औ, नौ a ship, ग्लौ moon."
—*Bopp.*

8. The Maráṭhí nouns ending in the anusvár are all neuter; मोतीं a pearl, कुंकूं a red powder, भांडें a vessel. Exc. गहूं *m.*

Note.—"The euphonic *n* is most frequently employed by the neuter gender, less so by the masculine, and most rarely by the feminine," in the Sanskṛit language.—*Bopp.*

9. A compound noun takes the gender of its last member; भाजीपाला vegetables, *m. sing.*, नाकडोळे nose and eyes, *m. plu.*, नवरानवरी bridegroom and bride *n. plu.*, आईबाप *m. plu.* father and mother.

§ 62. *Rules for determining the Gender of Substantives by their Signification.*

1. Names of living beings are according to their sex either masculine or feminine; मुलगा a boy, *m.*, मुलगी a girl, *f.*

Note.—Some nouns, expressing living beings, may denote either a male or a female; as माणूस a person; मांजर a cat; डुकर a hog or pig. When these nouns are used without any reference to the sex of the individual named, they are considered to be the neuter gender; तो पोर कुणब्याचा? Is it a Kuṇbi boy? तें पोर कोणाचें हो? Whose child is that? तें माणूस नाहीं? It is not a human being; या गांवांत मांजरें पुष्कळ आहेत. there are many cats in this town. When the sex of the individual is referred to, they assume the masculine or feminine gender; as, हा डुकर कोणी मारिला? who killed this hog, *m.*? ही मांजर उंदीर मारीत नाहीं, this cat (*f.*) does not kill rats.

2. The names of large and powerful inanimate objects are often masculine; डोंगर a mountain, समुद्र the sea, सूर्य the sun.

Note.—Some names of inanimate objects are of more than one gender; तारा a star, *f.*, *m.*; डग *n.*, *m.*, दुकान *n.*, *f.*, पितळ *f.*, *n.*, जागा place *m.*, *f.* The masculine gender is preferred in the Dakhan.

§ 63. Imperfect as these rules are, they will be found useful by the intelligent student of Maráṭhí. He will, however, be greatly helped in determining the gender of the nouns in the *reading lesson* by the *inflections* of the adjectives, pronouns, verbs and adverbs which may relate to them. Thus in the sentence हें मोठें पुस्तक रामानें चांगलें वाचिलें, Ráma read this large book well, the neuter gender of the noun पुस्तक is indicated by the demonstrative pronoun हें this, the adjective मोठें large, the adverb चांगलें well, and the verb वाचिलें read.

Rules for deriving Feminine and Neuter forms from Masculine Nouns.

§ 64. Substantives, denoting males, have sometimes corresponding feminine and neuter forms, and these feminine and neuter forms are of two kinds—

(1) Some are derived from the root by means of *suffixes*, and (2) some are *distinct original words* :—

1. Derivatives: मेंढा a ram, मेंढी a ewe; आजा a grandfather, आजी a grandmother.

2. Distinct words: उंट a he-camel, सांड a she-camel; पुरुष a man, स्त्री or बायको a woman.

§ 65. I.—*Derivative Forms.*

1. When a Maráṭhi word ending in आ indicates a living being, whether rational or irrational, it is usually in the masculine gender (see § 55, 2.), and assumes ई and एं to make up its feminine and neuter forms. The neuter form, however, is not so commonly derived as the feminine, particularly in reference to nouns denoting human beings. Thus:

Masculine.		*Feminine.*		*Neuter.*
आजा	a grandfather	आजी	a grandmother	
काका	a paternal uncle	काकी	a paternal aunt	
मामा	a maternal uncle	मामी	a maternal aunt	
दादा	an elderly man	दादी	an elderly woman	
मुलगा	a boy	मुलगी	a girl	मुलगें.
कुत्रा	a dog	कुत्री	a bitch	कुत्रें.
कोल्हा	a fox	कोल्ही	a vixen	कोल्हें.
घोडा	a horse	घोडी	a mare	घोडें.
बकरा	a he-goat	बकरी	a she-goat	बकरें.
मेंढा	a ram	मेंढी	a ewe	मेंढें.
लांडगा	a he-wolf	लांडगी	a she-wolf	लांडगें.

Note.—मावळा a maternal uncle, makes मावळण (Sk. मातुलानी) a maternal aunt, not मावळी.

Note.—Words denoting professions, characters, &c. substitute ईण for ई; hence, मराठा a Maráṭhá, मराठीण a Maráṭhá woman. (See § 60, 1.)

§ 66. Some nouns assume two neuter inflections, viz. ऊं and एं; as बकरा a he-goat, बकरी a she-goat, and बकरूं a kid, or बकरें. Of these two neuter forms the one in ऊं denotes a young animal, and that in एं, the species generally without reference to the sex, or an individual in contempt. Thus, तें बकरूं आण Bring that kid; हें बकरें कोणाचें? Whose goat is this? The form in ऊं may have a synonymous word, not cognate with it; as बकरूं or करडूं a kid; मेंढरूं or कोंकरूं a lamb. But sometimes the derivative form may be wanting; as घोडा a horse, घोडी a mare, and शिंगरूं a foal, not घोडूं.

Note.—The word लेक, denoting a son or daughter, has a neuter form in रूं, as लेंकरूं a child. The termination रूं makes up diminutive neuter forms.

Note.—When nouns take only the neuter ऊं, and not एं as well, the neuter form in ऊं may not imply a young animal, but only an individual in contempt; गायरूं a cow, in endearment or disparagement; वाघरूं a tiger; मांजरूं a cat, in endearment or contempt, or without reference to the sex.

§ 67. Nouns ending in any other vowel than आ, and implying living beings, rational as well as irrational, make up their feminine forms by affixing either ई or ईण. Some of these may assume the neuter ending रूं to form neuter diminutives. Thus, वाघ a tiger, वाघीण a tigress; वाघरूं a tiger in contempt. The terminations ई and ईण are affixed according to the following rules:—

1. Masculine nouns indicating *persons* are modified only if they express *surnames*, *characters*, *castes*, *professions*, &c.; and, then, they assume ईण alone. Thus, *surnames*: पवार Powar, *m.*, पवारीण *f.*; खिस्ती Khisti, *m.*, खिस्तीण *f.*; रानडा Ránadá, *m.*, रानडीण *f.*; चिपळोणकर Chiploṇkar, *m.*, चिपळोणकरीण *f.*; *Castes, professions*: सोनार a goldsmith, सोनारीण *f.*; भट a Brahman

5 *m*

priest, भटीण *f.*; मराठा a Maráthá, मराठीण *f.*; परभू a Parbhú. परभीण *f.*; धोबी a washerman, धोबीण *f.* *Characters*: पापी a sinner, पापीण *f.*; कोडी a leper, कोडीण *f.*

Note.—Surnames, words denoting castes, &c., may end in आ and yet take the feminine suffix ईण; as गोरा Gorá, गोरीण; कानडा a Kanarese man, कानडीण.

Note.—The words देव a god, ब्राह्मण a Brahman, दास a slave, शूद्र a Śúdra, which are pure Sanskṛit words, may assume only ई; as देवी a goddess, ब्राह्मणी a Brahman woman, दासी a female slave, शूद्री a Śúdrí. गवळी a cowherd, makes गवळण a cowherdess.

Note.—Some Persian words derived from Urdu, such as मोगल a Mogul, मेहतर a sweeper, take आणी for ईण; as मोगल, मोगलाणी *f.*; मेहतर, मेहतराणी *f.*

2. Masculine nouns indicating *irrational animals*, assume either ई or ईण to make up the feminine forms. These terminations are affixed in the following manner:—

(*a*) Maráṭhí words, composed only of two syllables, assume ईण; thus, उंट a camel, उंटीण *f.*; वाघ a tiger, वाघीण *f.*; सिंह a lion, सिंहीण *f.* (in poetry, सिंही); हत्ती an elephant, हत्तीण *f.*

(*b*) Pure Sanskṛit words of two syllables, not quite naturalised in the language, assume ई; thus मृग a deer, मृगी *f.*; हंस a swan, हंसी *f.*

(*c*) Maráṭhi polysyllabic words assume ई; thus उंदीर a mouse, उंदरी *f.*; गोचीड a dog-louse, गोचडी *f.*; गाढव an ass, गाढवी *f.*; ढेकूण a bug, ढेकणी *f.*; पोपट a parrot, पोपटी *f.*; बेडूक a frog, बेडकी *f.*; माकड a monkey, माकडी *f.*; सांबर an ell, सांबरी *f.*; हरण a deer, हरणी *f.*

§ 68. The names of inanimate objects are sometimes modified in Maráṭhí by the gender terminations, आ *m.*, ई *f.*, and एं *n.*, to express the following senses:—

1. The sense of *hugeness* or *clumsiness* is indicated by the masculine termination आ; thus, the radical form भाकर bread, by the addition of आ, becomes भाकरा, signifying a huge loaf of bread; from कातर a pair of scissors, कातरा a huge pair of scissors; गाडा a cart, from गाडी a carriage.

2. The sense of *softness* or *delicacy* is expressed by the feminine ई; भाकरी a loaf of bread, but भाकरा a huge loaf of bread; पोळा a large cake, पोळी a cake. When there are two feminine forms, one in अ and the other in ई, that in ई is softer than that in अ; as त्यानें भाकरी खाल्ली is softer than त्यानें भाकर खाल्ली he ate bread. The vigorous inhabitants of the Dakhan use the forms in अ, but the soft Konkanis, those in ई.

Note.—इ being a light and feeble vowel, naturally indicates the feminine gender. अ and आ are grander than the corresponding quantity of the vowel इ. "In Latin, also *i* may be considered as lighter than *a*."—*Bopp.*

3. The sense of *indifference* or *contempt* is denoted by the neuter inflection एं; गाडें from गाडी a carriage, denotes a carriage in contempt. Thus, ही गाडी कोणाची? whose carriage is this? हें गाडें कोणाचें! whose miserable apology for a carriage is this? हा गाडा कोणाचा? whose cart or waggon is this?

Note.—Sometimes डें is used to make up the neuter termination of contempt; गळ्यांत दोरडें (दोर + डें) बाळगून त्याचा आचार शूद्राचा though he wears the (sacred) cord (revilingly), he acts like a Súdra.

Note.—The neuter inflection डें and its masculine and feminine forms डा and डी, are affixed to nouns denoting persons, as well as things, to produce forms of contempt; हा कासारडा कशाला आला? why has this miserable fellow of a coppersmith come? ती भिकारडी आली that miserable beggar woman has come; असे भिकारडे चाळे काय कामाचे of what profit are such beggarly pranks?

The डा may also be employed by way of endearment; गरीब बापडा, कायकरील poor fellow, what could he do!

When the word is dissyllabic, it assumes उरडा instead of a simple डा; भट a Brahman priest, भटुरडा.

डा may be substituted by गा, टा, ला, का, &c.; गांव a village, गांवडें a small village.

Note.—The forms of the word दोर are peculiar; दोर a rope, *m.*, दोरा a thread, *m.*, दोरी a string, *f.*, दोरडें a string in contempt, *n.*

Note.—"The neuter prefers the greatest conciseness, and distinguishes itself from the masculine, not in the base only, but in the nominative and its perfect counterpart, the accusative; in the vocative also, where, this is the same as the nominative." The distinguishing sign of the neuter, which is the anusvár, is, as has been remarked above, the least personal and animated of all the grammatical sounds and therefore fitted to express the sense of contempt.—*Bopp.*

II.—Distinct Feminine Words.

§ 69. The following words do not derive the feminine forms from the root, but assume distinct words. Thus,

उंट a he-camel	सांड a she-camel.
काळवीट a male antelope	हरणी a female antelope.
दीर a brother-in-law	जाऊ a sister-in-law.
नवरा a husband	बायको a wife.
पिता a father	माता a mother.
पुरुष a man	स्त्री, बायको a woman.
बाप a father	आई a mother.
बैल an ox	गाय a cow.
बोकड a he-goat	शेळी a she-goat.
बोका a he-cat	मांजर, भाटी a she-cat.
भाऊ a brother	बहीण a sister.
मोर a peacock	लांडोर a pea-hen.
राजा a king	राणी a queen.
रेडा a he-buffalo	म्हैस a she-buffalo.
वाघ्या a male devotee	मुरळी a female devotee.
सासरा a father-in-law	सासू a mother-in-law.

CHAPTER VI.

Numbers of Substantives.

§ 70—§ 71.

§ 70. In Maráṭhì the plural of nouns is formed in the following way :—

Masculine Nouns.

1. All Masculine nouns, except those ending in आ, remain unchanged in the plural; the nouns ending in आ change their final vowel to ए.

(1) *Sing. and Plural* बाप a father, or fathers.
,, ,, माळी a gardener, or gardeners.
,, ,, लाडू a cake, or cakes.
,, ,, लाहो covetousness.
,, ,, पौ a mark, or marks on a die.

(2) *Sing.* आंबा a mango ; *Plu.* आंबे mangoes.
देशपांड्या a village officer ; देशपांडे.

Note.—In pure Maráṭhí words the य in conjunction is not accented as in Sanskṛit words, and is displaced in inflection ; as आगलाव्या, आगलावे ; भाट्या, भाटे. So also देशपांड्या + ईण, = देशपांडीण.

Note.—Honorific words in आ are not changed in the plural ; as, एथें दोन बाबा, आणि चार अण्णा आहेत there are here two Bábás and four Aṇṇás—persons of the names of Bábá and Aṇṇá ; तुमचे दादा आले आहेत Your brother has come. Surnames are changed ; गोपाळ साठा, गोपाळराव साठे ; रामा लोखंड्या, रामजी लोखंडे.

Note.—When any words, denoting family relations, are used as common nouns, they may optionally assume the plural form ; as तुम्हाला मामा or मामे किती आहेत How many maternal uncles have you?

Feminine Nouns.

2. All Feminine nouns, except the nouns ending in अ which belong to the first declension (§ 95), assume आ in the plural ; the nouns in अ of the first declension assume ई.

(1) *Singular.* *Plural.*

Singular.	*Plural.*
वाट a way	वाटा ways.
कथा a tale	कथा tales.
गाडी a carriage	गाड्या carriages.
बी a seed	बिया (or ब्या in the Dakhan) seeds.
ऊ a louse	उवा (or वा in the Dakhan) lice.

Singular.	*Plural.*
जळू a leech	जळवा leeches.
सवे (सवई or सवय) a habit	सवया habits.
तिवे (तिवई or तिवय) a tripod	तिवया tripods.
बायको a wife	बायका wives.

Note.—Some words of foreign origin ending in ऊ may not assume आ in the plural; as बाजू (Pers.) a side, *plu.* बाजू sides. In the Konkan they are sometimes inflected, as बाजू, बाज्वा.

Note.—The plural inflection आ, in union with the final ई and ऊ, is changed to या and वा respectively.

Note.—सू a needle makes सुया in the plural, as its genuine form is सुई (Sk. सूची); in the Konkan the form सुवा occurs. The word, पिसू a flea, makes पिस्वा or पिसा in the plural; the word ऊ a louse, makes उवा or वा in the plural. The latter forms are used chiefly in the Dakhan.

Note.—The words in pure ई and ऊ may or may not assume आ in the plural; as आई a mother, आई or आया mothers; जाऊ a sister-in-law, जाऊ or जावा sisters-in-law; गाई or गाय a cow, गाई or गाया cows.

(2) *Sing.* भिंत a wall, *plu.* भिंती walls.

Neuter Nouns.

3. All Neuter nouns, except those ending in एं, assume एं in the plural: the nouns ending in एं assume ईं in the plural.

(1) *Singular.*	*Plural.*
घर a house	घरें houses.
मोतीं a pearl	मोत्यें pearls.
लेंकरूं a child	लेंकरें children.
तारूं a ship	तारवें ships.

Note.—Nouns ending in ई and ऊ change the एं to ये and वे respectively. The neuter diminutives, (§ 100, *Note* 3,) which end in डूं, रूं, लूं, &c.; and others specified in § 100, *Note* 2, retain however the plural एं; as लेंकरूं a child, लेंकरें children; करडूं a kid, करडें kids; पिलूं a cub, पिलें cubs. The word निंबू a lime, makes निंबें limes.

(2) *Singular* तळें a tank. *Plural* तळीं tanks.

Masculine, Feminine and Neuter Nouns ending in इ *and* उ.

4. The nouns terminating in the short इ and उ are pure Sanskṛit words, and they do not change in the plural. Thus, *Masculine,* कवि a poet or poets; *Feminine,* मति intelligence or intelligences; अणु an atom or atoms; धेनु a cow or cows; *Neuter,* अस्थि a bone or bones.

Note.—Indeed, all pure Sanskṛit words ending in ई and ऊ, short or long, are not modified in the plural; as वधू a bride or brides; ब्राह्मणी a Brahman woman or women.

A Table of the Plural Inflections.

Masculine.	Feminine.	Neuter.
No change (or ए)	आ (or ई)	एं (or ईं)

Note.—(*a*) Names of materials and abstract nouns are usually used in the singular number, as तांबें copper; साखर sugar; चांगुलपणा goodness. The names of materials are employed in the plural when varieties are indicated; बाजारांतील सर्व साखरा पाहिल्या I saw all the sugars in the bazar; दोन्ही दुधें तापविलीं काय? Have you boiled both the milks?

(*b*) Nouns denoting grains are usually used in the plural, unless they denote kind or species; as, हे किती गहूं आहेत? How much (lit. how many) wheat is this? दोन मण Two maunds; एथें काय गहूं पेरला आहे? Is wheat sown here? दोन शेर मोहोऱ्या आणा Bring two seers of mustard. Bajri is always used in the singular; चार पायल्या बाजरी दळा Grind four measures of bajri; so also भात *n.* rice in the husk. Boiled rice is भात masculine, and is always singular.

(*c*) Some nouns have only a plural form; मुसक्या arms, as tied behind the back; गंडमाळा scrofula; देवी small-pox; वन्सें *n.* and *f. plu.*, word of respect for a husband's sister. The regular feminine form is वन्सा and is declined in that form; as वन्सांना बोलावा call वन्सा or वन्सें; कात्या the *plu.* the pleiades; आळेपिळे *m. plu.* or आळ्यापिळ्या *f. plu.* contortions.

(*d*) A singular noun may denote an individual as well as the species; हत्ती हें मोठें जनावर आहे the elephant is a large animal; वाघाच्या अंगावर पट्टे असतात, there are stripes on the body of the tiger; तिला वाघानें खाल्लें she was eaten by a tiger. The plural form may also be used to denote the species; ब्राह्मणांस or ब्राह्मणास दान द्यावें the Brahmans should be given a gift.

(*e*) Some nouns have both collective and plural forms; पैसा is singular in form, but denotes one or many; पैसे is plural. पैका is used only in the collective sense of पैसा. Thus, एक पैसा, दोन पैसे, चार पैसे one pice, two pice, four pice; त्याचा सर्व पैसा or पैका नाहींसा झाला, all his money was lost.

(*f*) Some nouns have two singular, but one plural form; नारळ or नारळी a cocoanut tree, *plural* नारळी cocoanut trees.

(*g*) Some nouns have two singular, and two plural forms; भाकरी or भाकर a loaf of bread, *plural* भाकऱ्या or भाकरी loaves of bread; धाबळी or धाबळ a woollen cloth; *plural* धाबळ्या or धाबळी; केळें or केळ a plantain, *plural* केळीं or केळें plantains. The latter forms are common in the Dakhan, and the former in the Konkan.

(*h*) Some words ending in ई or य in the singular, have corresponding forms in the plural; बाई or बाय a lady, *plural* बाई or बाया ladies; आई or आय, mother, *plural* आई or आया mothers; गाई or गाय a cow, *plural* गाई or गाया cows. The forms in ई, both singular and plural, are classical, and those in य and या colloquial. The plural forms in ई are used respectfully, as well as to denote the sense of plurality, while those in या simply express the latter sense; बाई आल्या होत्या, the lady had come; बाया आल्या होत्या, the ladies had come; आमच्या दोघींच्या आई जिवंत आहेत the mothers of both of us are alive.

§ 71. The following table will be found helpful in determining the plural form of a noun by the terminating vowel of its root. For instance, the plural inflection of बायको a woman, must be आ, making up बायका, as आ stands opposite to the vowel ओ in the column superscribed Feminine :—

Terminating Vowel of the Root.	Plural Inflections.		
	Masculine.	*Feminine.*	*Neuter.*
अ	No change.	आ, ई	एं
आ	ए	आ	......
इ	No change.	No change.	No change.
ई	No change.	आ	एं
उ	No change.	No change.	No change.
ऊ	No change.	अ	एं
ए	......	आ	ई
ऐ	......	आ	......
ओ	No change.	आ	......
औ	No change.	......	......

CHAPTER VII.

Cases of Substantives.

§ 72—§ 86.

§ 72. A case is that inflected form of the noun by which its relation to other words in the sentence is indicated; as तो प्रसंग शाहू राज्याच्या मरणानें निर्माण झाला that opportunity presented itself by the death of king Sháhú. In this sentence, the modified form राज्याच्या of the noun राजा, indicates its relation to the succeeding word मरणानें, and the modified form मरणानें is related to the compound verb निर्माण झाला.

§ 73. The inflections employed to modify nouns for this purpose are denominated विभक्तिप्रत्यय (case-endings), and there are *eight* principal relations (कारक) expressed by these inflections. Hence there are *eight Cases* (विभक्ति) in Maráṭhí.

Note.—In Sanskṛit कारक expresses the relation exsisting between a noun and a *verb*; any other relation would not be called कारक.

Note.—The Maráṭhi casé inflections are derived, as will be shown below, from the Sanskṛit through the Prâkṛit, and the Sanskṛit originals are, in their turn, modifications or corruptions of demonstrative pronouns.

"The case terminations express the reciprocal relations of nouns principally, and originally referred only to nouns, but from space were extended also to time and cause, the relations of the persons spoken of to one another."

"According to their origin they are, for the most part, pronouns." These "exponents of the relations of space have been naturally taken from those words which express personality, with their inherent secondary idea of room, of that which is near or more distant, of that which is on this or that side."

"In the more sunken, insensible sense of the language, the spiritually dead case terminations are, in their signification of space, replaced, supported, and explained by postpositions."—*Bopp.*

§ 74. The Maráṭhí eight cases are thus enumerated :—

1. *Nominative* or कर्त्तरी also (प्रथमा first).
2. *Accusative* or कर्मणी (द्वितीया second).
3. *Instrumental* or करणी (तृतीया third).
4. *Dative* or संप्रदानी (चतुर्थी fourth).
5. *Ablative* or अपादानी (पंचमी fifth).
6. *Genitive* or संबंधी (षष्ठी sixth).
7. *Locative* or अधिकरणी (सप्तमी seventh).
8. *Vocative* or संबोधन

§ 75. The Nominative case (कर्तरी) is the radical form of the noun, and expresses the agent (कर्त्ता) of an action, or the verb ; as हरि ईश्वराची प्रार्थना करितो Hari prays to God. In this sentence हरि Hari is the nominative case.

§ 76. The Accusative case (कर्मणि) is, like the Nominative, uninflected, and expresses the *immediate object* (प्रत्यक्ष कर्म) in which the action of the verb terminates ; as प्रथम बाबरानें हें शहर घेतलें, first Bábar took this city. The word शहर is the Accusative Case. The form of the Accusative does not differ from that of the Nominative.

Note.—In Sanskṛit, as well as in Prákṛit, the Nominative and Accusative have distinct inflections, both of which are dropped in Maráṭhí hence the identity of their forms :—

Nom. Sk. देवः, Prák. देवो, M. देव.
Acc. Sk. देवं, Prák देवं, M. देव.

Note.—The nasal sign of the accusative is dropped in several other languages besides Maráthí and the other Indian Aryan vernaculars. In Gothic substantives, as well neuter as masculine, the case sign *m* is wanting. "Even in Sánskṛit this *m* is dropped in words ending in इ and उ ; probably वारि was वारिम् and मधु, मधुम् ; in किम् from the stem कि, there is a trace of it."—*Bopp*.

Note.—The Accusative being the most dependent case, the most perfect counterpart of the Nominative, the nasal is its characteristic sign in many languages, such as Sanskṛit, Zend, Greek, Latin, &c. The nasal "is less personal, less animated, and hence appropriated to the accusative as well as to the nominative in the neuter."—*Bopp*.

Note.—Though this feebleness and inferiority of the accusative is not discernible in Maráthí, so far as its form is concerned, still it is quite clear from the *use* which is made of it in the language. It is never used when the object of a verb is a word denoting a *person;* तो गोविंदाला मारितो, he beats Govind, not तो गोविंद मारितो ; but तो दगड मारितो, he pelts stones, is correct, as दगड expresses an inanimate object. This incompetency of the accusative to represent a person is common to Hindi, Gujarati, &c. In Hindi, even a word denoting a lifeless object is put in the dative case, when it is necessary to make it emphatic; हरीने उस पथरको उठाया Hari took up that stone. The sentence, "Hari took up a stone," would be rendered with an accusative object; thus हरीने पथर उठाया. This idiom is not altogether foreign to Maráthí; ह्या नासक्या आंब्याला काय मी खाऊं? तुझा आग्रह असला तर खाऊन टाकीन, what, shall I eat this rotten mango? If you insist, I will eat it up. The accusative object would not be so emphatic; हा नासका आंबा काय मी खाऊं?

Note.—In Sanskṛit the indirect object denoting a person is usually in the dative case, but it may be optionally put in the accusative *when contempt is expressed*, with the verb मन् to think; न तृणाय तृणं वा मन्ये I do not consider thee to be worth a straw.—*Mr. Apte.*

§ 77. The Instrumental case (करणी) is inflected by means of the terminations नें singular and नीं plural, and indicates the instrument (करण) of an action; त्यानें तरवारीनें राजाचा शिरच्छेद केला, he beheaded the king with a sword; आपण डोळ्यांनीं पाहातों, we see with our eyes.

Note.—The instrumental termination is derived from the Sanskṛit through the Prákrit:—

Singular Instrumental Sk. देवेन, Prák. देवेण, M. देवानें.
Plural „ „ देवैः Prák. देवेहिं, M. देवांहीं-नीं.

The Plural नीं is evidently a modification of the Singular नें, and it has almost entirely superseded the old form हीं.

Note.—Since it is neuter nouns ending in एं that alone assume ईं in the plural, the case ending नें, which in the plural is changed to नीं, must originally have really had an anusvár over it, as all neuter nouns ending in एं have it, otherwise it could never have been changed to नीं in the plural; hence both नें and नीं should be nasalised. Besides, the old termination हिं (हीं) has it.

§ 78. The Dative case (संप्रदानी) is inflected by स, ला singular, and स, ला, ना plural, and expresses the idea of a recipient or donee; पातशाहानें अबदुल्लास जीवदान दिलें, the emperor spared Abdulla's life.

Note.—The inflections of the dative are partly derived from Sanskrit, and partly from Maráṭhí: the स and ना are of Sanskrit origin, and ला is a corruption of the Maráṭhí postposition लागीं near (लागणें to touch Sk. लग्). Both स and ना are modifications of the Sanskrit genitive terminations स्य and नां; thus,

Singular Genitive Sk. देवस्य, Prák. देवस्स, M. देवास (Dative).
Plural „ „ देवानां, Prák. देवाणं, M. देवांना (Dative).

The Prákrit, through which Maráṭhí is immediately derived, being deficient in the dative case, substituted the forms of the genitive for it; and hence the identity of the Maráṭhí dative inflections with those of the classical genitive. The Gujarati and Hindi dative forms claim the same origin.

§ 79. The Ablative case (अपादानी) is made up by the inflection ऊन or हून, and expresses the relation of separation; तो घरून आला, he came from home; मी पुण्याहून साताऱ्यास गेलों, I went from Poona to Sattara.

Note.—The Ablative हून or ऊन is a corruption of the Prákrit हिंतो or सुंतो.

§ 80. The Genitive case (संबंधी) is the substantive inflected by चा, and expresses the relation of origin, or possession, existing between two objects; त्या बलाढ्य वजीराचा मृत्यु छावणींत झाला, the death of this brave minister occurred in the camp. The relation between the two nouns वजीर and मृत्यु is indicated by the inflection चा.

§ 81. The Genitive case is adjectival in character, and may be said to qualify the noun by which it is governed. Hence it is modified like an adjective to agree with the noun it refers to:—

Masc. sing. त्याचा घोडा his horse, *plu.* त्याचे घोडे his horses.
Fem. „ त्याची घोडी his mare, „ त्याच्या घोड्या his mares.
Neut. „ त्याचें घोडें his horse, „ त्याचीं घोडीं his horses.

Note.—The genitive च्या is the modification of the Sanskṛit genitive inflection स्य, Prákrit स्स. In the dative form, which is derived from the same classical source, the स्य or स्स is reduced simply to स, but in the genitive, it is changed, by way of variety, to च or च्या. In Mahá-ráshtra, the स and च (*tsa*), which is the Maráṭhí sound of च (*cha*), are always interchangeable; thus सोसत नाहीं, I can't bear, or सोचत नाहीं; ठेस striking of the foot against a stone, or ठेच. In the upper provinces, where Hindi prevails, the letter क *ka* occupies the place of the Maráṭhí च, and स is frequently changed to क by the illiterate classes. The author heard the English word "station" pronounced as इसटेकन "istaken," at Jabalpur. The Hindi genitive and dative differ in form, only i. reference to the vowels of which they are composed: Dat. को *ko*, and Gen. का *ká*.

Note.—Of all the Aryan Indians, the Maráṭhís are most partial to the dento-palatal च *tsa* and the letter ळ *ḷa*; and the reason why they are so disposed to these sounds is their close proximity to the Dravidians, in whose vernaculars they are abundantly used. Moreover, in the principal Dravidian dialect, the Tamil, there is no sound or letter corresponding to स, and the letter स occurring in Sanskṛit words, is invariably substituted in that language by च *tsa*. It is no wonder, then, that the Maráṭhís should prefer the *tsa* sound of स *sa* to the *ka* of the Hindustanis, in the matter of the genitive termination. The change of *sa* to the Sanskṛit च *cha* would be violent, but not so its change to *tsa*.

Note.—The letter स *sa* has been displaced by several other letters in other languages. It is substituted by ज *ja*, र *ra*, ह *ha*, &c., and all these changes of *sa* are found to exist in the Indian languages. "A suffix, used in the formation of words which is peculiarly the property of neuter, is अस् *as*, which is still more frequently used in Zend than in Sanskṛit. In the *plural* these Zend neuters form *eṇhe* or *eñha*, and with this *ha* is evidently connected the lengthened हा in the New Persian." "As, however, the High German has, from its earliest period, repeatedly changed *s* into *r*, and *a* into *i*, I have no doubt that the *ir* the Middle, and High German *er*, is identified with the Sanskṛit neuter suffix अस्." "To the Latin, in like manner, belongs *rum* for *sum*; hence *istorum*, *istarum*."—*Bopp*.

§ 82. The Locative case (अधिकरणी, is inflected by ईं or आं, and indicates the relation of *position*; तूं आपल्या जागीं बैस sit in your own place; तो त्याच्या पायां पडला he prostrated himself at his feet). These inflections are not usually used in prose, but are superseded by the postposition आंत *in*. In poetry they are freely used; thus,

अंतरीं निर्मळ वाचेचा रसाळ, त्याचे गळां माळ असो नसो—*Tukárám*.

Note.—The Locative ईं or आं is derived from the Prákṛit termination अम्मि; thus, *Sing.* Sk. वृक्षे, Prák. वच्छे, वच्छम्मि, M. ईं or आं.

§ 83. The Vocative case (संबोधन) is a modified form of the substantive, identical with what is called the *crude-form* (§ 82), and is used in addressing a person; मुला, इकडे ये, child, come here.

Note.—Sometimes the Sanskṛit Vocative forms are used in dignified composition, especially in poetry; as हे हरे, for हरी, O Hari; हे गुरो (for गुरू) O Master! हे प्रभो (for प्रभू) O Lord; हे भगवन्, (for भगवाना) O God!

§ 84. The following is a table of the case-terminations:—

Cases (विभक्ति).	*Inflections* (प्रत्यय).
The Nominative	....
The Accusative	....
The Instrumental	नें *sing.*, नीं, *plu.*, by; शीं, *sing.* and *plu.*, with or against.
The Dative	स, ला, *sing.*, स, ला, ना, *plu.*, to.
The Ablative	हून, ऊन, from or than.
The Genitive	चा, *m sing.*, of.
The Locative	ईं, or आं, in.
The Vocative	*The Crude-form.*

§ 85. Besides these principal inflections, the following are also employed:—

Instrumental—नें, एं, *sing.*, नीं, ईं, हीं, *plu.*

Dative—तें and the *Crude-form.*

Note.—These instrumental case-endings are generally used in the Konkan, but they are not all admitted into the reading books. The inflections नें and नीं are affixed to pronouns,—the personal, relative and demonstrative; and Konkani writers always prefer these to those given in the text. ईं and its modification शीं in their original sense of *instrumental* agency, are, at present, confined to the popular dialects of the inhabitants of the Konkan, while शीं, in the sense of *with* or *against*, is universally employed ; तूं त्याशीं बोलूं नको do not speak with him ; झुलु लोक इंग्रजांशीं मोठ्या निकरानें लढले, the Zulus fought with great determination with or against the English. The forms एं and ईं chiefly occur in poetry ; also in old prose writings: मग राजानें बहुत सन्मानें भेट घेतली, then the king received him with great honour ; रघुनाथपंतीं जाऊन भेट घेतली Raghoonathpant went and saw him.

उपजला भावो तुझे कृपें सिद्धी जावो.—*Tukaram.*

हातीं हित आहे करील तयासी आपऊनी ऋषीं सांगितलें.—*Tukaram.*

Note.—The Dative तें is *exclusively* used in *poetry*.

§ 86. The following postpositions are sometimes substituted for the case-endings :—

Instrumental कडून, करून, करवीं, जवळून, द्वारें, by or through.

Dative पाशीं, जवळ, प्रत, to ; करितां, साठीं, अर्थ, स्तव, for.

Ablative पासून, जवळून, from ; पेक्षां, परीस, than.

Genitive ....

Locative आंत, मध्यें, in ; विषयीं, संबंधीं, about.

Vocative { अरे, रे, हे, अजी, अगा, गा O *m.* / अगे, गे, अगो, अजी, O *f.* } *sing.* अहो, अजी, O *m., f., plu.*

Note.—The postpositions are usually affixed instead of the case-terminations, when the relations to be expressed are of a material and sensible character ; the abstruse and metaphorical ones take the case endings, and chiefly those rarely used in prose ; त्याच्या हातीं (not हातांत) काय आहे ? what has he in his hands or power ?

Note.—The vocative particles are placed *before* the crude-form of the noun ; अरे मुला, O boy ; अहो बायांनों, O ladies.

Note.—All the above postpositions except करून, can be affixed to the crude-form of the noun but करून is affixed to the instrumental caseform of the noun in एं and the pronominal case-form in नें ; as शस्त्रें-करून by means of the weapon ; तेणेंकरून by means of it.

CHAPTER VIII.

Declension of Substantives.

DECLENSIONS ENUMERATED.

§ 87—§ 100.

§ 87. The inflection of a substantive by means of the case-terminations is called *Declension* or विभक्तिकरण. The following is an example of a substantive declined in all the cases :—

घर a house.

	Singular.	*Plural.*
Nom.	घर a house	घरें houses
Acc.	घर a house	घरें houses
Inst.	घरानें by a house घराशीं with a house	घरांनीं by houses घरांशीं with houses
Dat.	घरास, घराला to a house	घरांस घरांला, घरांना to houses
Abl.	घरून, घराहून from a house	घरांहून from houses
Gen.	घराचा of a house	घरांचा of houses
Loc.	घरीं in a house	घरीं in houses
Voc.	घरा O house	घरांनों O houses

§ 88 From the above example of the declension of the noun घर, it is evident that the noun changes its radical form before assuming the case-terminations. Thus, for instance, the above word घर becomes घरा before assuming the case-terminations. *The form which the noun assumes before taking the case-endings to make up its complete case-form or* विभक्ति *is called its* CRUDE-FORM, *i.e.*, the unfinished or imperfect form. The Maráṭhí grammarians call it the सामान्यरूप *Sámányarúpa i.e.*, a form *common* to nouns before the case-endings.

§ 89. THE CRUDE-FORMS ARE PRODUCED BY THE UNION OF THE DEMONSTRATIVE PRONOUNS या *yá* AND ई *í* WITH NOUNS; as, आंबा a mango + या = आंब्या ; भिंत a wall + ई = भिंती.

§ 90. THE MASCULINE AND NEUTER NOUNS ASSUME या, AND THE FEMININE NOUNS ASSUME ई.

§ 91. If the vowels in which Maráṭhí nouns terminate were of a uniform nature, all the nouns would regularly assume the या and ई; but the vowels are, as we have noticed in the chapters on Orthography, of various properties and powers (some being strong and others weak, some noble and others mean), and the nouns, consequently, assume the demonstratives somewhat irregularly.

§ 92. Some Nouns assume the Demonstratives in their Pure Forms, others in their Impure or Modified Forms, and the rest Entirely Reject them.

§ 93. Hence there are three classes of the crude-forms, or, in other words, there are Three Declensions (विभक्तिरूप कारणें) in Maráṭhí.

§ 94. The three Declensions are thus enumerated and described:—

I.—In the First Declension are included all those nouns which assume the या and ई in their pure forms.

II.—In the Second Declension are comprehended all those nouns which assume the या and ई in their impure forms.

III.—In the Third Declension are contained all those nouns which entirely reject the या and ई.

§ 95. The impure or modified forms of या and ई are आ and ए respectively. The आ is obtained by dropping the semi-vowel य् of या, and the ए, by changing the ई to its corresponding diphthong ए. (Sect. 11.)

Note.—Strictly speaking there is only one declension in Maráṭhí, viz., the first, and the other two may be considered its sub-divisions.

§ 96. The following is a table of the Distinguishing Terminations of the crude-form in the Three Declensions:—

First Declension.	Second Declension.	Third Declension.
या *m.*, *n.*, ई *f.*	आ *m.*, *n.*, ए *f.*	No change for the crude-form.

§ 97. The Maráṭhí Substantives are thus arranged under the Three Declensions:—

The First Declension.

Masculine Nouns.

1. All the Masculine nouns ending in आ and ई; thus, गाडा a cart, crude-form गाड्या; धोबी a washerman, crude-form धोब्या.

Feminine Nouns.

2. Most of the Feminine nouns ending in अ, and all those ending in ई; thus, भित a wall, crude-form भिंती; गाडी a carriage, crude-form गाडी.

Neuter Nouns.

3. All the Neuter nouns ending in ईं and एं; as, मिरीं a pepper, crude-form मिऱ्या; केळें a plantain, crude-form केळ्या.

The Second Declension.

Masculine and Neuter Nouns.

1. All Masculine and Neuter nouns ending in अ; as, Masc. देव a god, crude-form देवा; Neut. दार a door, crude-form दारा.

Feminine Nouns.

2. Some of the Feminine Nouns which end in अ, and all those ending in आ; thus, जीभ the tongue, crude-form जिभे; माता a mother, crude-form माते.

The Third Declension.

Masculine, Feminine, and Neuter Nouns.

1. All the nouns ending in short इ and उ; as कवि a poet, *m.*; धेनु a milch cow, *f.*; अक्षि an eye, *n.* *Though these nouns reject the demonstrative* या *and* ई, *they lengthen their terminating vowels before assuming the case-endings; as,* कवीनें *by a poet,* धेनूनें *by a cow.* These are pure Sanskrit words, and are not strictly amenable to the rules of Maráṭhí grammar.

2. All the nouns ending in ऊ; as, चाकू a penknife, चाकूला to a penknife.

3. All the nouns ending in the diphthongs, viz., ए (except the neuter nouns in ए), ऐ, ओ and औ; as, बायको a woman, बायकोला to a woman.

§ 98. The Maráṭhí nouns are arranged in the following Table according to their *Terminating Vowels* :—

First Declension.

Masculine. आ, ई.	Feminine. अ, ई.	Neuter. ई, ए.

Second Declension.

Masculine. अ.	Feminine. अ, आ.	Neuter. अ.

Third Declension.

Masculine. इ, उ, ऊ and the diphthongs.	Feminine. इ, उ, ऊ and the diphthongs.	Neuter इ, उ, and ऊ.

§ 99. It is thus evident that it is only those nouns which end in अ, आ, ई, ए, *four vowels*, that are changed in the crude-form, while the others remain unaltered. This is an important fact for the student to bear in mind as a knowledge of it would very much facilitate his study of the Declensions. To impress this important truth still further on the mind, we will give another Table, in which the terminating vowels of the nouns are given in their alphabetical order, and opposite to them the vowels terminating their crude-forms are put down in separate columns.

§ 100. This Table will, also, help the student to determine the crude-forms by means of the radical terminations of nouns. If the noun is Masculine, the termination of its crude-form wil, be found in the column marked " Masculine. " Thus, for instance, the crude-form of the neuter noun द्वार a door, is द्वारा, as आ stands opposite to अ in the Neuter column.

Root Terminations.	Crude-form Terminations.		
M., F., N.	Masculine.	Feminine.	Neuter.
अ	आ	ई or ए	आ
आ	या		०
ई	या	ई	या
एं (Neut.)	०	०	या
इ, उ, ऊ ए, ऐ, ओ, औ	No Crude-form Terminations.		

Note.—The information suggested by the above Table is embodied in the following rules, which may be committed to memory by the student.

Masculine Nouns.

1. All the Masculine nouns in अ assume आ.
2. All the Masculine nouns in आ and ई assume या.
3. All the remaining Masculine nouns remain unchanged.

Feminine Nouns.

1. The Feminine nouns in अ may assume either ई or ए.
2. All the Feminine nouns in आ assume ए.
3. All the Feminine nouns in ई assume ई.
4. All the remaining Feminine nouns remain unaltered.

Neuter Nouns.

1. All the Neuter nouns in अ assume आ.
2. All the Neuter nouns in ई and एं, assume या.
3. All the remaining Neuter nouns remain unchanged.

NOTE.

1. The employment of या and ई to make up the crude-forms of nouns, though suggested for the first time in this book, is not exclu-

sively confined to Maráṭhí, but extends to several other languages of the Indo-Aryan family. In the Hindi there is a trace of the demonstrative ई in the crude-forms of substantives ending in आ; as बेटा a son, the *crude-form* बेटे, and the *dative case-form* बेटेको, to a son. In Sanskṛit, the letter य is similarly used, as for instance, in the forms त्याम and स्याम, the य being combined with the pronominal bases त *ta* and स *sa*. The य in Sanskṛit is relative and not demonstrative. In the Gothic dialects, which bear a strong resemblance to the Pali and the Mahárástri (Maráṭhí), the demonstrative या is used in the form of य *ya* or यो *yo*, denoting he or तो. The य or यो is inserted between the adjective to be declined and the case-endings Sometimes the pronoun loses its semi-vowel य, as in Maráṭhí, and the terminations of the adjective are shortened. The Old Sclavonic, differing from the Lithuanian, declines only in some cases the adjective together with the appended pronoun, but in most cases, the latter alone. "While, however, in the Lithuanian, the approved pronoun has lost its य only in some cases, in the Old Sclavonic, that pronoun has lost, in many more, not only the य, but also its vowel, and therefore the whole base, and the termination alone is left" (as is the case in Maráṭhí in reference to the words of the Third Declension).—*Bopp.*

2. The demonstrative or relative या or यो came to be used by way of apposition to the noun; a kind of support to aid the noun in bearing the weight of the case-endings. And this appositional use of या in the crude-form is clearly established by the old archaic forms extant in Maráṭhí. In poetry these old forms are common; thus,

स्वगडियांस वदे वचनामृता.—*Wáman.*

In this line स्वगडियांस is written for the modern form स्वगड्यांस, and even, at present, Sástris unacquainted with the current modes of spelling, write the appositional demonstratives separate. Indeed, the presence of या is discovered in some forms of verbs, as well as nouns and the Maráṭhí verbs, etymologically nominal or participial, assume it when they end noun sentences, governed by a postposition; as, मूठमाती दिल्यावर घरीं जाऊं, we shall go home after we have buried him.

सोडविलियाविणें आग्नांसि सहसा नाहीं जाणें.—*Mukteshvar.*

In the old Bakhars या is usually written separate; राजियास घेऊन डेरियास जाणें Take the king and go to the camp.

3. The demonstrative forms या and ई were employed in Old Maráṭhí without distinction; hence the present crude-forms derived from the genitive and the adjectives are of two kinds, in या and ए; रामाच्या or रामाचे घरीं गेलों होतों, I went to Rama's house.

उन्हाळेमी (उन्हाळयानी) न तापे.—*Dnyánobá.*

भावेंवीण (भावावीण) भक्ति.—*Dnyánobá.*

4. The changes of या and ई in the Second Declension, or their utter rejection in the Third Declension, is easily explained. The अ is, indeed, a grave vowel, but being short, it is too feeble to bear the full weight of या, together with that of the case-ending; and it therefore changes the या to आ. The short vowels इ and उ are too delicate to assume the demonstratives, and, therefore, reject the demonstratives या and ई, though they are lengthened to bear the weight of the case-endings. The grave vowel आ usually submits to a mutilation by या; but it rejects it entirely when it comes at the end of a *proper name*, as derogatory to the dignity of a proper name. Indeed, all nouns resist changes of the crude-form as *degrading*, and when they are forced to submit, they usually become deteriorated. The words ending in the short vowels इ and उ being of Sanskṛit origin, are too shy to assume the या or ई, and therefore reject them, though they lengthen the short vowels to bear the weight of the case-endings. Thus, a proper noun, when modified by या or ई, degenerates into a form of contempt; as रामा Rámá, a man's name, राम्या a contemptuous form for Rámá; यमुनी Yamuni, a contemptuous form for यमुना, a woman's name. Even common nouns, when used honorifically, retain their radical form; माळी (for माळ्या) इकडे ये gardener, come here. In Hindi, also, those words of Sanskṛit origin which are not quite naturalised in the language, are not changed in the crude-form. Thus, घोडा a horse, becomes घोडे in the crude-form, but राजा a king retains its form, as राजाको to a king; दाताको to a donor. Even common Hindi words of honour remain unchanged; as काका a paternal uncle, काकाको; चचा a maternal uncle; लाला a schoolmaster, a title of respect. The vowel ऊ, and the diphthongs are too dignified (§ 19) to yield to a mutilation, and too strong not to be able to bear singly the weight of the case-endings. The feeble vowel ई, essentially characteristic of the feminine gender, and the neuter diphthong एं, weakened by the anusvár, bend their necks without the least resistance to the absolute domination of the demonstratives या and ई. The feminine nouns ending in आ, and a few in अ derived from Sanskṛit nouns in आ, are too proud to submit

tamely to the modifying influences of a purely vernacular or vulgar inflection. Painfully conscious, however, of their feminine weak nature they assume the Sanskṛit ए rather than the vulgar ई, in conformity with the laws of combination, denominated संधि; not an unusual mode of submission among proud mortals, who, when forced to submit, seek to bow the head in a dignified manner.

When it is necessary to express extreme contempt, a double inflection is employed, in Maráṭhi, in utter defiance of the rules of grammar; पोर a child, usually in contempt, of which पोरा is its regular crude-form, and पोऱ्या = पोरा + या, is its doubly inflected form, indicative of extreme contempt; रे पोऱ्या O you brat, instead of रे पोरा O child.

CHAPTER IX.

Declension—*continued.*

THE FIRST DECLENSION.

§ 101—§ 108.

Masculine Substantives.

§ 101. Masculine Nouns ending in आ and ई assume या.

Examples.

Root, आंबा A mango; crude-form, आंब्या.

	Singular.	*Plural.*
Nom.	आंबा a mango	आंबे mangoes
Acc.	आंबा a mango	आंबे mangoes
Instr.	आंब्यानें by a mango	आंब्यांनीं by mangoes
	आंब्याशीं with a mango	आंब्यांशीं with mangoes
Dat.	आंब्याला-स to a mango	आंब्यांला-स-ना to mangoes
Abl.	आंब्याहून than a mango	आंब्यांहून than mangoes
Gen.	आंब्याचा of a mango	आंब्यांचा of mangoes
Loc.	आंब्यांत in a mango	आंब्यांत in mangoes
Voc.	आंब्या O mango	आंब्यांनों O mangoes

Note.—The ablative termination हून oftener expresses *comparison* than ablation or separation, and may be expressed in English by "than" as well as "from." It has the ablative sense chiefly when affixed to nouns of locality or place; as, तो पुण्याहून आला he came *from* Poona, but तो रामाहून मोठा आहे he is bigger *than* Rama. The postposition पासून expresses the ablative sense of "from."

Root, माळी A gardener; crude-form, माळ्या.

	Singular.	*Plural.*
Nom.	माळी a gardener	माळी gardeners
Acc.	माळी a gardener	माळी gardeners
Instr.	माळ्यानें by a gardener	माळ्यांनीं by gardeners
	माळ्याशीं with a gardener	माळ्यांशीं with gardeners
Dat.	माळ्याला-स to a gardener	माळ्यांला-स-ना to gardeners
Abl.	माळ्याहून than a gardener	माळ्यांहून than gardeners
Gen.	माळ्याचा of a gardener	माळ्यांचा of gardeners
Loc.	माळ्यांत in a gardener	माळ्यांत in gardeners
Voc.	माळ्या O gardener	माळ्यांनों O gardeners

Note.—Proper names of persons and respectful appellations reject the या in the crude-form; thus, आबा a respectful word for a father makes आबाला to a father, and not आब्याला; रावजी Rávjí, रावजीला to Rávjí, not रावज्याला; so also मुनशी a Mahomedan teacher, मुनशीला to a Munshí; स्वामी a lord; स्वामीला to a lord. The abstract noun in आ as चांगुलपणा, and Sanskṛit words not naturalised in the language may not assume the या; चांगुलपणाला to goodness; चंद्रमा, the moon, चंद्रमाला to the moon.

Note.—The word हत्ती an elephant, is irregularly declined; it does not assume या. Some Sanskṛit words in ई, not naturalised in the language, reject the या; as करी an elephant; केसरी a lion.

	Singular.	*Plural.*
Nom.	हत्ती an elephant	हत्ती elephants
Acc.	हत्ती an elephant	हत्ती elephants
Instr.	हत्तीनें by an elephant	हत्तींनीं by elephants
	हत्तीशीं with an elephant	हत्तींशीं with elephants
Dat.	हत्तीला to an elephant	हत्तींला-स-ना to elephants
Abl.	हत्तीहून than an elephant	हत्तींहून than elephants
Gen.	हत्तीचा of an elephant	हत्तींचा of elephants
Loc.	हत्तींत in an elephant	हत्तींत in elephants
Voc.	हत्ती O elephant	हत्तींनों O elephants

Note.—The word राजा *rádzá*, a king, is often written in the crude-form without the या, but pronounced as if united with या; राजा a king, राज्याला *rájálá*, to a king.

Note.—The words in स are usually written with श, instead of स्य; as आरसा a looking-glass, आरशाला or आरस्याला to a looking-glass.

Note.—Words ending in या in the root do not append an additional या; as वाटाड्या a guide, वाटाड्याला to a guide.

Neuter Substantives.

§ 102. Nouns ending in ई and ए assume या.

Examples.

Root, मोती A pearl; crude-form, मोत्या.

	Singular.	*Plural.*
Nom.	मोती a pearl	मोत्यें pearls
Acc.	मोती a pearl	मोत्यें pearls
Instr.	मोत्यानें by a pearl	मोत्यांनीं by pearls
	मोत्याशीं with a pearl	मोत्यांशीं with pearls
Dat.	मोत्याला-स to a pearl	मोत्यांला-स-ना to pearls
Abl.	मोत्याहून than a pearl	मोत्यांहून than pearls
Gen.	मोत्याचा of a pearl	मोत्यांचा of pearls
Loc.	मोत्यांत in a pearl	मोत्यांत in pearls
Voc.	मोत्या O pearl	मोत्यांनों O pearls

Note.—बीं seed collectively; dative, बियाला to seed.

Root, तळें A tank; crude-form, तळ्या.

	Singular.	*Plural.*
Nom.	तळें a tank	तळीं tanks
Acc.	तळें a tank	तळीं tanks
Instr.	तळ्यानें by a tank	तळ्यांनीं by tanks
	तळ्याशीं with a tank	तळ्यांशीं with tanks
Dat.	तळ्याला-स to a tank	तळ्यांला-स-ना to tanks
Abl.	तळ्याहून than a tank	तळ्यांहून than tanks
Gen.	तळ्याचा of a tank	तळ्यांचा of tanks
Loc.	तळ्यांत in a tank	तळ्यांत in tanks
Voc.	तळ्या O tank	तळ्यांनों O tanks

Feminine Substantives.

§ 103. Feminine nouns ending in अ and ई assume ई.

There are in all 2,500 feminine nouns ending in अ in the Maráṭhí language, out of which all except some 290 that belong exclusively to the Second Declension and are given below (§ 106,) fall under this, *i. e.*, the First Declension.

Example.

Root, भिंत A wall; crude-form, भिंती.

	Singular.	*Plural.*
Nom.	भिंत a wall	भिंती walls
Acc.	भिंत a wall	भिंती walls
Instr.	{ भिंतीनें by a wall भिंतीशीं with a wall	भिंतींनीं by walls भिंतींशीं with walls
Dat.	भिंतीला-स to a wall	भिंतींला-स-ना to walls
Abl.	भिंतीहून than a wall	भिंतींहून than walls
Gen.	भिंतीचा of a wall	भिंतींचा of walls
Loc.	भिंतींत in a wall	भिंतींत in walls
Voc.	भिंती O wall	भिंतींनो O walls

Note.—The Maráthi nouns which come under this declension are principally of this description :—

(*a*) Such words as are derived from Sanskrit nouns ending in ई:—

आग fire (Sk. अग्नि *m.*)
कूस side (Sk. कुक्षि *m.*)
केळ a plantain tree (Sk. कदली)
गांठ a knot (Sk. ग्रंथि)
चूल a fireplace (Sk. चुल्ली)
धूळ dust (Sk धूलि)
भिंत a wall (Sk. भित्ति)
मूठ a fist (Sk. मुष्टि)
रास a heap (Sk. राशि)
वात a wick (Sk. वर्त्ति)
वेल a creeper (Sk. वल्ली)
सवत a rival wife (Sk. सपत्नी)
सुंठ dry ginger (Sk शुंठी)

(*b*) Such nouns as are derived from Maráthi verbs :—

ओळख acquaintance, from ओळखणें to be acquainted.
चाळण a sieve, from चाळणें to strain.
ठेव a deposit, from ठेवणें to keep.
तुट a deficiency, from तुटणें to break (*intrans. verb*).
तोड a device, from तोडणें to break (*trans. verb*).
भेट a meeting, from भेटणें to meet.
वांक a bending, from वांकणें to bend.
सूट an abatement, from सुटणें to get loose.

(*c*) Such nouns as are derived from Persian and Arabic, ending in त, द, न, र, श, स :—

जामीन a security	तरवार (1st and 2nd) a sword
जाहिरात an advertisement	दऊत an inkstand
तकरार striving	नांद intoxication
तब्यत disposition	मिजास temper

(*d*) English words introduced into the language, when viewed as feminine, usually assume ई ; thus—

टिकीट a ticket	स्लेट a slate
पेनसिल a pencil	नोटिस a notice

When the penultimate इ of English words is changed to अ, the word is usually considered as neuter ; ती टिकीट that ticket, *f.* ; तें टिकट *n.*

Note.—The feminine monosyllabic words in अ remain undropped ; as बला विचारा ask mother.

Root गाडी a carriage; crude-form, गाडी (= गाडी + ई.)

	Singular.	*Plural.*
Nom.	गाडी a carriage	गाड्या carriages
Acc.	गाडी a carriage	गाड्या carriages
Instr.	गाडीनें by a carriage गाडीशीं with a carriage	गाड्यांनीं by carriages गाड्यांशीं with carriages
Dat.	गाडीला-स to a carriage	गाड्यांला-स-ना to carriages
Abl.	गाडीहून than a carriage	गाड्यांहून than carriages
Gen.	गाडीचा of a carriage	गाड्यांचा of carriages
Loc.	गाडींत in a carriage	गाड्यांत in carriages
Voc	गाडी O carriage	गाड्यांनों O carriages

Note.—The words स्त्री a woman, बी a seed, &c., may be optionally declined as follows :—

	Singular.	*Plural.*
Nom.	स्त्री a woman	स्त्रिया women.
Instr.	स्त्रियेनें (स्त्रीनें) by a woman	स्त्रियांनीं by women.
Dat.	स्त्रियेस (स्त्रीस) to a woman	स्त्रियांस to women.
Voc.	स्त्रिये (स्त्री) O woman	स्त्रियांनों O women.

When the plural form of बी a seed is made ब्या, instead of बिया (Sect. 70), the plural inflected forms are as ब्यांनीं by the seeds, ब्यांला to the seeds, &c.

Note.—The य in these forms comes from Sanskṛit, thus :—

Sanskṛit Declension.

	Singular.	*Plural.*
Nom.	स्त्री: a woman	स्त्रियः
Instr.	स्त्रिया by a woman.	स्त्रीभि:
Dat.	स्त्रियै to a woman	स्त्रीभ्य:

THE SECOND DECLENSION.

Masculine Substantives.

§ 104. Masculine nouns ending in अ assume आ.

Examples.

Root, बाप A father ; crude-form, बापा.

	Singular.	*Plural.*
Nom.	बाप a father	बाप fathers
Acc.	बाप a father	बाप fathers
Instr.	बापानें by a father	बापांनीं by fathers
	बापाशीं with a father	बापांशीं with fathers
Dat.	बापाला-स to a father	बापांला-स-ना to fathers
Abl.	बापाहून than a father	बापांहून than fathers
Gen.	बापाचा of a father	बापांचा of fathers
Loc.	बापांत in a father	बापांत in fathers
Voc.	बापा O father	बापांनों O fathers

Note.—The letters of the Alphabet, क *ka*, ख *kha*, ग *ga*, &c., do not assume आ ; as कला to *ka;* बला to *ba ;* ह्या. डपासून काय शिकावें ? What can we learn from this blockhead ?

Note.—The genitive forms of nouns ending in अ, when used as *adjectives*, do not inflect the noun in the crude-form ; as घरचा household, घराचा of the house : आह्मी घरचे वांसे आणिले आहेत, बाजारचे नाहींत, We have brought house-hold rafters, and not those from the bazaar. To also हातचें, पाडचें, पहरचें, रानचें, सरकारचें, &c. The general sense of such forms may be expressed in English by the phrase "*relating to.*"

Note.—Pure adjective forms could be substituted for such forms ; गुजराथचा or गुजराथी of Gujarat ; पैठणचें or पैठणी of Paithan ; नागपुरचें or नागपुरी of Nagpur ; बाजारचें or बाजारी तूप Bazaar ghee. The word प्रकार variety, usually takes the form प्रकारचा of variety.

Note.—Words in अ expressing *time* assume the genitive termination without any inflection: as सकाळ morning, सकाळचा of the morning; काल yesterday, कालचा of yesterday.

Note.—The masculine and neuter names of places in अ, having long vowels or nasalised syllables, usually take the dative ला without undergoing any inflectional change; तो इंग्लंडला भुलला he was fascinated by England; इराणला गेलों होतों. I went to Persia. But नगराला गेलों नव्हतों I did not go to Nagar.

Feminine Substantives.

§ 105. Feminine nouns ending in आ, and a few nouns ending in अ, assume ए.

Examples.

Root, कथा A tale; crude-form, कथे.

	Singular.	*Plural.*
Nom.	कथा a tale	कथा tales
Acc.	कथा a tale	कथा tales
Instr.	कथेनें by a tale कथेशीं with a tale	कथांनीं by tales कथांशीं with tales
Dat.	कथेला-स to a tale	कथांला-स-ना to tales
Abl.	कथेहून than a tale	कथांहून than tales
Gen.	कथेचा of a tale	कथांचा of tales
Loc.	कथेंत in a tale	कथांत in tales
Voc.	कथे O tale	कथांनों O tales

Note.—The names of females, when used respectfully, do not assume ए in the crude-form; thus, यमुना Yamuná, dat. यमुनाला To Yamuná; यमुनेला, the regular form, is not respectful.

Root, खाट A cot; crude-form, खाटे.

	Singular.	*Plural.*
Nom.	खाट a cot	खाटा cots
Acc.	खाट a cot	खाटा cots
Instr.	खाटेनें by a cot खाटेशीं with a cot	खाटांनीं by cots खाटांशीं with cots
Dat.	खाटेला-स to a cot	खाटांला-स-ना to cots
Abl.	खाटेहून than a cot	खाटांहून than cots
Gen.	खाटेचा of a cot	खाटांचा of cots
Loc.	खाटेंत in a cot	खाटांत in cots
Voc.	खाटे O cot	खाटांनों O cots

§ 106. The number of words in अ under this declension is about 290 (§ 70), and they are the following :—

अटक	खाट	झडप	तार	पैज	मांडणूक	लवंग
अडक	खारीक	झीक	तारीख	फातमा	मात	लशुन
अलंग	खीज	झूम	तालीम	फाम	मांद	लांक
अहेव	खूण	झूर	तिडक	फिरंग	मादवान	लाख
अळवीण	खूप	झोप	तिडीक	फुंक	मांदस	लांच
आउंज	खेप	टांग	तींज	फौज	मान	लाज
आत	खेम	टिच	तीट	ब	मानणूक	लाट
आंब [वस	खेव	टिवाटीव	तूळ	बग	माय	लाण
आवोस,आं	गजक	टीक	तेरीख	बाग	माव	लात
इरजीक	गंजीफ	टीच	तेरीज	बाज	माळ	लाताड
ईट	गप	टीप	तोफ	बाम	मेंग	लालूच
ईद	गरज	डांक	दरज	बीज	मोच	लांव
उणीव	गुंज	डांग	दाढ	बीद	मोट	लाळ
ऊब	गुंफ	डेग	दुरव	बूज	मोहनमान	लीख
एळ	गुराब	डेंग	दुशाख	बैत	मोहोर	लीद
एरीण	गोद	ढांग	धूव	बाद	मोहीम	लोंग
काड	चपडास	ढेंग	धोप	बोंब	मौज	वखटीक
कणीक	चाईन	ढेलच	नजर	भाक	म्हसक	वकणूक
कंबरor क-	चार	तज	नणंद	भांग	रकम	वर्त्तणूक
करप [मर	चिंच	तजवीज	नथ	बाज	रयत	वस्त
कथ	चितंग	तन	नमाज	भाड	राख	वहाणं
कांच	चिवार	तनाव	नरद	भाष	राखूळ	वाट
काव	चीच	तरफ	नाव	भांस	रांग	वाफ
कास	चीढ or ड	तलफ	नीज	भिकाळ	रांड	वाभळ
किलच	चीप	तवसाळ	नीद	भिक्षाळ	रांडमुंड	वांव
किलीच	चीर	तसर	नेणीव	भीक	रानघोळ	विलायत
किळळ	चील	तसरीफ	पईज	भीड	रीघ	वीज
कुमक	चुणूक	तहान	पखाजorस	भूक	रीझ	वीट
कुळीक	जंजीर	तळवाट	पश्चिम	भूज	रीप	वीड
कैद	जट	तक्षीम	पहाट	भोवंड	रीस	वीळ
कोईल or	जांग	ताऊज	पाच	भोवळ	रेघ	वेंग
कोईळ	जाग	ताज	पीण	मध	रेब	वेण
खच	जांघ	ताजीम	पुनव	मसक	रेंव	वेल
खडव	जाणीव	तान	पुन्येव	मसूर	रेवड	वेळ
खरूज	जिव्हorव्हे	तान्ह	पूर्व	महमाय	रोंय	शाकor स्व
खाक	जीभ	तांब	पेंठ	माठ	लंब	शाल

शाळ	शिव	शेंस	सवन	साव	सून	हुरमूज
शिक	शेंक	सकाळ	सहाण	सांव	सोंड	
शिणक	शेंज	सडक	साखर	सिक	सोनकाव	
शिप	शेंच	सदर	सांज or झ	सिकाल	हाक	
शीर	शेंद	समीध	सांड	सींव	हांव	
शिलक	शेंप	सव	साण	सूज	हुरडभूज	

Note.—Of the above feminine nouns, most are derived from Sanskṛit words ending in आ, and it is on this account that they, in spite of their altered form in a final अ, conform to the classical mode of declension. We shall, for illustration, trace a few Maráṭhí words in अ to their Sanskṛit originals in आ :—

M. आंब an acid — Sk. आम्ला
M. ईट or वीट a brick — Sk. इष्टिका
M. कणीक flour — Sk. काणिका
M. कास udder — Sk. कच्छा
M. खाट a cot — Sk. खट्वा
M. चीर a crevice — Sk. चिरा
M. जीभ the tongue — Sk. जिव्हा
M. नीज sleep — Sk. निद्रा
M. भीक alms — Sk. भिक्षा
M. माळ a garland — Sk. माला
M. राख ashes — Sk. रक्षा
M. लाज shame — Sk. लज्जा
M. सांज evening — Sk. संध्या
M. साळ a school — Sk. शाला

Note.—Some of these feminine words are derived from nouns ending in other vowels than आ—

M. वाट a way, Sk. वाट *m.*
M. वाफ vapour, Sk. बाष्प *m.*
M. मध honey, Sk. मधु *n.*

Note.—Some Maráṭhí words, though derived from Sánskṛít nouns in आ, assume ई in the crude-form; कावीळ jaundice (Sk. कामिला), Dative काविळीला to jaundice; so also हळद turmeric (Sk. हरिद्रा), Dative हळदीला, to turmeric.

Note.—Some words are declined either with इ or ए; as शिंप or शिंपी a shell, Dative शिंपेला or शिंपीला to a shell ; तरवार a sword, तरवारीला or तरवारेला to a sword.

Neuter Substantives.

§ 107. Neuter nouns ending in अ assume आ.

Examples.

Root, घर a house; crude-form, घरा.

	Singular.	*Plural.*
Nom.	घर a house	घरें houses
Acc.	घर a house	घरें houses
Instr.	घरानें by a house घराशीं with a house	घरांनीं by houses घरांशीं with houses
Dat.	घराला-स to a house	घरांला-स-ना to houses
Abl.	घराहून than a house	घरांहून than houses
Gen.	घराचा of a house	घरांचा of houses
Loc.	घरांत in a house	घरांत in houses
Voc.	घरा O house	घरांनो O houses

THE THIRD DECLENSION.

Masculine Substantives.

§ 108. Masculine Substantives in ऊ, ओ and औ reject the आ. There are no masculine nouns ending in the diphthongs ए and ऐ. (§ 54, 6.)

Examples.

चाकू, A penknife.

	Singular.	*Plural.*
Nom.	चाकू a penknife	चाकू penknives
Acc.	चाकू a penknife	चाकू penknives
Instr.	चाकूनें by a penknife चाकूशीं with a penknife	चाकूंनीं by penknives चाकूंशीं with penknives
Dat.	चाकूला-स to a penknife	चाकूंला-स-ना to penknives
Abl.	चाकूहून than a penknife	चाकूंहून than penknives
Gen.	चाकूचा of a penknife	चाकूंचा of penknives
Loc.	चाकूंत in a penknife	चाकूंत in penknives
Voc.	चाकू O penknife	चाकूंनो O penknives

Note 1.—A few words ending in ऊ assume वा in the form of वा, व being the semi-vowel corresponding to ऊ (§ 20). In the Dakhan, however, the inflection in वा is almost entirely ignored, except in the words गहूं wheat, and भाऊ a brother; ह्या गव्हाला to this grain of wheat; भावाला to a brother. When भाऊ is used as a respectful appellation, it is not inflected; भाऊला आमंत्रण आहे, पण माझ्या भावाला नाहीं, Bhau is invited, but not my brother.

Note 2.—The following seven words may take, or reject, the वा: गू fœces, चाटू a ladle, नारू a guinea-worm, पणतू a great-grandson, लाडू a sweet cake, विस्तू fire, वेळू a bamboo, सांकू a kind of bridge, साडू a brother-in-law.

Note 3.—The following two substantives may assume वा or आ, or remain unchanged: नातू a grandson, विंचू a scorpion.

Note 4.—The following four words may retain their form, or assume आ: तट्टू a pony, परभू a Parbhu, यात्रेकरू a pilgrim, वाटसरू a traveller.

Obs. The student may, except the words गहूं and भाऊ a brother, always reject the या or वा.

Examples,

(2) लाडू A cake.

	Singular.	*Plural.*
Nom.	लाडू a cake	लाडू cakes
Instr.	लाड्वानें or लाडूनें by a cake	लाड्वांनीं or लाडूंनीं by cakes
Gen.	लाड्वाचा or लाडूचा of a cake	लाड्वांचा or लाडूंचा of cakes
Voc.	लाड्वा or लाडू O cake	लाड्वांनो or लाडूंनो O cakes

(3) नातू A grandson.

Singular.

Nom.	नातू a grandson
Instr.	नात्वानें, नातानें or नातूनें by a grandson
Voc.	नात्वा, नाता, नातू O grandson

Plural.

Nom.	नातू grandsons
Instr.	नात्वांनीं, नातांनीं, नातूंनीं by grandsons
Voc.	नात्वांनो, नातांनो, नातूंनो O grandsons

(4) यात्रेकरू A pilgrim.

Singular.

Nom.	यात्रेकरू a pilgrim
Instr.	यात्रेकरूनें or यात्रेकरानें by a pilgrim
Voc.	यात्रेकरू or यात्रेकरा O pilgrim

Plural.

Nom.	यात्रेकरू pilgrims
Instr.	यात्रेकरूंनीं or यात्रेकरांनीं by pilgrims
Voc.	यात्रेकरूंनों or यात्रेकरांनों O pilgrims

लाहो, Covetousness.

	Singular.	*Plural.*
Nom.	लाहो covetousness	लाहो covetousness
Instr.	लाहोनें by covetousness	लाहोंनीं by covetousness
Voc.	लाहो O covetousness	लाहोंनों O covetousness

पौ, A mark on a die.

	Singular.	*Plural.*
Nom.	पौ a mark on a die	पौ marks on a die
Instr.	पौनें by a mark on a die	पौंनीं by marks on a die
Voc.	पौ O mark on a die	पौंनों O marks on a die

Note.—Masculine nouns in ओ and औ are few and not in common use, § 54, 7. The words डोहो *m.*, a deep hole in a river, and मोहो *m. n.*, a bee's nest, are better written as डोह and मोह, and inflected with आ.

Feminine Substantives.

109. The Feminine nouns in ऊ, ए, ऐ and ओ, do not change in the crude-form. There are no feminine nouns in औ.

Examples.

दारू, Spirituous liquor; crude-form, दारू.

	Singular.	*Plural.*
Nom.	दारू liquor	दारू liquors
Acc.	दारू liquor	दारू liquors
Instr.	दारूनें by liquor दारूशीं with liquor	दारूंनीं by liquors दारूंशीं with liquors
Dat.	दारूला-स to liquor	दारूंला-स-ना to liquors
Abl.	दारूहून than liquor	दारूंहून than liquors
Gen.	दारूचा of liquor	दारूंचा of liquors
Loc.	दारूंत in liquor	दारूंत in liquors
Voc.	दारू O liquor	दारूंनों O liquors

Note.—A good many feminine words in ऊ are inflected with वे in the Konkan, but the student should adhere to the above rule. Thus:—

	Singular.	*Plural.*
Nom.	जळू a leech	जळवा leeches
Instr.	जळूनें or जळवेनें, by a leech	जळवांनीं by leeches
Voc.	जळू or जळवे O leech	जळवांनों O leeches

बायको, A woman.

	Singular.	*Plural.*
Nom.	बायको a woman	बायका women
Instr.	बायकोनें by a woman	बायकांनीं by women
Voc.	बायको O woman	बायकांनों O women

Neuter Substantives.

§ 110. The Neuter Substantives in ऊं usually retain the ऊं. There are no neuter nouns ending in the diphthongs, except those which terminate in the nasalised एं, and they belong to the First Declension, § 94.

Example.

राजाळूं, A vegetable.

	Singular.	*Plural.*
Nom.	राजाळूं a vegetable	राजाळें vegetables
Acc.	राजाळूं a vegetable	राजाळें vegetables
Instr.	राजाळूनें by a vegetable	राजाळ्यांनीं by vegetables
Dat.	राजाळूला-स to a vegetable	राजाळ्यांला-स-ना to vegetables
Abl.	राजाळूहून than a vegetable	राजाळ्यांहून than vegetables
Gen.	राजाळूचा of a vegetable	राजाळ्यांचा of vegetables
Loc.	राजाळूंत in a vegetable	राजाळ्यांत in vegetables
Voc.	राजाळू O vegetable	राजाळ्यांनों O vegetables

Note.—1. The noun तारूं a ship is, always, declined with वा:

Example.

तारूं, A ship.

	Singular.	*Plural.*
Nom. & Acc.	तारूं a ship	तारवें ships
Instr.	तारवानें by a ship	तारवांनीं by ships
Voc.	तारवा O ship	तारवांनों O ships

Note.—2. The following nouns may be declined either in ऊ, या, or आ, the last inflection being most generally employed :—

कुंकूं a particular powder
कुसूं a town wall
गुरूं a horned cattle
गोखरूं a particular shrub
पिपरूं a drum-stick
तट्टूं a pony
थरूं a haft
निंबूं a lime
परसूं a yard
फाळूं a part of a plough
रताळूं a sweet potato
सुकाणुं a helm

Note.—3. The diminutives in कूं, डूं, रूं and लूं invariably assume आ. The following are the principal :—

करडूं a kid
किरडूं a reptile
कोंकरूं a lamb
गायरूं a cow
पाखरूं a bird
पिलूं a cub
मांजरूं a cat
मेंढरूं a sheep
रेडकूं a buffalo calf
वासरूं a calf
शेरडूं a goat
लेंकरूं a child
वाघरूं a tiger

Example.

पाखरूं, A bird.

	Singular.	*Plural.*
Nom. & Acc.	पाखरूं a bird	पाखरें birds पाखरें birds
Instr.	पाखरानें by a bird	पाखरांनीं by birds
Voc.	पाखरा O bird	पाखरांनों O birds

निंबु, A lime.

Nom. & Acc.	निंबूं a lime	निंबें limes
Instr.	निंबानें by a lime	निंबांनीं by limes
Voc.	निंबा O lime	निंबांनों O limes

Words ending in short इ *and* उ.

§ 111. The words in short इ and उ are pure Sanskṛit words, and they simply lengthen the final इ and उ in the crude-form.

Examples.

कवि A poet; crude-form, कवी.

	Singular.	*Plural.*
Nom.	कवि a poet	कवि poets
Acc.	कवि a poet	कवि poets
Instr.	कवीनें by a poet कवीशीं with a poet	कवींनीं by poets कवींशीं with poets
Dat.	कवीला-स to a poet	कवींला-स-ना to poets
Abl.	कवीहून than a poet	कवींहून than poets
Gen.	कवीचा of a poet	कवींचा of poets
Loc.	कवींत in a poet	कवींत in poets
Voc.	कवी O poet	कवींनों O poets

भानु the sun; crude-form भानू.

	Singular.	*Plural.*
Nom. & Acc.	भानु the sun	भानु suns
Instr.	भानूनें by the sun	भानूंनीं by suns
Voc.	भानू O sun	भानूंनों O suns

CHAPTER X.

The Adjective.

§ 112—§ 149.

§ 112. The Adjective is a word which is joined to a substantive, to qualify it; माझ्या बापानें हरजीला चांगली शिक्षा केली, My father gave Harji a good punishment; एक सगळा महिना झाला असावा, It must be one whole month since.

§ 113. The adjective may describe a noun, or limit its signification. Hence adjectives are considered as adjectives of quality, or adjectives of number, or numerals; त्या दुष्ट मनुष्याला मरून तीस वर्षे झालीं, It is thirty years since the death of that wicked man. In this sentence दुष्ट wicked is an adjective of quality, and तीस thirty is a numeral.

§ 114. When the adjective ends in आ, it is inflected, to show its agreement with the noun which it qualifies. The inflections which it assumes are the *General Gender Terminations* specified in § 46:—

Sing. चांगला *m.* चांगली *f.* चांगलें *n.*, good.
Plu. चांगले *m.* चांगल्या *f.* चांगलीं *n.*, good.

§ 115. Before an inflected noun, the adjective in आ assumes its crude-form made up with the demonstrative या; काळा black; काळ्या घोड्यानें by the black horse; मोठ्या घरांना, to large houses. Sometimes ए is optionally substituted for the demonstrative या; भल्या or भले बायकोचा Of a good woman.

Note.—In poetry sometimes the adjective takes the case-terminations of the noun it qualifies. In the following line the adjective उदासीन, takes the instrumental case-ending of the noun मानस:—

शस्य करावें भावें न असावें मानसें उदासीनें.

§ 116. When the adjective does not end in आ, it remains unaltered before the noun it qualifies; आंबट फळें Sour fruits; कडू भोपाळ्याला काय करूं, What shall I do with the bitter gourd?

Note.—In poetry the adjectives that do not end in आ may be inflected:—

मेनिका आली कौशिकनाथ सालंकारा, सुवक्त्रा.—Mukteshwar.
हें सांग सादिलें या रूपें अनंतें पुढें ही बहुतें करणें आहे.—Tukaram.
ऐशा प्रकारें खळ गर्व हंता, हरी तयाची सकळा अहंता.—Wáman.

Note.—The adjective in अ is sometimes inflected to agree with the noun it is joined to even in prose, especially when the adjective is emphatic in excited discourse:—माझे शूरा मुला, मला तुझा मुका घेऊं दे O my brave boy, let me kiss thee; आहा माझ्या पूज्या मामा तूं माझे अपराध क्षमा करशील? O my most worthy uncle, will you pardon my faults?

§ 117. If the final vowel of the root is changed to आ, the adjective becomes subject to inflectional changes like any ordinary adjective in आ. Thus लहान small, may be changed to लहाना; कडू bitter, to कडवा, &c; लहान्या तोंडांत in the small mouth; कडू or कडवें तूप bitter ghee, *n.*

§ 118. When an adjective is used as a substantive, it is declined like a substantive; बऱ्यांची संगत धरा associate with the good; वाइटाची फेड बऱ्यानें करा return good for evil. The masculine, feminine, and neuter adjectives ending in आ, ई and एं respectively, follow the First Declension, those ending in अ follow the Second, and the rest the Third:—

शहाणा. Wise.

Singular.

	Masculine.	*Neuter.*	*Feminine.*
Nom.	शहाणा	शहाणें.	शहाणी.
Acc.	शहाणा	शहाणें.	शहाणी.
Inst.	शहाण्यानें		शहाणीनें
Dat.	शहाण्याला-स		शहाणीला-स
Abl.	शहाण्याहून		शहाणीहून
Gen.	{ शहाण्याचा-ची-चें *sing.* / चे-च्या-चीं *plu.* }		{ शहाणीचा-ची-चें / शहाणीचे-च्या-चीं
Loc.	शहाण्यांत		शहाणींत
Voc.	शहाण्या		शहाणे
Attributive crude-form	शहाण्या		शहाण्या

Plural.

Nom.	शहाणे	शहाणीं	शहाण्या
Acc.	शहाणे	शहाणीं	शहाण्या
Instr.		शहाण्यांनीं	
Dat.		शहाण्यांला-स-ना	
Abl.		शहाण्यांहून	
		{ शहाण्यांचा *m.*, ची *f.*, चें *n.*, *sing.* / चे *m.*, च्या *f.*, चीं *n.*, *plu.*	
Loc.		शहाण्यांत	
Voc.		शहाण्यांनों	
Attributive crude-form		शहाण्यां	

वाईट, Bad.

	Singular.	*Plural.*
Nom. & Acc.	वाईट	वाईट
Instr.	वाइटानें	वाइटांनीं
Dat.	वाइटाला-स	वाइटांला-स
Voc.	वाइटा	वाइटांनों

कडू, Bitter.

	Singular.	*Plural.*
Nom. & Acc.	कडू	कडू
Instr.	कडूनें	कडूंनीं
Dat.	कडूला-स	कडूंला-स
Voc.	कडू	कडूंनों

Numerals.

§ 119. There are six kinds of Numerals, *viz.*, the Cardinals (संख्यावाचक), Ordinals (क्रमवाचक), Fractionals (संख्यांशवाचक), Distributives (भेदवाचक), Multiplicatives (गुणांक), and Indefinites (अनिश्चित संख्यावाचक).

1. *The Cardinal Numerals.*

§ 120. The Cardinals denote the *number* of objects, and answer to the question, *how many*? As, एक one, पन्नास fifty.

§ 121. In compound numerals, such as एकवीस twenty-one, बावीस twenty-two, &c., &c., the smaller number comes first in Maráṭhí, while in English it is just the reverse.

Note.—In Maráṭhí the elements of the compound word designating the numeral, cannot often be distinguished, as for instance in the compound बावन, बा stands for two, and वन, for fifty. बा is the modified form of बे (Sk. द्वि or द्वे two) and वन is derived from पन्नास (Pr. पण्णासा, Sk. पंचाशत् fifty). In Maráṭhí प is often changed to व in composition.

Note.—In Maráṭhí the numerals above one hundred are not used with "and," as in English; "one hundred *and* five," would be in Maráṭhí एकशें पांच, one hundred five; one thousand nine hundred *and* six, एक हजार नऊशें सहा.

§ 122. The idea of indefiniteness is expressed by the cardinals by joining two numbers together, without the conjunction "and" or "or;" thus, दहा पांच माणसें आलीं होतीं, some five or ten men had come; पांच सहा वर्षांत फळें येतील, it will bear fruit in five or six years; लाख सवालाख जमले होते, a lac or a lac and a quarter had assembled; चार पांच जण होते, some four or five men were present.

§ 123. When a cardinal is repeated, it makes up a distributive form: दोन दोन, two a piece; पांच पांच, by fives; एक एकाला दोन दोन भाकऱ्या दिल्या, each had two loaves given to him.

§ 124. The idea of multitude, expressed in English by the preposition "by," is denoted in Maráṭhí by inflecting the aggregate or collective cardinals, such as a hundred, a thousand, a lac, and a crore, by the particle ओं; as, "rupees by lacs," लाखों

रुपये ; अशीं म्यां शेंकडों शहरें पाहिलीं, I have seen such cities by hundreds. The following aggregates are thus inflected :— शेंकडा a hundred, शेंकडों by hundreds ; हजार a thousand, हजारों by thousands ; लाख a hundred thousand, लाखों by lacs ; क्रोड ten millions, क्रोडों by ten millions. The collective numeral शंभर a hundred, assumes the form of शेंकडा, and then takes the ओं.

This same idea of multitude is expressed, also, by the employment of the Sanskṛit forms of these aggregate numerals, combined with the word अवधि a limit ; as, सहस्रावधि by thousands ; कोट्यावधि लोकांच्या तोंडीं हीच वार्ता, this same story was in the mouths of millions of people.

§ 125. The numeral एक one, joined to another cardinal numeral, expresses the sense of indefiniteness denoted in English by the preposition "about ;" पांच एक रुपये द्यावे, please give him about five rupees ; शंभर एक माणसें आलीं होतीं, about a hundred men had come. It may only be used with words denoting quantity ; मण एक तूप आणा, bring about a maund of ghee.

§ 126. The cardinal numerals denote the idea of frequency by assuming the particle शां (Sk. शः) ; एकशां once ; शंभरशां a hundred times.

§ 127. The cardinals are thus written and pronounced :—

1	१	एक.	13	१३	तेरा.
2	२	दोन.	14	१४	चवदा, चौदा.
3	३	तीन.	15	१५	पंधरा.
4	४	चार.	16	१६	सोळा.
5	५	पांच.	17	१७	सत्रा.
6	६	सहा.	18	१८	अठरा.
7	७	सात.	19	१९	एकुणीस.
8	८	आठ.	20	२०	वीस.
9	९	नऊ, नव.	21	२१	एकवीस.
10	१०	दहा.	22	२२	बावीस, बेवीस.
11	११	अकरा.	23	२३	तेवीस.
12	१२	बारा.	24	२४	चोवीस, चौवीस, चव्वीस.

25	२५	पंचवीस.
26	२६	सव्वीस.
27	२७	सत्तावीस.
28	२८	अठ्ठावीस.
29	२९	एकुणतीस.
30	३०	तीस.
31	३१	एकतीस.
32	३२	बत्तीस.
33	३३	तेतीस, तेहतीस,
34	३४	चवतीस, चौतीस.
35	३५	पस्तीस.
36	३६	छत्तीस.
37	३७	सदतीस, सततीस.
38	३८	अडतीस, अठतीस.
39	३९	एकुणचाळीस.
40	४०	चाळीस.
41	४१	एकेचाळीस.
42	४२	बेचाळीस.
43	४३	त्रेचाळीस.
44	४४	चव्वेचाळीस.
45	४५	पंचेचाळीस.
46	४६	शेचाळीस.
47	४७	सत्तेचाळीस.
48	४८	अठ्ठेचाळीस.
49	४९	एकुणपन्नास.
50	५०	पन्नास.
51	५१	एकावन्न.
52	५२	बावन्न.
53	५३	त्रेपन्न.
54	५४	चौपन्न, चोपन्न.
55	५५	पंचावन्न.
56	५६	छप्पन्नं.
57	५७	सत्तावन्न.
58	५८	अठ्ठावन्न.
59	५९	एकुणसाठ.
60	६०	साठ.
61	६१	एकसष्ट.
62	६२	बासष्ट.
63	६३	त्रेसष्ट.
64	६४	चवसष्ट, चौसष्ट.
65	६५	पांसष्ट.
66	६६	सासष्ट.
67	६७	सदसष्ट, सत्सष्ट.
68	६८	अडसष्ट, अडुसष्ट.
69	६९	एकूणहत्तर.
70	७०	सत्तर.
71	७१	एकाहत्तर, एक्केहत्तर.
72	७२	बाहत्तर.
73	७३	त्रेहत्तर, त्र्याहत्तर.
74	७४	चौऱ्याहत्तर.
75	७५	पंचेहत्तर, पंचाहत्तर.
76	७६	शाहत्तर, शेहत्तर.
77	७७	सत्याहत्तर, सत्तेहत्तर.
78	७८	अठ्ठ्याहत्तर, अठ्ठेहत्तर.
79	७९	एकुणऐंशी.
80	८०	ऐंशी.
81	८१	एक्यांयशी.
82	८२	ब्यांयशी.
83	८३	त्र्यांयशी.
84	८४	चौऱ्यांयशी.
85	८५	पंचांयशी.
86	८६	शांयशी.
87	८७	सत्यांयशी.
88	८८	अठ्ठ्यांयशी.
89	८९	एकुणनव्वद, नव्यांयशी.
90	९०	नव्वद.
91	९१	एक्याण्णव.
92	९२	ब्याण्णव.
93	९३	त्र्याण्णव.
94	९४	चौऱ्याण्णव.
95	९५	पंचाण्णव.
96	९६	शाण्णण.
97	९७	सत्याण्णव.
98	९८	अठ्ठ्याण्णव.
99	९९	नव्याण्णव.
100	१००	शंभर.

101	१०१ एकशें एक.
102	१०२ एकशें दोन..
200	२०० दोनशें.
300	३०० तीनशें.
400	४०० चारशें.
500	५०० पांचशें.
1,000	१,००० हजार (Sk. सहस्त्र).
10,000	१०,००० दहाहजार (Sk. दशसहस्त्र).
1,00,000	१,००,००० लाख (Sk. लक्ष).
10,00,000	१०,००,००० दहालाख (Sk. दशलक्ष).
1,00,00,000	१,००,००,००० कोट, क्रोड (Sk. कोटि).

Note.—1. The Maráṭhi figures, indicating the numerals, being the same as the Sanskṛit, are modifications of the initial letters of the Sanskṛit names of the cardinals, and in their original forms as existing in ancient inscriptions, the initial letters can be distinctly recognized:—

१=ए in एक	one	(1)		६=ष in षट्	six	(6)
२=द in द्वि	two	(2)		७=स in सप्त	seven	(7)
३=त्र in त्रि	three	(3)		८=अ in अष्ट	eight	(8)
४=च in चतुर्	four	(4)		९=न in नव	nine	(9)
५=प in पंच	five	(5)		१०=द in दश	ten	(10)

Note.—2. In bills and notes the cardinals 101, 102, &c. are written as एकोत्तरशें (= एक + उत्तर exceeding + शें, one exceeding a hundred) दुवोत्तरशें, &c, instead of as एकशेंएक, एकशेंदोन, &c,

Note.—3. The numerals 24 चोवीस, 40 चाळीस and its compounds, and 54 चोपन्न, though written with च, are usually pronounced as if written with च्य.

Obs.—The English figures correspond to the Maráṭhi, and are denominated Arabic figures; but the figures, though originally introduced into Europe from Arabia, were not invented by the Arabs but by the Hindus, and the Arabs acknowledge their Indian origin.

§ 128. Except the first four, the rest of the cardinal numerals are regularly declined—those ending in अ take आ in the crude-form, and all the others remain unchanged. Thus,

(अ)	सात	seven,	Dat.	साताला to seven.
(आ)	सहा	six.	Dat.	सहाला to six.
(ई)	ऐशीं	eighty.	Dat.	ऐशींला to eighty.

When used before inflected or uninflected nouns they do not undergo any change : सात माणसें or माणसांला seven men or to seven men ; पांचशें रुपये or पांचशें रुपयांनीं five hundred rupees or with five hundred rupees.

Note.—शें a hundred, used in numeral compounds, changes the एं to आ in the crude-form ; दोनशें two hundred, दोनशांला to two hundred, पांचशांला to five hundred.

§ 129. The numeral एक one takes आ in the crude-form, but when it refers to a feminine noun, it assumes ई :—

Nom.	एक one, *m.*, *n.*	एक one, *f.*
Dat.	एकाला to one	एकीला to one
Gen.	एकाचा of one	एकीचा of one

§ 130. The numerals दोन two, तीन three, and चार four are changed to दोहों, तिहीं and चोहों respectively, in the crude-form :—

Nom.	दोन two	*Dat*	दोहोंला to two
Nom.	तीन three	*Dat.*	तिहींला to three
Nom.	चार four	*Dat.*	चोहोंला to four

Note.—दोन or दोहों is sometimes changed to दों, chiefly in poetry :— गर्भ त्यागुनि अनादरें, दोघें गेलीं दों पंथीं.—Mukteshwar.

§ 131. When दोन two, तीन three, and चार four refer to a noun denoting a person, they assume the following forms :—

दोन = दोघे *m.*	दोघी *f.*	दोघें *n.*
तीन = तिघे *m.*	तिघी *f.*	तिघें *n.*
चार = चौघे *m.*	चौघी *f.*	चौघें *n.*

Note.—These forms are usually substituted for nouns denoting persons, or applied attributively to them when the persons they refer to have been mentioned in the previous part of a discourse, or when they constitute the whole number; दोन माणसें खालीं आलीं आहेत, two persons have come downstairs, but ते दोघे आले आहेत, those two persons have come, or both have come.

Note.—When the other cardinal forms are used for persons, the word जण persons is usually used with them ; पांच जण आले होते five men had come; दहा जणीला द्या give to ten women. जण when used with two, three and four, the numerals assume the forms दोघे, तिघे,

चौघे; दोघी जणी two women, चौघे जण four men; कोणी चौघे जण खालीं आहेत some four men are downstairs.

Note.—जण is the corruption of the Sanskṛit word जन, and is used in all the three genders. Its plural forms are जण *m.* जणी *f.* जणें *n.* It is usually used with a numeral जण हरावें, जण चोरावें of the people some side with the robbed, some with the robber.

Note.—The Sanskṛit form जन may mean a collective body generally; मनुष्यजन the human race, श्वजन the canine race. Also, it means man individually or generally. In the masculine and neuter gender it denotes the people or the world generally; ऐकावें जनाचें, करावें मनाचें listen to what people say, but follow your own mind.

§ 132. The neuter forms दोघें, तिघें and चौघें are used to denote the common gender, a male and female; गर्भ त्यागुनि अनाथरें, दोघें गेलीं दों पंथीं.—*Mukteshwar*.

§ 133. The above numerals are thus declined:—

Nom.	दोघे *m.*, दोघें *n.*, two	दोघी *f.*, two
Dat.	दोघांला-स-ना to two	दोघींला to two
Gen.	दोघांचा of two	दोघींचा of two

§ 134. The numerals दोन two, तीन three, and चार four with ही "even," make up the number denoting definiteness or totality; thus, दोन्ही both, तिन्ही all the three, and चान्ही all the four; but with the other numerals ही is written separately, as पांचही जण all the five persons. Sometimes the न of दोन्ही and तिन्ही is dropped; as दोहीं both, तिहीं all the three; दोहीं सांज, both in the morning and evening. चान्ही is changed to चोही or चहूं; चोहींकडे or चौहूंकडे on all sides. These definite forms are used for both *persons* and things; आमचीं दोन्ही मुलें आजारी आहेत both of our children are ill.

§ 135. These numerals, when qualifying an inflected noun, assume their crude-form; त्या दोघां माणसांनीं or दोघां जणांनीं, (जण Sk. जन person,) by those two men; म्यां एका बाईला पाहिलें, I saw a lady.

Note.—Before an inflected noun, the crude-form of एक may be एक, एका, एके or एक्या: एका is preferable to the others.

II.—The Ordinal Numerals.

§ 136. The Ordinals denote the *order* or succession of objects ; as पहिला first, दुसरा second.

§ 137. The Ordinals, except the first four numbers, are made up by adding वा to the Cardinals : पांच five + वा = पांचवा fifth ; आठ eight + वा = आठवा eighth; from एकुणीस nineteen and onwards the ordinals change the final vowel of the cardinal to आ before taking वा; as एकुणिसावा nineteenth, शंभरावा hundredth. The following are the ordinal forms of the first four numbers:—

पहिला first, *m.*	पहिली *f.*	पहिलें *n.*
दुसरा second, *m.*	दुसरी *f.*	दुसरें *n.*
तिसरा third, *m.*	तिसरी *f.*	तिसरें *n.*
चौथा fourth, *m.*	चौथी *f.*	चौथें *n.*

§ 138. The ordinals are declined like चांगला in the First Declension :—

पहिला the first.

Singular.

Nom.	पहिला the first, *m.*	पहिली *f.*	पहिलें *n.*
Dat.	पहिल्याला to the first	पहिलीला	पहिल्याला
Gen.	पहिल्याचा of the first	पहिलीचा	पहिल्याचा

Plural.

Nom.	पहिले the first, *m.*	पहिल्या *f.*	पहिलीं *n.*

Dat. पहिल्यांला to the first
Gen. पहिल्यांचा of the first.

सातवा the seventh.

Singular.

Nom.	सातवा seventh, *m.*	सातवी *f.*	सातवें *n.*
Dat.	सातव्याला to the seventh	सातवीला	सातव्याला

Plural.

Nom.	सातवे *m.*	सातव्या *f.*	सातवीं *n.*

Dat. सातव्यांला

Note.—The instrumental case of the ordinals is used adverbially; as पहिल्यानें or पहिल्यान first or at first ; सातव्यानें a seventh time.

III.—The Multiplicatives.

§ 139. The Multiplicatives denote how many fold a thing is; as एकपट one-fold, or single; दुप्पट two-fold, or double. These forms are made up by adding पट (Sk. पट, a fold) to the cardinal numeral; as पांच five + पट = पांचपट five-fold.

§ 140. The numerals, दोन two, तीन three, चार four, and दहा ten, are changed to दु, ति, चौ and दस respectively before पट, and the प of पट is doubled in the forms of दोन and तीन. Thus,

दुप्पट double	चौपट four-fold
तिप्पट treble	दसपट ten-fold

Note.—The forms दु, ति and चौ are the forms assumed by दोन two, तीन three and चार four in composition; as चौकट, a frame, चौकडा, an ear-ring, चौकोनी quadrangular, चौपायी four-legged, चौपदरी, four-folded. चार takes the form of चहुं in चहुंकडे all around; तिमजली three-storied; तिबाजू three-sided; दुकसबी clever; दुकाठी a two-masted vessel.

Note.—The word गुण fold or time is joined to numerals in their Sanskrit forms; as द्विगुण two-fold; त्रिगुण three-fold; चतुर्गुण four-fold.

Note.—The forms एकेरा or एकेरी single, दुहिरी-रा or दुहेरी double, तिहिरी or तिहेरी-रा three-fold, are used chiefly in reference to the *folding of cloth*, or *a rope*; दुहेरी दोरा a double thread. From four and onwards the word पदरी, the adjectival form of पदर a fold, is joined to the numerals; चौपदरी कंठी a necklace with four folds. पदर may be optionally used for all the other numerals; एकपदरी single.

IV.—Fractionals.

§ 141. The Fractionals denote one or more parts of a whole number; as सव्वा or सवा one and a fourth; पाव a fourth.

§ 142. The fractionals may be used with the cardinals, simple or aggregate; as सव्वादोन two and a quarter, or सव्वाशें one hundred and twenty-five. When the fractionals are united with the cardinals, they are put first and then the cardinals, which is just the reverse of what is done in English; साडेचार four and a half. The following are the fractional numbers, with their peculiar signs:—

Fractional Numbers.

$\frac{1}{4}$ ·।· पाव.
$\frac{1}{2}$ ·॥· अर्धा-र्धी-र्धें, &c.
$\frac{3}{4}$ ·।॥· पाऊण.
$1\frac{1}{4}$ १।· सव्वा.
$1\frac{1}{2}$ १॥· दीड.
$1\frac{3}{4}$ १।॥· पावणेदोन, पाउणेदोन.
$2\frac{1}{4}$ २।· सव्वादोन.
$2\frac{1}{2}$ २॥· अडीच.
$2\frac{3}{4}$ २।॥· पावणेतीन, पाउणेतीन.
$3\frac{1}{4}$ ३।· सव्वातीन.
$3\frac{1}{2}$ ३॥· साडेतीन.
$3\frac{3}{4}$ ३।॥· पावणेचार, पाउणेचार.

§ 143. The numbers from three and onwards are regularly denominated. Like सव्वातीन ($3\frac{1}{4}$) we have सवाचार ($4\frac{1}{4}$), सवापांच ($5\frac{1}{4}$), and so on. The words सव्वा and दीड prefixed to the cardinal signify $\frac{1}{4}$ and $\frac{1}{2}$ plus, while पाउणे prefixed to the cardinal, signifies $\frac{1}{4}$ minus. Thus पावणेदोन means $2-\frac{1}{4}$ $(=1\frac{3}{4})$; but सव्वादोन means $2+\frac{1}{4}$ $(=2\frac{1}{4})$; साडेतीन $3+\frac{1}{2}$ $(=3\frac{1}{2})$.

§ 144. The fractionals may be reduced still lower in Maráthí:—

$\frac{1}{4}$ पाव a fourth, a quarter.
$\frac{1}{8}$ अधपाव.
$1\frac{1}{2}$ of $\frac{1}{4} = \frac{3}{8}$ दीडपाव.
$2\frac{1}{2}$ of $\frac{1}{2} = \frac{5}{8}$ अडीचपाव.

Note.—One-eighth ($\frac{1}{8}$) of a measure is called नवटांक or छटांक.

§ 145. The fractionals are thus employed with the aggregate numbers :—

पाउणशें $(100 - \frac{1}{4}$ of $100)$ 75.
सव्वाशें $(100 + \frac{1}{4}$ of $100)$ 125.
दीडशें $(1\frac{1}{2}$ of $100)$ 150.
पाउणेदोनशें $(200 - \frac{1}{4}$ of $100)$ 175.
सव्वादोनशें $(200 + \frac{1}{4}$ of $100)$ 225.
अडीचशें $(2\frac{1}{2}$ of $100)$ 250.

§ 146. In this way any fraction might be joined to thousands, lacs, crores, &c. Beyond the number two, as दोन two, दोनशें two hundred, दोन हजार two thousand, &c., the word साडे is used to denote a half; as साडेतीन हजार 3,500; साडेदहा हजार 10,500.

Note.—"The symbols for pice, annas, and rupees are these—)। one pice,)।। two pice,)।।। three pice, -) one anna, =) two annas, ≡) three annas, ।) four annas, ॥) eight annas, ॥।) twelve annas, ।-)। five annas and one pice, ।=)।। six annas and two pice, ॥।≡)।।। fifteen annas and three pice, १) one rupee, ५०॥) fifty rupees and eight annas, ६३४॥=)।।। six hundred and thirty-four rupees ten annas and three pice."—*Hindi Grammar.*

§ 147. The fractionals are regularly declined. Those ending in अ are of the Second Declension, and those in आ, ई and ए of the First. सव्वा is irregular; as सव्वाला to one and a quarter, not सव्व्याला.

V.—Distributive Numerals.

§ 148. The distributive numerals indicate how many each time a thing is; as हरएक, दरएक, प्रत्येक each, every. The sense of distribution is usually expressed by repeating the cardinals; एकएकानें यावें you may come one by one; दोन दोन आंबे आणा bring two mangoes at a time; पन्नास पन्नास जेवायाला बसले they sat down to dine by fifties.

Note.—By affixing ला to some numeral ending in आ, the distributive sense is expressed; सगळाला द्या, अर्धाला देऊं नका give a whole to each, do not give a half; अर्धाला खांब पूर fix the posts, each half deep.

VI.—The Indefinite Numerals.

§ 149. The indefinite numerals denote a number indefinitely; as बहुत many; थोडे a few, *m.* plural; सर्व, अवघा, all, *m.* The indefinite numerals are regularly declined like the adjectives of quality, § 114; बहुत many, बहुतांला to many; अवघा all, अवघ्यांला to all.

CHAPTER XI.

Pronouns.

§ 150—§ 177.

§ 150. A pronoun is a word which supplies the place of a noun, or refers to a noun mentioned before or after it; as रामा म्हणतो मी येणार आहे Rámá says that he intends to come; जो मनुष्य काल आला होता तो हाच आहे this is the very man that came yesterday.

§ 151. There are six kinds of pronouns, viz., the Personal पुरुषवाचक, the Personal Indefinite सामान्य पुरुषवाचक, the Relative संबंधी, the Interrogative प्रश्नार्थक, the Demonstrative दर्शक, and the Indefinite सामान्य.

§ 152. The Pronouns, with the exception of the First and Second Personal Pronouns, are regularly declined. The masculine pronouns in आ or ओ are changed to ई in the feminine, and to ए in the neuter gender; as तो he, ती she, and तें it, and are declined like the adjectives of quality in आ, § 114.

1. *The Personal Pronouns.*

§ 153. The Personal Pronouns (पुरुषवाचक सर्वनामें) are chiefly employed as substitutes for the names of *persons*, and represent *three* persons, viz., the speaker, the person spoken to, and the person spoken of. The form indicating the *speaker* is called the *First Person*, the form for the person *spoken to* is called the *Second Person*, and the form denoting the person *spoken of* is called the *Third Person*. The following are the forms for the three persons:—

Sing.	1st *Pers.*	मी I *m., f., n.*	*Plu.*	आम्ही we *m., f., n.*
,,	2nd ,,	तूं thou *m., f., n.*	,,	तुम्ही you *m., f., n.*
,,	3rd ,,	तो he, ती she, तें it.	,,	ते *m.*, त्या *f.*, तीं *n.*, they

Note.—The personal pronouns are thus derived from the Sanskṛit language, through the Prákṛit:—

Singular.

1st *Pers.*	Sk. अहं,	Prák. अहम्मि,	Mar. मी I
2nd *Pers.*	Sk. त्वं,	Prák. तुं,	Mar. तूं thou

Plural.

1*st* *Pers.* Sk. वयं, Prák. अम्हे (also वअं), Mar. आह्मी we
2*nd* *Pers.* Sk. यूयं, Prák. तुम्हे, Mar. तुह्मी you

§ 154. The Third Personal forms are also demonstrative in sense, and donote *that* and *those*, as well as *he*, *she*, *it*, and *they*.

Note.—The Sanskrit base त *ta*, feminine ता *ta*, from which these forms are derived, signifies he, "this, that." The Zend forms are identified with the Sanskrit.—*Bopp*.

§ 155. The pronouns मीं I and तूं thou are thus declined :—

मीं I.

	Singular.	*Plural.*
Nom.	मीं I	आह्मी we
Acc.	मीं me	आह्मी us
Instr.	म्यां by me	आह्मीं by us
	मजशीं with me	आह्मांशीं with us
Dat.	मला-मजला to me	आह्माला-स to us
Abl.	मजहून than me	आह्मांहून than us
Gen.	माझा *m.* of me	आमचा *m.* of us
Loc.	माझ्यांत in me	आह्मांत in us

तूं Thou.

	Singular.	*Plural.*
Nom.	तूं thou	तुह्मी you
Acc.	तूं thee	तुह्मी you
Instr.	त्वां by thee	तुह्मीं by you
	तुजशीं with thee	तुह्मांशीं with you
Dat.	तुला, तुजला to thee	तुह्माला-स to you
Abl.	तुजहून than thee	तुह्मांहून than you
Gen.	तुझा *m.* of thee	तुमचा *m.* of you
Loc.	तुझ्यांत in thee	तुह्मांत in you

Note.—The instrumental singular of these pronouns is usually written with the anusvár, though etymologically there is no warrant for it ; but there is sufficient authority for the nasalisation of the plural form.

Note.—The nominative मीं I and तूं thou are now usually used for the instrumental म्या by me and त्वा by thee; as, मीं (for म्या) तें सर्व लिहिलें *lit.* it has been written by me; तूं (for त्वा) तें करायाचें होतें, *lit.* it should have been done by thee. These are purely Konkani constructions.

Note.—The inflected forms of मीं I and तूं thou are thus derived from Sanskṛit:—

मी I.

Sing.	*Nom.*	Sk. अहं,	Prák. अहम्मि,	Mar. मीं, I
,,	*Acc.*	Sk. मां,	Prák. मं,	Mar. मीं, me
,,	*Instr.*	Sk. मया,	Prák. मे or मए,	Mar. म्या, by me

तूं Thou.

Sing.	*Nom.*	Sk. त्वं,	Prák. तुमं or तं,	Mar. तूं thou
,,	*Acc.*	Sk. त्वां,	Prák. तुमं or तं or तुं,	Mar. तूं thee
,,	*Instr.*	Sk. त्वया,	Prák. तुमे or तइ or तए,	Mar. त्वा by thee
Plu.	*Instr.*	Sk. अस्माभि,	Prák. अम्हेहिं,	Mar. आम्हीं by us
,,	,,	Sk. युष्माभि,	Prák. तुम्हेहिं,	Mar. तुम्हीं by you

§ 156. Before inflected nouns मीं I and तूं thou assume their crude-forms:—

1*st Per.*	*Sing.*	मज	*Plu.*	आम्हां
2*nd* ,,	,,	तूज	,,	तुम्हां

They may take also their case-forms; as, मज गरीबाला to me a poor man, or मला गरीबाला. In the instrumental singular only the case-forms of the pronouns are used; as, म्या रामानें by me Rama.

§ 157. The Third Personal Pronouns तो he, ती she, and तें it, are thus declined:—

Masculine.

	Singular.	*Plural.*
Nom.	तो he	ते they
Acc.	तो him	ते them
Instr.	त्यानें by him	त्यांनीं by them; त्यांशीं or त्यांजशीं with them
Dat.	त्याला, त्याजला, त्यास to him	त्यांला, त्यांजला, त्यांस, त्यांना, to them
Abl.	त्याहून, त्याजहून than him	त्यांहून त्यांजहून than them
Gen.	त्याचा of him	त्यांचा of them
Loc.	त्यांत in him	त्यांत in them
Crude-form	त्या	त्यां

Feminine.

	Singular.	*Plural.*
Nom.	ती she	त्या they
Acc.	ती her	त्या them
Instr.	तिनें by her.	त्यांनीं by them त्यांशीं or त्यांजशीं with them
Dat.	तिला, तिजला, तीस to her	त्यांला, त्यांजला, त्यांस, त्यांना to them
Abl.	तिहून, तिजहून than her	त्यांहून, त्यांजहून than them
Gen.	तिचा of her	त्यांचा of them
Loc.	तींत in her	त्यांत in them
Crude-form	त्या	त्यां

Neuter.

	Singular.	*Plural.*
Nom.	तें it	तीं they
Acc.	तें it	तीं them
Instr.	त्यानें by it	त्यांनीं by them त्यांशीं or त्यांजशीं with them
Dat.	त्याला-स to it	त्यांला, त्यांजला, त्यांस, त्यांना to them
Abl.	त्याहून than it	त्यांहून, त्यांजहून than them
Gen.	त्याचा of it	त्यांचा of them
Loc	त्यांत in it	त्यांत in them
Crude-form	त्या	त्यां

§ 158. The Third Personal Pronouns तो he, ती she, तें it, as well as the Relative जो who, the Demonstrative हा this, and all the other pronouns ending in आ or ओ assume only their crude-forms before an inflected noun; त्या बायांनीं by those ladies; ह्या लोकांस to these people; ज्या मनुष्याचा कुत्रा मेला the man whose dog died.

The Indefinite Personal Pronoun.

§ 159. The Indefinite Personal Pronoun is आपण one's self, and refers to persons. It is substituted for all the personal pronouns, both in the singular and plural, and may be translated as I or myself; thou or thyself; he or himself; she or herself, as well as their plural forms; as, नंतर आपण निघून गेला afterwards he went away; मी आपणास ओळखितों, महाराज, पण तुम्ही आपणास ओळखीत नाहीं I know you, Sir, but you do not know yourself.

§ 160. The adverbial form स्वत: of one's self, is used sometimes for आपण, especially when it is used to emphasize the personal pronouns; as, मीं स्वत: तिकडे गेलों होतों I myself went there; so also स्वत:चें अनहित केलें he has injured himself. When स्वत: is used in this way as a pronoun, it is an Indefinite Personal Pronoun.

Note.—आपण is derived from the Sanskṛit word आत्मन् self, changed to आपणो in Prákrit; and आत्मन्, in the former language, is used in all the genders, numbers, and persons. स्वत: is the Sanskṛit ablative of स्व self, and in the form स्वयं self, is used as freely as आत्मन्; स्वयं वृतवान्, I chose it myself, or thou chosest it thyself, or he or she chose it himself or herself; स्वयं वृतवत: we, you, or they chose it of ourselves or yourselves or themselves.—*Max Müller.*

§ 161. आपण and स्वत: are declined as follows:—

आपण Oneself.

Nom.	आपण	oneself
Acc.	आपण	oneself
Instr.	आपण	by oneself
Dat.	आपणाला-स	to oneself
Abl.	आपणाहून	than oneself
Gen.	आपला *m.*	of oneself
Loc.	आपणांत	in oneself

Crude-form आपणा.

Note.—In poetry the instrumental may be inflected; राजाज्ञा नसतां तुम्हांसि मिथिले नेऊं नये आपणें.—*Vithal.*

स्वत: Self.

Nom.	स्वत:	self	*Abl.*	स्वत:हून	than self
Acc.	स्वत:	self	*Gen.*	स्वत:चा	of self
Instr.	स्वत:	by self	*Loc.*	स्वतांत	in self
Dat.	स्वत:ला-स	to self	Crude-form	स्वत:	

Note.—In the plural the crude-form of आपण assumes the anusvára; त्यांनीं आपणांस मारून घेतलें, they killed themselves.

Note.—The genitive आपला is often erroneously substituted for आपण; ते आपल्याला (for आपणांला) भेटायास येणार आहेत, they are going to come to see your honour. But आपला one's own or of oneself may be used as a noun like the adjective चांगला good, and then it can be declined in all the cases; आपल्यांला आपण पाहावें, we should see to our own (people); आपण आपलें ठेवावें, we should keep what is our own.

Note.—Some change स्वत: in the crude-form to स्वतां; as त्यानें स्वतांला (स्वत:ला) ठकाविलें he cheated himself.

III.—The Relative Pronoun.

§ 162. The Relative Pronoun has a relational force, and always refers to some other word or phrase in the sentence; जो मुलगा येणार होता तो आला आहे, the boy who intended to come has come. In the sentence, जो is a relative, referring to मुलगा a boy, followed by the demonstrative तो that.

Note.—जो is derived from the Sanskrit यः who, changed to जो in the Prakṛit.

§ 163. The relative जो assumes the forms जी feminine, and जें neuter, and is declined like the adjective in आ.

§ 164. There are some relative forms which are made up with the help of the demonstrative pronouns, Sect. 172; as, जसा such as; जसला of such kind as; जितका, जेवढा as much as, as great as; जितकाला, जेवढाला as much as to each person; जितका, जेवढा, of the number which.

§ 165. The relative pronoun, together with the noun to which it refers, makes up one sentence, to which another is joined beginning with the Demonstrative pronoun तो that, so that the relative pronoun has the force of a conjunction—the particle which joins two sentences together; as जो मनुष्य प्रामाणिकपणानें वागेल (1) तो गरीबही असेल (2) The man who will act honestly may be even poor. The demonstrative which follows the relative is called a correlative परस्परसंबंधी.

Singular.

Nom.	जो *m.* who	जी *f.* who	जें *n.* which
Acc.	जो whom	जी	जें which
Instr.	ज्यानें by whom	जिनें	ज्यानें by which
Dat.	ज्याला-स-ज्याजला to whom	जिला-जीस-जिजला	ज्याला-स-ज्याजला to which
Abl.	ज्याहून-ज्याजहून than whom	जिहून-जिजहून	ज्याहून-ज्याजहून than which
Gen.	ज्याचा *m.* of whom	जिचा *m.*	ज्याचा *m.* of which
Loc.	ज्यांत in whom	जींत	ज्यांत in which
Crude-form	ज्या	ज्या	ज्या

Plural.

Nom.	जे *m.* who	ज्या *f.* who	जीं *n.* which
Acc.	जे whom	ज्या whom	जीं which

Instr.	ज्यांनीं by whom or which
Dat.	ज्यांला-स-ज्यांजला to whom or which
Abl.	ज्यांहून-ज्यांजहून than whom or which
Gen.	ज्यांचा *m.* of whom or which
Loc.	ज्यांत in whom or which
Crude-form	ज्यां

IV.—*The Demonstrative Pronouns.*

§ 166. The Demonstrative Pronoun directly points out the word or phrase to which it refers; हा मुलगा this boy; तो चाकर that servant.

§ 167. There are two demonstrative pronouns, *viz.*, हा this, pointing to an object near the speaker, and तो that, pointing to a distant object.

§ 168. The declension of तो that, is given under the Personal Pronouns (§ 157).

§ 169. The pronoun हा is changed to ही feminine, and हें neuter, and is thus declined:—

Singular.

Nom.	हा *m.* this	ही *f.*	हें *n.*
Acc.	हा this	ही	हें
Instr.	ह्यानें by this	हिनें	ह्यानें
Dat.	ह्याला-स-ह्याजला to this	हिला-हीस-हिजला	ह्याला-स-ह्याजला
Abl.	ह्याहून-ह्याजहून than this	हिहून	ह्याहून
Gen.	ह्याचा *m.* of this	हिचा *m.*	ह्याचा *m.*
Loc.	ह्यांत in this	हींत	ह्यांत
Crude-form	ह्या	ह्या	ह्या

Plural.

Nom.	हे these *m.*	ह्या	हीं *n.*
Acc.	हे these *m.*	ह्या	हीं

Instr.	ह्यांनीं by these	*m. f. n.*
Dat.	ह्यांला-स-ह्यांजला to these	*m. f. n.*
Abl.	ह्यांहून-ह्यांजहून than these	*m. f. n.*
Gen.	ह्यांचा of these	*m. f. n.*
Loc.	ह्यांत in these	*m. f. n.*

Crude-form ह्यां.

§ 170. या is also substituted for ह्या, and इ for हि in the crude-form, which are the older forms; याला or ह्याला to this; इला or हिला to this, *f.*:—

आर्या आर्यासि रुचे, इच्या ठायीं जशी असे गोडी ।
आहे इतरा छंदीं गोडी, परि या परीस ती थोडी ॥

Note.—हा is derived from the Sanskrit असस् that or this, changed in Prákṛit to the indeclinable अह.

§ 171. The following demonstrative derivatives are important, by the aid of which corresponding relative, interrogative, and several other pronominal forms may be derived:—

1. Forms denoting *number*: इतका so many. (Sk. इयत्.)

2. Forms denoting *quantity*: एवढें so much. (Sk. एतावत्, Prák. एद्दहं).

3. Forms of number and quantity denoting *distribution*: इतकाला, एवढाला so much to any or each person; इतकाला देऊं नका do not give so much to each.

4. Forms denoting *order* or *series*: इतकावा, एवढावा, so much*th* (if we may coin an equivalent expression).

5. Forms indicating *kind* or *sort*: असा, असला, असलाला such. (Sk. ईदृशः Prák. एरिसो.) असलाला is distributive in force; as असलाले आंबे दिले they gave such mangoes to each; असलाला पेरू खाला each ate such a guava.

Note—असा is often used at the end of a word with the elision of अ; as तो रामचंद्रपंतसा वाटतो he appears to be like Ramchandrapant; गोर गरिबांस अन्न द्यावेसें वाटतें, परंतु अनुकूळ नाहीं I feel inclined to give food to the poor, but have no means; आज पाऊस पडेलसा वाटतो it looks as if it would rain to-day.

§ 172. When the relative जो, the interrogative कोण, and the demonstrative तो are united with the above demonstrative

12 *m*

forms, they simply retain their initial consonants, ज, क and त; कोण who? + असा = कसा, how? जो + असा = जसा as; तो + असा = तसा so..

Relative जो ज	Demonstrative तो त	Interrogative कोण क

V.—The Interrogative Pronouns.

§ 173. The Interrogative Pronouns are used to form questions; as, कोण आहे? who is there? त्याला काय पाहिजे? what does he want?

§ 174. The interrogative pronouns are कोण who? कोणता or कोणचा which or what one? कोणी or कोण्ही any one; काय what? किती, कितीक how many?

Note.—कोण is derived from the Prákṛit कोण्णे, Sk. कः who? + अन्यः other = कोन्यः; किती how many? from Sk. कति? and काय from Sk. किम्, Prákṛit कीआ, (क्या Hindi).

Note.—कोण्हीं is composed of कोण + ही, and occurs in poetry. It is also commonly used in the Deckan, but कोणी is now preferred to it.

§ 175. The interrogatives are declined in the following manner:—

(1) कोण who? takes आ; कोण who? कोणाला to whom?

(2) कोणता or कोणचा which one? is inflected in the three genders, and is declined like the adjective in आ (Sect. 114.)

(3) किती how many? remains unchanged in the crude-form.

(4) कितीक how many? is declined with आ in the masculine and neuter, and with ई in the feminine; as कितिकांना to how many *m. n.*; कितिकींना to how many (women)? कितीक is derived from किती + एक, and agrees in declension with एक (129). Before inflected nouns it remains unchanged; as कितीक माणसांनीं हें केलें, How many men did this?

(5) काय what? is irregularly declined.

Examples.

कोण who?

	Singular.	*Plural.*
Nom. & Acc.	कोण who	कोण
Instr.	कोणीं by whom	कोणीं
Dat.	कोणाला-स to whom	कोणांला-स
Abl.	कोणाहून than whom	कोणांहून
Gen.	कोणाचा of whom	कोणांचा
Loc.	कोणांत in whom	कोणांत.
Crude-form	कोणा	कोणां

Note.—Before inflected nouns कोणा is preferable to कोण्या or कोणे.

कोणता which one?

Singular.

Nom. & Acc.	कोणता, *m.*	कोणती, *f.*	कोणतें, *n.*
Instr.	कोणत्यानें	कोणतीनें	कोणत्यानें
Dat.	कोणत्याला-स	कोणतीला-स	कोणत्याला स
Crude-form	कोणत्या	कोणत्या	कोणत्या

Plural.

Nom. & Acc.	कोणते, *m.*	कोणत्या, *f.*	कोणतीं, *n.*
Instr.	कोणत्यांनीं.		
Dat.	कोणत्यांला-स-ना.		
Crude-form	कोणत्यां.		

किती how many?

Nom. & Acc.	किती how many?
Instr.	कितीनीं by how many?
Dat.	कितींला to how many?
Crude-form	कितीं

काय what?

	Singular.	*Plural.*
Nom. & Acc.	काय what	काय
Instr.	कशानें by what	कशांनीं
Dat.	कशाला-स to what	कशांला-स-ना
Abl.	कशाहून than what	कशांहून
Gen.	कशाचा of what	कशांचा
Loc.	कशांत in what	कशांत
Crude-form	कशा	कशां

§ 176. Besides the interrogative forms given above there are others derived with the help of the demonstrative pronouns: कितका, केवढा how many or how much; कितकाला, केवढाला how much in order? कसा, कसला, कसलाला of what kind? Sect. 171.

VI.—The Indefinite Pronouns.

§ 177. The Indefinite Pronouns express an indefinite generality. They are these: कोण, some one; कोणी, any one; कोणएक, some one; कोणसा, some one; कोणता, any one; कैक many a one; अमुक, अमका, फलाणा, a certain one; अमका, तमका, some particular person or thing; उभय, उभयतां, both; कित्येक, several; कांहीं, something, some; कांहींएक some few; कांहींक (कांहीं + एक) a few; कांहींकांहीं some individuals of a number; आणिक, अणखी, अन्य another; अन्योन्य, परस्पर, mutual; इतर, वरकड, others; अवघा, सर्व, सगळा, all; एक some one. Of these words, those ending in आ are declined like the adjectives in आ; those in अ assume आ in the crude-form; and the rest remain unchanged in the crude-form.

CHAPTER XII.

THE VERB.

The Classification of Verbs.

§ 178—§ 187.

§ 178. A verb is the chief word in the sentence, and affirms *being, action* and *suffering* of some person or thing; देव आहे God is (being); रामा चालतो Rama walks; गोविंदा पोथी वाचितो Govindá reads a book (action); चारशें मनुष्यें मारिलीं गेलीं four hundred men were killed (*suffering.*)

§ 179. The verb almost always expresses action, and especially the *chief* action of the mind, *viz.,* the assertion or denial of a proposition, and it is consequently called क्रियापद an ACTION—WORD in Marathi.

§ 180. The noun or pronoun of which an action is affirmed by the verb, is called the *Subject* (कर्ता), and the noun or pronoun towards which the action of the verb tends, is called the *Object* (कर्म). In the above sentence गोविंदा पोथी वाचितो Govinda reads a book, गोविंद । is the subject, and पोथी is the object of the verb वाचितो.

§ 181. The subject of the verb is often the agent or doer (कर्ता) of the action denoted by it.

§ 182. Verbs may be thus classified according to their *signification, derivation,* and *conjugation*:—Transitive (सकर्मक) or Intransitive (अकर्मक), Potential (शक्य), Causal (प्रयोज्य), Auxiliary (सहाय्य), Defective (गौण), Regular (नियमित) or Irregular (अनियमित), Anomalous (विधिभंजक), Passive (कर्मणि), and Impersonal (भावकर्तृक)

§ 183. When an action denoted by the verb passes on to the object, it is *transitive* (सकर्मक), and when the action terminates in the subject, it is *intransitive* (अकर्मक); as, रामा आंबा खातो, Rámá eats a mango (transitive); रामा येतो, Rámá comes (intransitive). This is a division of verbs exclusively according to their *signification.*

§ 184. The Marathi verbs may be *changed in form,* or *used with other words,* to express some new idea, and the forms thus produced are called *Causal* verbs, *Potential* verbs, and *Compound* verbs. This is a division of verbs according to *Derivation.*

(1) The Causal verb chiefly expresses the sense of *instrumental agency*; as रामा पुस्तक वाचितो Rámá reads the book; *Causal,* रामाकडून गोविंद पुस्तक वाचवितो Govind causes Rámá to read the book.

(2) The Potential verb expresses the idea *of ability* or *power;* as, रामा झाड मोडितो Rámá breaks the tree; *Potential,* रामाच्यानें झाड मोडवतें Rámá can break the tree.

(3) The Compound verb, which is composed of two words, conveys a simple idea; as अंगांत घालणें to wear, lit., to put in the body; धुऊन टाकणें to wash out, lit., to throw away after washing.

185. The Marathi verbs may be divided *according to their Conjugation into Auxiliary* verbs, *Defective* verbs, *Regular* or *Irregular* verbs, *Anomalous* verbs, *Impersonal* verbs, and *Passive* verbs.

(1) The Auxiliary verbs are used to make up the forms of the verbal *Tenses* and *Moods*; as रामा चालत आहे Rámá is walking; मला गेलें पाहिजे I must go.

(2) The Defective verbs are deficient in some forms of conjugation; as पाहिजे It is wanted; नलगे It is not necessary.

(3) The Regular verbs are conjugated in the *past tense* in the common way, and the Irregular in an uncommon way; as, चाल Walk thou, चालला He walked, Reg.; जा Go thou, गेला He went, Irreg.

(4) The Anomalous verbs are conjugated irregularly *in the constructions* or प्रयोग; as, रमा आपला धडा शिकली Ramá has learnt her lesson.

(5) When the Transitive verb is conjugated with its object *as the subject*, it is called a Passive or Suffering verb; as, झाड मोडलें The tree fell; झाड मोडिलें गेलें The tree was felled.

(6) When the intransitive verb is conjugated without a subject, *its subject being concealed in it*, it is called *Impersonal*; काल माझ्या पोटांत कळमळत होतें I was sick at the stomach yesterday—I was affected with nausea.

§ 186. The verbs may, also, be divided according to the *Agential relation* of the *subject to the action* which the verb expresses, and considered as *Active*, *Passive* and *Neuter*.

1. When the verb represents the subject as the *agent* or doer of the action expressed by it, then it is *Active*; as रामा बसतो Rámá sits; रामा भाकर खातो Rámá eats bread. The active verb may be either Transitive or Intransitive.

2. When the verb represents the subject as *acted upon* by some other agent, or by itself, then it is *Passive*; as, रोहिले इंग्लिशांकडून मारिले गेले The Rohillas were killed by the English; झाड मोडतें The tree breaks. (Sect. 186, 5.)

Note.—Strictly speaking when the subject of the verb is acted upon *by itself*, it is distinct from the true Passive, which necessarily implies *foreign agency*. The former may be called a verb of the *Middle Voice*, that is, a verb the subject of which is both the *agent* and the *object* of the action; as, दार उघडलें the door opened.

Note.—Sometimes the Transitive verb, without any change of conjugation, has the force of an Intransitive; त्याच्या ओटीवर झड मारील, the spray will beat upon his veranda. The verb expresses the sense of *repeated* or *vigorous* action.

Note.—When the Transitive verb expresses the performance of the act denoted by it in a *general* way, it is used intransitively, without any change of conjugation; तो चांगलें वाचितो he reads well; तो कांहीं वाईट म्हणत नाहीं he does not at all recite badly.

3. When the Intransitive verb represents its subject as *neither the agent* of the action denoted by it, *nor the object* affected by it, the Intransitive verb is called *Neuter;* as, झाड पडतें The tree falls; गाई सुटली The cow got loose; रामा चांगला आहे Rámá is good; रामा बरा दिसत नाहीं Rámá does not look well.

Note.—The verb सुटली, got loose in गाई सुटली, the cow got loose, and पडलें fell in झाड पडलें, the tree fell, may be regarded as verbs of the Active form with the Passive sense, like the verbs of the Middle Voice; only those are Intransitive and these Transitive

Note.—Corresponding to these Neuter Intransitives there are Active Transitives; as सुटणें to get loose, सोडणें to loose; मरणें to die, मारणें to kill; पडणें to fall, पाडणें to fell; फिटणें to get loose, फेडणें to unloose.

Note.—Sometimes Active Intransitives have a neuter force; रामा खुरचीवर बसतो Rámá sits on the chair, Active; रामानें हातोड्यानें खिळा बसविला, पण तो चांगला बसला नाहीं Rámá fixed the nail with a hammer, but it was not (or did not get) well fixed.

§ 187. The last three divisions of verbs, based on the *agential relation* of the subject, are commonly denominated *Voices* or वाच्यें.

Note.—"These distinctions, however, rest in many cases, in Sanskṛit as well as Greek, on peculiar conceptions which it is difficult to analyse or realise; and in Sanskṛit, as well as Greek, the right use of the Active and Middle voices is best learnt by practice. Thus नी

to lead, is used as parasmaipada in such expressions as गंडं विनयति he carries off a swelling; but as atmanepada, in क्रोधं विनयते he turns away or dismisses with wrath; a subtle distinction which it is possible to appreciate when stated, but difficult to bring under any general rules."—*Max-Muller*.

CHAPTER XIII.

The Inflection of Verbs.

§ 188—§ 216.

§ 188. The verb is given in the Maráṭhi Dictionary in what is called its gerundial form, *i. e.*, it is given with the particle णें affixed to it; करणें to do.

§ 189. A verbal root (धातु) is the form which remains after the णें is dropped; as, मारणें to strike; मार strike thou.

§ 190. The verbal root, when employed to predicate action of a noun, is modified, by means of certain particles, called *personal-endings*, to indicate its relation to the noun. Thus, the gerund, बोलणें to speak; the root, बोल speak thou; the inflected form, बोलतो speaks (= बोल + तो); हरि बोलतो Hari speaks. the तो in बोलतो is a *personal-ending*.

§ 191. The personal-endings indicate the following particulars:—

1. The Genders (लिंग)—Masculine, Feminine, and Neuter.
2. The Numbers (वचन)—Singular and Plural.
3. The Persons (पुरुष)—the First, the Second, and the Third.
4. The Tenses (काळ)—the Present, the Past, and the Future.
5. The Moods (अर्थ)—the Indicative, the Conditional, the Subjunctive, the Imperative, and the Infinitive.
6. The Constructions (प्रयोग or *Prayogas*)—The Subjective, the Objective, and the Neuter.
7. The Participles and the Verbal Nouns (धातुसाधितें)—four Participles, and two Verbal Nouns.

§ 192. The mode or manner in which the verbal inflections or personal-endings are joined to the root, is called *Conjugation* (आख्यातरूप).

TENSES.

§ 193. A tense (Lat. *tempus*, time) is the form of the verb made up by inflection, or by the aid of the auxiliary verbs (§ 186, 1), in order to indicate the *time* of the action signified by it; thus, बोलतो he speaks; बोलेल he will speak, the root being बोल speak thou. The forms that are produced *by inflection* are called *Simple Tenses*, and those made up by the aid of *the auxiliary verbs* are denominated *Compound Tenses*.

§ 194. There are four Simple Tenses in Maráṭhí, three of which indicate the principal divisions of time—the *Present*, the *Past*, and the *Future*; the fourth expresses a particular feature of past time, and is called the *Past Habitual Tense*.

§ 195. (1) The *Present Tense* (वर्तमानकाळ) is that form of the verb which denotes that an action is going on in the present time; घोडा चालतो the horse walks; साधु सर्वांवर दया करितात virtuous men show kindness to all.

§ 196. (2) The *Past Tense* (भूतकाळ) expresses an action as completed in time already past or spent; हरण पाशांत पडला the deer fell into the snare; माशाचें हंसणें आजपर्यंत कोणीं पाहिलें किंवा ऐकिलें नाहीं until this day no one has seen or heard of the laughter of a fish.

§ 197. (3) The *Future Tense* (भविष्यत्काळ) expresses an action to occur in time subsequent to the present; मीं मरून देवाजवळ जाईन after I die I shall go to God; ते सांगतील तें मीं मागेन I shall ask what they will bid.

§ 198. (4) The *Habitual Past Tense* (रीतिभूतकाळ) indicates the habitual doing of an action in past time; रामा रोज चार तास वाचीत बसे Rámá used to sit reading four hours a day; तो बाहेर निघे व कमरेस चार पांच चिरगुटें बांधी he was in the habit of sallying forth, and tying four or five pieces of cloth around his loins.

§ 199. The following are the *Inflections* which make up the forms of the simple tenses:—

PRESENT TENSE.
1st and 2nd Conjugations.

	Singular.			*Plural.*
	M.	*F.*	*N.*	*M. F. N*
1.	तों	तें	तें	तों
2.	तोस	तेस	तेंस	तां
3.	तो	ते	तें	तात

PAST TENSE.
1st Conjugation.

	Singular.			*Plural.*
	M.	*F.*	*N.*	*M. F. N.*
1.	लों	लें	लें	लों
2.	लास	लीस	लेंस	लां
3	ला	ली	लें	ले ल्या लीं

FUTURE TENSE.

1st Conjugation.

	Singular.	*Plural.*
	M. F. N.	*M. F. N.*
1.	एन	ऊं
2.	शील (or सील)	आल
3.	एल	तील

2nd Conjugation.

	Singular.	*Plural.*
	M. F. N.	*M. F. N.*
1.	ईन	ऊं
2.	शील (or सील)	आल
3.	ईल	तील

Note.—The Second Singular शील is preferable to सील.

PAST HABITUAL.

1st Conjugation.

	Singular.	*Plural.*
	M. F. N.	*M. F. N.*
1.	एं	ऊं
2.	एस	आं
3.	ए	अत

2nd Conjugation.

	Singular.	*Plural.*
	M. F. N.	*M. F. N.*
1.	ईं	ऊं
2.	ईस	आं
3.	ई	ईत

Note.—अस is sometimes substituted for the Second Singular Intransitive Past Habitual एस.

Note.—The inflections of the tenses are of *two* kinds; those directly derived from Sanskṛit through the Prákṛit, and those of a purely Maráṭhi origin. It has not yet been ascertained when the latter terminations came into use, but the former, which make up the Past

Habitual forms, are found in the oldest Maráṭhí poetical works. These are, in fact, the source from which all the existing forms of the tenses are derived, and they are found, with slight changes, in Hindi and Gujaráti serving the purpose of the aorist. What we have designated purely Maráṭhí forms are produced by the union of the demonstrative pronoun तो that, (used, also, as the Third Personal Pronoun,) with the Past Habitual inflections. Thus,

The pronoun तो *m.* + P. H. एं = तों; चालतों I walk, *sing.* 1*st pers.*
,, तो *m.* + P. H. एस = तोस; चालतोस *sing.* 2*d pers.*
,, तो *m.* + P. H. ए = तो; चालतो *sing.* 3*rd pers.*
,, तो *m.* + P. H. ऊं = तों; चालतों *plu.* 1*st pers.*
,, तो *m.* + P. H. आं = तां; चालतां *plu.* 2*nd pers.*
,, तो *m.* + P H. अत = तात; चालतात *plu.* 3*rd pers.*

In the same way the feminine and neuter inflections are derived :—

	Feminine.	*Neuter.*
Sing. 1	ती + एं = तें (or त्यें)	तें + एं = तें
,, 2.	ती + एस = तेस (or त्येस)	तें + एस = तेंस
,, 3.	ती + ए = ते (or त्ये)	तें + ए = तें
Plu. 1.	ती + ऊं = तों	तें + ऊं = तों
,, 2	ती + आं = तां	तें + आं = तां
,, 3.	ती + अत = तात	तें + अत = तात

The Feminine forms in त्ये are employed in the Konkan. In the Dakhan the third person singular is ती, instead of ते or त्ये, and the neuter first person singular is तों. The Dakhan forms have no etymological authority. Nor are the singular forms in त्ये of much authority, as the plural forms do not take य. Besides, according to the Maráthí rules of combination , when two vowels are united, the weaker is displaced by the stronger.

Note.—The inflections of the past tense are derived from those of the present tense by a slight change. For the vowels of the second and third personal inflections are substituted the general gender terminations specified in § 46 ; and the forms thus produced are joined to the past participiple in ल or ला.

In the first person the vowels do not submit to a displacement, as personality is most emphatically asserted in the forms for that person.

Note.—The modified forms of the present tense, before they are united with the past participle ला, are the same as those of the Conditional Mood, § 202.

Note.—The following are the modified forms of the present tense used to make up the forms of the past tense and the conditional mood :—

Sing. 1. तों	तों M.	*Plu.* तों	तों M.
,, 2. तोस + आ = तास M.		,, तां + आं = तां M.	
,, 3. तो + आ = ता M.		,, तात + ए = ते M.	

Note.—The above modified forms of the present tense are thus combined with ला to make up the past forms :—

Sing. 1. ला + तों = लों M.	*Plu.* ला + तों = लों M.
,, 2. ला + तास = लास M.	,, ला + तां = लां M.
,, 3. ला + ता = ला M.	,, ला + ते = ले M.

Note.—The feminine and neuter forms are derived in the same way as the masculine: —ला + तें = लें *f. 1st Sing.*; ला + ती = ली *f. 3rd Sing.*

Note.—The Future and the Past Habitual retain their classical forms. The Past Habitual is the original Maráṭhí tense, immediately derived from Sanskṛit through Prákṛit, and from it the Future is derived :—

First Conjugation (Sk. *Atmanepada*).

				Past Habitual.	Future.
Sing.	1.	Sk. ए,	Prák. मि	Mar. एं	Mar. एन
,,	2.	,, से	,, ए	,, एस	,, शील
,,	3.	,, ते	,, ए	,, ए	,, ए
Plu.	1.	,, महे	,, मु	,, ऊं	,, ऊं
,,	2.	,, ध्वे	,, ह (धं, ध्या) आं	,, आं	,, आल
,,	3.	,, अंते	,, आते	,, अत	,, तील

Second Conjugation (Sk. *Parsamuipada*).

				Past Habitual.	Future.
Sing.	1.	Sk. मि,	Prák. मि,	Mar. ई	Mar. ईन
,,	2.	,, सि	,, सि	,, सी. ईस	,, शील
,,	3.	,, ति	,, ति	,, ई	,, ईल
Plu.	1.	,, मः	,, मू	,, ऊं	,, ऊं
,,	2.	,, थ	,, ह	,, आं	,, आल
,,	3.	,, अन्ति	,, अंति	,, ईत or आत	,, तील

Note.—The letter ल which distinguishes the future form is a modification of the Sanskrit स changed to ह in Prákṛit ; Sanskrit करिष्यति he will do, Prák. करिस्सदि, Mar. करील.

Note.—Not only are the Present and Past inflections pronominal in regard to their origin, but even the Past Habitual and the Future are so. Such is the case with the personal-endings in most languages, "although, in the course of time, they are no longer recognized and felt to be that which by their demonstrable origin, they imply and are." "It appears to me most probable that the majority of them are pronouns, through which action or quality which is expressed in the root, in abstract, becomes something concrete, *e. g.*, the expression of the idea 'to love' becomes the expression of the person 'who loves.' This person, however, is more closely defined by the personal terminations, whether it be 'I,' 'thou,' or 'he.'" — *Bopp.* The anusvára of the first person, the स of the second, and the त of the third, are existing remnants of the Sanskṛit personal pronouns, which are found as verbal terminations in all the Aryan languages.

Moods.

§ 200. A mood is the inflected form of the verb, expressing the *manner* of the action denoted by the verb as *positive*, *conditional*, or *obligatory* ; and there are FIVE such forms or moods in Maráṭhí, *viz.*, the *Indicative* (स्वार्थ), the *Conditional* (संकेतार्थ), the *Subjunctive* (विध्यर्थ), the *Imperative* (आज्ञार्थ), and the *Infinitive* (उद्देशार्थ).

§ 201. (1) The *Indicative* denotes whether the action expressed by the verb actually does or does not take place ; as, साधु कोठेंही गेले तरी मान्यता पावतात wherever virtuous men might go, they obtain respect ; माझ्याजवळ तुझी भूक जाई असा पदार्थ नाहीं there is not anything by me that would satisfy your hunger ; तो काय उपाय करील तें नकळे I do not know what remedy he will use.

Note.—The Indicative strictly speaking is no mood, as in it only "relations of time are expressed. The absence of modal accessory notions is its characteristic."—*Bopp.*

§ 202. (2) The *Conditional* expresses an action which is thought of as contingent,—as one which may or may not happen; तो उद्यां येता तर बरें होतें it would be well if he came to-morrow. The essential sense of the conditional is that of suppositiveness—an uncertainty and indecision; it makes a supposition, which may or may not be realized. The inflections of the conditional are modified forms of those of the indicative present (§ 199), and are the following:—

	Singular.			*Plural.*		
	M.	*F.*	*N.*	*M.*	*F.*	*N.*
1.	तों	तें	तें		तों	
2.	तास	तीस	तेंस		तां	
3.	ता	ती	तें	ते	त्या	तीं

Note.—In Sanskṛit the conditional form resembles partly the future, and partly the past, forms, and expresses that the completion of a wish that had been entertained was not actually realized; thus, the Sanskṛit अदास्यम् I would give, or I would have given, answers to the future दास्यामि I will give, together with the privative अ of the past tense अदाम् I gave. This composite character of the Sanskṛit conditional exists most perfectly in the Maráṭhí forms. They also denote the *possible* unrealization of a felt desire or expectation, and assume the past inflectional vowels; तो हंसता तर मीही हंसतों if he had laughed I too would have laughed, *i.e.* I believed, that he might laugh, but he did not, and my expectation was not realized.

Note.—The conditional inflections are derived from the indicative present by the aid of the gender terminations which make up the tenses of the indicative past (§ 199, *Note.*)

Note.—We have given elsewhere a verbal form which expresses conditionality most absolutely. It is the dative of the past tense or the past participle: श्लोक काढल्यास (काढला+यास) त्यांची परिक्षा होईल whenever he shall produce his slokas, they will be examined. The dative particle expresses purpose is fulfilled in future time; but the dative termination, by being affixed to a *past* form, comes to denote a purpose whose fulfilment is uncertain, *i.e.*, a mere supposition. The same dative particle, on the other hand, by being united to a future participle, expresses a purpose most emphatically; as तो शिकायास (शिकूं+यास, § 215) गेला he has gone to learn.

§ 203. (3) The *Subjunctive* denotes the *propriety* or *impropriety* of an action; जें न मिळालें तें मिळवावें, मिळालें तें रक्षावें, रक्षिलेलें वाढवावें, वाढविल्याचा सत्पात्रीं व्यय करावा we should acquire that which has not been obtained; preserve that which has been acquired; increase that which has been preserved; and expend in good works what has been increased; ही स्त्री कोणास द्यावी हें सांगावें let it be said to whom this woman should be given. The following are the inflections of the subjunctive:—

	Singular.			*Plural.*		
	M.	*F.*	*N.*	*M.*	*F.*	*N.*
1.	आवा	आवी	आवें	आवे	आव्या	आवीं
2.	आवास	आवीस	आवेंस	आवेत	आव्यात	आवींत
3.	आवा	आवी	आवें	आवे	आव्या	आवीं

Note.—The monosyllabic roots in ए and ई are changed to या in combination with the subjunctive suffix; ने lead thou; न्यावा (ने+आवा *m.*) it ought to be led; पी drink thou; प्यावा it ought to be drunk.

Note.—The subjunctive terminations आवा, &c., are derived from the Sanskrit participial particle तव्य denoting the sense of futurity as well as that of obligation. The तव्य is changed to अव्व in Prákṛit and to आव in Maráṭhí, combined with the principal gender terminations (§ 46.)

Note.—The Potential Passive participial तव्य (also अनीय and य) denotes "that the action or state expressed by the root or derivative base *must* or *ought* to be done or undergone." The sense conveyed is that of fitness, obligation, or necessity; मया तत् कर्त्तव्यं I must do.

§ 204. (4) The *Imperative* expresses command, advice, exhortation, or benediction; तूं आपलें काम मुकाट्यानें कर mind your own business quietly; आज आपलें राज्य पांडव पावोत may the Pándavs obtain their kingdom to-day; गोष्ट खरी पण मीं काय करूं ?

it is true, but what can I do? The imperative has the following inflections:—

	Singular.	Plural.
	M. F. N.	*M. F. N.*
1.	ऊं	ऊं
2.	अ	आ
3.	ओ	ओत

Note.—The ओ and ओत are changed to वो and वोत when the monosyllabic verb ends in ई or ए; दे give thou, देवो (for देओ) may he give; पिवोत (for पीओत) may they drink. So also the 2nd plural आ changes the monosyllabic ई or ए to या; घे take thou, घ्या take ye; पी drink thou, प्या drink you.

Note.—Sometimes ऊ and ऊत, the original forms, are substituted for ओ and ओत of the third person.

Note.—In poetry, ईं is affixed to the 2nd person imperative singular of the transitive verb, and एं to that of the intransitive; घेंईं for घे take thou; पावें reach thou. These modified forms are more respectful and urgent.

घेंईं घेंईं माझे वाचे, गोड नाम विठोबाचें.—*Tukaram.*

नारायणा आठवि सर्पराणा पावें ह्मणे गा पुरुषा पुराणा.—*Waman.*

Note.—The imperative terminations are thus derived from Sanskrit:—

1.	*Sing.*	Sk.	अनि	Prák.	मु	M.	ऊं
2.	,,	,,	अ	,,	अ	,,	अ
3.	,,	,,	तु	,,	उ	,,	ऊ or ओ
1.	*Plu.*	,,	अम	,,	मो	,,	ऊं
2.	,,	,,	त	,,	ह	,,	आ
3.	,,	,,	न्तु	,,	तु	,,	ऊत or ओत

§ 205. (5) The *Infinitive* expresses the action as dependent upon another action, and is chiefly employed to make up compound verbal forms; तो जाऊं लागला he began to go; राजा एक सारखी टक लावून त्या पुत्राकडे पाहूं लागला the king began to look intently at that son; मला जाऊं द्या let me go. The inflection of the infinitive is ऊं; कर do thou; करूं to do.

Note.—The Infinitive termination ऊं is a modification of the Sanskrit infinitive तुं changed in Prákrit to दुं or उं. The Sanskrit तुं expresses "to be requisite, or to will, in the sense of the future."

THE PRAYOGAS, OR CONSTRUCTIONS.

§ 206. The terminations assumed by the verb in conjugation (§ 217) indicate whether it agrees in *gender*, *number* and *person* with the nouns to which it is related, or stands neutral.

§ 207. This agreement or disagreement of the verb with the nouns to which it is related, indicated by the inflections which it assumes in conjugation, is called प्रयोग or construction.

§ 208. The noun with which the verb agrees may be either its *subject* or its *object*. Sometimes it may agree neither with the subject nor with the object, but may be *neutral*, *i.e.*, indifferent to both.

§ 209. There are, consequently, *three* forms of construction—the *Subjective*, the *Objective*, and the *Neuter*.

§ 210. In the Subjective or कर्तरि construction, the verb agrees with the subject; मुलगा पोथी वाचितो the boy reads a book.

2. In the Objective or कर्मणि construction, the verb agrees with the object; गांवकऱ्यांनीं सरकाराचा महसूल दिला नाहीं the villagers did not pay the revenue of the Government.

3. In the Neuter or भावे construction, the verb agrees neither with the subject nor with the object, but is conjugated *in the neuter singular*; पंतोजीनें मुलास फार मारिलें the schoolmaster beat the boys severely.

Obs.—Ignorance or indifference is always indicated in Maráṭhi by the neuter gender, and hence the verb that is indifferent both to the subject and object is put in the neuter gender. In the following sentences the neuter gender is used to denote ignorance or indifference; कोण हाक मारितें who calls out to me? तें कोण येतें who is that coming there? कोणी माणूस येतें some human being is coming.

§ 211. The noun with which the verb agrees, whether it be the subject or the object, is always *uninflected*. The un-inflected case of the subject is the Nominative, and the uninflected case of the object is the Accusative. Consequently in the Subjective construction, the subject is in the Nominative case, and in the Objective construction the object is in the Accusative case.

§ 212. Since in the Neuter construction, the verb agrees neither with the subject nor the object, *both* the nouns are *inflected*. The inflected subject is usually in the Instrumental case, and the inflected object is in the Dative case. Sometimes the inflected subject is in the Dative case.

Note.—Inflection, which in reality is a mutilation, is a sign of weakness, and the inflected subject and object are therefore incapable of influencing the verb.

Obs.—The Prayogas are, strictly speaking, a department of Syntax, but we have anticipated it as it is impossible to understand the principles of Maráṭhi conjugation without some knowledge of it.

THE PARTICIPLES AND THE VERBAL NOUNS.

* 213. The *Partciples* are forms derived from verbs, and are chiefly employed to make up compound tenses. They are the *Present*, the *Past*, tho *Pluperfect*, and the *Future*.

1. The Present Participle denotes currency of action, and assumes त, ता *m.*, तां or तांना to make up its forms; चाल walk thou; चालत, चालता, चालतां, or चालतांना walking; मीं मारीत आहें I am beating.

Note.—The *Present Participle* in त, of which ता, तां and तांना are modifications, is derived from the Sanskṛit present participle in अत्; भू to be + अत् = भवत् becoming; जि to conquer + अत् = जयत् conquering. The forms in तां and तांना are the locatives of the Maráṭhi त denoting "duration."

Note.—The forms of the Present tense are strictly speaking produced by affixing the personal-endings to the Present Participles, and not to the roots, the Participial terminations being joined to the roots; as चाल + त = चालत walking (Present Participle) + तो = चालतो he walks. One of the त s is elided in union.

2. The *Past Participle* implies a past action, and assumes ला or लेला *m.*; तारला or तारलेला saved; कोण्ही एके दिवशीं ती वनांत रडत पडली होती on a certain day she lay weeping in the forest.

Note.—The past participle ला m. is derived from the Sanskṛit past participle passive त, changed in Prákṛit to द ; thus, श्रुत heard, Prák. सुद, and द, being changed to ल. In Maráṭhí as well as in Sanskṛit, the participle is both active and passive in sense.; स तत्र गतः he went there ; तेनेदमुक्तं this was said by him. The passive ending applied to verbs denoting motion, to intransitive verbs, and a few other roots has an active sense ; गतोऽहं he went.—*Mr. Apte.*

In the Sclavonic languages, the passive participle त is transferred to the active voice, "with the retention of the meaning of past time," and is also weakened to *l*, probably by first becoming changed to *d*. In Persian it is usually active, and in Georgian, it becomes *l*.—*Bopp.*

3. The *Pluperfect Participle* denotes an action that takes place before that mentioned in the principal cause, and assumes ऊन ; जाऊन having gone; मामापुढें जाऊन मी पायां पडेन I will go into the presence of my uncle, and on my knees beg pardon.

Note.—The Pluperfect Participle ऊन is derived from the Sanskṛit indeclinable participle त्वा, which is changed to तूण or ऊण in Prákṛit. In the Prákṛit prose, "there are a few instances of त्वा being relaxed to ड्डा, as गड्डा for कत्वा."—*Cowell.*

4. The *Future Participle* expresses the intention of the agent to do the action denoted by the verb, and takes the termination णार or णारा ; ये come thou, येणार being about to come ; तो येणार आहे he is about to come.

Note.—The Future Participle णार is a modification of the Sanskṛit future participal form in तृ or तार. The Sanskṛit form is employed both as a participle and as a noun of agency, and the Maráṭhí form is also used in the same manner. When the Maráṭhí participle is used in the latter sense, the final अ is lengthened : तो बोलणार आहे, he is about to speak ; बोलणारा a speaker. In Sanskṛit, as in Maráṭhi, the future participle is generally used with the verb " to be," as Sk. दातास्मि, I will give, M. मी देणार आहे.

Note.—"It is requisite to observe here that, in the history of languages, the case not unfrequently occurs, that one and the same form is, in the lapse of time, split into several, and then the different forms are applied by the spirit of the language to different words. Thus, in Sanskṛit, दाता from the base दातृ,तार, means both the giver and 'he that will give'; but in Latin, this one form, bearing two different meanings has been parted into two, of which the one has assumed to itself alone the task of representing a future participle, while the other appears. like the Greek δοτηρ *doter*, only a name of agent."—*Bopp.*

§ 214. The participles that end in आ (not the locative आं) are declinable, and the rest are indeclinable; तो येता झाला he commenced to come; ती येती झाली she commenced to come.

Note.—The declinable participles being, by derivation, adjectival, they are capable of being used both as adjectives and nouns; वाहातें पाणी a flowing stream; पळत्याच्या पाठीस लागणें to pursue one that is running; मेलेलें लेंकरूं a dead child; मेलेल्यांस जिवंत करणें to restore the dead to life; ही रडणारी मुलगी this weeping girl; हसणारांचे दांत the teeth of those who laugh.

Note.—Though the participles may be employed as *finite verbs*, as is the case with the past participle ला, they retain their nominal character, and are, sometimes, inflected by means of the case-terminations, and the postpositions, as ordinary nouns, giving the whole sentence a nominal character; फौज परगण्यांतून गेल्यावर (गेली + वावर) गांवकरी कलेक्टर साहेबांकडे खोटी फिर्याद करितात कीं, शिपायांनीं आम्हांस लुटलें after troops have passed through a district, the inhabitants go to the Collector and complain falsely that the soldiers have plundered them; मुलींच्या सासूचीं माणसें जवळ असलीं म्हणजे त्या लाजून कांहीं बोलत नाहींत आणि कांहीं पुसल्यावर (पुसलें + वावर) उत्तरही देत नाहींत in the presence of the relations on the side of the mothers-in-law, girls will scarcely speak for shyness or reply to a single question.

§ 215. The *Verbal Nouns*, distinct from the Participles, are two, viz. the *Gerund and* the *Supine*.

1. The *Gerund* is a neuter substantive, derived from the verbal root by the use of the suffix णें, and denotes action in a general way; करणें to do = कर do thou + णें. It is declined like a neuter substantive in एं in all the cases.

Note.—The Gerundial suffix is a modification of the Sanskṛit अन employed to produce abstract nouns; thus, सीव् + अन = सीवन, Prák. सीवणा, M. शिवणें to sew. "The German infinitive in *an* (standan) belongs to the class of the Sanskṛit abstract अन, as बंधनं, the binding = Gott bind."—*Bopp.* In Hindi the gerund is in आना.

2. The *Supine* is a case or cases of the Infinitive Mood, viz., the Dative and the Genitive. The dative form expresses the idea of *purpose*, and the genitive, that of *suitableness* or *requisiteness*; as, तो त्यास मारावास गेला, he went to beat him; त्याला तिकडे जायाचें आहे he has to go there; आम्हास देशांतरीं जायाचें पडेल we shall be under the necessity of going abroad.

Note.—"A case of the Infinitive mood (according to C. F. Becker) ending in Latin in *um* and *u*, that in *um* being sometimes called the *former supine*, and that in *u* the *latter supine*." *Supine* is derived "from *supineness*, bent or thrown backward, probably because, although furnished with substantive case-endings, it throws itself back as it were, on the verb."—*Webster's Dictionary*.

§ 216. The supine forms are thus produced:—

The *Infinitive* करूं to do.
The *Dative* करावयास-ला or करायास-ला (= करूं + यास).
The *Genitive* करावयाचा or करायाचा (= करूं + याचा).

Note.—The Sanskṛit infinitive तुं is used as an adjective, as in भोक्तुं कालः the time of eating, or as an "expression of purpose," as in कृष्णं द्रष्टुं व्रजति he goes to see Krishn; and the Maráthí infinitive though originally conveying both these senses in the language, now usually employs its case-forms (or the Supines) for this purpose. In the older editions of the Bálmitra, the infinitive occurs used as an adjective, though at present it is invariably displaced by its genitive supine; याचा नेसूं (नेसायाचा) पंचा कोठें आहे? Where is his wearing garment? In the more southerly parts of the Konkan, where many archaic forms have still general currency, the infinitive is used as extensively as in Sanskṛit; तो त्याका भेटूं आलो असा (M. तो त्याला भेटायास आला आहे), he has come to see him. It is only to convey the sense of a dependent action that the infinitive is used now by the Maráṭhis: तो पाहूं or पाहायास लागला he began to see.

CHAPTER XIV.

CONJUGATION.

§ 217—§ 222.

§ 217. The affixing of the personal-endings (प्रत्यय) to the verb or the verbal root, is called *Conjugation* (रूप चालविणें.)

§ 218. The verbal roots assume the personal-endings in TWO WAYS ; they either *modify their terminating vowels before taking the personal-endings*, or *remain unchanged before them.*

§ 219. The radical form of the verb, whether modified, or unmodified, is called, in reference to the personal-endings, the *base* (अंग).

§ 220. The verbs according to their *bases* are divided into TWO classes or CONJUGATIONS, viz., the FIRST CONJUGATION and the SECOND CONJUGATION.

1. The FIRST CONJUGATION includes all those verbs *which do not change in the base* ; as, root, चाल walk thou ; base, चाल, the same as the root ; present participle, चालत walking.

2. The SECOND CONJUGATION includes all those verbs *which assume* ई *in the base;* as, root, कर do thou ; base, करी=कर+ई ; present participle, करीत doing.

Note.—The intermediate ई, when shortened, as when the personal-ending has an initial long vowel, (कर+ई+तो=करितो he does) is usually omitted in conversation, but it should never be elided in writing. The illiterate affix it even to verbs of the first conjugation ; for instance, they would say बोलितो, and even बोलीतो, for बोलतो he speaks.

Note.—The two Maráṭhí conjugations correspond to the Sanskṛit *Atmanepada* (Intransitive) and *Parasmaipada* (Transitive) conjugations. The distinctive ई of the second conjugation characterises the corresponding Sanskṛit conjugation, viz., the *Parasmaipada*. The इ is the original personal-ending, the Sanskṛit ए being produced from it by the insertion of अ before it. The इ is a remnant of मि, "the weakened form of the syllable म which in Sanskṛit and Zend lies at the foundation of the oblique cases of the simple pronoun as its theme."—*Bopp.*

Note.—"In general, however, the Sanskṛit language, as it at present exists, disposes of both forms in an arbitrary manner. Of the cognate languages, only the Zend, the Greek, and the Gothic have retained their primitive form."—*Bopp.* In Maráṭhí the verbs regularly conform to these principles of conjugation.

§ 221. The Maráṭhí verbs are thus arranged under the two Conjugations:—

THE FIRST CONJUGATION.

1. All *Intransitive* verbs; बस, बसतो he sits.
2. All *Anomalous* verbs; शीक, शिकतो he learns.
3. All *Potential* verbs; करव, करवतें I can do it.

4. All *Monosyllabic* verbs, whether transitive or intransitive, and all the *verbs ending in* ह (except लिहिणें to write), *in the present tense only*; दे, देतो he gives; पाह, पाहतो he sees; but लीह, लिहितो he writes.

THE SECOND CONJUGATION.

1. All *Transitive* verbs; सोड, सोडितो he looses.

2. All the *verbs ending in* ह, *in the past tense only*; राह, राहिलें it remained.

§ 222. The Personal-endings for both the Conjugations are alike, except those of the Indicative Past Habitual and Future tenses. (Sect. 199).

Paradigma.

FIRST CONJUGATION.

Root ऊठ; Base ऊठ; उठतों I rise.

INDICATIVE MOOD.

Present Tense (*Kartari Prayoga*).

Singular.

	M.	*F.*	*N.*
1.	मीं उठतों	मीं उठतें	मीं उठतें I rise
2.	तूं उठतोस	तूं उठतेस	तूं उठतेंस thou risest
3.	तो उठतो	ती उठते	तें उठतें he, she, or it rises

Plural.

1. आम्ही उठतों we rise *m.*, *f.*, *n.*
2. तुम्ही उठतां you rise *m.*, *f.*, *n.*
3. ते उठतात *m.*, त्या उठतात *f.*, तीं उठतात *n.*, they rise

Past Tense (Kartari Prayoga).

Singular.

	M.	*F.*	*N.*
1.	मीं उठलों	मीं उठलें	मीं उठलें I rose
2.	तूं उठलास	तूं उठलीस	तूं उठलेंस thou rosest
3.	तो उठला	ती उठली	तें उठलें he, she, or it rose.

Plural.

1. आम्ही उठलों *m.*, *f.*, *n.*, we rose
2. तुम्ही उठलां *m.*, *f.*, *n.*, you rose
3. ते उठले *m.*, त्या उठल्या *f.*, तीं उठलीं *n.*, they rose

Future Tense (Kartari Prayoga).

Singular.

1. मीं उठेन I shall rise *m.*, *f.*, *n.*
2. तूं उठशील thou shalt rise *m.*, *f.*, *n.*
3. तो, ती, तें उठेल, he, she, or it shall rise

Plural.

1. आम्ही उठूं we shall rise *m.*, *f.*, *n.*
2. तुम्ही उठाल you shall rise *m.*, *f.*, *n.*
3. ते, त्या, तीं उठतील they shall rise

Past Habitual (Kartari Prayoga).

Singular.

1. मीं उठें I used to rise *m.*, *f.*, *n.*
2. तूं उठेस thou usedst to rise *m.*, *f.*, *n.*
3. तो, ती, तें उठे he, she, or it used to rise

Plural.

1. आम्ही उठूं we used to rise *m.*, *f.*, *n.*
2. तुम्ही उठां you used to rise *m.*, *f.*, *n.*
3. ते, त्या, तीं उठत they used to rise

CONDITIONAL MOOD.

(Kartari Prayoga.)

Singular.

	M.	*F.*	*N.*	
1.	मीं उठतों	मीं उठतें	मीं उठतें	had I risen, or I should have risen
2.	तूं उठतास	तूं उठतीस	तूं उठतेंस	hadst thou risen, or thou shouldest have risen
3.	तो उठता	ती उठती	तें उठतें	had he, she, or it risen, or he, she, or it should have risen

Plural.

1. आम्ही उठतों *m.*, *f.*, *n.*, had we risen, or we should have risen
2. तुम्ही उठतां *m.*, *f.*, *n.*, had you risen, or you should have risen
3. ते उठते *m.* / त्या उठत्या *f.* / तीं उठतीं *n.* } had they risen, or they should have risen

SUBJUNCTIVE MOOD.

(*Kartari Prayoga.*)

Singular.

	M.	*F.*	*N.*	
1.	मीं उठावा	मीं उठावी	मीं उठावें	I may or might rise
2.	तूं उठावास	तूं उठावीस	तूं उठावेंस	thou mayest or mightest rise
3.	तो उठावा	ती उठावी	तें उठावें	he, she, or it may or might rise

Plural

1. आम्ही उठावे, आम्ही उठाव्या, आम्ही उठावीं we may or might rise
2. तुम्ही उठावेत, तुम्ही उठाव्यात, तुम्ही उठावींत you may or might rise
3. ते उठावे, त्या उठाव्या, तीं उठावीं they may or might rise

(*Bháve Prayoga.*)

Singular.

M. F. N.

1. म्या उठावें I should or ought to rise
2. त्वा उठावें thou shouldest or oughtest to rise
3. त्यानें, तिनें, त्यानें उठावें he, she, or it should or ought to rise

Plural.

1. आम्हीं उठावें we should or ought to rise
2. तुम्हीं उठावें you should or ought to rise
3. त्यांनीं उठावें they should or ought to rise

IMPERATIVE MOOD.

(*Kartari Prayoga.*)

	Singular. *M. F. N.*	*Plural.* *M. F. N.*
1.	मीं उठूं let me rise	आम्ही उठूं let us rise
2.	तूं ऊठ rise thou	तुम्ही उठा rise ye
3.	तो, ती, तें उठो let him, her, or it rise	ते, त्या, तीं उठोत let them rise

INFINITIVE MOOD.

उठूं to rise

PARTICIPLES.

Present उठत, उठता *m.*, उठतां, उठतांना rising

Past उठला *m.*, उठलेला *m.* risen
Pluperfect उठून having risen
Future उठणार being about to rise

Gerund.

उठणें to rise, or rising

Supines.

Dat. उठायास or उठायाला, उठावयास or उठावयाला to rise or for rising
Gen. उठायाचें or उठावयाचें to rise, of rising

Second Conjugation.

Root मोड ; Base मोडी ; मोडितों I break.

Indicative Mood.

Present Tense (Kartari Prayoga).

Singular.

	M.	*F.*	*N.*
1.	मीं मोडितों	मीं मोडितें	मीं मोडितें I break
2.	तूं मोडितोस	तूं मोडितेस	तूं मोडितेंस thou breakest
3.	तो मोडितो	ती मोडिते	तें मोडितें he, she or it breaks

Plural.

1. आह्मी मोडितों we break *m.*, *f.*, *n.*
2. तुह्मी मोडितां you break *m.*, *f.*, *n.*
3. ते, त्या, तीं मोडितात they break

Past Tense (Karmani Prayoga).

M. F. N.

Singular.

1. म्या	*Sing.*	मोडिला *m.*	मोडिली *f.*	मोडिलें *n.*
		I broke (him, her, or it)		
	Plu.	मोडिले *m.*	मोडिल्या *f.*	मोडिलीं *n.*
		I broke (them, *m.*, *f.*, *n.*)		
2. त्वा	*Sing.*	मोडिला *m.*	मोडिली *f.*	मोडिलें *n.*
		thou brokest (him, her, or it)		
	Plu.	मोडिले *m.*	मोडिल्या *f.*	मोडिलीं
		thou brokest (them)		
3. त्यानें *m.*, *n.* तिनें *f.*	*Sing.*	मोडिला *m.*	मोडिली *f.*	मोडिलें *n.*
		he, she, or it broke (him, her, or it)		
	Plu.	मोडिले *m.*	मोडिल्या *f.*	मोडिलीं *n.*
		he, she, or it broke (them)		

Plural.

1. आम्हीं	*Sing.*	मोडिला *m.*	मोडिली *f.*	मोडिलें *n.*	we broke (him, her or it)
	Plu.	मोडिले *m.*	मोडिल्या *f.*	मोडिलीं *n.*	we broke (them)
2. तुम्हीं	*Sing.*	मोडिला *m.*	मोडिली *f.*	मोडिलें *n.*	you broke (him, her or it)
	Plu.	मोडिले *m.*	मोडिल्या *f.*	मोडिलीं *n.*	you broke (them)
3. त्यांनीं	*Sing.*	मोडिला *m.*	मोडिली *f.*	मोडिलें *n.*	they broke (him, her or it)
	Plu.	मोडिले *m.*	मोडिल्या *f.*	मोडिलीं *n.*	they broke (them)

(*Bhâve Prayoga.*)

Singular.

1. म्यां मोडिलें I broke
2. त्वां मोडिलें thou brokest
3. त्यानें *m.*, *n.*, तिनें *f.*, मोडिलें he, she, or it broke

Plural.

1. आम्हीं मोडिलें we broke
2. तुम्हीं मोडिलें you broke
3. त्यांनीं मोडिलें they broke

Future Tense (*Kartari Prayoga*).

Singular.

M. F. N.

1. मीं मोडीन I shall or will break
2. तूं मोडिशील thou shalt break
3. तो, ती, तें मोडील he, she, or it shall break

Plural.

M. F. N.

1. आम्ही मोडूं we shall break
2. तुम्ही मोडाल you shall break
3. ते, त्या, तीं मोडितील they shall break

Past Habitual (Kartari Prayoga).

Singular.

M. F. N.

1. मीं मोडीं I used to break
2. तूं मोडीस thou usedst to break
3. तो, ती, तें मोडी he, she, or it used to break

Plural.

M. F. N.

1. आम्ही मोडूं we used to break
2. तुम्ही मोडा you used to break
3. ते, त्या, तीं मोडीत they used to break

CONDITIONAL MOOD.

(*a*) Were I to break, or had I broken
(*b*) I would break, or would have broken

Singular.

	M.	*F.*	*N.*	
1.	मीं मोडितों	मीं मोडितें	मीं मोडितें	had I broken
2.	तूं मोडितास	तूं मोडितीस	तूं मोडितेंस	hadst thou broken
3.	तो मोडिता	ती मोडिती	तें मोडितें	had he, she, or it broken

Plural.

M. F. N.

1. आम्ही मोडितों had we broken
2. तुम्ही मोडितां had you broken
3. ते मोडिते, त्या मोडित्या, तीं मोडितीं had they broken

SUBJUNCTIVE MOOD.

(*Karmaṇi Prayoga.*)

Singular.

1. म्या 2. त्वा 3. त्यानें *m.*, *n.*, तिनें *f.*	मोडावा *m.*, मोडावी *f.*, मोडावें *n.*, *Sing.* मोडावे *m.*, मोडाव्या *f.*, मोडावीं *n. Plu.*	I, thou, or he, she, or it should have broken, or should break.

Plural.

1. आम्हीं 2. तुम्हीं 3. त्यांनीं	मोडावा *m.*, मोडावी *f.* मोडावें *n.* *Sing.* मोडावे *m.*, मोडाव्या *f.*, मोडावीं *n.* *Plu.*	We, you, or they should have broken, or should break.

(*Bháve Prayoga.*)

Singular.

M. F. N.

1. म्या मोडावें I should break
2. त्वा मोडावें thou shouldst break
3. त्यानें *m.*, *n.*, तिनें *f.*, मोडावें he, she, or it should break

Plural.

1. आम्हीं मोडावें we should break
2. तुम्हीं मोडावें you should break
3. त्यांनीं मोडावें they should break

IMPERATIVE MOOD.

Singular.

1. मीं मोडूं let me break
2. तूं मोड break thou
3. तो *m.*, ती *f.*, तें *n.*, मोडो let him, her or it break

Plural.

1. आम्ही मोडूं let us break
2. तुम्ही मोडा break ye
3. ते, त्या, तीं मोडोत let them break

INFINITIVE MOOD.

मोडूं to break.

PARTICIPLES.

Present मोडीत, मोडिता, *m.*, मोडितां, मोडितांना breaking
Past मोडिला *m.*, मोडिलेला *m.*, broken
Pluperfect मोडून having broken
Future मोडणार being about to break

GERUND.

मोडणें to break, breaking

SUPINES.

Dat. मोडायास or मोडायाला ; मोडावयास or मोडावयाला to break
Gen. मोडायाचें or मोडावयाचें to be broken

CHAPTER XV.

CONJUGATION—*continued*.

1. The Causal Verb.

§ 223—§ 230

§ 223. The Causal Verb is derived by affixing अव to the root of the Maráṭhí verb ; as मोड+अव=मोडव+लें=मोडवलें, म्या मोडविलें I caused it to be broken. (§ 184. (1))

§ 224. The Causal Verb, being, in all its forms, essentially transitive, invariably follows the Second Conjugation.

SECOND CONJUGATION.

INDICATIVE MOOD.

Present Tense.

मीं मोडवितों I cause it to be broken.

	Singular.	*Plural.*
1.	मीं मोडवितों *m.*, तें *f.*,-तें *n.*	आह्मी मोडवितों *m.*, *f.*, *n.*
2.	तूं मोडवितोस *m.*, तेस *f.*, तेंस *n.*	तुह्मी मोडवितां *m.*, *f.*, *n.*
3.	तो, ती, तें मोडवितो *m.*, ते *f.*, तें *n.*	ते, त्या, तीं मोडवितात *m.*, *f.*, *n.*

Past Tense.

(*Karmani Prayoga.*)

म्या मोडविला I caused it to be broken.

Singular.	1.	म्या *m.*, *f.*, *n.*	*Sing.* मोडविला *m.*,-ली *f.*,-लें *n.* *Plu.* मोडविले *m.*,-ल्या *f.* ला *n.*
	2.	त्वा *m.*, *f.*, *n.*	
	3.	त्यानें *m.*, *n.*, तिनें *f.*	
Plural.	1.	आह्मीं *m.*, *f.*, *n.*	*Sing.* मोडविला *m.*,-ली *f.*,-लें *n.* *Plu.* मोडविले *m.*,-ल्या *f.*,-लीं *n.*
	2.	तुह्मीं *m.*, *f.*, *n.*	
	3.	त्यांनीं *m.*, *f.*, *n.*	

(*Bhâve Prayoga.*)

म्या or मीं मोडविलें I caused it to be broken.

Singular and Plural.

1. म्या or आम्हीं *m., f., n.* } मोडविलें
2. त्वा or तुम्हीं *m., f., n.*
3. त्यानें *m.*, तिनें *f.*, त्यानें *n.*
   त्यांनीं *m., f., n.*

Future Tense.

मीं मोडवीन I shall cause it to be broken.

	Singular.	*Plural.*
1.	मीं मोडवीन *m., f., n.*	आम्ही मोडवूं *m., f., n.*
2.	तूं मोडविशील *m., f., n.*	तुम्ही मोडवाल *m., f., n.*
3.	तो, ती, तें मोडवील	ते, त्या, तीं मोडवितील.

Past Habitual.

मीं मोडवीं I used to cause it to be broken.

	Singular.	*Plural.*
1.	मीं मोडवीं *m., f., n.*	आम्ही मोडवूं *m., f., n.*
2.	तूं मोडवीस *m., f., n.*	तुम्ही मोडवा *m., f., n.*
3.	तो, ती, तें मोडवी	ते, त्या, तीं मोडवीत

CONDITIONAL MOOD.

1*st Sing*. मीं मोडवितों had I caused it to be broken; I should have caused it to be broken.

Singular.

1. मीं मोडवितों *m.*,-तें *f.*,-तें *n.*
2. तूं मोडवितास *m.*,-तीस *f.*, तेंस *n.*
3. तो, ती, तें मोडविता *m.*,-ती *f.*,-तें *n.*

Plural.

1. आम्ही मोडवितों.
2. तुम्ही मोडवितां.
3. ते, त्या, तीं मोडवितें *m.*,-त्या *f.*,-तीं *n.*

SUBJUNCTIVE MOOD.

(*Karmani Prayoga.*)

1*st Sing*. मीं or म्या मोडवावा I may or might cause it to be broken.

M. F. N.

Singular.	1.	म्या	*Sing.* मोडवावा *m.*,-वी*f.*,-वें*n.*
	2.	त्वा	*Plu.* मोडवावे*m.*,-व्या *f.*,-वीं *n.*
	3.	त्यानें *m.*, तिनें *f.*, त्यानें *n.*	
Plural.	1.	आह्मीं	
	2.	तुह्मीं	
	3.	त्यांनीं	

(*Bhâve Prayoga.*)

Singular and Plural.

1.	म्या or आह्मीं	मोडवावें
2.	त्वा or तुह्मीं	
3.	त्यानें *m.*, *n.*, तिनें *f.*, त्यांनीं	

IMPERATIVE MOOD.

1*st* *Sing.* मीं मोडवूं let me cause it to be broken.

	Singular. *M. F. N.*	*Plural.* *M. F. N.*
1.	मीं मोडवूं	आह्मीं मोडवूं
2.	तूं मोडव or मोडीव	तुह्मी मोडवा
3.	तो *m.*, ती *f.*, तें *n.*, मोडवो	ते *m.*, त्या *f.*, तीं *n.*, मोडवोत

INFINITIVE MOOD.

मोडवूं to cause it to be broken.

PATICIPLES.

Present मोडवीत, मोडविता, मोविती-तांना
Past मोडविला-लेला
Pluperfect मोडवून
Future मोडविणार

GERUND.

मोडवणें to cause it to be broken.

SUPINES.

Dat. मोडवायास-ला to cause to be broken.
Gen. मोडवायाचा of causing to be broken.

§ 225. The अव is affixed both to transitiveand intransitive verbs :—Intr. बसणें to sit, बसविणें to cause to sit ; रामा बसतो Rama sits; त्यानें रामाला बसविलें he caused Rama to sit. Trans. मारणें to strike, मारविणें to cause to strike ; रामा गाईला मारितो Rama strikes a cow ; तो रामाकडून गाईला मारवितो he causes Rama to strike a cow. The intransitive becomes transitive in its causal form.

§ 226. When the Intransitive verb is made causal, the original subject becomes the *object* of the causal form ; as, रामा निजतो Rama sleeps; तो रामाला निजवितो he causes Rama to sleep.

§ 227. When the Transitive verb is made causal, the original subject becomes the *instrumental* or *indirect agent* of the causal form, and another agent is introduced as the subject of the causal form, influencing the action of the instrumental or original agent ; as, हरि पोथी वाचितो Hari reads a book ; गोविंदा हरीकडून पोथी वाचवितो Govind causes Hari to read a book.

§ 228. When the simple *Transitive* verb becomes causal, it expresses *two agencies*—one direct, and the other indirect or instrumental ; as सुतारांकडून भीमरावांनीं घर बांधविलें Bhimrao got the house built by carpenters, or caused the house to be built by carpenters. *Bhimrao* is the direct agent, and carpenters, the indirect.

§ 229. When the simple *Intransitive* assumes the causal form, it expresses *only one agency*—the *direct* ; as रामरावांनीं पाटिलबावाला सत्रंजीवर बसविलें Ramrao caused the patil to sit on the carpet. Ramrao is the direct agent.

§ 230. By the insertion of an additional व, the simple intransitive becomes capable of expressing the indirect as well as the direct agency ; as रामरावांनीं पाटलाकडून त्या घोडयास चालव-विलें Ramrao caused that horse to walk through the patil.

§ 231. By the use of an additional व the simple transitive becomes a double causal ; as, रामा तें काम करितो Rama does the work,—*Simple* Trans. ; विठू रामाकडून तें काम करवितो Vithu causes Rama to do the work,—*Causal*; विठू रामाकडून गोविंदाच्या हातून तें काम करववितो Vithu causes Rama to get the work done by Govind,—*Double Causal.*

§ 232. The subject of the causal verb, when denoting *indirect* agency, is inflected by the postposition कडून by means of, while the direct agent may be either in the nominative or the instrumental case; रामानें वानरांकडून पराक्रम करविले Rama wrought wonders by the agency of the monkeys; हा मुलगा आपल्या भावाकडून पाणी भरवितो this boy causes his brother to fill water; दाईनें मुलाला निजविलें the nurse put the child to sleep; दाई मुलाला खुर्चीवर बसविते the nurse seats the child in the chair.

Note—In Sanskṛit the subject of the simple verb is put in the instrumental case in the causal form; as रामो भार्यां त्यजति, Rama abandons his wife; *Causal*,—(स) रामेण भार्यां त्याजयति (he) makes Rama abandon his wife.

Note.—Etymologically the Passive and Causative forms are alike in form and sense, but convey their present difference of sense only by their forms of conjugation and construction with a foreign agent.

2. The Potential Verb.

§ 233. The Potential Verb is derived from the simple verb by affixing व to the Root; चाल walk thou + व=चालव; मला चालवतें I can walk.

§ 234. The Potential Verb, whether transitive or intransitive, is of the First Conjugation, and does not take ई to make up its base; माझ्यानें सोडवतें I can unloose it; माझ्यानें सोडवलें I was able to unloose it.

§ 235. The Potential Verb never takes the *Kartari* construction, with the subject in the nominative case, but only the *Karmani* or the *Bhave*, with the subject in the *dative* or in the *instrumental form derived from the genitive* case; मला or माझ्यानें बसवतें I can sit; त्याला or त्याच्यानें भाकर खाववते he can eat bread; तिला or तिच्यानें हा सगळा ग्रंथ वाचवला she could read this whole book; रामाला or रामाच्यानें चोराला धरवलें Rámá could catch the thief.

Note.—In Sanskrit the Potential Passive Participle has the agent either in the genitive or the instrumental case ; मया or मम सेव्यः, सेवितव्य : or सेवनीयो हरि Hari should be worshipped by me. In Prakrit the genitive is changed to the dative. Hence the case of the Maráṭhí Potential is either the dative, or the instrumental derived from the genitive ; मला or माझ्यानें चालवतें I can walk. In Sanskrit the subject is never put in the dative case.

§ 236. The Potential intransitive verb always takes the *Bháve* construction, and the transitive, either the *Karmani* or the *Bháve*.

§ 237. It is only when the object denotes a *person*, that the potential transitive verb takes the *Bháve* construction, otherwise it is habitually conjugated in the *Karmani*.

Note.—In poetry the simple instrumental is sometimes used for that derived from the genitive ; आम्हीं शक्तिहीनें कैसें करवेल तें नेणें.—*Tukáram.*

§ 238. The Anomalous verbs, in their potential forms, take either the *Bháve* or the *Karmani* construction, like the ordinary transitive potentials :—

Simple Anomalous—मीं धडा शिकलीं I learnt the lesson (*Kartari Prayoga*).

Potential Anomalous : मला or माझ्यानें धडा शिकवला I could learn the lesson (*Karmani Prayoga*); मला or माझ्यानें त्याला शिकवलें I could teach him (*Bháve Prayoga*).

Paradigm.

INDICATIVE MOOD.

Present Tense (*Bháve Prayoga*).

माझ्यानें or मला चालवतें I can walk ; माझ्यानें or मला मोडवतें I can break.

Singular.	1. माझ्यानें or मला		चालवतें *Intrans.* मोडवतें *Trans.*
	2. तुझ्यानें or तुला		
	3. त्याच्यानें or त्याला	*m., n.*	
	तिच्यानें or तिला *f.*		
Plural.	1. आमच्यानें or आम्हांला		
	2. तुमच्यानें or तुम्हांला		
	3. त्यांच्यानें or त्यांला		

(*Karmani Prayoga.*)

माझ्यानें (मोडवतो)*m.* I can break.

Singular.
1. माझ्यानें or मला
2. तुझ्यानें or तुला
3. त्याच्यानें or त्याला *m.,n.* / तिच्यानें or तिला

Plural.
1. आमच्यानें or आम्हांला
2. तुमच्यानें or तुम्हांला
3. त्यांच्यानें or त्यांला

} *Sing.* मोडवतो *m.*, ‘ते *f.*, तें *n.* / *Plu.* मोडवतात *m.*, *f.*, *n.* } Trans.

Past Tense (*Bháve Prayoga*).

1*st Sing.* माझ्यानें or मला चालवलें I could walk, *Intrans.*
,, ,, माझ्यानें or मला मोडवलें. I could break, *Trans.*

(*Karmani Prayoga.*)

1*st Sing.* माझ्यानें or मला मोडवला *m.* I could break.

M. F. N.

Singular.
1. माझ्यानें or मला
2. तुझ्यानें or तुला
3. त्याच्यानें or त्याला / तिच्यानें or तिला

Plural.
1. आमच्यानें or आम्हांला
2. तुमच्यानें or तुम्हांला
3. त्यांच्यानें or त्यांला

} *Sing.* मोडवला *m.*,-ली *f.*,-लें *n.* / *Plu.* मोडवले *m.*,-ल्या *f.*,-लीं *n.*

Future Tense.

1*st Sing.* माझ्यानें or मला चालवेल. I shall be able to walk.
,, ,, माझ्यानें or मला मोडवेल I shall be able to break.

M. F. N.

Singular.
1. माझ्यानें or मला
2. तुझ्यानें or तुला
3. त्याच्यानें or त्याला / तिच्यानें or तिला

Plural.
1. आमच्यानें or आम्हांला
2. तुमच्यानें or तुम्हांला
3. त्यांच्यानें or त्यांला

} चालवेल *Intrans.* / मोडवेल *Trans.*

Habitual Past.

1*st Sing.* माझ्यानें or मला चालवे I used to be able to walk.
,, ,, माझ्यानें or मला मोडवे I used to be able to break.

		M. F. N.	
Singular.	1.	मांझ्यानें or मला	चालवे *Intrans.* मोडवे *Trans.*
	2.	तुझ्यानें or तुला	
	3.	त्याच्यानें or त्याला / तिच्यानें or तिला	
Plural.	1.	आमच्यानें or आम्हांला	
	2.	तुमच्यानें or तुम्हांला	
	3.	त्यांच्यानें or त्यांला	

CONDITIONAL MOOD.

(*Bháve Prayoga.*)

1*st Sing.* माझ्यानें or मला चालवतें if I can or could walk.
,, ,, माझ्यानें or मला मोडवतें if I can or could break.

		M. F. N.	
Singular.	1.	माझ्यानें or मला	चालवतें *Intrans.* मोडवतें *Trans.*
	2.	तुझ्यानें or तुला	
	3.	त्याच्यानें or त्याला / तिच्यानें or तिला	
Plural.	1.	आमच्यानें or आम्हांला	
	2.	तुमच्यानें or तुम्हांला	
	3.	त्यांच्यानें or त्यांला	

(*Karmani Prayoga.*)

1*st Sing.* माझ्यानें or मला मोडवता *m.*, I can or could break.

		M. F. N.	
Singular.	1.	मांझ्यानें or मला	*Sing.* मोडवता-ती-तें / *Plu.* मोडवते-त्या-तीं *Tran.*
	2.	तुंझ्यानें or तुला	
	3.	त्याच्यानें or तिला	
Plural.	1.	आमच्यानें or आम्हांला	
	2.	तुमच्यानें or तुम्हांला	
	3.	त्यांच्यानें or त्यांला	

SUBJUNCTIVE MOOD.

(*Bháve Prayoga.*)

1st *Sing.* माझ्यानें or मला चालवावें I may or might, should or would be able to walk.

" " माझ्यानें or मला मोडवावें I may or might, or should, or would be able to break.

(*Karmani Prayoga.*)

1st *Sing.* माझ्यानें or मला मोडवावा I might or should or would be able to break.

M. F. N.

Singular.	1.	माझ्यानें or मला	*Sing.* मोडवावा-वी-वें *Plu.* मोडवावे-व्या-वीं
	2.	तुझ्यानें or तुला	
	3.	त्याच्यानें or त्याला तिच्यानें or तिला	
Plural.	1.	आमच्यानें or आम्हांला	
	2.	तुमच्यानें or तुम्हाला	
	3.	त्यांच्यानें or त्यांला	

IMPERATIVE MOOD.

1st *Sing.* माझ्यानें or मला चालवो let me be capable of walking.

" " माझ्यानें or मला मोडवो let me be capable of breaking.

M. F. N.

Singular.	1.	माझ्यानें or मला	चालवो *Intrans.* मोडवो *Trans.*
	2.	तुझ्यानें or तुला	
	3.	त्याच्यानें or त्याला तिच्यानें or तिला	
Plural.	1.	आमच्यानें or आम्हांला	
	2.	तुमच्यानें or तुम्हाला	
	3.	त्यांच्यानें or त्यांला	

PARTICIPLES.

Present चालवत, चालवता, चालवतां, चालवतांना being capable of walking, *Intrans.*

Present मोडवत, मोडवता, मोडवतां, मोडवतांना being capable of breaking, *Trans.*

Past चालवला-लेला having been capable of walking

,, मोडवला-लेला having been capable of breaking

GERUND.

मोडवणें to be able to break, *Trans.*

चालवणें to be able to walk, *Intrans.*

Note.—The Potential forms from the Subjunctive mood downwards are rarely used, but are given simply for reference.

3. THE ANOMALOUS VERB.

§ 239. The Anomalous Verbs are conjugated intransitively, *i. e.*, in the first Conjugation (§ 185, 4); as, ती धडा शिकली she has learnt her lesson. They always take the Subjective or *Kartari* construction. The following are the exceptions :—

1. In the Subjunctive mood the Anomalous Verbs take the *Karmani* or the *Bhâve* construction, like the other transitives : त्या ती ग्रंथ पढावा I should learn that book.

2. In the Potential form, the Anomalous Verbs take the *Karmaní* or the *Bhâve* construction, § 238 ; as, मला or माझ्यानें ती पोथी शिकवली I could learn that book.

Note.—All the verbal terminations derived from the Sanskṛit passive participle retain their sympathy with the suffering object with which they, by their nature, agree, and hence these particles, whenever they are affixed to transitive verbs, force them to agree with the object, whatever might be their incidental peculiarities. The past participle ला has lost much of its original passive character and energy, and it consequently does not exert any influence upon such irregular forms as the Anomalous verbs; whereas the subjunctive and potential particles are not so commonly used in the language as ला and have not, therefore, lost any of their original passive force.

INDICATIVE MOOD.

Present Tense.

1*st Sing.* मीं शिकतों (not शिकितों) I learn

Past Tense.

Kartari Prayoga (*not the Karmani or Bhâve.*)
1*st Sing.* मीं शिकलों I learnt

Future Tense.

1*st Sing.* मी शिकेन (not शिक्रीन) I shall learn

Past Habitual.

1*st Sing.* मीं शिकें (not शिकीं) I used to learn

CONDITIONAL MOOD.

1*st Sing.* मी शिकतों had I learnt (not शिकितों)

SUBJUNCTIVE MOOD.

Bhâve Prayoga.

1*st Sing.* म्या शिकावें I should or ought to learn

Karmani Prayoga.

1*st Sing.* म्या शिकावा *m.* I should or ought to learn

IMPERATIVE MOOD.

1*st Sing.* मीं शिकूं let me learn

INFINITIVE MOOD.

शिकूं to learn

PARTICIPLES.

Present शिकत, शिकता, शिकतां, शिकतांना learning
Past शिकला-लेला learnt or learned
Pluperfect शिकून having learnt
Future शिकणार being about to learn

GERUND.

शिकणें to learn

SUPINES.

Dat. शिकायास—ला or शिकावयास—ला
Gen. शिकायाचा or शिकावयाचा

§ 240. The following are the Anomalous verbs in the language :—

आचरणें practise
ओकणें to vomit
चावणें to bite
चुकणें to miss
जनणें to bear
जिंकणें to conquer
जेवणें to dine
झोंबणें to seize hold of
डसणें to bite
तरणें to pass over
थुंकणें to spit
नेसणें to gird on
पढणें to study
पसवणें to foal
पांघरणें to clothe
पावणें to obtain
पिणें to drink
पोहणें to swim
प्रसवणें to bring forth
बोलणें to tell
मुकणें to lose
म्हणणें to say
लागणें to touch
लेणें to put on
विणें to bring forth
विसरणें to forget
शिंकरणें to blow the nose
शिवणें to touch
समजणें to understand
स्मरणें to remember
हरणें to lose

Note.—The verb सांगणें is transitive, but does not take the intermediate ई, or the transitive future and past habitual inflections. In regard to the *Prayogas*, it is regular.

Note.—The word जेवणें is irregular in construction or प्रयोग, but regular in the matter of the inflections and the base; मीं जेवितों I dine; तो जेवील he will dine. In the past tense the इ is dropped; मी जेवलों I dined, not जेविलों.

Note.—The verbs चावणें to bite, झोंबणें to grasp rudely, डसणें to bite, शिवणें to touch, मुकणें to lose, and लागणें to touch take the object in the dative case; तो कुत्रा माझ्या पायाला डसला the dog bit my leg; माझ्या कापडांला शिवला he touched my clothes; तूं जिवाला मुकशील you will lose your life.

Note.—Some of the above Anomalous verbs are also used intransitively; थुंकणें to spit, पोहणें to swim, विणें to bring forth, etc. शिंकरणें to blow the nose may also be conjugated in the objective construction त्यानें नाक शिंकरलें (obj. cons.), or तो नाक शिंकरला he blew the nose.

4. The Irregular Verbs.

§ 241. Several verbs, both transitive and intransitive, form their *past tense* irregularly, and the following is a list of them. They are arranged in *three* groups :—

1st.—Those which change the final vowel of the root to आ before assuming the past termination ला.

2ndly.—Those which modify the root by means of *vowels*, *consonants*, and *semi-vowels*.

3rdly.—Those which have a past tense formed from another root.

(1) *Roots which* assume आ :—

Root.	*Past Tense.*
नीघ go out	निघाला
पळ flee	पळाला
म्हण say	म्हणाला
रीघ penetrate by force	रिघाला
हींव be cold	हिंवाला

Note.—The above verbs have only the *specified* forms for the past tense.

जीर soak into	जिराला or जिरला
ढळ slip aside	ढळाला or ढळला
तीड crack	तिडाला or तिडला
नीभ get out of	निभाला or निभला
भीज be wetted	भिजाला or भिजला
मुर be absorbed	मुराला or मुरला

Note.—The second past form is in general use.

ऊड fly	उडाला or उडला
दड lie hid	दडाला or दडला
नीम cease	निमाला or निमला
नीव cool	निवाला or निवला
बूड sink	बुडाला or बुडला
मीळ meet with	मिळाला or मिळला
वीर melt	विराला or विरला

Note.—The first past form is in general use.

ऊभ cease for a time	उभाला or उभला
खीज grate	खिजाला or खिजला
गळ leak	गळाला or गळला
जळ burn	जळाला or जळला
झीज wear away	झिजाला or झिजला
दब yield or give way	दबाला or दबला

दीप be dazzled	दिपाला or दिपला
बूज start	बुजाला or बुजला
बूझ understand	बुझाला or बुझला
रीझ be delighted with	रिझाला or रिझला
लप lie hid	लपाला or लपला
वीझ be extinguished	विझाला or विझला

Note.—Both the forms are equally used.

(2) Verbs which substitute different consonants and vowels for some of the letters of the root, in order to make up the past tense :—

गा sing	गाइलें or गालें
ध्या meditate	ध्याइलें or ध्यालें
मा hold	माइलें or मालें
घे take	घेतलें
पी drink	प्यालें
धू wash	धुतलें
भी fear	भ्यालें
वी bear	व्याल
ले wear	ल्यालें
दे give	दिलें
बघ see	बघितलें
माग ask	मागितलें
सांग tell	सांगिनलें
खण dig	खणलें or खंटलें
म्हण say	म्हटलें
हाण slay	हाटलें
घाल put	घातलें
कर do	केलें
मर die	मेलें
खा eat	खाल्लें

(3) Verbs that have a past tense formed from another root :—

Root.	*Past Tense.*
जा go	गेला
ये come	आला
हो beecom	झाला

§ 242. We give below two irregular verbs conjugated in the various tenses :—

कर do (*Transitive Verb*).

Present Tense.

Singular.	*Plural.*
मीं करितों I do	आम्हीं करितों we do

Past Tense.

मीं or म्या केलें I did	आम्हीं केलें we did
तूं or त्वा केलें thou didst	तुम्हीं केलें you did
त्यानें केलें he did	त्यांनीं केलें they did

Future Tense.

Singular.	*Plural.*
मीं करीन I shall do	आम्ही करूं we shall do
तूं करशील thou shalt do	तुम्ही कराल you shall do
तो करील he shall do	ते, त्या, तीं करतील they shall do

जा Go (*Intransitive Verb*).

Present Tense.

मीं जातों I go	आम्ही जातों we go

Past Tense.

मीं गेलों I went	आम्ही गेलों we went
तूं गेलास thou wentest	तुम्ही गेलां you went
तो गेला he went, *m.*	ते गेले they went, *m.*

Future Tense.

मीं जाईन I shall go

तूं जाशील thou shalt go, &c., &c.

CHAPTER XVI.

The Auxiliary Verbs.

§ 243—§ 257.

§ 243. The verbs employed to make up the compound *forms* of the Tenses and Moods are called *Auxiliary* or helping verbs ; thus, मला गेलें पाहिजे I must go ; पाहिजे it is necessary, is a helping verb. The verbs united with the Auxiliaries are called, in contradistinction, Principal Verbs.

§ 244. The Auxiliary verbs are divided into two classes—those which make up the forms of the Tenses, and those which make up the forms of the Moods.

§ 245. The Auxiliary verbs which make up the Compound forms of the tenses are **असणें** to be and **होणें** to become, and both denote existence; **रामचंद्र राजा होता**, Ramchandra was a king; **शिवाजी राजा झाला** Sivaji became a king. These Auxiliary verbs are called *Substantive verbs*, or verbs expressing existence.

§ 246. The Negative forms of **असणें** and **होणें** are **नसणें** no to be, and **होत नाहीं** one does not become, respectively.

§ 247. The Auxiliary verbs which make up the Compound forms of the Moods are **पाहिजे** it is wanted, and **लागणें** to touch, and both express the *necessity* or *obligation* of performing the action denoted by the principal verb; **मला गेलें पाहिजे** I must go; **मला जावें लागतें** it is necessary for me to go. These Auxiliary Verbs may be called Modal Verbs, or verbs relating to the Moods.

§ 248. The Negative forms corresponding to **पाहिजे** and **लागणें** are **नको** it is not wanted and **नलगे** it is not necessary or incumbent, respectively.

§ 249. There is a third Negative Modal form in **नये**, which expresses impropriety or unsuitableness; **म्या तें करूं नये** I should not do it.

§ 250. The Modal verbs make up the Compound forms of the Subjunctive and Imperative moods.

§ 251. Most of the Auxiliary Verbs, both the Substantive and Modal, are deficient in forms of conjugation, and are therefore denominated *Defective Verbs*. (Sect. 171.)

I. The Substantive Verbs.

असणें to be.

§ 252. The verb **असणें** has three distinct forms for the present Indicative—**आहें**, **होय** and **असतों** I am.

§ 253. आहे is employed to express the existence of objects as well as their properties ; रामा घरीं आहे Rama is at home, *existence* ; रामा शहाणा आहे Rama is wise, *property*. But the form in होय is used only for affirming qualities of objects ; मनुष्यांच्या तारणोपायास श्रद्धा मुख्य साधन होय the principal instrument for effecting man's salvation is faith. We cannot say तो एथें होय, but तो एथें आहे he is here.

§ 254. The present form in असतो has usually the sense of the present habitual or the present continuative ; रामा आजारी असतो Rama is usually ill.

§ 255. We give below the conjugation of the verb असणें to be :—

INDICATIVE MOOD.

Present Tense (First Form.)

Singular.	*Plural.*
1. मीं आहें I am	आम्ही आहों we are
2. तूं आहेस thou art	तुम्ही आहां you are
3. तो, ती, तें आहे he, she, or it is	ते, त्या, तीं आहेत they are

Note.—These forms are derived from the Sanskṛit present form of the verb "to be." The inflections of the habitual past of the first conjugation are combined with the first person singular of the present tense :—

Sk. अस्मि, Prák. अम्हि, O. M. आहे, M. आहें.

Singular.	*Plural.*
1. आहें I am=आहे+एं	आहों we are=आहे+ऊं
2. आहेस thou art=आहे+एस	आहां you are=आहे+आं
3. आहे he is=आहे+ए	आहेत they are= आहे+अत

The forms in Old Maráṭhí corresponded more closely with the Sanskṛit forms of the present :—

Sing. 1.	Sk. अस्मि I am	Prák. अम्हि, O. M. आहें
,, 2.	Sk. असि thou art,	Prák. असि, O. M. असि
,, 3.	Sk. अस्ति he is,	Prák. अत्थि, O. M. आथि

Present Tense (Second Form).

	Singular.	*Plural.*
1.	मीं होय I am	आम्ही व्हॉं we are
2.	तूं होस thou art	तुम्ही व्हां you are
3.	तो, ती, तें होय he, she, or it is	ते, त्या, तीं होत they are

Note.—(1) The first personal singular form is sometimes nasalised; as मीं होय or हॉंय, and the authority for the nasalization will be seen in the following note. The first personal plural form is sometimes given as हॉं or होऊं.

(2). The forms in होय I am, are derived from the Sanskrit भू to be or to become, changed in Prákṛit to हो, in combination with the inflections of the past habitual intransitive:—

	Singular.	*Plural.*
1.	हॉंय = हो + एं Sk. भू; Prák. हो	व्हॉं = हो + ऊं
2.	होस = हो + (ए) स	व्हां = हो + आं
3.	होय = हो + ए	होत = हो + अत

Present Tense (Third Form).

मीं असतों I usually am.

	Singular.	*Plural.*
1.	मीं असतों *m.*,-तें *f.*,-तें *n.*	आम्ही असतों *m.*, *f.*, *n.*
2.	तूं असतोस *m.*,-तेस *f.*,-तेंस *n.*	तुम्ही असतां *m.*, *f.*, *n.*
3.	तो असतो *m.* ती असते *f.* तें असतें *n.*	ते *m.*, त्या *f.*, तीं *n.*, असतात.

Past Tense.

मीं होतों I was.

	Singular.	*Plural.*
1.	मीं होतों *m.*, -तें *f.*,-तें *n.*, I was	आम्ही होतों we were
2.	तूं होतास *m.*,-तीस *f.*,-तेंस *n.*, thou wast	तुम्ही होतां you were
3.	तो होता *m.*, he was ती होती *f.*, she was तें होतें *n.*, it was	ते होते *m.* त्या होत्या *f.* तीं होतीं *n.* } they were

Note.—These forms are the conditional forms of the verb होणें to become, but used also as the past Indicative forms of the verb असणें to be.

Future Tense.

मीं असेन I shall or will be.

Singular.

1. **मीं असेन** I shall be
2. **तूं असशील** (or **असशिल**) thou shalt be
3. **तो, ती, तें असेल** he, she, or it shall be

Plural.

1. **आम्ही असूं** we shall be
2. **तुम्ही असाल** you shall be
3. **ते, त्या, तीं असतील** they shall be

Note.—The form **असशील** is not so old as **असशिल**, but it is usually used at present.

Past Habitual.

मीं असें I used to be or usually was.

Singular.

1. **मीं असें** I usually was
2. **तूं असस** thou usually wast
3. **तो, ती, तें असे** he, she, or it usually was

Plural.

1. **आम्ही असूं** we usually were
2. **तुम्ही असा** you usually were
3. **ते, त्या, तीं असत** they usually were

CONDITIONAL MOOD.

मीं असतों were I, had I been, or I would be, or would have been.

	Singular.	*Plural.*
1.	**मीं असतों** *m.*, **-तें** *f.*, **-तेंं** *n.*	**आम्ही असतों** *m.*, *f.*, *n.*
2.	**तूं असतास** *m.*, **-तीस** *f.*, **-तेस** *n.*	**तुम्ही असतां** *m.*, *f.*, *n.*
3.	**तो असता** *m.*	**ते असते** *m.*
	ती असती *f.*	**त्या असत्या** *f.*
	तें असतें *n.*	**तीं असतीं** *n.*

Dubitative Conditional.

मीं असलों should I be.

	Singular.	*Plural.*
1.	मीं असलों *m.*, -लें *f.*, -लें *n.*	आम्ही असलों *m.*, *f.*, *n.*
2.	तूं असलास *m.*, -लीस *f.*, -लैस *n.*	तुम्ही असलां *m.*, *f.*, *n.*
3.	तो असला *m.*	ते असले *m.*
	ती असली *f.*	त्या असल्या *f.*
	तें असलें *n.*	तीं असलीं *n.*

Note.—मीं त्यांच्या घरीं असलों तर माग ये should I be at his house, hen only come.

Subjunctive Mood (*Kartari Prayoga*).

मी असावा I may, can, might, could, would, or should be, or have been.

	Singular.	*Plural.*
1.	मीं असावा *m.*,-वी *f.*,-वें *n.*	आम्ही असावे *m.*,-व्या *f.*,-वीं *n.*
2.	तूं असावास *m.*,-वीस *f.*,-वेंस *n.*	तुम्ही असावेत *m.*,-व्यात *f.*,-वींत *n.*
3.	तो असावा *m.*	ते असावे *m.*
	ती असावी *f.*	त्या असाव्या *f.*
	तें असावें *n.*	तीं असावीं *n.*

(*Bháve Prayoga.*)

म्या असावें I should or might be.

	Singular.	*Plural.*
1.	म्या असावें	आम्हीं असावें
2.	त्वा असावें	तुम्हीं असावें
3.	त्यानें *m.*, तिनें *f.*, त्यानें *n.*, असावें	त्यांनीं असावें

Imperative Mood.

मीं असूं let me be

	Singular.	*Plural.*
1.	मीं असूं	आम्ही असूं
2.	तूं अस or ऐस	तुम्ही असा
3.	तो, ती, तें, असो	ते, त्या, तीं असोत.

INFINITIVE MOOD.

असूं to be usually.

PARTICIPLES.

Present असत, असता, असतां, असतांना being
Past. असला *m.*, असलेला *m.* been.
Plu. असून having been.
Fut. असणार about to be.

GERUND.

असणें to be or being.

SUPINES.

Dat. असायाला-स or असावयाला-स.
Gen. असायाचें or असावयाचें.

II. The verb होणें to become.

§ 256. This verb is regularly conjugated, except in the past tense.

Note.—होणें is derived from the Sanskṛit verb भू to be or to become hrough the Prakṛit.

IDICATIVE MOOD.

Present Tense.

	Singular.	*Plural.*
1.	मीं होतों I become	आह्मी होतों we become
2.	तूं होतोस thou becomest	तुम्ही होतां you become
3.	तो होतो he becomes ती होते she becomes तें होतें it becomes	ते, त्या, तीं होतात they become

Past Tense.

	Singular.	*Plural.*
1.	मीं झालों I became	आह्मी झालों we became
2.	तूं झालास thou becamest	तुम्ही झालां you became
3.	तो झाला *m.*, he became ती झाली *f.*, she became तें झालें *n.*, it became	ते झाले त्या झाल्या तीं झालीं they became

Future Tense.

1.	मीं होईन I shall become	आम्ही होऊं we shall become
2.	तूं होशील (or शील) thou shalt become	तुम्ही व्हाल you shall become
3.	तो, ती, तें होईल he, she, or it will become	ते, त्या, तीं होतील they shall become

Past Habitual.

1.	मीं होईं I used to become	आम्ही होऊं we used to become
2.	तूं होईस thou usedst to become	तुम्ही व्हा you used to become
3.	तो, ती, तें होई he, she, or it used to become	ते, त्या, तीं होत they used to become

CONDITIONAL MOOD.

मीं होतों were I to become, or would become, or have become.

	Singular.	*Plural.*
1.	मीं होतों *m.*,-तें *f.*,-तें *n.*	आम्ही होतों
2.	तूं होतास *m.*,-तीस *f.*,-तेंस *n.*	तुम्ही होतां
3.	तो होता *m.*	ते होते
	ती होती *f.*	त्या होत्या
	तें होतें *n.*	तीं होतीं

SUBJUNCTIVE MOOD.

(*Kartari Prayoga.*)

मीं व्हावा I may, might, could, would, or should become or have become.

	Singular.	*Plural.*
1.	मीं व्हावा *m.*, व्हावी *f.*, व्हावें *n.*	आम्ही व्हावे *m.*, -व्या *f.*, -वीं *n.*
2.	तूं व्हावास *m.*, व्हावीस *f.*, व्हावेंस *n.*	तुम्ही व्हावेत *m.*,-व्यात *f.*,-वींत *n.*
3.	तो व्हावा	ते व्हावे
	ती व्हावी	त्या व्हाव्या
	तें व्हावें	तीं व्हावीं

(*Bháve Prayoga.*)

	Singular.		*Plural.*	
1.	म्या *m.*, *f.*, *n.*	व्हावें	आम्हीं *m.*, *f.*, *n.*	व्हावें
2.	त्वा *m.*, *f.*, *n.*		तुम्हीं *m.*, *f.*, *n.*	
3.	त्यानें *m.*, तिनें *f.*, त्यानें *n.*		त्यांनीं *m.*, *f.*, *n.*	

IMPERATIVE MOOD.

मीं होऊं let me become.

1.	मीं होऊं	आम्ही होऊं
2.	तूं हो	तुम्ही व्हा
3.	तो, ती, तें होवो (ऊ)	ते, त्या, तीं होवोत (ऊत)

INFINITIVE MOOD.

होऊं to become.

PARTICIPLES.

Present होत, होता *m.*, होतां, होतांना becoming
Past झाला *m.*, झालेला *m.*, become
Pluperfect होऊन having become
Future होणार about to become

GERUND.

होणें to become.

SUPINES.

Dat. व्हावयास-ला ; व्हायास-ला to become
Gen. व्हावयाचें-व्हावाचें is to become

§ 257. We give below the Negative forms of असणें to be and होणें to come.

I. The Negative Forms of असणें to be.

INDICATIVE MOOD.

Present Tense.

(First form, corresponding to आहें.)

	Singular.	*Plural.*
1.	मीं नाहीं I am not	आम्ही नाहीं we are not
2.	तूं नाहींस thou art not	तुम्ही नाहीं you are not
3.	तो, ती, तें नाहीं he, she, or it is not	ते, त्या, तीं नाहींत they are not

Note.—This form is used to make up the negative forms of आहे; मीं आहें I am, मीं नाहीं I am not; मी करीत आहें I am doing, मीं करीत नाहीं I am not doing; म्या केलें I did, म्या केलें नाहीं I did not do; मी करीन I will do, मी करणार नाहीं I will not do.

(Second form, corresponding to होय.)

	Singular.	*Plural.*
1.	मीं नव्हें I am not	आम्ही नव्हों we are not
2.	तूं नव्हस, नव्हेस thou art not	तुम्ही नव्हां you are not
3.	तो, ती, तें नव्हे he, she, or it is not	ते, त्या, तीं नव्हेत or नव्हत they are not

(Third form, corresponding to असणें.)

मीं नसतों I am not in the habit of being.

	Singular.	*Plural.*
1.	मीं नसतों *m.*, -तें *f.*, -तें *n.*	आम्ही नसतों
2.	तूं नसतोस *m.*, -तेस *f.*, -तेंस *n.*	तुम्ही नसतां
3.	तो नसतो *m.* ती नसते *f.* तें नसतें *n.*	ते, त्या, तीं नसतात

Past Tense.

(Corresponding to होतों I was.)

मीं नव्हतों I was not.

	Singular.	*Plural.*
1.	मीं नव्हतों *m.*,-तें *f.*,-तें *n.*	आम्ही नव्हतों
2.	तूं नव्हतास *m.*,-तीस *f.*,-तेंस *n.*	तुम्ही नव्हतां
3.	तो नव्हता *m.* ती नव्हती *f.* तें नव्हतें *n.*	ते नव्हते त्या नव्हत्या तीं नव्हतीं

Future Tense.

मीं नसेन I shall not usually be.

1.	मीं नसेन	आम्हीं नसूं
2.	तूं नसशील	तुम्ही नसाल
3.	तो, ती, तें नसेल	ते, त्या, तीं नसतील

Past Habitual Tense.

मीं नसें I was not in the habit of being.

1.	मीं नसें	आम्ही नसूं
2.	तूं नसस	तुम्ही नसा
3.	तो, ती, तें नसे	ते, त्या, तीं नसत

Conditional Mood.

मीं नसतों were I not, had I not been, or would not be, or would not have been.

	Singular.	*Plural.*
1.	मीं नसतों *m.*, -तें *f.*, -तें *n.*	आम्ही नसतों
2.	तूं नसतास *m.*, -तीस *f.*, -तेंस *n.*	तुम्ही नसतां
3.	तो नसता *m.*	ते नसते
	ती नसती *f.*	त्या नसत्या
	तें नसतें *n.*	तीं नसतीं

Dubitative Tense.

मीं नसलों should I not be.

1.	मीं नसलों *m.*, -लें *f.*, -लें *n.*	आम्ही नसलों
2.	तूं नसलास *m.*, -लीस *f.*, -लेंस *n.*	तुम्ही नसलां
3.	तो नसला *m.*	ते नसले
	ती नसली *f.*	त्या नसल्या
	तें नसलें *n.*	तीं नसलीं

Subjunctive Mood.

(*Kartari Prayoga.*)

मीं नसावीं I may or might not have been.

1.	मीं नसावा *m.*, -वी *f.*, वें *n.*	आम्ही नसावे
2.	तूं नसावास *m.* , -वीस *f.*, -वेंस *n.*	तुम्ही नसावेत
3.	तो नसावा *m.*, ती नसावी *f.*, तें नसावें *n.*	ते नसावे, त्या नसाव्या, तीं नसावीं

(*BhávePrayoga.*)

म्या नसावें I should not be.

1.	म्या	नसावें	आम्हीं	नसावें
2.	त्वा		तुम्हीं	
3.	त्यानें *m.*, *n.* तिनें *f.*		त्यांनीं	

(2nd Form.)

1.	म्या	असूं नये	आम्हीं	असूं नये
2.	त्वा		तुम्हीं	
3.	त्यानें *m.*, *n.*, तिनें *f.*		त्यांनीं	

Imperative Mood.

	Singular.	*Plural.*
2.	तूं असूं नको do not be thou	तुम्ही असूं नका
3.	तो, ती, तें नसो let him not be	ते, त्या, तीं नसोत

Infinitive Mood.

नसूं not to be.

Participles.

Present नसत, नसता *m.*, नसतां, नसतांना not being
Past नसला *m.*, नसलेला *m.*, not been
Pluperfect नसून having not been
Future नसणार not about to be

Gerund.

नसणें not to be.

Supines.

Dat. नसायास-ला; नसावयास-वयाला not to be
Gen. नसायाचें-वयाचें is not to be

II. The Negative Forms of होणें to become.

Indicative Mood.

Present Tense.

	Singular.	*Plural.*
1.	मीं होत नाहीं I am not becoming	आम्ही होत नाहीं
2.	तूं होत नाहींस	तुम्ही होत नाहीं
3.	तो, ती, तें होत नाहीं	ते, त्या, तीं होत नाहींत

Past Tense.

1.	मीं झालों नाहीं I did not become	आम्ही झालों नाहीं
2.	तूं झाला नाहींस	तुम्ही झालां नाहीं
3.	तो झाला नाहीं, ती झाली नाहीं, तें झालें नाहीं	ते झाले नाहींत, त्या झाल्या नाहींत, तीं झालीं नाहींत

Note.—Another negative past form is मीं न झालों I did not become, तूं न झालास thou didst not become ; but the one given in the paradigm is the more common.

Future Tense.

	Singular.	*Plural.*
1.	मीं होणार नाहीं I shall not become	आम्ही होणार नाहीं
2.	तूं होणार नाहींस	तुम्ही होणार नाहीं
3.	तो, ती, तें होणार नाहीं	ते, त्या, तीं होणार नाहींत

Note.—The form in न होईन is occasionally used ; मीं न होईन I shall not become, तूं न होशील thou shalt not become, &c.

Past Habitual.

	Singular	Plural
1.	मीं होईना I was not wont to become	आम्ही होऊंना
2.	तूं होईसना, or होईनास	तुम्ही व्हाना, or व्हानात
3.	तो, ती, तें होईना	ते, त्या, तीं होतना, or होईनात

Note.—This form is also used : मीं न होई I was not wont to become, तूं न होईस, तो न होई, &c.

Pluperfect.

	Singular	Plural
1.	मीं झालों नव्हतों *m.*, I had not become	आम्ही झालों नव्हतों
2.	तूं झाला नव्हतास *m.*	तुम्ही झालां नव्हतां
3.	तो झाला नव्हता *m.*	ते झाले नव्हते
	ती झाली नव्हती *f.*	त्या झाल्या नव्हत्या
	तें झालें नव्हतें *n.*	तीं झालीं नव्हतीं

CONDITIONAL MOOD.

मीं न होतों were I not to become.

	Singular.	*Plural.*
1.	मीं न होतों *m.*, -तें *f.*, -तें *n.*	आम्ही न होतों
2.	तूं न होतास *m.*, -तीस *f.*, -तेंस *n.*	तुम्ही न होतां
3.	तो न होता *m.*	ते न होते
	ती न होती *f.*	त्या न होत्या
	तें न होतें *n.*	तीं न होतीं

SUBJUNCTIVE MOOD.

म्या होऊं नये I should not become.

	Singular.	*Plural.*
1.	म्या } होऊं नये	आम्ही } होऊं नये
2.	त्वा } होऊं नये	तुम्ही } होऊं नये
3.	त्यानें *m.*, *n.*, तिनें *f.* } होऊं नये	त्यांनीं } होऊं नये

Note.—The forms in नव्हावें are also used ; म्या, त्वा, त्यानें, &c. न व्हावें I should not become.

IMPERATIVE MOOD.

	Singular	Plural
2.	तूं होऊं नको do not thou become	तुम्ही होऊं नका
3.	तो, ती, तें न होवो let him, her, or it not become	ते, त्या, तीं न होवोत

INFINITIVE MOOD.

न होऊं not to become.

PARTICIPLES.

Present न होत, न होता *m.*, न होतां, न होतांना not becoming
Past न झाला *m.*, न झालेला *m.*, not become
Pluperfect न होऊन not having become
Future न होणार not about to become

GERUND.

न होणें not to become.

SUPINES.

Dat. न व्हायास-ला, न व्हावयास-ला not to become
Gen. न व्हायाचें, न व्हावयाचें is not to become

CHAPTER XVII.

THE AUXILIARY VERBS—(*Continued*).

II. THE MODAL VERBS.

§ 258—§ 285.

§ 258. The Verbs used to make up the Compound forms of the Moods are called *Modal* Verbs. (Sec. 247.) They are पाहिजे it is wanted and लागणें to touch, together with their Negative forms नको.it is not wanted, नलगे it is not necessary and नये it is not necessary or suitable.

(1) पाहिजे It is wanted.

§ 259. The verb पाहिजे is an old passive form of the verb पाहणें to see, and though it etymologically means " it may be seen," it conveys at present, the sense of " it is wanted ; " as, मला एक रुपाया पाहिजे a Rupee is wanted by me, or I want a Rupee.

Note.—पाहिजे it is wanted, necessary, incumbent ; *i. e.*, it should be *looked* after, or seen about.

Note.—The जे *je* in the form पाहिजे is the corruption of the Sanskṛit य ya, the sign of the passive verb ; the य is changed to इअ or इज्ज in Prakṛit, and the Prakṛit इज्ज is changed to ज or जे in

Marathi ; as, Sk. पठ्यते, Prak. पढिज्जइ, M. पढिजेते it is studied. When Sanskrit passive constructions are literally translated into Marathi, the forms in ज or जे are usually used ; as, विष्णुना प्रपंचः क्रियते,=विष्णुनें प्रपंच करिजेतो the world was created by Vishnu. In poetry the forms in जे occur frequently, but in prose they are rarely used. An imperative of dignity, formed with जे, is often used in letters, as दिजे give please, किजे do please. These forms are more courteous than those in the simple imperative or subjunctive :—

माझे मनोरथ पूर्ण किजे देवा, केशवा, माधवा, नारायणा.

Námdeva.

Note.—The forms पाहिजे it is wanted, and म्हणजे (literally, " it is said ") that is, then, are the only two words which are used in ordinary Marathi prose ; the one is a verb, and the other a conjunction.

§ 260. The subjunctive व्हावें of the verb होणें to become is optionally used for पाहिजे ; मला आंबा पाहिजे or व्हावा I want a mango. The form हावा or हवा may be substituted for व्हावा.

§ 261. The verb पाहिजे is joined either to the past tense, or to the dative supine of the principal verb, to make up the compound subjunctive forms ; as मला गेलें or जावयास पाहिजे I must go. The latter form is uncommon and inelegant.

Note.—The supine may be either in the dative स or ला. The form with the ला is more common in the Deccan.

§ 262. पाहिजे, like the English word " to want, " expresses two distinct ideas in regard to its sense of requisiteness or necessity : (1) it may mean "to have occasion for, to require" as, in winter we *want* a fire ; or " to feel need of, to desire, " as I *want* to speak to you about something.

This two-fold sense is, expressed also, by the Marathi verb पाहिजे : (1) मला गेलें पाहिजे or जायास पाहिजे I have occasion to go or I must go ; I am required to go. (2) मला जायास पाहिजे I feel the need of going, or I want or wish to go. The latter sense is expressed only by the form made up with the dative supine.

§ 263. The subject of the Compound subjunctive form in पाहिजे may take the subject in the Nominative, Instrumental, or the Dative case.

(1) The Compound form constructed with a nominative or dative subject denotes a kind of necessity or requisiteness that is not moral ; त्याचा सर्व अभिमान गेला (or जावास) पाहिजे. he must get rid of all his vanity ; तूं कांहीं खाल्लें नाहींस, तुला फलाहार केला (or करायास) पाहिजे you have not eaten anything and you must take some refreshment.

Note.—The nouns or third personal pronouns denoting inanimate objects or irrational animals usually take the subject in the Nominative case.

(2) When the Compound form takes an instrumental subject, it indicates a moral necessity or duty ; त्वा आलें पाहिजे you ought to come.

§ 264. We give below the conjugation of the verb पाहिजे :—

INDICATIVE MOOD.

Present Tense.

	Singular.	*Plural.*
1.	मीं पाहिजे I am wanted	आम्ही पाहिजे we are wanted
2.	तूं पाहिजेस thou art wanted	तुम्ही पाहिजे or पाहिजेस you are wanted
3.	तो, ती, तें पाहिजे he, she, or it is wanted	ते, त्या, तीं पाहिजेत they are wanted

Note.—Sometimes the present form is compounded with आहे, as the past (the following form) is made up with होता ; मीं पाहिजे आहें I am wanted.

Past Tense.

	Singular.	*Plural.*
1.	मीं पाहिजे होतों I was wanted	आम्ही पाहिजे होतों
2.	तूं पाहिजे होतास *m.*, तीस *f.*, —तेंस *n.*, thou wast wanted	तुम्ही पाहिजे or पाहिजेत होतां
3.	तो पाहिजे होता he was wanted	ते पाहिजे होते
	ती पाहिजे होती she was wanted	त्या पाहिजे होत्या
	तें पाहिजे होतें it was wanted	तीं पाहिजे होतीं

Future Tense.

1. मीं पाहिजे or पाहिजेन I shall be wanted आम्ही पाहिजे

2.	तूं पाहिजे or पाहिजेस thou shalt be wanted	तुम्ही पाहिजे or पाहिजेत
3.	तो, ती, तें पाहिजे or पाहिजेल he, she, or it shall be wanted	ते, त्या, तीं पाहिजेत

§ 265. Besides these Indicative forms, there are some conditional and dubitative forms in use, of which those made up with असतें and असेल are the most common; त्याला तो आंबा पाहिजे असता तर बरें होतें it would be well if the mango were required by him; त्याला तें पाहिजे असेल he might want it.

§ 266. The person for whom or by whom a thing is wanted is put in the dative case; मला ते रुपये पाहिजेत the rupees are wanted by me.

Present Tense.

(2) नको it is not wanted.

	Singular.	*Plural.*
1.	मीं नको I am not wanted	आम्ही नको we are not wanted
2.	तूं नको thou art not wanted	तुम्ही नको you are not wanted
3.	तो, ती, तें नको he, she, or it is not wanted	ते, त्या, तीं नकोत they are not wanted

§ 267. The past form is made up with the auxiliary होता; thus Present tense, मला द्रव्य नको money is not wanted by me; Past tense, मला द्रव्य नको होतें money was not wanted by me. The present form serves the purpose of the future: मला पेढे उद्यांच्या मेजवानीकरितां नकोत I do not want the sweetmeat for to-morrow's feast.

Note.—नको may imply dislike or disapprobation as well absence of demand or necessity; मला कोणताही पदार्थ नको I care not for anything; त्याला काम करायास नको he dislikes work.

Note.—नको नको होणें to be averse or disinclined; तो तिला अगदीं नको नकोसा झाला होता she disliked him completely.

Note.—नको may be an adverb; नको, नको, त्याला मारूं नको No. Forbear! do not beat him.

§ 268. The verb नको is used to make up the Compound Negative forms of the Imperative and the Subjunctive mood.

(1) It is joined to the infinitive mood of the principal verb to make up the imperative forms, and only the second singular and plural forms are thus produced :—

Singular.	*Plural.*
तूं देऊं नको do not thou give	तुम्ही देऊं नका do not you give.

Note.—In the Konkan the second personal singular is नकोस ; तूं देऊं नकोस do not give.

2. It is joined to the dative supine to form the Negative forms of the compound subjunctive made up with पाहिजे ; मला गेलें or जायास पाहिजे I must or have to go,—मला जायास नको it is not necessary for me to go ; त्याला यावयास पाहिजे he wants or wishes to come,—त्याला यावयास नको he does not want or wish to come.

§ 269. For the Negative of the Compound form with an instrumental agent, the negative of the simple subjunctive in आवें is usually used ; as, म्या गेलें पाहिजे I should go ; म्या जाऊं नये I should not go. म्या गेलें न पाहिजे would be the regular Negative form.

Note.—Other idiomatic expressions are also used for the negative form ; त्याला गेलें पाहिजे he will have to go ; Neg. – त्याला जाण्याची गरज नाहीं—अगत्य नाहीं; त्याला जायास नको.

(3) लागणें to be wanted or necessary.

§ 270. The verb लागणें originally means to touch, as तूं त्याला लागूं नको, विटाळ होईल do not touch him, he will contract defilement ; but it is used in its *secondary* sense of " to be wanted," " to be necessary, " as a grammatical form ; as, तूं मला लागतोस thou art wanted by me, or necessary to me, or suitable for me. It is thus conjugated :—

Present Tense.

Singular.

1. मीं लागतों *m.*, -तें *f.*, *n.*, I am wanted
2. तूं लागतोस *m.*, -तेस *f.*, -तेंस *n.*, thou art wanted
3. { तो लागतो *m.*, he is wanted
   ती लागते *f.*, she is wanted
   तें लागतें *n.*, it is wanted

Plural.

1. आह्मी लागतों we are wanted
2. तुह्मी लागतां you are wanted
3. ते *m.*, त्या *f.*, तीं *n.*, लागतात they are wanted

Past Tense.

मीं लागलों I was wanted आम्ही लागलों we were wanted

Future Tense.

मीं लागेन I shall be wanted आम्ही लागूं we shall be wanted

Past Habitual.

मीं लागें I used to be wanted आम्ही लागूं we used to be wanted

The other tenses, Conditional, Subjunctive, &c., are regularly formed throughout.

§ 271. This verb is used as an auxiliary verb, to make up the compound forms of the subjunctive mood; as मला जावें लागतें it is necessary for me or incumbent upon me to go; मला जावें लागलें it was necessary for me to go; मला जावें लागेल it will be necessary for me to go. The simple subjunctive conveys the sense of propriety or ethical necessity, but the compound form with लागणें denotes *simple necessity or requisiteness*: मला जावें लागेल would literally mean,—"the propriety of going will be incumbent upon me." The agent of this compound subjunctive is in the dative case.

Note.—Since the compound form takes only the dative for the agent the simple Subjunctive form, making up a part of it, may be regarded as a substantive, being the subject of the verb लागणें, and taking the dative of the noun or pronoun joined to it; as, मला जावें लागतें, for me (मला) the propriety of going (जावें) is necessary (लागतें) = The propriety of going is incumbent upon me. The subjunctive inflection आवें is nominal by origin (Sect. 203).

§ 272. The dative supine may be substituted for the simple subjunctive making up the compound form; मला जावें लागेल or जायास लागेल it would be necessary for me to go. Both the compound forms have the same sense.

§ 273. There is a third compound subjunctive form existing in Marathi, which is produced by joining लागणें to the gerund;

as सांगणें लागतें, it is necessary to tell; करणें लागतें it is necessary to do.

आहा तुम्ही माझे कीं हो यजमान, म्हणोनि सांगणें लागे आम्हांला

Ramdas.

Oh, you are our patron, it becomes us therefore to tell you that.

मज कां करणें लागला विचार why was it necessary for me to consider? *Tukaram.*

This form is more courteous than that with the simple subjunctive, as the gerundial form is more indefinite than the simple subjunctive.

Note.—There are some other compound subjunctive verbs made up with other auxiliary verbs, such as पडणें to fall, आहे is, etc., for which see the Compound Verbs.

Note.—The verb लागणें is used for making up other compound verbal forms, for which see the Compound Verbs.

(4) नलगे It is not necessary.

§ 274. नलगे is a negative form of लागणें to be wanted, derived from its Past Habitual form लागे it used to be wanted, the ला being contracted to ल; as, "अकस्मात् लागे जावें" we may have to go away suddenly, the negative construction of which would be अकस्मात जावें नलागे or नलगे.

§ 275. नलगे may be used by itself, or with other verbs to make up compound forms. In the following sentence it is used by itself—तुझें वस्त्र नलगे your dress is not wanted.

§ 276. It is joined to the *simple subjunctive*, or to *the gerund* to make up the compound forms; as, मला जावें नलगे it is not necessary for me to go; तीस त्याला बोध करणें नलगे it is not necessary for her to give him instruction. The subject of the compound forms is in the dative case. The compound forms may be regarded as compound subjunctives.

Note.—The compound form, made up by joining नलगे to the simple subjunctive, sometimes expresses what is reasonable or probable; तसा दिवस पुन्हा यावा नलगे such a day is not likely to come again.

§ 277. The negative form नलगे is more courteous than नको it is not wanted; हे पेढे घ्यावे you may take these sweet balls. You may refuse by saying either नकोत they are not wanted, or नलगेत they are not necessary. The latter form implies that the person who declines the offer has no choice in the matter but is controlled simply by necessity, and it is therefore more courteous than the former which is an expression of a desire or wish.

§ 278. The verb नलगे is conjugated only in the third person. Thus,

3rd Person Singular तो, ती, तें नलगे he, she, or it is not wanted.
3rd Person Plural ते, त्या, तीं नलगेत they are not wanted.

नये It will not come.

§ 279. The negative form नये (न + येणें) literally means "that will not come," and is used usually to make up the negative forms of the subjunctive mood in आवें; त्यानें जावें he should go,—Neg. त्यानें जाऊं नये he should not go; त्यापासुन पोटभर खाणे मिळावेत belly-ful food would be got from him;—Neg. त्यापासून पोटभरही खाणे मिळूं नयेत even belly-ful food could not be got from him; बसविलेले दगड निसकूं नयेत याजकरितां लोखंडाच्या पट्टीनें बसवितात in order that the fixed stones may not come out, they fix them with bars of iron.

§ 280. The compound negative form is produced by joining नये to the infinitive mood; as, करूं + नये = करूं नये should not do.

§ 281. The chief use of this negative form, like the simple subjunctive, is to express the ethical sense of duty or propriety, and for this purpose it is usually employed. The form नये, therefore, expresses what is *not proper or advisable*; as, आपण लोकांचा अनादर करूं नये we should not show disrespect to people.

§ 282. There is another negative subjunctive form produced by joining नये to the present participle in तां; as, मला करितां नये I should not do it.

§ 283. Of these two subjunctive negative forms the former in the infinitive mood is stronger than the latter. The former expresses a prohibition on the ground of moral impropriety or wrongness, and the latter on the ground of disadvantageousness or inutility. Thus, रावसाहेबानें मना केलेली गोष्ट म्यां करूं नये I should not do what the gentleman has prohibited, lest I should do what is wrong, *i.e.*, against my conscience; but when a person says रावसाहेबानें मना केलेली गोष्ट म्यां करितां नये, I should not do what the gentleman has prohibited, he states that he is afraid to do the thing, not so much because it is against his conscience, but because it has been forbidden by his superior, and he would do harm to himself by doing it. He might have done it if he had not the dread of incurring the displeasure of the gentleman.

§ 284. The stronger form is not so courteous as the weaker, and a person uses the latter when he wants to express a refusal politely; as, म्या येऊं नये, I ought not to come, is less courteous than म्या or मला येतां नये I cannot with propriety come. In the latter form the speaker speaks more of his inability than his unwillingness, and therefore does not question the essential propriety of the demand made upon him.

§ 235. The form in the infinitive mood, being strictly ethical, and therefore directly expressive of choice or will, takes the subject only in the instrumental case, while the other, which is not so ethical, takes the subject either in the instrumental or the dative; म्या वाचूं नये I ought not to read; मला or म्या तें वाचतां नये I can not with propriety read it. The instrumental case being more personal than the dative usually expresses a moral sense.

§ 286. Like the simple subjunctive, the compound negative form is conjugated in all the three constructions.

Subjective Construction.

तो, ती, तें मिळूं नये, he, she or it could not be found.	ते, त्या, तीं मिळूं नयेत, they could not be found

Objective Construction.

म्या or आम्हीं त्वा or तुम्हीं त्यानें, तिनें, or त्यानें or त्यांनीं	खाऊं नये I, thou, he, she, or it should not eat it खाऊं नयेत I, etc., should not eat them.

Neuter Construction.

म्या or आम्हीं
त्वा or तुम्हीं
त्यानें, तिनें, त्यानें or त्यांनीं } चालूं नये I, etc., should not walk.
मारूं नये I, etc., should not beat.

CHAPTER XVII.

Compound Verbs.

§ 287—§ 312.

§ 287. The number of the simple verbs in the Maráṭhi language is limited, and their deficiency is made up by a combination of two or more words. Thus the simple idea of "to love" is rendered in the language by two words "प्रीति करणें" "to make love," प्रीति love, being a noun, and करणें, to do, a verb. The whole phrase प्रीति करणें to love, is called a *compound verb*.

Note.—There are not a few phrases in English which are analogous to what we denominate compound verbs; thus, "to make a trial" परीक्षा or पारख करणें; "to do battle" युद्ध करणें. Sometimes English compound verbs can be expressed in Maráṭhí only by simple verbs as "to give away," "to take down," &c.; thus, "he *gave away* a hundred rupees in charity," will be in Maráṭhí त्यानें धर्मार्थ शंभर रुपये दिले; take *down* that turban, will be तें पागोटें उतर or उतरून दे.

§ 288. The compound verb may combine a ***noun*** and a *verb*, or ***two distinct verbal*** forms. When the compound verb combines a *noun* and a *verb*, it is called a *Nominal*, and when *both* the members are *verbs*, it is denominated a *Verbal Compound*.

Note.—Sometimes Sanskrit participles are joined to verbs to make up compound verbs; उत्पन्न करणें to beget; निर्माण करणें to create सिद्ध करणें to accomplish.

§ 289. The *Nominal Compound* expresses a *simple* idea, and usually such an idea as is incapable of being expressed in the language in any other way; while the *verbal compound* simply *modifies* the sense of the verb which forms its first member. The modifying verb is called a *servile*, and the verb modified, the *principal* verb. Thus, अंगांत घालणें "to wear" is a nominal, and expresses the simple notion of wearing, and खाऊन टाकणें "to eat up" is a verbal compound, and denotes that the act of "eating," expressed by the principal participle खाऊन, is done to *perfection* by the addition of the servile टाकणें "to throw." So also, धुऊन टाक wash it thoroughly.

§ 290. The compound verbs, whether nominal or otherwise, may be transitive or intransitive in *sense*, and when they are transitive, they take an object. The object of a compound verb may be Accusative, Dative, Genitive, or Locative.

(1) *The Accusative Object: (Verbal comp.)* घर धुऊन टाक wash the house thoroughly; (*Nominal*) तें अंगांत घाल wear it.

(2) *The Dative Object: (Verbal comp.)* म्या त्याला न्हाऊं घातलें I bathed him; (*Nominal*) तिला शिक्षा केली they punished her.

(3) *The Genitive Object: (Nominal)* त्याचा कोणीं विश्वास धरूं नये none should trust him; माझी तिला दया आली she pitied me.

(4) *The Locative Object: (Nominal)* आपल्या आईबापांवर प्रीति ठेवा love your parents.

§ 291. The compound verb is conjugated like any simple verb, and can be conjugated in all the tenses in which its servile is conjugated. Thus, for instance, the servile पाहिजे is defective, and therefore the compound composed of it is deficient in the forms of conjugation. It is thus the servile alone that undergoes the changes of conjugation; thus, तो जाता झाला he commenced to go; तो जाता होईल he will commence to go (*inceptive compound*); ती करूं शकते she can do its मी करूं शकेन I shall be able to do it (*potential compound*).

Obs.—The Maráṭhí people take pleasure in using the compound verbs, even when corresponding simple verbs may exist in the language; and this somewhat extended mode of expression has a dignity and force which are wanting in the other forms of speech. The student will find very valuable information on this interesting subject, which is more a matter of idiom than of grammar, in *Molesworth's Maráthi Dictionary*, under the several serviles which are employed to make up the compound forms.

1.—The Nominals.

§ 292. The Nominals are composed chiefly of the following serviles :—

करणें to do   देणें to give   मांडणें to place

खाणें to eat   धरणें to hold   मारणें to strike

घालणें to put   फोडणें to break   येणें to come

घेणें to take   बसणें to sit   लागणें to touch

ठेवणें to place   बाळगणें to preserve   लावणें to apply

§ 293. The serviles in a Nominal Compound may be united with inflected , or uninflected, nouns.

1. *Inflected Nouns* : अंगांत घालणें to wear, अंगांत is the locative case, united with the servile घालणें to put.

2. *Uninflected Nouns* : मार खाणें to receive a beating, मार is the accusative case, united with the servile खाणें to eat.

§ 294. When the servile is transitive, it agrees with the *uninflected* noun—the internal object, (§ 295) that is joined with it ; त्यानें फार मार खाल्ला he got a severe beating ; त्वा त्याला मुका दिला you let yourself be kissed by him.

But if the noun making up the compound is inflected, the transitive servile agrees with the uninflected noun which it takes as the object of the whole nominal compound ; त्यानें अंगांत आंगरखा घातला he wore a coat. In this sentence आंगरखा is the object of the whole Nominal अंगांत घातला wore, and the servile घातला agrees in gender and number with आंगरखा.

§ 295. The Nominal made up with an uninflected accusative noun may take another noun as its object, just as the Nominal made up with an inflected noun. The uninflected accusative noun composing the Nominal may be called its *Internal Object*, and the other noun governed by the whole Nominal its *External Object*. The External Object is always inflected.

§ 296. The External Object may be in one of these three cases—the Dative, the Genitive, and the Locative.

1. When the primary sense of the *servile* is that of *giving* or analogous to it, the External Object is dative ; त्यांनीं त्याला

फार मार दिला they beat him severely ; लोकांनीं मला उगीच भय घातलें the people for nothing frightened me.

2. When the *nominal* conveys a moral or *spiritual* sense, the External Object is often genitive, as the genitive is the least sensuous of the cases ; राज्याचा कोणीं हेवा करूं नये no one should envy the king ; आपण त्याचा विचार करूं we shall consider it ; त्याचा विश्वास धरूं नये we should not trust him ; त्या बाळाचा मुका घे kiss that child ; त्याची ममता लावून घ्यावी we should win his affections.

Note.—ममता लावून घेणें to win affection is a double compound verb.

Note.—"Verbs implying to be masters, such as ईश्, भू with प्र ; दय् to pity, and words implying remembering (with regret), to think of, &c. govern their objects in the genitive case.—*Apte.*

3. When the primary sense of the *servile* is that of *place*, the external object is locative ; देवावर प्रीति ठेवा love God. The servile means "to place," "to keep" in a place.

Note.—The nominal प्रीति करणें ought to take only a *genitive* object, but it takes the locative ; बहिणभावांवर प्रीति करावी we should love our brothers and sisters. But this expression, so foreign to the Maráthí idiom, may have been introduced into the language by those conversant with English. It ought to take the genitive object, as the expressions प्रीति धरणें,-बाळगणें-असणें to love.

Note.—But when the result of an emotion is indicated, in some tangible shape, the nominal very naturally takes the locative object ; त्यावर त्यांनीं दया केली or उपकार केला they conferred a favour upon him ; but when the subjective act itself is denoted, the genitive object is appropriately employed ; त्यांना त्याची दया आली they felt pity for him.

Note.—When there is any indefiniteness implied by the nominal compound in regard to the mental act, the object is not put in the genitive case, but in the locative preceded by विषयीं ; मीं त्याविषयीं विचार करीन or simply पाहीन I wll consider about it ; मीं त्याविषयीं यत्न करीन I will try about it ; so also मेहनत घेईन I will take pains.

§ 297. Some Nominals, made up of transitive serviles, express the sense of *reflexive or passive verbs* (§ 167, 1), and this passive sense is conveyed especially by such verbs as singly *denote* acts which are apparently performed *for the benefit of the agent*. Thus खाणें to eat, expresses an action whose natural result is the benefit of the agent, the eater, and hence compounds made up with its aid are *reflexive* or *passive* in sense; as त्यानें मार खाल्ला he was beaten, literally he ate a beating. The instrumental subject here is not active, but suffers the effects of its own action. The real agent or doer of the action is put in the genitive case; त्यानें रामाचा मार खाल्ला he was beaten by Ráma. Another verb like खाणें to eat, is घेणें to take; मीं त्याचा उपका कां घ्यावा ? why should I bear his reproach?

Note.—The fact that the Maráthi compound *reflexive* or *passive* forms are made up with the aid of such verbs as singly express acts which are *apparently performed for the benefit of the agent*, may lead to the more intelligible apprehension of those distinctions of conjugation, existing in Sanskṛit as well as Greek, which perplex the modern student. पचति he cooks, *Active Voice*; पचते he cooks for himself, *Middle Voice*. These peculiarities of conjugation are preserved in the Maráthi *Anomalous Verbs* § 167, 2.

Note.—The reflexive sense may be indicated, also, by Nominals made up with intransitive serviles; as, त्याला धैर्य आलें he became bold; त्याला दया आली he was affected with pity; धाक असणें to be in dread.

Note.—There are active forms corresponding to the passive or reflexive expressions:—

Transitive Passive मार खाणें to be beaten; *Transitive Active* मार देणें to beat. *Intransitive Passive* भय वाटणें to be afraid, to fear; *Transitive Active* भय घालणें to frighten.

Note.—The Reflexive or Passive Nominals differ in sense according to the nature of the serviles employed to make them up. Those with the intransitive serviles resemble the Deponents, or the verbs of the Middle Voice, and those with the transitive serviles are strictly passive, implying foreign agency.

§ 298. The serviles are thus arranged according to the cases of their External Objects:—

I. *The Dative Object*: घालणें to put; देणें to give; लावणें to apply.

2. *The Genitive Object* : आणणें to bring ; करणें to do ; धरणें to hold; बाळगणें to preserve, cherish ; मांडणें to place; येणें to come ; वाटणें to feel. The verb करणें is variously employed.

3. *The Locative Object* : ठेवणें to place ; बसणें to sit ; लागणें to touch ; लावणें to apply.

§ 299. When an *inflected* noun is joined to a transitive servile, the servile agrees with the uninflected object of the nominal ; त्यानें पायांत जोडा घातला he put the shoes on his foot. When the servile is intransitive, the nominal takes the Kartari construction ; ती फार रागें भरली she was very angry.

§ 300. When the nominal is made up with an inflected noun, the inflected noun may be in any one of the following *three* cases ; thus, *the Instrumental*—रागें भरणें to be angry ; *the Dative* —सिद्धीस नेणें to finish ; दृष्टीस पडणें to be seen ; *the locative*—अंगांत घालणें to wear.

Obs.—This is quite a new department of Maráthi grammar opened up to the intelligent student of the language, who will, however, find abundant illustration and confirmation of the principles announced here in the speech of educated natives, as well as in works written by them. Mr. Molesworth's *Maráthi Dictionary* is a storehouse of most valuable information on this point.

II.—Verbal Compounds.

§ 301. The Verbal Compounds have been divided according to their *signification* into *eight* classes, viz. (1) the *Potentials*, (2) the *Passives*, (3) the *Intensives*, (4) the *Continuatives* and *Frequentives*, (5) the *Desideratives*, (6) the *Inceptives*, (7) the *Permissives*, and 8 the *Obligationals*. They are conjugated in all the tenses in which their serviles are.

1. *The Potentials.*

§ 302. Three verbs are employed to make up the potential forms : the verbs शकणें to be able, पावणें to obtain, to be able, and येणें to come, to be able.

1. The verb शकणें to be able is united with the *infinitive* of the principal verb ; and the compound can be used as

widely as the potential derivative in व; माझ्यानें करवतें; I can do it, or मीं करूं शकतें. The compound, however, is not much used in common conversation, but chiefly employed in official transactions.

Note.—This potential form is neither unidiomatic nor inelegant as is often alleged, since it corresponds to the Sanskṛit form कर्तुं शक्नोमि I am able to do, and is used in Maráthi Proverbs, the most idiomatic expression in the language. For instance, it occurs in this proverb : फुटलें मोतीं तुटलें मन सांधूं न शके विधाता God cannot mend a broken pearl or an injured mind.

2. A more idiomatic expression is that made up with पावणें; तुला दोन काठ्या रगडून लाविल्या म्हणजे तूं हांसूं पावणार नाहींस you will not be able to laugh if I should give you two hard stripes on the back; मी तुला बळकट धरिलें आहे; तूं आतां सुटूं पावणार नाहींस I have held you fast; you cannot now get loose from me. But this idiom is falling into disuse.

3. The verb येणें to come, is joined either to the present participle in तां, or the dative supine of the principal verb; मला लिहितां येतें I can write, or मला लिहायास येतें. This compound verb is constructed with the dative of the agent. It expresses (on 1 p. 161.)

The various senses of the compound potential forms with येणें can be easily traced to the original signification of the servile; येणें to come unto,—*i.e*, to be *known unto*, or to be performed by. It expresses *possibility of doing*, especially theresulting power from the possession of adequate strength, wealth, talent or authority; मला चालतां or चालायास येतें I am able to walk, *i. e.*, I possess the strength necessary to walk; मला लिहितां or लिहावयास येतें I can write, *i. e*, I have the ability of writing or acquaintance with the art of writing; मला आंत जातां येतें I can go in, *i. e.*, I have the needful authority or freedom to go in; मला विकत घेतां or घ्यायास येईल, I can buy, *i. e.*, I shall have money enough to buy; त्याचें वय पाहून त्याकडे दोष म्हणून लावितां येत नाहीं, considering his age I can hardly impute any blame to him;

ते धनी पडले त्यांसीं उत्तर करितां येत नाहीं he is the master and it will not do to answer him. This form cannot be used as widely as that in शकणें to be able or पावणें to be able.

There is a slight difference between the form made up with तां and that with the dative supine : ऐकतां येणें and ऐकायास येणें. The former always denotes a *capacity in the agent*, while the latter does not ; मला तुमचें बोलणें लांबून ऐकतां आलें I was able to hear your speech from a distance ; मला तुमचें बोलणें लांबून ऐकायास आलें, your speech was audible to me from a distance, it was capable of being heard. The form in तां is always active, and that in आयास may be either active or passive.

The form in तां may express *expediency* or *propriety* as well as active potentiality ; as, ते धनी पडले त्यांसीं उत्तर करितां येत नाहीं, प्रसंग पाहून बोलायास येईल, he is the master and it does not become us to speak to him ; we shall speak to him when the suitable opportunity comes.

The verb येणें may also be joined to the infinitive mood ; as, ऐकूं येणें to be possible to be heard. This form has a passive force, and not active as in the form made up with the present participle in तां ; as, मला तें ऐकतां येतें I am able to hear it ; तें ऐकूं or ऐकायास येतें it is capable of being heard ; it is audible. It is only a few verbs that make up the potential form with the aid of the infinitive ; the supine is generally substituted for the infinitive.

2. *The Passives.*

§ 303. The Marathi compound Passive forms (कर्मकर्तरि), like those of the potential in शकणें to be able, are chiefly limited to business transactions. The verb जाणें to go is joined to the past participle in ला of the transitive verb, in order to make up the passive form ; as, मारला गेला he was beaten, literally, he was gone beaten.

§ 304. In conjugation the whole verb agrees with the subject ; thus—

Present Tense.

मीं मारला जातों I am beaten.

	Singular.	*Plural*
1.	मीं मारिला जातों *m.*	आम्ही मारिले जातों
2.	तूं मारिला जातोस *m.*	तुम्ही मारिले जातां
3.	तो मारिला जातो *m.*	ते मारिले जातात

Past Tense.

मीं मारिला गेलों I was beaten.

1.	मीं मारिला गेलों *m.*	आम्ही मारिले गेलों
2.	तूं मारिला गेलास *m.*	तुम्ही मारिले गेलां
3.	तो मारिला गेला *m.*	ते मारिले गेले

Future Tense.

मीं मारिला जाईन I shall be beaten.

1.	मीं मारिला जाईन *m.*	आम्ही मारिले जाऊं
2.	तूं मारिला जाशील *m.*	तुम्ही मारिले जाल
3.	तो मारिला जाईल *m.*	ते मारिले जातील

§ 305. Instead of employing this compound passive, the Marathis usually adopt the following modes of expression :

1. The agent, when known, is supplied ; प्रलयकालीं ईश्वर जगाचा लय करील God will destroy the world at the last day, for प्रलयकालीं जगाचा लय केला जाईल the world will be destroyed, &c.

2. The third plural indicative is used ; as, असें म्हणतात they say so, for "it is said".

3. The perfect and pluperfect indicative tenses of transitive verbs, which are in reality passives, are employed without their instrumental agent ; thus, पुराणांत सांगितलें आहे it is narrated in the Purans ; गाय बांधली होती the cow was tied up ; म्हटलें आहे it is said.

4. An intransitive verb (the deponents, § 167, 1) of the same meaning, is substituted ; तो तरेल, he will be saved, for तारिला जाईल ; तो लढाईंत मेला he was slain in battle.

5. A noun of a suitable sense with an auxiliary verb is used ; त्याचा उद्धार होईल he will be saved.

6. The pluperfect participle of the corresponding intransitive verb with जाणें is used ; तें जळून जाईल it will be burnt up.

7. The past participle in इत with होणें is used ; तो संतोषित or संतुष्ट झाला आहे he is satisfied.

8. Compound passive forms made up with nominals are used ; त्यानें मार खाल्ला he was beaten.

Obs.—"Whoever wishes to be understood must not content himself with using words that might convey the idea intended, but not in the way such as the natives themselves employ to express it, and take care, too, that those words are arranged in the order to which the Maráṭhás are accustomed."—*Dr. Stevenson.*

Note.—Read in connection with the passive verbs, the observations on the reflexive or passive nominals, § 297.

Note.—In Sanskṛit and Prákṛit the passive form is made up by inflection, as Sk. क्रियते, Prák. करिज्जेतें it is done. The letter य is inserted to make up the passive form in Sanśkṛit, which is changed to ज in Prakṛit, and thus the Sanskṛit य is the abbreviated form of या to go. The full form of या is still used in Bengali to produce the passive verb ; as करायाइ I am made, lit. I go in making. In Sanskṛit, compound passive forms occur, besides the simple in य, as in Latin. The Latin *amatum iri* to be loved, is literally to be gone in love."—*Bopp.*

3. *The Intensives.*

§ 306. The Intensives *intensify* the sense indicated by the verb which forms their first member, and which is put in the pluperfect participle ; as, तें तुम्ही शिवून टाका finish off the sewing of it. The intensives express a state of completion : what is completely, wholly, quite, effected, as in the English phrases to cut up, to drink up, to turn up, to sew up a rent, etc.

§ 307. The serviles employed with the pluperfect participle are chiefly the following :—

घेणें to take	टाकणें to throw	बसणें to sit
चुकणें to miss	ठेवणें to keep	येणें to come
जाणें to go	देणें to give	सोडणें to unloose

1. आपण स्नान करून घ्यावें you may finish off your ablutions; म्या त्यास ठेवून घेतलें आहे I have managed to get him to stay. Sometimes these serviles are redundant, and are employed simply to round a period.

2. तो सर्व करून चुकला, बाकी त्यानें कांहीं ठेविलें नाहीं he has done all he possibly could do; he has left nothing untried. This servile is used in reference to matters that are evil or calamitous; सर्व उपाय करून चुकलों, गुण कांहीं आला नाहीं we have tried all possible remedies, but to no effect.

3. तळ्यांतून पाणी अटून गेलें the water of the tank is dried up; तो सगळी वाट चालून गेला he walked up the whole way. Sometimes the servile is redundant; तिला मरून जाऊन दहा वर्षें झालीं it is ten years since her decease. Emphatic imperatives are produced by joining जाणें to go, to the verbal root: आण जा bring it at once; दे जा give it at once. The servile जाणें is used with intransitive participles, like the servile टाकणें with the transitive; तो मरून गेला he is dead and gone; त्यास मारून टाकिलें they beat him to death, or killed him.

4. रोहिल्यांस आरबांनीं तरवारीनें मारून टाकिलें the Arabs put the Rohillas to the sword; पिऊन टाक drink it off.

5. पत्र लिहून ठेवा write off the letter and have it ready; पिठांत पाणी घालून ठेव put water in the flour and have it ready. The servile ठेवणें corresponds with the above servile टाकणें to throw in that both express the finishing of an action; but टाकणें means that after the action is completed, nothing more is to be done with it, while ठेवणें implies that after the completion of the action care is to be taken to have its effects preserved: ती पोथी वाचून टाक read the book and be done with it; whereas ती पोथी वाचून ठेव means, read the book carefully so that the knowledge acquired might be serviceable afterwards.

6. हें टाकून द्या throw this away; राजपुत्रानें प्रधानपुत्रास हांकून दिलें the prince drove away the son of the prime minister; त्यानें त्याला लावून दिलें he sent him off, *packed him off.*

7. तो सर्व गिळून बसला he has swallowed up everything, *i. e.*, robbed; तो दिवाळें काढून बसला आहे, he has become quite insol-

vent. बसणें differs from टाकणें, but agrees with ठेवणें in reference to the *continuance* of the effects of the act denoted by the principal verb.

8. त्यानें त्यांस मारून सोडिलें he gave them a sound thrashing.

Note.—Great care should be taken to distinguish between what is really a servile, and what *appears* to be so. In a verbal compound the servile has no *independent sense or use*; it simply serves the purpose of modifying the sense of the verb that is united with it. When it expresses more than this, it is not a servile, and it does not combine with the verbal form preceding it. Thus, बांधून ठेवणें to tie up, may be or may not be a compound; गाय बांधून ठेव tie up the cow; पोथी पेटींत बांधून ठेव tie up the book, and keep it in the box.

4. *Continuatives and Frequentives.*

§ 308. The Continuatives express *persistence* in a certain course of action, and the Frequentives a *recurrence* of a certain action, and both are made up by the present participle in त of the principal verb, and the servile जाणें to go, बसणें to sit, राहणें to remain, येणें to come, &c. Thus, रोज औषध घेत जा continue to take the medicine every day; बाळा, तूं येत जा हो mind that you come frequently, child; चांगुणा शिवायाचें सोडुन भाऊबरोबर गप्पा मारीत बसते Tsánguna, neglecting her sewing, keeps chatting with Bhâu; तो नेहमीं गात राहतो he always keeps singing; तो तसेंच करीत आला he has been always acting so.

Note.—While the form in राहणें expresses continuance or persistence of action, that in जाणें denotes a single act; मीं त्याला सांगितलें तरी तो निजून राहिला he kept sleeping in spite of my orders; तो निजून गेला he fell asleep. Moreover the form in राहणें expresses an intentional act, and जाणें either an intentional or unintentional act.

5. *Desideratives.*

§ 309. The Desideratives express a *wish* or *desire*, and join the servile पाहणें to see, to the infinitive or the dative supine of the principal verb; हा मुलगा तुमच्याशीं बोलूं पाहातो this boy desires to speak with you, or, this boy stands ready to speak with you; वाटतें मला खायाला पाहतो I fancy he wants to eat me up.

Note.—The subjunctive form in पाहिजे may be considered as desiderative ; आपणाला आलें पाहिजे (see the etymology of पाहिजे, § 259) your honour must come, *i. e.*, I earnestly desire that you may be pleased to come.

6. *Inceptives.*

§ 310. The Inceptives express the *beginning* of an action, and there are two serviles used to make up their forms, *viz.*, लागणें to touch, होणें to become.

(1) लागणें is united either with the infinitive mood, or the dative supine ; तो चालूं or चालायास लागला he commenced to walk ; तो वाचायास लागला नाहीं इतक्यांत त्याची वाचा बंद झाली no sooner did he begin to read, than he became dumb.

(2) The verb होणें is joined to the present participle in ता ; राजा बोलता झाला the king began to speak ; चालते व्हा you may set off ; देते व्हा begin to give (begin and go through the act).

7. *Permissives.*

§ 311. The Permissives are composed of the infinitive mood and the verb देणें to give ; मला जाऊं द्या permit me to go ; वारा लिहूं देत नाहीं the wind will not let me write ; मीं त्याला येऊं देणार नाहीं I will not let him do come.

8. *Obligationals.*

§ 312. These compounds express obligation or moral necessity. The serviles employed to make up these forms are पडणें to fall, पाहिजे it is necessary, लागणें to touch, and असणें to be.

1. The servile पडणें is joined either to the dative, or the genitive supine of the principal verb ; तूं ज्वरमस्त झालास म्हणून मला खेपा घालायास or घालायाच्या पडतात as you are suffering from fever, I am obliged to go backwards and forwards ; तेथपर्यंत मला चालायाचें or चालायास पडलें I was under the necessity of walking up to there. The verb is conjugated throughout with the subject in the dative case ; but when the principal verb is intransitive, the servile पडणें is put in the neuter singular, and when it is transitive, it agrees with its object : त्याला फेऱ्या घालायास or घालायाच्या पडतात he is forced to go about.

2. पाहिजे has been previously considered under the Modal verbs (Sect. 259). It is used with the past tense of the principal verb; आज रात्रीस मला गेलें पाहिजे it is necessary for me to go to-night. It expresses either a physical or moral necessity, and takes the subject either in the instrumental or dative case. The verb with the instrumental subject usually expresses a moral necessity ; म्या ऐकलें पाहिजे I ought to hear.

The verb with the subject in the nominative case expresses what is necessary or essential to an event, and conveys intensively the sense that a verb with the subjunctive of असणें to be does ; जर त्यानें चोरी केली म्हणावी तर तो तेथें गेला पाहिजे if we should say that he committed the theft, then he must even have gone there; his going there is essential to the supposition that he stole. तो गेला असावा expresses a supposition in a general way.

3. The servile लागणें is joined either to the subjunctive mood, or to the dative supine ; त्याच्या हातून आमचें कार्य न झाल्यास आपणास तसदी द्यावी लागेल should he not succeed in doing our business, we shall be under the necessity of troubling you ; खंडू पळून गेला, म्हणून रुपये रामजीस द्यायास लागतील since Khandu has run away, Ramji will have to pay the money. It speaks of a responsibility or duty which may or may not be moral, and is used as a courteous form of urgency ; रावसाहेबांना जावें लागेल your honour will have to go (Sect. 272.)

4. The genitive supine of the principal verb is joined to the tenses of the verb असणें ; तुम्हांस आतांच जायाचें आहे you have to go even now. It denotes an incumbency expressed by the English phrase made up with "have," followed by an infinitive, as you *have to go* to-night.

The form can be used regularly in the present and past tenses only—मला जायाचें आहे I have to go ; मला जायाचें होतें I had to go : in the future tense, पडेल is usually employed ; मला जायाचें पडेल I shall have to go. The regular future with असेल is usually dubitative; मला जायाचें असेल I may have to go.

The subject of this form is usually in the dative case ; but in the past tense, it may take the instrumental case, when it denotes a moral responsibility ; as, म्या जायाचें होतें I should have gone. It has the same force as the past tense of the simple subjunctive ; म्या जावें होतें or जायाचें होतें.

Note.—The form may express the intention of the agent in an emphatic way ; ते उद्यां जायाचे आहेत they have decided to go to-morrow.

Note.—It may denote what is necessarily dependent upon the disposition or nature of a person or thing ; तो एखादे दिवशीं अनर्थ करायाचा he is such a man as will surely one day or other do mischief ; धोंडा कानास लागला तो तुटायाचाच पण थोडक्यांत चुकलें the stone struck his ear, and it (the ear) was ready to break off, but the act was deficient by a little, *i. e.*, the ear was within an ace of being struck off.

CHAPTER XVIII.

The Compound Tenses.

§ 313—§ 331.

§ 313. The Simple Tenses given in Chapter XIII. do not answer all the purposes of expression, and consequently compound forms are made up by the aid of the substantive verbs The substantive verbs are joined, either to *the participles* of the principal verb, or to its *simple tenses* ; thus, तो लिहीत आहे he is writing ; मावशीनें माझे वाढदिवशीं ही आंगठी दिली होती my maternal aunt gave me this ring on my birthday. In the latter sentence the substantive verb is joined to a simple tense (the past) of the principal verb, and in the former, to a participle (the present) of the principal verb.

§ 314. Both the members of the compound tense are inflected in conjugation, unless the first is a participle ending in the inherent अ ; as मीं बसत होतों I was sitting, मीं बसलों होतों I had sat. In the former sentence the participle बसत is not inflected, but in the latter, both the verbs are inflected.

§ 315. The Compound Tenses express MODIFICATIONS of the Principal Simple Tenses—The Present, the Past, and the Future.

§ 316. **The Principal Simple Tenses denote time in a general way, and are therefore called Indefinite Tenses, while the Compound Tenses, express their particular senses. Thus, तो लिहितो he writes, simply means that the action of writing actually takes place in present time ; but लिहीत आहे denotes that the present action is *still going on*, and *not finished*.**

§ 317. **Each simple tense has several corresponding compound forms, and we give the following table by way of illustration :—**

	Simple Tenses.	Compound Tenses.			
	Indefinite.	*Imperfect.*	*Perfect.*	*Habitual.*	*Prospective.*
Present.	मीं चालतों I walk.	मीं चालत आहें I am walking.	मीं चाललों आहें I have walked.	मीं चालत असतों I usually walk.	मीं चालणार आहें I am about to walk.
Past.	मीं चाललों I walked.	मीं चालत होतों I was walking.	मीं चाललों होतों I had walked.	मीं चालत असें I usually walked.	मीं चालणार होतों I was about to walk.
Future.	मीं चालेन I shall walk.	मीं चालत असेन I shall be walking	मीं चाललों असेन I shall have walked.		मीं चालणार असेन I shall be about to walk.

The Indicative Mood.

§ 318. The Indicative has *six* compound forms for the Present, *six* for the Past, and *five* for the Future.

Present Tense.

§ 319. 1. The *Present Imperfect* or *Progressive* is formed of the present participle in त, and the present tense of the verb to be ; तो वाचीत आहे he is reading.

2. The *Present Imperfect Emphatic* is the present tense with the verb आहे ; तो रडतो आहे he is crying.

3. The *Present Perfect* is the past tense with the verb आहे ; मीं बसलों आहें I have sat.

4. The *Present Habitual* is the present participle in त and the present tense of the verb असणें; मासे समुद्रांत रहात असतात fishes live in the sea.

5. The *Present Prospective* is the future participle with the verb आहे; मीं शिकणार आहें I am about to learn.

6. The *Present Dubitative* is formed with the present participle and असावा ; तो मरत असावा he must be dying.

Past Tense.

§ 320. 1. The *Past Imperfect* or *Progressive* is the present participle in त with the past tense होता was; इतक्यांत एक वाघ येत होता at that instant a tiger was approaching.

2. The *Past Perfect* or *Pluperfect Tense* is formed witht the past tense and the past tense होता ; त्यांनीं तिला ताटीवर निजविलें होतें तेव्हां म्या पाहिलें just after they had placed her on the bier I saw her ; ती थंड झाली होती she had become cold.

3. The *Past Habitual* is the present participle in त and the past habitual tense of असणें ; माळा करून तो ब्राह्मण नित्य बसत असे having erected a temporary watchtower, that Brahman was in the habit of daily sitting on it.

4. The *Inceptive Past* is formed of the present participle ending in ता with the past tense of the verb होणें ; धृतराष्ट्र बोलता झाला Dhritaráshtra began to speak.

5. The *Dubitative Past* is formed with the past tense of the verb and असावा ; तो चालला असावा he must have walked.

6. The *Past Prospective* is the future participle with the past tense of the verb आहे ; तुम्हीं माणूस पाठविला तेव्हां मीं लिहिणार होतों I was going to write when you sent the man.

Future Tense.

§ 321. 1. The *Future Imperfect* or *Progressive* is the present participle with असेन ; मीं बारा वाजतां तुझी वाट पाहत असेन I shall be waiting for you at twelve o'clock.

2. The *Future Inceptive* is the present participle in ता and the future tense of होणें; तो चालता होईल he will begin to go away.

3. The *Future Perfect* is the past tense with असेन; मीं चाललों असेन I shall have walked; तुम्हीं प्रातःकाळीं याल त्यावेळेस मीं स्नान केलें असेल I shall have bathed when you will come to-morrow early in the morning.

4. The *Future Prospective* is the future participle in णार with असेन; तुम्ही याल तेव्हां मीं लिहिणार असेन I shall be going to write when you come.

5. The *Future Dubitative* is made up with the future participle and असावा; तो जाणार असावा he must be going.

The Conditional Mood.

§ 322. The Conditional has *two* compound forms for the Present Tense, *two* for the Past, and *two* for the Future.

Present Tense.

§ 323. 1. The *Present Progressive* is the present participle in त with the present conditional of असणें; तो जर काम करीत असता तर असा अनर्थ कशानें घडता? had he been employed at his work, how could such an accident have occurred?

2. The *Present Dubitative* is the present participle in त with असलों; तो जात असला, तर तें काम त्याला सांगा should he be going, then entrust the business to him.

Past Tense.

§ 324. 1. The *Past Indefinite* is made up of the past indicative and the simple conditional of the verb असणें; तें थोडक्यांत चुकलें, नाहीं तर ती पडली असती it missed by a little, otherwise she would have fallen (she narrowly escaped a fall).

2. The *Past Dubitative* is the past tense with असलों; मीं अशी लबाडी केली असली, तर मग मीं द्वाड खरा should I really have been guilty of such roguery, then truly I am a blackguard.

Future Tense.

§ 325. 1. The *Future Indefinite* is the future participle in णार with the simple conditional of असणें; तो जाणार असता तर बरें होतें it would have been well if he had been going.

2. The *Future Dubitative* is the future participle in णार with असला; जर तो जाणार असला, तर मला सांगा should he be going, then tell me.

THE SUBJUNCTIVE MOOD.

§ 326. The subjunctive proper expresses *duty ;* and the subjunctive form in आवें, when employed with the subject in the instrumental case, usually expresses this sense; म्या जावें I ought to go.

Note.—The subjunctive with the subject in the nominative case expresses doubt or uncertainty, and produces the dubitative forms of the indicative. The simple subjunctive form is made up with the termination आवें joined to the simple verb (Sect. 203), and the compound subjunctive with the auxiliary verb असणें joined to the simple subjunctive ; म्या जावें होतें I ought to have gone.

Note.—The subjunctive has other compound forms which are given under the *Modal verbs* (Chap. VII).

§ 327. The subjunctive has *one* compound form for the Present Tense, and *two* for the Past. It has none for the Future.

Note.—Duty is ever present, and the verbal forms therefore usually denote *present* acts of duty. An accomplished act of duty may be viewed as past, but a duty that is not performed always remains present ; and hence the subjunctive mood is deficient in future forms.

Note.—There are however some future forms produced irregularly to express the sense of future obligation. There are four such forms ; मला जावें लागेल I shall have to go ; मला गेलें पाहिजेल it shall be incumbent on me to go ; म्या गेलें पाहिजेल it shall be my duty to go : मला जावें पडेल I shall be under the necessity of going.

Present Tense.

§ 328. The *Present Imperfect* is formed with the present participle and the simple subjunctive of असणें; म्या जागत असावें I should be watching.

Past Tense.

§ 329. (1) The *Past Indefinite* is made up with the simple subjunctive and होता; त्वा सांगावें होतें you should have told.

Note.—म्या सांगायाचें होतें and म्या सांगितलें पाहिजे होतें have the same sense as सांगावें होतें, but are more commonly used.

(2) The *Past Imperfect* is produced by joining होता to the present imperfect subjunctive; म्या लिहीत असावें होतें I should have been writing.

Participles.

Present.

§ 330. The Present Participle is made up of the present participle of the verb in त, and the present participle in तां or तांना of the verb असणें; भोजराजा राज्य करीत असतां or असतांना एका ब्राम्हणानें नवी भूमी साधून शेत पेरिलें होतें during the reign of Bhoja Rájá a certain Bráhman, having acquired a piece of waste land, sowed it with grain.

Past.

§ 331. The Past Participle is the past participle with असतां; तो खालीं आला असतां त्याची बुद्धि पुनः पूर्ववत् व्हावी, whenever he came down, his disposition would become the same as before.

CHAPTER XIX.

PARADIGMAS OF VERBS.

§ 332. We give below all the tenses, simple and compound, in their full forms of conjugation :—

1. FIRST CONJUGATION.

(Intransitive Verb.)

THE INDICATIVE MOOD.

Present Tense.

(1) *The Present Indefinite.*

I walk.

	Singular.	*Plural.*
1.	चालतों-तें-तें	चालतों
2.	चालतोस-तेस-तेंस	चालतां
3.	चालतो-ते-तें	चालतात

(2) *The Present Imperfect.*

I am walking.

1.	चालत आहें	चालत आहों
2.	चालत आहेस	चालत आहां
3.	चालत आहे	चालत आहेत

(3) *The Present Imperfect Emphatic.*

I am walking.

1.	चालतों *m.*, -तें *f.*, -तें *n.*, आहें	चालतों आहों
2.	चालतोस *m.*, -तेस *f.*, -तेंस *n.*, आहेस	चालतां आहां
3.	चालतो *m.*, -ते *f.*, तें *n.* आहे	चालते-त्या-तीं आहेत

(4) *The Present Perfect.*

I have walked.

1.	चाललों-लें-लें आहें	चाललों आहों
2.	चालला-ली-लें आहेस	चाललां आहां
3.	चालला-ली-लें आहे	चालले-ल्या-लीं आहेत

(5) *The Present Habitual.*

I am wont to walk.

1.	चालत असतों *m.*, -तें *f.*, -तें *n.*	चालत असतों
2.	चालत असतोस *m.*, -तेस *f.*, -तेंस *n.*	चालत असतां
3.	चालत असतो *m.*, -ते *f.*, -तें *n.*	चालत असतात

(6) *The Present Prospective.*

I am about to walk.

1.	चालणार आहें	चालणार आहों
2.	चालणार आहेस	चालणार आहां
3.	चालणार आहे	चालणार आहेत

(7) *The Present Dubitative.*

I must be walking.

1.	चालत असावा-वी-वें	चालत असावे-व्या-वीं
2.	चालत असावास-वीस-वेंस	चालत असावेत-व्यात-वींत
3.	चालत असावा-वी-वें	चालत असावे-व्या-वीं.

Past Tense.

(1) *The Past Indefinite.*

I walked.

	Singular.	*Plural.*
1.	चाललों *m.*, -लें *f.*, -लें *n.*	चाललों
2.	चाललास *m.*, -लीस *f.*, -लेंस *n.*	चाललां
3.	चालला *m.*, -ली *f.*, लें *n.*	चालले-ल्या-लीं

(2) *The Past Imperfect.*

I was walking.

1.	चालत होतों-तें-तें	चालत होतों
2.	चालत होतास-तीस-तेंस	चालत होतां
3.	चालत होता-होती-होतें	चालत होते-त्या-तीं

(3) *The Pluperfect Tense.*

I had walked.

1.	चाललों होतों-तें-तें	चाललों होतों
2.	चालला होतास-तीस-तेंस	चाललां होतां
3.	चालला होता	चालले होते
	चालली होती	चालल्या होत्या
	चाललें होतें	चाललीं होतीं

(4) *The Past Habitual.*

(*First form.*)

मीं चालें I was wont to walk

1.	चालें	चालूं
2.	चालेस	चाला
3.	चाले	चालत

(*Second form.*)

I was wont to walk.

1.	चालत असें	चालत असूं
2.	चालत असेस	चालत असां
3.	चालत असे	चालत असत

(6) *The Inceptive Past.*

I began to walk.

	Singular.	*Plural.*
1.	चालता झालों-ती झालें-तें झालें	चालते-त्या-तीं झालों
2.	चालता झालास-ती झालीस-तें झालेंस	चालते-त्या-तीं झालां
3.	चालता झाला-ती झाली-तें झालें	चालते झाले-त्या झाल्या-तीं झालीं

(7) *The Past Prospective.*

I was going to walk.

1.	चालणार होतों-तें-तें	चालणार होतों
2.	चालणार होतास-तीस-तेंस	चालणार होतां
3.	चालणार होता-ती-तें	चालणार होते-त्या-तीं

(8) *The Dubitative Past.*

I must have walked.

1.	चाललों असावा-लें असावें-लें असावें	चाललों असावे-ल्या-वीं
2.	चालला असावास-ली असावीस-लें असावेंस	चालला असावेत -ल्यात-वींत
3.	चालला असावा-ली असावी -लें असावें	चालले असावे-ल्या असाव्या-लीं असावीं

Future Tense.

(1) *The Future Indefinite.*

I shall walk.

1.	चालेन	चालूं
2.	चालशील	चालाल
3.	चालेल	चालतील

(2) *The Future Imperfect.*

I shall be walking.

1.	चालत असेन	चालत असूं
2.	चालत असशील	चालत असाल
3.	चालत असेल	चालत असतील

(3) *The Future Inceptive.*

I will begin to walk.

	Singular.	*Plural.*
1.	चालता-ती-तें होईन	चालते-त्या-तीं होऊं
2.	चालता-ती-तें होशील	चालते-त्या-तीं व्हाल
3.	चालता-ती-तें होईल	चालते-त्या-तीं होतील

(4) *The Future Perfect.*

I shall have walked.

1.	चाललों-लें-लें असेन	चाललों असूं
2.	चालला-ली-लें असशील	चाललां असाल
3.	चालला-ली-लें असेल	चालले-ल्या-लीं असतील

(5) *The Future Prospective.*

I shall be going to walk.

1.	चालणार असेन	चालणार असूं
2.	चालणार असशील	चालणार असाल
3.	चालणार असेल	चालणार असतील

(6) *The Future Dubitative.*

I must be going about to walk.

1.	चालणार असावा-वी-वें	चालणार असावे-व्या-वीं
2.	चालणार असावास-वीस-वेंस	चालणार असावेत-व्यात-वींत
3.	चालणार असावा-वी-वें	चालणार असावे-व्या-वीं

The Conditional Mood.

Present Tense.

(1) *The Present Indefinite.*

Were I to walk, I should walk.

1.	चालतों-तें-तें	चालतों
2.	चालतास-तीस-तैंस	चालतां
3.	चालता-ती-तें	चालते-त्या-तीं

(2) *The Present Imperfect.*

Had I been walking, or I should have been walking.

1.	चालत असतों-तें-तें	चालत असतों
2.	चालत असतास-तीस-तैंस	चालत असतां
3.	चालत असता-ती-तें	चालत असते-त्या-तीं

(3) *The Present Dubitative.*

Should I be walking.

	Singular.	*Plural.*
1.	चालत असलों-लें-लें	चालत असलों
2.	चालत असलास-लीस-लैंस	चालत असलां
3.	चालत असला-ली-लें	चालत असले-ल्या-लीं

Past Tense.

(1) *The Past Indefinite.*

Should I have walked, or I should have walked.

1.	चाललों असतों *m.*,-लें असतें *f.*, *n.*	चाललों असतों
2.	चालला असतास-ली असतीस-लें असतैंस	चाललां असतां
3.	चालला असता-ली असती-लें असतें	चालले असते-ल्या असत्या -लीं असतीं

(2) *The Past Dubitative.*

Should I really have walked.

1.	चाललों असलों *m.*,-लें असलें *f.*, *n.*	चाललों असलों
2.	चालला असलास-ली असलीस -लें असलैंस	चाललां असलां
3.	चालला असला-ली असली-लें असलें	चालले असले-ल्या असल्या-लीं असलीं

Future Tense.

(1) *The Future Indefinite.*

Had I to walk, or I had to walk.

1.	चालणार असतों *m.*,-तें *f.*, *n.*	चालणार असतों
2.	चालणार असतास-तीस-तैंस	चालणार असतां
3.	चालणार असता-ती-तें	चालणार असते-त्या-तीं

(2) *Future Dubitative.*

Should I be about to walk.

1.	चालणार असलों *m.*, -लें *f.*,*n.*	चालणार असलों
2.	चालणार असलास-लीस-लेंस	चालणार असलां
3.	चालणार असला-ली-लें	चालणार असले-ल्या-लीं

THE SUBJUNCTIVE MOOD.

Present Tense.

(1) *The Present Indefinite.*

I should or ought to walk.

1.	म्यां चालावें	आम्हीं चालावें
2.	त्वां चालावें	तुम्हीं चालावें
3.	त्यानें *m.*, *n.*, तिनें *f.*, चालावें	त्यांनीं चालावें

(2) *The Present Imperfect.*

I should be walking.

1.	म्यां चालत असावें	आम्हीं चालत असावें
2.	त्वां चालत असावें	तुम्हीं चालत असावें
3.	त्यानें *m.*, *n.*, तिनें *f.*, चालत असावें	त्यांनीं चालत असावें

(3) *The Present Dubitative.*

I might walk.

	Singular.	*Plural.*
1.	मीं चालावा-वी-वें	आम्ही चालावे-व्या-वीं
2.	तूं चालावास-वीस-वेंस	तुम्ही चालावेत-व्यात-वींत
3.	तो चालावा	ते चालावे
	ती चालावी	त्या चालाव्या
	तें चालावें	तीं चालावीं

Past Tense.

(1) *The Past Indefinite.*

I should or ought to have walked.

1.	म्यां चालावें होतें	आम्हीं चालावें होतें
2.	त्वां चालावें होतें	तुम्हीं चालावें होतें
3.	त्यानें *m.*, *n.*, तिनें *f.*, चालावें होतें	त्यांनीं चालावें होतें

(2) *The Past Imperfect.*

I should have been walking.

1.	म्या चालत असावें होतें	आम्हीं चालत असावें होतें
2.	त्वा चालत असावें होतें	तुम्हीं चालत असावें होतें
3.	त्यानें *m.*, *n.*, तिनें *f.*, चालत असावें होतें	त्यांनीं चालत असावें होतें

Future Tense.

(1) *First Form.*

म्या गेलें पाहिजेल I shall be morally bound to go.

(2) *Second Form.*

मला गेलें पाहिजेल I shall be under the necessity of going.

(3) *Third Form.*

मला जावें लागेल I shall be under the necessity of going.

(4) *Fourth Form.*

मला जायाचें पडेल I shall be under the necessity of going.

THE IMPERATIVE MOOD.

मीं चालूं let me walk.

1.	चालूं let me walk	चालूं let us walk
2.	चाल walk thou	चाला walk ye
3.	चालो may he, she, or it walk	चालोत may they walk.

THE INFINITIVE.

चालूं to walk.

THE PARTICIPLES.

Simple Present चालत, चालता, चालतां, चालतांना walking.
Comp. Present चालत असतां, चालत असतांना while walking.
Simple Past चालला-चाललेला walked.
Comp. Past चालला असतां if or while engaged in walking.
Future चालणार-चालणारा about to walk.

THE GERUND.

चालणें to walk.

THE SUPINES.

Dat. चालायास-चालावयास to walk.
Gen. चालायाचा-चालावयाचा of walking.

THE SECOND CONJUGATION.

THE INDICATIVE MOOD.

Present Tense.

(1) *The Present Indefinite.*

मीं वाचितों I read.

	Singular.	*Plural.*
1.	वाचितों *m.*, -तें *f.*, *n.*	वाचितों *m.*, *f.*, *n.*
2.	वाचितोस *m.*, -तेस *f.*, -तेंस *n.*	वाचितां *m.*, *f.*, *n.*
3.	वाचितो *m.*, -ते *f.*, तें *n.*	वाचितात *m.*, *f.*, *n.*

(2) *The Present Imperfect.*

मीं वाचीत आहें I am reading.

1.	वाचीत आहें *m.*, *f.*, *n.*	वाचीत आहों
2.	वाचीत आहेस *m.*, *f.*, *n.*	वाचीत आहां
3.	वाचीत आहे	वाचीत आहेत

(3) *The Present Imperfect Emphatic.*

मीं वाचितो आहें I am reading.

1. मीं वाचितों आहें *m.*, वाचितें आहे *f.*, *n.* वाचितों आहों *m.*, *f.*, *n.*
2. वाचितो *m.*, वाचिते *f.*, -तें *n.*, आहेस वाचिते *m.*, त्या *f.*,-तीं *n.* आहां
3. वाचितो *m.*, -ते *f.*, -तें *n.*, आहे वाचिते *m.*, -त्या *f.*,-तीं *n.*, आहेत

(4) *Present Perfect.* (*The Objective Construction.*)

म्या वाचिला आहे I have read.

1. म्या or आम्हीं *m.*, *f.*, *n.*
2. त्वा or तुम्हीं *m.*, *f.*, *n.*
3. त्यानें *m.*, *n.* तिनें, त्यांनीं

} वाचिला-ली-लें आहे *Sing.* वाचिले-ल्या-लीं आहेत *Plu.*

(*The Neuter Construction.*)

म्या वाचिला आहे I have read.

1. म्या or आम्हीं *m.*, *f.*, *n.*
2. त्वा or तुम्हीं *m.*, *f.*, *n.*
3. त्यानें *m.*, *n.*, तिनें *f.*, or त्यांनीं

} वाचिलें आहे.

(5) *The Present Habitual.*

मीं वाचीत असतों I am wont to read.

	Singular.	*Plural.*
1.	वाचीत असतों *m.*, -तें *f.*, *n.*	वाचीत असतों *m.*, *f.*, *n.*
2.	वाचीत असतोस *m.*, -तेस *f.*, -तेंस *n.*	वाचीत असतां *m.*, *f.*, *n.*
3.	वाचीत असतो *m.*, -ते *f.*, -तें *n.*	वाचीत असतात *m.*, *f.*, *n.*

(6) *The Present Prospective.*

मीं वाचणार आहें I am going to read.

1.	वाचणार आहें *m., f., n.*	वाचणार आहों
2.	वाचणार आहेस *m., f., n.*	वाचणार आहां
3.	वाचणार आहे *m., f., n.*	वाचणार आहेत

Past Tense.

(1) *The Indefinite Past. (The Objective Construction.)*

म्या वाचिलें I read.

1. म्या or आम्हीं *m., f., n.*
2. त्वा or तुम्हीं *m., f., n.*
3. त्यानें *m., n.,* तिनें *f.,* or त्यांनीं *m., f., n.*

} वाचिला *m.,*-ली *f.*-लें *n. Sing.* वाचिले, -ल्या, -लीं *Plu.*

(The Neuter Construction.)

म्या वाचिलें I read.

1. म्या or आम्हीं *m., f., n.*
2. त्वा or तुम्हीं *m., f., n.*
3. त्यानें *m., n.,* तिनें *f.* or त्यांनीं

} वाचिलें

(2) *The Past Imperfect.*

मीं वाचीत होतों I was reading.

1.	वाचीत होतों *m.,* -तें *f., n.*	वाचीत होतों *m., f., n.*
2.	वाचीत होतास *m.,* -तीस *f.,* तेंस *n.*	वाचीत होतां *m., f., n.*
3.	वाचीत होता *m.,*-ती *f.,* -तें *n.*	वाचीत होते, -त्या *f.,* तीं *n.*

(3) *Pluperfect Tense.*

(The Objective Construction.)

म्या वाचिला होता I had read

1. म्या or आम्हीं *m., f., n.*
2. त्वा or तुम्हीं *m., f., n.*
3. त्यानें *m., n.,* तिनें *f.,* or त्यांनीं

} वाचिला होता,-ली होती,-लें होतें *Sing.* वाचिले होते,-ल्या होत्या,-लीं होतीं *Plu.*

(The Neuter Construction.)

1. म्या or आम्हीं
2. त्वा or तुम्हीं
3. त्यानें *m., n.* तिनें *f.,* or त्यांनीं

} वाचिलें होतें I had read.

(4) *The Past Habitual.*

(1) मीं वाचीं I was wont to read.

1.	वाचीं *m., f., n.*	वाचूं *m., f., n.*
2.	वाचीस *m., f., n.*	वाचा *m., f., n.*
3.	वाची *m., f., n.*	वाचीत *m., f. n.*

(2) मीं वाचीत असें I was wont to read.

1.	वाचीत असें *m., f., n.*	वाचीत असूं *m., f., n.*
2.	वाचीत असेस *m., f., n.*	वाचीत असां *m., f., n.*
3.	वाचीत असे *m., f., n.*	वाचीत असत *m., f., n.*

(5) *The Past Inceptive.*

I began to read.

1.	मीं वाचिता झालों *m.*	आम्ही वाचिते झालों
	,, वाचिती झालें *f.*	,, वाचित्या झालों
	,, वाचितें झालें *n.*	,, वाचितीं झालों
2.	तूं वाचिता झालास *m.*	तुम्हीं वाचिते झालां
	,, वाचिती झालीस *f.*	,, वाचित्या झालां
	,, वाचितें झालेंस *n.*	,, वाचितीं झालां
3.	तो वाचिता झाला *m.*	ते वाचिते झाले
	ती वाचिती झाली *f.*	त्या वाचित्या झाल्या
	तें वाचितें झालें *n.*	तीं वाचितीं झालीं

(6) *Past Dubitative.*

(*The Objective Construction.*)

म्या वाचिलें असावें I must have read.

1.	म्या or आम्हीं *m., f., n.*	वाचिला असावा *m.*, - ली असावी *f.*, -लें असावें *n.* *Sing.*
2.	त्वा or तुम्हीं *m., f., n.*	
3.	त्यानें *m., n.*, तिनें *f.*, or त्यांनीं	वाचिले असावे *m.*, -ल्या असाव्या *f.*, लीं असावीं *n.* *Plu.*

(*Neuter Construction.*)

म्या वाचिलें असावें I must have read.

1.	म्या or आम्हीं *m., f., n.*	वाचिलें असावें
2.	त्वा or तुम्हीं *m., f., n.,*	
3.	त्यानें *m., n.*, तिनें *f.*, or त्यांनीं	

(7) *Past Prospective.*

मी वाचणार होतों I was about to read.

1.	वाचणार होतों *m.*, -तें *f.*, *n.*	वाचणार होतों *m.*, *f.*, *n.*
2.	वाचणार होतास *m.*,-तीस *f.*, -तेंस *n.*	वाचणार होतां *m.*, *f.*, *n.*
3.	वाचणार होता *m.*,-ती *f.*,-तें *n.*	वाचणार होते *m.*, होत्या *f.*, होतीं *n.*

Future Tense.

(1) *Future Indefinite.*

मी वाचीन I shall read.

	Singular.	*Plural.*
1.	वाचीन *m.*, *f.*, *n.*	वाचूं
2.	वाचिशील *m.*, *f.*, *n.*	वाचाल
3.	वाचील *m.*, *f.*, *n.*	वाचितील

(2) *The Future Imperfect.*

मी वाचीत असेन I shall be reading.

1.	वाचीत असेन *m.*, *f.*, *n.*	वाचीत असूं *m.*, *f.*, *n.*
2.	वाचीत असशील *m.*, *f.*, *n.*	वाचीत असाल *m.*, *f.*, *n.*
3.	वाचीत असेल *m.*, *f.*, *n.*	वाचीत असतील *m.*, *f.*, *n.*

(3) *The Future Inceptive.*

मी वाचिता होईन I shall begin to read.

1.	मी वाचिता होईन *m.*	आम्ही वाचिते होऊं *m.*
	,, वाचिती होईन *f.*	,, वाचित्या होऊं *f.*
	,, वाचितें होईन *n.*	,, वाचितीं होऊं *n.*
2.	तूं वाचिता होशील *m.*	तुम्ही वाचिते व्हाल *m.*
	,, वाचिती होशील *f.*	,, वाचित्या व्हाल *f.*
	,, वाचितें होशील *n.*	,, वाचितीं व्हाल *n.*
3.	तो वाचिता होईल *m.*	ते वाचिते होतील *m.*
	ती वाचिती होईल *f.*	त्या वाचित्या होतील *f.*
	तें वाचितें होईल *n.*	तीं वाचितीं होतील *n.*

(4) *Future Perfect.*

(*The Objective Construction.*)

म्या वाचिलें असेल I shall have read.

	Singular.	*Plural.*
1.	म्या or आम्हीं *m., f., n.*	वाचिला *m.*, -ली *f.*, -लें *n*, असेल *Sing.*
2.	त्वा or तुम्हीं *m., f., n.*	वाचिले *m.*,-ल्या *f.*,-लीं *n.*, असतील *Plu.*
3.	त्यानें *m., n.*, तिनें *f.*, or त्यांनीं	

(*The Neuter Construction.*)

1.	म्या or आम्हीं *m., f., n.*	वाचिलें असेल
2.	त्वा or तुम्हीं *m., f., n.*	
3.	त्यानें *m.,n.*, तिनें *f.*, or त्यांनीं	

(5) *The Future Prospective.*

मीं वाचणार असेन I shall be going to read.

1.	वाचणार असेन *m., f., n.*	वाचणार असूं
2.	वाचणार असशील *m., f., n.*	वाचणार असाल
3.	वाचणार असेल *m., f., n.*	वाचणार असतील

THE CONDITIONAL MOOD.

Present Tense.

(1) *The Present Indefinite.*

मीं वाचितों were I to read, I should read.

	Singular.	*Plural.*
1.	वाचितों *m.*, -तें *f.*, *n.*	वाचितों *m., f., n.*
2.	वाचितास *m.*, -तीस *f.*, -तेंस *n.*	वाचितां *m., f., n.*
3.	वाचिता *m.*, -ती *f.*, -तें *n.*	वाचिते, वाचित्या, वाचितीं

(2) *The Present Progressive.*

मीं वाचीत असतों had I been reading, or I should have been reading.

1.	वाचीत असतों *m.*, -तें *f*, *n.*	वाचीत असतों
2.	वाचीत असतास *m.*, -तीस, *f.*, -तेंस *n.*	वाचीत असतां
3.	वाचीत असता *m.*, -ती *f.*, -तें *n.*	वाचीत असते-त्या-तीं

(3) *Present Dubitative.*

मीं वाचीत असलों should I be reading.

	Singular	Plural
1.	वाचीत असलों *m.*, -लें *f.*, *n.*	वाचीत असलों
2.	वाचीत असलास *m.*,-लीस *f.*,-लेंस *n.*	वाचीत असलां
3.	वाचीत असला *m.*, -ली *f.*, -लें *n.*	वाचीत असले *m.*, असल्या *f.*, असलीं *n.*

Past Tense.

(1) *The Past Indefinite.*

(*Objective Construction.*)

म्या वाचिला असता should I have read, or I should have read.

1. म्या or आम्हीं *m.*, *f.*, *n.*
2. त्वा or तुम्हीं *m.*, *f.*, *n.*
3. त्यानें *m.*, *n.*, तिनें *f.*, or त्यांनीं

} वाचिला असता, *m.*, -ली असती *f.*, -लें असतें *n. Sing.* वाचिले असते *m.*, -ल्या असल्या *f.*, -लीं असतीं *n. Plu.*

(*Neuter Construction.*)

1. म्या or आम्हीं *m.*, *f.*, *n.*
2. त्वा or तुम्हीं *m.*, *f.*, *n.*
3. त्यानें *m.*, *n.*, तिनें *f.*, or त्यांनीं

} वाचिलें असतें

(2) *Past Dubitative.*

(*Objective Construction.*)

म्या वाचिला असला should I really have read.

1. म्या or आम्हीं *m.*, *f.*, *n.*
2. त्वा or तुम्हीं *m.*, *f.*, *n.*
3. त्यानें *m*, *n.*, तिनें *f.*, or त्यांनीं

} वाचिला असला, -ली असली, -लें असलें *Sing.* वाचिले असले, -ल्या असल्या, -लीं असलीं *Plu.*

(*Neuter Construction.*)

1. म्या or आम्हीं
2. त्वा or तुम्हीं
3. त्यानें *m.*, *n.*, तिनें *f.*, or त्यांनीं

} वाचिलें असलें

Future Tense.

(1) *The Future Indefinite.*

मीं वाचणार असतों were I going to read, or I should be going to read.

1.	वाचणार असतों *m.*,-तें *f.*, *n.*	वाचणार असतों
2.	वाचणार असतास *m.*, तीस *f.*, -तेंस *n.*	वाचणार असतां
3.	वाचणार असता *m.*,-ती *f.*, -तें *n.*	वाचणार असते,असत्या,असतीं

(2) *The Future Dubitative.*

मीं वाचणार असलों should I be going to read.

1.	वाचणार असलों *m.*, -लें *f.*, *n.*	वाचणार असलों
2.	वाचणार असलास*m.*, -लीस *f.*-लेंस*n.*	वाचणार असलां
3.	वाचणार असला *m.*, -ली *f.* -लें *n.*	वाचणार असले, असल्या, असलीं

SUBJUNCTIVE MOOD.

Present Tense (First Form).

(*The Neuter Construction.*)

म्या वाचावें I should read.

1. म्या or आम्हीं *m.*, *f.*, *n.*
2. त्वा or तुम्हीं *m.*, *f.*, *n.*
3. त्यानें*m.*, *n.*,तिनें *f.*,or त्यांनीं

} वाचावें

(*The Objective Construction.*)

म्या वाचावा I should read.

1. म्या or आम्हीं *m.*, *f.*, *n.*
2. त्वा or तुम्हीं *m.*, *f.*, *n.*
3. त्यानें *m.*, *n.*, तिनें *f.*, or त्यांनीं

} वाचावा, वाचावी, वाचावें *Sing.* वाचावे, वाचाव्या, वाचावीं *Plu.*

(*Second Form.*)

(*The Objective Construction.*)

मला वाचावा लागतो it is necessary for me to read.

1. मला or आम्हांला *m.*, *f.*, *n.*
2. तुला or तुम्हांला *m.*, *f.*, *n.*
3. त्याला *m.*, *n.*, तिला *f.*, or त्यांला

} वाचावा लागतो *m.*, -वी लागते, *f.*, -वें लागतें *n.*, *Sing.* वाचावे *m.*, -व्या *f.*,-वीं *n.*, लागतात *Plu.*

(*Third Form.*)

(*The Objective Construction.*)

मला वाचिला पाहिजे I must read.

1. मला or आम्हांला 2. तुला or तुम्हांला 3. त्याला *m., n.*, तिला *f.*, or त्यांला	वाचिला *m.*,-ली *f.*,-लें *n.* पाहिजे *Sing.* वाचिले *m.*, -ल्या *f.*, -लीं पाहिजेत *Plu.*

(*Fourth Form.*)

(*The Objective Construction.*)

मला वाचायाचा आहे I have to read.

1. मला or आम्हांला 2. तुला or तुम्हांला 3. त्याला *m., n.*, तिला *f.*, or त्यांला	वाचायाचा-ची-चें आहे. वाचायाचे-च्या-चीं आहेत.

Past Tense (*First Form*).

म्या वाचावें होतें I should have read.

(*The Neuter Construction.*)

1. म्या or आम्हीं *m., f., n.* 2. त्वा or तुम्हीं *m., f., n.* 3. त्यानें *m., n.*, तिनें *f.*, or त्यांनीं	वाचावें होतें

(*The Objective Construction.*)

1. म्या or आम्हीं 2. त्वा or तुम्हीं 3. त्यानें *m., n.*, तिनें *f.*, or त्यांनीं	वाचावा होता *m.*,-वी होती *f.*, -वें होतें *n., Sing.* वाचावे होते *m.*,-व्या होत्या *f.*,-वीं होतीं *n., Plu.*

(*Second Form.*)

मला वाचावा लागला it was necessary for me to read.

1. मला or आम्हांला 2. तुला or तुम्हांला 3. त्याला *m., n.*, तिला *f.*, or त्यांला	वाचावा लागला *m.*,-वी लागली *f.*,-वें लागलें *n., Sing.* वाचावे लागले *m.*, -व्या लागल्या *f.*, -वीं लागलीं *n., Plu.*

(*Third Form.*)

मला वाचिला (*m.*) पाहिजे होता I must have read.

(*Fourth Form.*)

मला वाचायाचा होता (*m.*) I had to read.

Future Tense (*First Form*).

(*The Objective Construction.*)

मला वाचावा लागेल it will be necessary for me to read.

1.	मला or आम्हांला	वाचावा *m.*,-वी *f.*,-वें *n.*, लागेल
2.	तुला or तुम्हांला	वाचावे *m.*,-व्या *f.*, -वीं *n.*, लागतील
3.	त्याला *m.*, *n.*, तिला *f.*, त्यांला	

(*Second Form.*)

मला वाचिला पाहिजेल it shall be incumbent on me to read.

(*Third Form.*)

ला वाचावयाचा पडेल it shall be necessary for me to read.

IMPERATIVE MOOD.

मीं वाचूं let me read.

1.	मा वाचूं	आम्ही वाचूं
2.	तूं वाच	तुम्ही वाचा
3.	तो, ती, तें वाचो	ते, त्या, तीं वाचोत

INFINITIVE MOOD.

वाचूं to read.

PARTICIPLES.

Present : वाचीत, वाचिता, वाचितां, वाचितांना reading.
,, वाचीत असतां, वाचीत असतांना while reading.
Past : वाचिला, वाचिलेला read.
,, वाचिला असतां, or वाचिला असतांना if read.
Future : वाचणार, वाचणारा about to read.
Pluperfect : वाचून having read.

GERUND.

वाचणें to read.

SUPINES.

Dat. वाचायास or वाचावयास for reading.
Gen. वाचायाचा or वाचावयाचा of reading.

III.—*Negative Conjugation.*

§ 333. The Negative forms of the Tenses given under the First and Second Conjugations are produced by employing the Negative forms of the verbs असणें to be and होणें to become, given under Section 255. Thus—

INDICATIVE MOOD.

Present Indefinite.

मीं चालतों I walk : *Neg.* मीं चालत नाहीं I do not walk.

1.	मीं चालत नाहीं	आम्हीं चालत नाहीं.
2.	तूं चालत नाहींस	तुम्हीं चालत नाहीं.
3.	तो, ती, तें चालत नाहीं	ते, त्या, तीं चालत नाहींत.

Past Tense.

मीं चाललों I walked : *Neg.* मीं चाललों नाहीं I did not walk.

1.	मीं चाललों नाहीं *m.*	आम्हीं चाललों नाहीं.
2.	तूं चालला नाहींस *m.*	तुम्हीं चाललां नाहीं.
3.	तो चालला नाहीं *m.*	ते चालले नाहींत *m.*

Future Tense.

मीं चालेन I shall walk. मीं चालणार नाहीं I shall not walk.

1.	मीं चालणार नाहीं	आम्ही चालणार नाहीं.
2.	तूं चालणार नाहींस	तुम्हीं चालणार नाहीं.
3.	तो, ती, तें चालणार नाहीं	ते, त्या, तीं चालणार नाहींत.

§ 334. From the forms given above the student will be able to produce forms for the other tenses; but we shall give below the First Person Singular form for each tense by way of guidance :—

INDICATIVE MOOD.

Present	*Indef.*	मीं चालत नाहीं I do not walk.
„	*Imp.*	मीं चालत नाहीं I am not walking.
„	*Perf.*	मीं चाललों नाहीं I have not walked.
„	*Hab.*	मीं चालत नसतों I am not wont to walk.
„	*Prosp.*	मीं चालणार नाहीं I am not going to walk.
„	*Dub.*	मीं चालत नसावा I must not be walking.

Past Indef. मीं चाललों नाहीं (or मीं न चाललों) I did not walk.
,, *Imp.* मीं चालत नव्हतों I was not walking.
,, *Incep.* मीं चालता झालों I began to walk.
,, *Perf.* मीं चाललों नव्हतों I had not walked.
,, *Hab.* (1) मीं चालेना (or मीं न चालें) I was not wont to walk.
,, *Hab.* (2) मीं चालत नसें I was not wont to walk.
,, *Prosp.* मीं चालणार नव्हतों I was not going to walk.
,, *Dub.* मीं चाललों नसावा I must not have walked.
Future Indef. मीं चालणार नाहीं (or मीं न चालेन) I shall not walk.
,, *Imp.* मीं चालत नसेन I shall not be walking.
,, *Incep.* मीं चालता होणार नाहीं I shall not begin to walk.
,, *Perf.* मीं चाललों नसेन I shall not have walked.
,, *Dub.* मीं चालणार नसावा I must not be going about to walk.

Conditional Mood.

Present Indef. मीं न चालतों (or चालतोंना) were I not to walk.
,, *Imp.* मीं चालत नसतों had I not been walking.
,, *Dub.* मा चालत नसलों should I not be walking.
Past Indef. मीं चाललों नसतों if I should not have walked.
,, *Dub.* मीं चाललों नसलो if I really should not have walked.
Future Indef. मीं चालणार नसतों if I had not been about to walk.
,, *Dub.* मीं चालणार नसलों if I should not be about to walk.

Subjunctive Mood.

Present Indef. म्या चालूं नये (sometimes म्या न चालावें) I should not walk.
,, *Imp.* म्या चालत असूं नये or म्या चालत नसावें I should not be walking.
Past Indef. म्या चालूं नये होतें or चालावयाचें नव्हतें I should not have walked.
,, *Imp.* म्या चालत असावयाचें नव्हतें I should not have been walking.
Future. (1st Form) म्या न गेलें पाहिजेल or म्या गेलें न पाहिजेल I shall not be bound to go.
,, (2nd ,,) मला न गेलें पाहिजेल or गेलें न पाहिजेल It will not be necessary for me to go.

Future (3rd Form) मला जावें लागणार नाहीं I shall not be under the necessity of going.

„ (4th „) मला जायावें पडणार नाहीं I shall not be under the necessity of going.

IMPERATIVE MOOD.

1.	मीं चालूं नको or नको चालूं shall I not walk ?	आम्ही चालूं नको or नको चालूं shall we not walk ?
2.	तूं चालूं नको do not walk thou.	तुम्ही चालूं नका do not you walk.
3.	तो, ती, तें न चालो let him, her or it not walk.	ते, त्या, तीं न चालोत let them not walk.

INFINITIVE MOOD.

न चालूं not to walk.

PARTICIPLES.

Present. न चालतां, न चालत असतां not walking.
Past. न चाललेला, न चालला असतां not walked.
Pluperfect. न चालुन having not walked.
Future. न चालणार, न चालणारा not being about to walk.

GERUND.

न चालणें, not to walk.

SUPINES.

Dat. न चालायास not to walk. *Gen.* न चालायाचा of not walking.

CHAPTER XX.

THE PARTICLES OR INDECLINABLE WORDS.

The Adverb.

§ 335—§ 360.

§ 335. An adverb is a word which qualifies an adjective, a verb, or another adverb ; तो फार शहाणा आहे he is very wise ; तिकडे जा go there ; जरा हळूं चालावें you should walk a little slowly.

§ 336. The adverbs are generally undeclined or uninflected but whenever they end in an unnasalised आ, and denote quality or manner, they assume inflections either in agreement with the subject or with the object of the verb which they qualify; त्यानें चांगलें गायन केलें he sang well; तो असा फिरला he turned so.

§ 337. Nouns may be used adverbially either in their (1) *original*, or (2) in their *inflected* forms :—

(1) तो दोन दिवस जागत राहिला he remained awake two days; तो चार कोस चालला he walked four miles; त्यानें चार वार कापड घेतलें he took four yards of cloth; तो काय दगड लिहितो he is utterly incapable of writing anything. These uninflected nouns, denoting *time, place* and *measure* or *standard,* are used adverbially. They may be called Adverbial accusatives, as they are in the Accusative case.

(2) In the following sentences *inflected* nouns and adjectives are used adverbially:—तो रात्रीस आला he came at night (Dative); सकाळच्या कोठें होतास where were you in the morning? (Gen.); इतक्यांत तो बसला in the meantime he sat down (Loc.); मुकाट्यानें आला he came quietly; मोठ्यानें ओरडला he cried out loudly (Instrumental). Some more words are—अनवाणी, barefooted; अनशेंपोटीं on an empty stomach; लोकरित्या by general practice, etc.

§ 338. Sometimes pronouns are used adverbially; आपले आपण or आपल्या आपण of itself, of one's own accord; आपाप of one's self; आपसांत amongst ourselves, or yourselves or themselves; तस्मात् (Sk.) therefore.

§ 339. Adjectives may be employed adverbially in their original form; as, रामानें वाईट वाचिलें. Rama read badly; ती चांगली चालली She walked well.

§ 340. Participles may be employed adverbially; as, तिनें जाणून केलें She did it intentionally; विचार करून बोलावें we should speak considerately; ती रडत गेली she went away weeping; बिछान्यांत पडल्या पडल्या तें मीं लिहून टाकिलें I wrote it off while lying in bed. The participial adverbs are thus distinguished :—

(1) The reduplicated present participle in त expresses the *manner of an act*; as, अंधारांत पडतपडत आला he came stumbling in the dark.

(2) The reduplicated present participle in तां expresses the *currency* or continued course of an act; as, वाचतां वाचतां तो निजला he slept while reading.

(3) The reduplicated past participle, inflected by या or यां, expresses usually *the continuance* of either a *posture* or position of the body, or a *state of mind*; बसल्या बसल्या त्यानें तें संपवून टाकिलें as he kept sitting he finished it off; उठल्या बसल्या (whether standing or sitting) त्याला ती मारीत असे she used to beat him at all times; त्यानें घाबऱ्यां घाबऱ्यां ती गोष्ट सांगितली she told the story with consternation. Sometimes the या or यां is joined to an adjective expressive of an attitude; उभ्यां उभ्यां जाऊन येतें I will go and come back immediately.

Note.—The या or यां is an abbreviation of the instrumental case: तो उभ्यानें or उभ्यां; निजल्यानें or निजल्यां.

Note.—The form in या is sometimes used *conditionally*; तो कांहीं केल्या एथून जात नाहीं he will not go hence, do whatever you might. केल्या is more forcible than केल्यानें.

(4) The reduplicated pluperfect participle expresses manner forcibly; त्यानें आपणास मारून मारून घेतलें he beat himself most cruelly; मीं बसून बसून थकलों I got tired by sitting ever so long.

§ 341. (5) The simple present participle in त, and the pluperfect participle in ऊन, are used adverbially, to denote the *manner* in which an action is done; ती रडत गेली she went away weeping; त्यानें जाणून केलें he did it intentionally; आपण हें मिळून करावें we should do it unitedly; विचार करून बोलावें we should speak considerately.

§ 342. By the aid of the genitive case-endings, the indeclinable adverbs are made into adjectives; त्याची आतांची स्थिति उत्तम आहे his present state of life is very good; आजच्या दिवशीं त्यानें मला भेटावें होतें he should have come to see me to-day.

§ 343. The sense of some adverbial indeclinables is modified by the use of some of the case-terminations, as well as the postpositions ; तो तिकडून (तिकडे+ऊन) आला he came that way ; कोठपर्यंत जाणार? how far do you mean to go? कोठला तूं? of what place are you? कोठून आलास whence have you come?

§ 344. The following pronominal adverbs are a source of most useful compounds in the language :—

Class.	Pronouns.	Adverbs.				Condition.
		Time.	Place.	Manner.	Quantity.	
Relative.	जो who	जेव्हां when	जेथें where	जसा as	जितका, जेवढा as much	जर if जरी although
Demonstrative.	तो that हा this	तेव्हां then एव्हां now	तेथें, तिकडे there, एथें, here इकडे hither	तसा so असा so	तितका, that much, इतका, एवढा this much	तर then तरी still
Interrogative	कोण who ?	केव्हां, कधीं when ?	कोठें where	कसा how ?	कितका, केवढा how much ?	

Note.—When there are two pronominal adverbs expressing the same relation, they somewhat differ in sense.

(1) There are two interrogative forms indicating time, viz. केव्हां and कधीं when : केव्हां refers to recent time, and कधीं to a remote period ; आपण सभेस केव्हां आलां तें नकळे I do not know when you came to the meeting ; यमुनाबाई काशीस राहत असतात त्या इकडे आल्या तरी कधीं Yamunabai resides at Benares ; when did she ever come here ?

(2) There are two demonstrative forms ; एथें and इकडे here. एथें (Sk. अत्र here) denotes simply rest in a place, and इकडे (हा this + कड side, direction), both rest in a place, and motion to a place. एथें would be translated into English by here, and इकडे by here and hither, hitherwards. The corresponding forms for एथें and इकडे are तेथें there, and तिकडे there or thither ; आपण एथें बसावें please sit here ; तूं इकडे ये come here.

एथें and इकडे are used substantively; आमच्या एथें असा प्रकार पाहावयास मिळावयाचा नाहीं you will not see such things at our house; तुमच्या इकडे त्यानें राहणें किती दिवस होईल ? how long will he stay at your house ?

(3) The uses of कितका, केवढा how much तितका, तेवढा, इतका, so much, एवढा, so much, जितका, जेवढा as much, are given under the uses of the pronouns.

Note.—जर and जरी are always conjunctions, but तर and तरी are adverbs as well. तर means "indeed", "but," "however," &c.; मी तर त्याचा बाप आणि असें कृत्य म्या कसें करावें I am indeed his father, and how could I do such an act ? तुम्ही तर लाख रुपये मागतां आणि मी तर केवळ गरीब पडलों, You indeed ask a lac of rupees and I am but quite a poor man. तरी denotes "at least" ; दोनशें रुपये तरी खर्च झाला असेल At least two hundred rupees might have been expended.

§ 345. One of the pronominal adverbs is repeated, or joined to another adverb, to make up adverbial compounds. The following are compound adverbs denoting time:—

कधीं कधीं now and then, sometimes
जेव्हां जेव्हां whenever
जेव्हां तेव्हां always
जेव्हां केव्हां sometimes
जेव्हां कधीं whensoever
कधा नाहीं never
कधींना कधीं { some time or other / some time or ever }
कधीं तरी now and again
केव्हां कधीं indefinitely

§ 346. Compound adverbs of place, manner, &c., could be produced in the same manner: जेथें जेथें wherever; जसा तसा, जसा कसा somehow or other; एथें तेथें here and there, everywhere, &c.

§ 347. Any other adverbs might be employed to make up adverbial compounds: रोज रोज daily ; वारंवार frequently; पुनः पुनः again and again.

§ 348. The adverbial particles are thus classified :—

(1) *Adverbs of Time* (कालवाचक).

(*a*) *Point of Time.*

आज to-day (Sk. अद्य, Pr. अज्ज)
आतां (Sk. अतः), एव्हां now
सांप्रत at present (Sk.)
तूर्त (Sk. त्वरित) presently
झटकन instantly
अकस्मात, (Sk.) एकाएकीं suddenly
एकदम at once
तत्काळ, तत्क्षणीं immediately (Sk.)
हुल्लीं lately
लवकर soon
आज काल now-a-days
जेव्हां when
तेव्हां then
केव्हां when ?
पूर्वी, (Sk. पूर्व) अगोदर before, formerly
नंतर afterwards (Sk. अनंतर)
मग, पश्चात (Sk.) hereafter
उद्यां to-morrow (Sk. उदय)
काल yesterday (Sk. कालः time)
परवां two days ago, or two days hence (Sk. परश्वस्)
तेरवां three days ago, or three days hence
शेवटीं at last

Note.—एव्हां "at this very time" is more emphatic than आतां, being equivalent to आतांच at this very time; मीं एव्हां जात नाहीं I do not go just now. When reduplicated, it expresses 'about this time of the day, about this hour,' and is used in speaking of an occurrence upon a past day; काल आपण तेथून एव्हां एव्हां निघालों नाहीं बरें ? Did we not start yesterday about this time of the day ?

Note.—मग as an adverb means "then," "upon that," "afterwards."; It is also a conjunction, expressing, like तर, "then," "in that case" तो गेला, मग तुला जायास काय झालें, he has gone; what harm is there, then, in your going ?

Note.—तेव्हां then, at that time, is always adverbial in sense and use; it is never a conjunction.

(*b*) *Duration of Time.*

नेहमी, (Sk. नियत) नित्य, सर्वदा, सदा always (Sk.)
सतत continually (Sk.)
प्रतिदिवशीं, रोज (Pers.) रोज रोज, रोजच्या रोज daily
सनातन eternally (Sk.)
कधीं ever (Sk. कदा)
कधीं नाहीं never
दिवसानुदिवस, दिवसेंदिवस day after day
अजून, यद्यपि (Sk.) as yet

Note.—दिवसानुदिवस or दिवसेंदिवस describes an act as daily increasing or decreasing, while प्रतिदिवशीं does not involve any notion of an increase or diminution.

(c) *Repetition of Time.*

वारंवार often (Sk. वार)
पुनः पुनः frequently (Sk.)
पुनः again (Sk.)
रोज रोज day by day

(2) *Adverbs of Place.*

(a) *Rest in a place.*

एथें here (Pr. एत्थ, Sk. अत्र)
तेथें there (Pr. तत्थ, Sk. तत्र)
जेथें तेथें everywhere
कोठें where? (Pr. कुत्थ, Sk. कुत्र)
कोठें नाहीं nowhere
जवळ, समीप (Sk.) near
सर्वत्र everywhere (Sk.)
वर above (Sk. उपरि)
खालीं below
मध्यें within (Sk. मध्य)
मागें behind
पुढें, समोर before
पलिकडे, पल्याड beyond
आसपास on all sides, in the neighbourhood (Sk. पार्श्व)
सभोंवतें around (Sk. भ्रमण)

(d) *Motion to or from a place.*

इकडे hither
तिकडे thither
दूर far (Sk.)
जवळ, समीप (Sk.) near
इकडून hence
तिकडून thence

(3) *Adverbs of Manner.*

(e) *Manner, strictly so called.*

असें so (Prak. एसो, Sk. एषः)
येणेंप्रमाणें thus
बरें well (Sk. वरं)
एकत्र together (Sk.)
यथार्थ properly (Sk.)
कदाचित् perhaps (Sk.)
तसें so (Prak. तहा, Sk. तथा)
कसें how? (Prak. कहं, Sk. कथं)
जसें as (Prak. जहा, Sk. यथा)
सवें or सवेंच spontaneously (in poetry)
एऱ्हवीं, उगाच, उगेंच, उगीच, उगा merely, or for no reason
अकस्मात्, अचानक suddenly (Sk.)
निरर्थक to no purpose (Sk.)
व्यर्थ in vain (Sk. वृथा)
फुकट *gratis*, free of charge
स्वतः of one's self (Sk.)
बहुशः abundantly (Sk. बहुशस्) बहुतकरून.

(*f*) *Degree.*

फार (M.), अतिशय (Sk.), exceedingly
अत्यंत eminently (Sk.)
अगदीं or ही quite
किंचित् scarcely (Sk.)
जरा (A.) nearly, a little
पूर्ण, पुरता fully
मात्र, केवळ only (Sk.)
प्राय: for the most part, usually (Sk.)
लवकर (M.), शीघ्र (Sk.), जलद (P.),
झटपट quickly
अधिक more (Sk.)
कमी less (Sk.)
हळू slowly
अवश्य necessarily (Sk.)
च, ही, ना, पण, देखील even
निदान (Sk.) at least

Note.—च, ही, ना, पण are emphatic adverbs ; आतांच जा go just now ; तूंच ये you alone come ; तूं ही ये you too come ; तूं ना येतोस ? are *you* coming, or is somebody else coming ?

Note.—हा धोतरजोडा पुरता दाहा हात नाहीं this pair of dhotars is not fully ten cubits long.

(4) *Adverbs of Quantity.*

(*g*) *Measure.*

फार much
थोडा a little
पुरें enough
कांहीं or कांहींसा somewhat
अगदीं entirely
बहुत much (Sk.)

(*h*) *Number or Order.*

एकदां once
शंभरपट, शंभरदां a hundred-fold
पहिल्यानें, प्रथमत: firstly
दुसऱ्यानें secondly
शेवटीं, अखेरीं, अंतीं lastly
आरंभीं at the beginning

(5) *Adverbs of Mood.*

(*i*) *Affirmation.*

होय yes ; खचीत certainly ; नि:संशय (Sk.) undoubtedly; खरोखर truly.

(*j*) *Negation.*

नाहीं, न, ना not ; बिलकूल नाहीं, किमपी नाहीं not at all ; कधीं नाहीं never.

(*k*) *Probability and Doubt.*

Sk. कदाचित् perhaps ; बहुधा, प्राय: for the most part.

(6) *Adverbs of Relation.*

जेथें where ; जेव्हां when ; जेथें कोठें wheresoever ; जसा as ; जिकडे whither.

(7) *Adverbs of Demonstration.*

एथें here ; तेथें there ; एव्हां now ; तेव्हां then ; असा like this, so ; तसा like that, so ; इकडे hither ; तिकडे thither.

(8) *Adverbs of Interrogation.*

केव्हां when ? कोठें where ? कशाला why ? कोणीकडे where ? कां why ? कसा how ?

(9) *Adverbs of Imitation.*

झण झण, झण झणां with a clang, quickly, briskly.

फट, फटकन, फटकर, फटकनशीं, फटदिशी, pop ! at once.

गट, गटकन, गटकर, गटदिनी, गटदिशी, गटगट, गटगटां, gulpingly.

II.—*Postpositions.*

§ 349. A Postposition is a word which shows the relation of a noun or pronoun to some other word in the sentence; तो आपल्या जाग्यावर बसला he took his seat.

Note.—" At the bottom of all genuine postpositions, at least in their original sense, there exists a relation between two opposite directions ; thus, "over," "from," "before," "to" have the relations "under," "in," "towards," "from," as their counterpoles and points of comparison, as the right is opposed to the left."—*Bopp.*

Note.—Postpositions, as well as all other particles, were originally nouns, verbs, &c. ; (1) *Postpositions* :—कडे at, from कड a side ; मध्यें inside, from मध्य middle ; विषयीं about, from विषय matter ; करून by means of, from करणें to do ; (2) *Conjunctions* :—कारण "for," from कारण a reason ; ह्मणून therefore, from ह्मणणें to say. When particular nominal or verbal forms become stereotyped as relational words by constant use, their original character gradually comes to be forgotten and often their original form is modified. Thus, कडे at, is the crude form of कड a side, and signifies nothing but " at, " " to, " " towards. " Its full dative form is, also, sometimes used ; ह्याकडेस towards this ; त्याकडेस towards that.

§ 350. The noun to which a postposition is joined assumes its crude-form (§ 88) before the postposition ; घर a house, घरा,घरापासून from a house. The postposition serves, in fact, the same purpose that a case-ending does ; त्याला or त्याजवळ or त्यापाशीं दे, give it to him. Sometimes the noun may not assume its crude-form before a postposition ; सकाळपर्यंत till morning. It is chiefly words denoting time that remain unaltered.

§ 351. The postpositions may be optionally joined to the simple crude-form of the noun, or its genitive crude-form; घराबाहेर or घराच्या बाहेर out of the house.

§ 352. The postpositions ending in an unnasalised आ, are inflected like the adverbs (§ 278), to agree in gender and number with the nouns to which they refer ; त्या तोफेच्याभों-वताले दहा हत्ती उभे होते there were ten elephants standing round that cannon. In fact, the postposition and its noun are an adverbial phrase, and are consequently subject to the same laws of concordance or agreement that the adverbs ending in आ are. (§ 278.)

§ 353. The postpositional phrase could be changed into an attributive or adjective phrase, by means of adjectival suffixes ; पुण्यासभोंवतील गांवें the villages round about Puna ; आमच्या घरापलिकडलें घर the house beyond ours ; त्यांविषयींच्या गोष्टी ऐ-किल्या आहेत काय ? have you heard the accounts about them ?

Note.—The postposition करून is joined to the instrumental in एं-आपल्या कृपेंकरून आम्ही या स्थितीस पोंहचलों आहों we have attained this state by your favour. It is, also, joined to the instrumental case of the pronouns in णें ; तेणेंकरून through it. In Sanskrit and other classical languages the postpositions usually govern various cases.

§ 354. Adverbs when governed by postpositions are not inflected, as कालपासून since yesterday ; but they may take the genitive crude-form, कालच्यापासून since yesterday.

§ 355. The postpositions are thus classified according to the relations signified by them :—

Time.

आंत in	पर्यंत until
पुढें, नंतर after	अगोदर, पूर्वी before

Note.—नंतर chiefly means " after a certain *action* or event " as well as after a certain period of time ; बोलल्यानंतर or वर, after speaking ; but पुढें denotes " in a time future to a *time* specified; " ह्या गोष्टीचा ह्यापुढें कधीं विचार करूं we shall consider this matter some time after this.

Space.

आंत, ठायीं, in, amongst
मध्यें in, between
बाहेर out
पाशीं, समीप, सन्निध near
समक्ष, देखतां, पुढें, समोर before
मागें behind
परोक्ष, in the absence of
खालीं under
वर on
अलिकडे on this side
पलिकडे beyond

Note.—मध्यें is more forcible than आंत, and is chiefly used to denote purely local relations; while आंत, is more generally used. All metaphorical and other non-sensuous relations are usually denoted by आंत, never by मध्यें. The word ठायीं is used only in learned discourse for आंत; आमच्या ठायीं ईश्वरें अनेक शक्ति ठेविल्या आहेत God has put within us various powers.

Motion to or from a place.

आंतून from within
कडे at, towards
पर्यंत, पावेतों till
वरून from above
मधून from the middle.
खालून from below
पासून from

Instrumentality.

कडून, करवीं, द्वारां, द्वारें, हातीं by or through

Miscellaneous Relations.

पैकीं out of
खेरीज, शिवाई or शिवाय, वांचून, विना without
बदल, ऐवजीं, मोबदला, instead of
समान, सरसा, सारखा, प्रमाणें like
जवळ, पाशीं near to
भोंवता around
पुरता sufficient for
साठीं for
विषयीं about
बरोबर, संगें, संगतीं, सवें, सह, सहित, सहवर्तमान with
जोगा suitable
विरुद्ध, उलटें against
सुद्धां together with

Note.—वांचून and विना signify only "without or except;" तेरकविना or वांचून येऊं नको do not come without taking it, but शिवाय expresses some more ideas. It expresses (1) besides, (2) without or except, in composition, additional or extra; याशिवाय त्यानें आणखी कांहीं म्हटलें besides this he said someting else; माझ्याशिवाय जाऊं नको do not go without me; शिवाय जमा or खेरीज जमा extra-collections. The postposition खेरीज agrees with शिवाय in all the senses of शिवाय. खेरीज is used, in addition, to express the sense of exclusion, with certain verbs like करणें to do, ठेवणें to keep; मला खेरीज करून or ठेवून बाकीच्यांस बोलावणीं केलीं excepting me all the others were invited.

Note.—शिवाय expresses "besides" as well as "without" or "except," while वांचून has only the latter meaning; त्यावांचून मला दुसरा कोणी नाहीं I have none except him; या दोघांशिवाय मला आणखी दोन भाऊ आहेत I have two brothers besides these two.

Note.—The postposition सवें along with; is used in poetry.

III.—*Conjunctions.*

§ 356. A conjunction is a word used to connect the different parts of an extended sentence, or two affirmations; औरंगझेब बऱ्हाणपूर सोडून माळव्यांत शिरून गेला, आणि मुरादास जाऊन मिळाला. Aurungzebe, having left Barhanpur, went to Malwa and joined Murad; त्याची रीति बोलून चालून मनमिळाऊ असे, त्यामुळें बहुधा लोक त्यावर प्रीति करीत; परंतु कोंकणामध्यें मोठमोठे दरवडे पडले त्यांत हा सामील होता, असा त्याच्यावर वहमा होता, he was generally liked for his pleasing address, but was suspected to have taken part in the great robberies in the Konkan.

Note.—Even when the conjunction appears only to connect two words, it really connects two sentences. Postpositions connect two notions; conjunctions, two propositions.

§ 357. The conjunctions are thus classified:—

1. Those which unite sentences, in form as well as in meaning, are called Copulative Conjunctions, आणि, आणखी, व, न and; कीं, जे that; ही, देखील, also; पण also, likewise; म्हणजे that is; किंबहुना nay; thus, तूं लबाड काय, चोर पण आहेस you are not only a liar, but also a thief; घोडा व बैल a horse and an ox.

Note.—जे that, is used chiefly in old writings; तेथें लिहिलें होतें जे, सला करून तुम्ही आम्ही एक व्हावें, It was written there that we should make peace and become one.

2. Those which join sentences together, but *disconnect their meaning*, are called Disjunctive Conjunctions: किंवा, अथवा कीं, अगर, का or. Thus, रामानें किंवा त्याच्या भावानें हें केलें असावें Rama or his brother must have done it.

3. Those which connect sentences, but express *contrariety* of senses, are called Adversative Conjunctions: पण, परंतु, परि, तरी but, यद्यपि, जरी though, तरी, तथापि still. Thus, त्यांमध्यें माझा कांहीं दोष नाहीं असें शहाजीनें खातरीपूर्वक सांगितलें तथापि तें विजापुरच्या दरबारास खरें वाटलें नाहीं, Shahaji assured them that he was not implicated in it, still the court of Bijapoor did not believe him; या धास्तीनें शिवाजी अतिशय घाबरला, तरी अशा विश्वासघातक शत्रूस तो शरण गेला नाहीं Shivaji was very much distressed by this apprehension, but he did not submit to such a treacherous enemy.

4. Those which state a reason, or purpose, are called Causative Conjunctions; कां कीं, कारण, कारण कीं because, in order that; म्हणून therefore, in order that; अत एव, वास्तव, या करितां therefore; आतां now, in present circumstances. Thus, तो आपला सूड उगवील अशी त्यास भीति पडली, म्हणून यानें मारेकरी घालून त्यास एकदम मारण्याचा हुकूम केला he apprehended that he would take revenge on him, and therefore he ordered him at once to be assassinated.

Note.—म्हणून is derived from म्हणणें to say, and means literally, this being said, this being the fact. It has these senses:—

1. It has the sense of "therefore;" त्यानें मला शिवी दिली म्हणून म्या त्याच्या तोंडांत मारिलें he abused me and therefore I slapped him in the face.

2. It has the force of the demonstrative pronoun हें, used at the end of a sentence to make it distinct and prominent; मी तुझे घरीं येईन म्हणून म्हणाला he said that he would come to your house; आंबा म्हणून फार चांगलें फळ आहे mango is a good fruit.

3. It has the sense of "called"; इसाक म्हणून आब्राहामाचा पुत्र होता there was a son of Abraham, called Isaac.

5. Those which express a condition or supposition are designated Conditional Conjunctions; जर if (correlative तर then); जरी although (correlative तरी still); नाहींतर otherwise, else; म्हणजे then, की then. Thus, तुम्ही जर बरोबर लोक आणिले तर मी भिऊन जाईन if you should bring any people with you, I shall feel frightened; एथें पाणी पडलें की वाळून जाईल should water fall here it would at once dry up.

Note.—म्हणजे is an ancient polite imperative form of म्हणणें to say denoting "please to say, allow, grant," and has these senses:—

1. It expresses "that is to say," "namely," &c.; अश्व म्हणजे घोडा *aśva* signifies a horse.

2. It expresses "then indeed," "that being the case"; तुम्ही बोललां म्हणजे माझें कार्य होईल should you speak, then indeed my business will be done.

6. Those which are declarative; की that; म्हणून saying, &c.

7. Those which express comparison; पेक्षां, परीस than.

Note.—पेक्षां, also, denotes "since, seeing that," &c.; being constructed with ज्या, ह्या, त्या; ज्या पेक्षां or पेक्षीं तुम्हीं आलां त्या पेक्षां or पेक्षीं वस्तु दिली पाहिजे I must give the thing since you have come.

Note.—का, कां, करितां, काय are frequently joined to जर as expletives, जर का तो आला तर मी देईन if he should come I will give it.

IV.—Interjections.

§ 358. An Interjection is a word which expresses very sudden emotion of the mind, but no definite thought; छत्! मिरू असें म्हणूं नये बरें pshaw, you should not say so, Miru; आहा! ती ती येत आहे oh, there there she comes.

§ 359. Interjections are thus classified according to the *emotions* they express:—

1. Those expressing *joy*: ओहो, आहा oh!

2. Those expressing *approbation*: वाहवा, ठीक, भले शाबास, धन्य bravo! excellent.

3. Those expressing *surprise*: आहा oh; अबब, अलल, अहाहा oh.

4. Those expressing *displeasure*: (*a*) *contempt*: छे, छत्, छी, छी छी, धिक्, फें, fie! shame! (*b*) *disgust*: इश्श, इश्शायो, शिव yah!

fagh! त्राहि त्राहि save! save! mercy! (*c*) *reproach*: हत्, उदेव shame! (*d*) *prohibition*: उंहूं or ऊंहूं no don't! चुप! hush! (*e*) *indifference*: अं: umph!

5. Those used in addressing persons: masculine, अरे, रे, हे O! fem. अगे, गे O! अजी masc. or fem.; plu., masc. or fem. अहो O!

Note.—अरे and रे are not respectful forms, but are frequently used in contempt or endearment: the same is true of अगे, जसें अरे माझ्या बाळा कां तूं असा रडतोस, O my child, why dost thou cry so? अगे प्रिये, तुझें बाळ तुला पुन: त्या सुखस्थानीं भेटेल O beloved, you will see your child again in that Happy Land; अरे मूर्खा तुला काय सांगावें O fool, what shall I say to thee? हे is singular, but respectful; हे देवा, तूं मला तार O God, save me. अहो, which is plural, is used in addressing superiors and others to whom we wish to be formally courteous; अहो यांत त्याचा दोष नाहीं sir, in this he is not blamable; अहो भक्तजन, देवाची स्तुति करा, O worshippers, praise God. A religious mendicant or teacher, whose religious character gives him a superiority over even kings, might say हे राजा, तुझें कल्याण असो, O king, may thou be happy; but every other person would use अहो. अजी is used familiarly, though respectfully, in addressing a man or woman; अजी महाराज आपण तें सर्व विसरलां, O sir! you have forgotten it all.

§ 360. There are a few words in the language, which are not necessary to make up the sense of a sentence; but are sometimes inserted to fill a vacancy, or for ornament; मी आपला वाचीत बसेन, I will just sit reading; मी आपला एथून उठलों, व आपला त्याच्या घरीं गेलों I quietly arose from here, and went quietly to his house; हें तूं आणलेलें पागोटें का? is this indeed the turban brought by you? कां रामराव? आज तुम्हास कसें वाटतें? why, Ramrao, how do you feel to-day? The following are a few Maráṭhí expletives; आपला, का, कां, कीं, मातबयाने, तें कीं नाहीं, आणि, &c. Sometimes whole sentences are thus inserted; आणि काय सांगूं? and what shall I say? देव तुमचें बरें करो may God bless you, &c. Some of the expletives have, it must be confessed, a force and meaning which other words have not, and without them the Maráṭhí language would be deprived of not a little of its idiomatic vigour and grace, as is illustrated in the above sentences with आपला, one's own.

Note.—आपला is an expletive denoting *content*; कां, *surprise*; कीं, a *strong affirmation* or *surprise*; तूं येतोस कीं? (कीं ending a question), you mean to come, don't you?—*emphasis*; मीं देतों कीं, I am giving it, don't you see? (रे is often joined to कीं; आलों किरे, जातों किरे, बसतों किरे.

PART II.

CHAPTER XXI.

DERIVATION.

The Origin and Composition of the Maráṭhi Language.

§ 361—§ 381.

§ 361. The Hindus of the higher classes or castes are denominated Aryas (nobles, but etymologically cultivators), a name which is also given to many other races whose ancient languages, literatures, and religions are analogous to those of the Hindus. As the majority of the Aryan nations inhabit Europe and India, they are also designated Indo-European or Indo-Germanic races.

§ 362. The Indo-European races are the Greeks, the Romans, the Celts, the Teutons, the Sclavoṇes, the Persians, and the Hindus. They are descended from one common stock, and their languages coincide chiefly in regard to vocables of a purely private or domestic nature.

Note.—"It is precisely those words and elements which are the most primitive, the most fundamental, and the most essential parts of each language which they have in common. I mean, first, those words which express the natural relations of father, mother, &c., and kindred generally; secondly, the pronouns; thirdly, the prepositions and particles; fourthly, the words expressing number; and fifthly, the forms of inflection."—*Dr. Muir.*

§ 363. The vocables of the different Aryan languages differ in form, but their identity of origin can be easily traced. Their variations are such as can be accounted for by supposing such causes for them as "caprice, alteration fo physical circumstances, differences of education, and varieties in the organs of speech, which are peculiar to different races." The following letters are exclusively peculiar to Sanskṛit: the palatals च, छ, ज, झ, ञ, and श; the linguals ट, ठ, ड, ढ, and ण;

and the guttural nasal ङ. These letters are modifications of certain letters which are common to all the Indo-European dialects. Thus, च् and छ् are derived from क्, ज् from ग्, the linguals from the dentals त, थ, &c., and ङ from म् or न् "in consequence of certain phonetic laws."

§ 364. The affinity of origin between the Sanskrit and three other Aryan languages, viz., the Greek, the Latin and the Zend, will be seen from the following table :—

Sk.	Zend.	Gr.	Lat.	Pers.	
पितृ	*patar*	*patēr*	*pater*	*padar*	a father
मातृ	*mátar*	*mētēr*	*mater*	*mádar*	a mother
भ्रातृ	*brátar*	*phratria* (a clan)	*frater*	*bráthar*	a brother
स्वसृ	*quanhar*		*soror*	*khwáhar*	a sister
दुहितृ	*dughdhar*	*thugater*		*dukhtar*	a daughter
नप्तृ नपात्	*napa*	*anepsios*	*nepos*		a grandson, cousin
जामातृ	*zámátar*	*gambros*	*gener*	*dâmád*	a son-in-law
श्वशुर	*qasúra*	*hekuros*	*socer*	*khusra*	a father-in-law
वीर		*hērōs*	*vir*		a hero, man
पति	*paiti*	*posis*	*potis*		a lord, husband, able
अन्		*anemos*	*animus*		wind, mind
अक्षि	*aspi*	*ops, okos*	*oculus*		an eye
पद् or पाद	*pádh*	*pous,podos*	*pes,pedis*	*pá*	a foot
देव	*daeva*	*theos*	*deus*		a god
नक्तम्		*nukta*	*noctem*		night
स्तार, तारा	*stare*	*aster*	*astrum*		a star
सम	*ham*	*sun*	*con*		with
उपरि	*upairi*	*huper*	*super*	*bar*	above
प्र	*fra*	*pro*	*pro*		before
नूनम्	*nu*	*nun*	*nunc*		now
द्वि	*dva*	*duo*	*duo*	*do*	two
सप्तन्	*haptan*	*hepta*	*septem*	*haft*	seven
प्रथमः	*fratemo*	*protos*	*primus*		first

27 *m*

Sk.	Zènd.	Ger.	Lat.	Pers.	
द्विज	*bis*	*dis*	*bis*		twice
दा, ददामि	*dadhámi*	*didōmi*	*do*	*dádan*	to give
भर	*bar*	*pherō*	*fero*	*burdan*	to bear
जन्	*zan*	*gennao*	*gigno*	*zádan*	to beget
भू	*bu*	*phuō*	*fui*	*búdan*	to be
ज्ञा		*mnaomai*	*memini*		I think

§ 365. Sanskṛit is regarded as the oldest of the Aryan languages, and exists in its primitive form in the Vedas, the oldest literary books of the Hindus. It continued as the literary as well as the popular language of the Hindu Aryans, who were emigrants from Central Asia, up to about 900 B.C., after which it ceased to be their vernacular, although it continued to be sedulously cultivated for all the higher purposes of literature and religion. For popular purposes the Aryans used several new dialects which had sprung up among them by a mixture of their own language with those of the aborigines among whom they had settled. The popular dialects were denominated *Prákṛit.*

Note.—"The word prákṛita came from prakṛiti (procreative) 'nature,' and means 'derived,' the several Prákṛita dialects being regarded as derivatives of Sanskṛit either directly or mediately. The original language from which a her springs is called *prakṛiti* or sound. Thus, Hema Chundra says, 'Prákṛit has its origin in Sanskṛit ; that which is derived, or comes from the latter, is called Prákṛita.' The expressions Sanskṛit and Prákṛit are opposed to each other in another sense, when the former word denotes men of cultivated minds, and the latter those who are uncultivated. The term Prákṛit is therefore also applied to vulgar and provincial forms of speech."—*Lassen.*

Note.—In the Sanskṛit dramas that are extant, the women and servants are represented as conversing in the Prákṛit, while the priests, the kings, and other persons of rank and education in the Sánskṛit. The changes which Sanskṛit vocables, as well as inflections, have undergone in the Prákṛit, are such as would be effected by illiterate people using the learned language. "Thus, *stri* became *istri*, *rakta* became *rakat*, and *kshatriya* became *khatriya*, *khittia*, or *chhattaya*."

§ 366. Vararuchi, the author of the oldest and most authoritative grammar of the Prákṛits, mentions four dialects, among which he assigns the foremost place to Mahárásḥṭrí, the immediate source of Maráṭhí. It is *par excellence* the Prákṛit, and he devotes to it nine chapters out of the twelve into which his book is divided.

§ 367. The four Prákṛit dialects mentioned by Vararuchi are distinguished by the names of the provinces in which they are said to have flourished. The *Mahárásḥtri* was current in Maharashtra; the *Mágadhi*, in Magadha, the modern Bahar; the *Śauraseni* in Súrasena, the region round about Mathura; and the *Paiśáchi* was the language of the Pisáchas, barbarous hill-tribes.

§ 368. Sanskṛit words underwent the following changes in the Prákṛits:—

I.—The Vowel Changes.

§ 369. 1. The Prákṛits usually retain all the vowels, except ऋ, ॠ, ऌ, ॡ, ऐ and औ.

(*a*) ऋ is changed to रि, as ऋण a debt, Pr. रिण, M. रीण; but if the ऋ is combined with a consonant, it is changed to अ, इ or उ; thus, Sk. तृण grass, Pr. तण, M. तन; Sk. दृष्टि sight, Pr. दिट्ठि, M. दीट; Sk. ऋतु season, Pr. उदू.

(*b*) ऐ becomes ए or अइ, rarely इ or ई; Sk. कैलास, Pr. केलासो; Sk. दैत्य a demon, Pr. दइच्चो; Sk. दैव fate, Pr. दइवं or दव्वं, M. दैव; सैन्धव produced in Sindh, Pr. सिंधवं; Sk. धैर्य firmness, Pr. धीर, M. धीर.

(*c*) औ is changed to ओ or अउ; sometimes to उ; Sk. यौवनम् youth, Pr. जोव्वणं, M. ज्वान; Sk. पौर a citizen, Pr. पउरो, M. पवार; Sk. कौशल welfare, Pr. कौसल or कोसल, M. कुशाळ.

2. अ is sometimes changed to इ, ए and ओ:

(*a*) Sk. पक्व cooked, Pr. पिक्क, M. पिकें, ripe.
Sk. व्यजनं a fan, Pr. विजणो, M. विजणा, a fan.
Sk. अंगारः a live coal, Pr. इंगलो, M. इंगळ or इंगोल.

(b) Sk. शय्या a bed, Pr. सेज्जा, M. शेज.
Sk. वल्लि a creeper, Pr. वेल्ली, M. वेल.

(c) The अ becomes ओ when followed by व; Sk. लवणं salt, Pr. लोणं, M. लोण saltness in a soil.

3. A long vowel followed by a double letter is shortened :—
Sk. मार्गः a way, Pr. मग्गो, M. माग a trace, track.
Sk. दीर्घः long, Pr. दिग्घो.
Sk. पूर्व, Pr. पुव्व.

Note.—Sometimes the long vowel is retained, and the conjunct simplified; Sk. ईश्वरः a lord, Pr. इस्सरो or ईसरो.

4. A short vowel followed by a conjunct is sometimes lengthened, and the conjunct simplified; Sk. जिव्हा a tongue, Pr. जीहा, M. जीभ.

5. The short vowels इ and उ, followed by conjuncts, are usually changed to ए and ओ respectively, retaining the conjuncts :—

Sk. पिण्डः a lump	Pr. पेंडं	M. पेंड
Sk. सिन्दूरः red lead	Pr. सिं or सेंदूरं	M. शेंदूर
Sk. तुण्डं the face	Pr. तोडं	M. तोंड
Sk. मुक्ता a pearl	Pr. मोत्ता	M. मोती

II.—The Simple Consonants.

§ 370. 6. The single consonants श, ष, न, and य are usually changed in the Prákṛits: for the two sibilants स is substituted, ण for न, and ज for य:—

Sk. शब्दः a sound	Pr. सद्दो	M. साद
Sk. षंढः a eunuch	Pr. संढो	
Sk. नदी a river	Pr. णई	

Note.—At Ratnagiri नई is the word for नदी, a river.

Sk. यशस् glory	Pr. जसो
Sk. यक्षः a demi-god	Pr. जक्खो M. जख्ख exceedingly old and infirm.

7. The aspirates are changed to ह:—

Sk. सखी a female friend	Pr. सही	M. सई a name of a woman
Sk. कथनं a saying	Pr. कहणं	M. कहाणि a story
Sk. साधु a merchant	Pr. साहु	M. साहू
Sk. भू to be	Pr. हो	M. हो become thou

8. The consonants क्, ग्, च्, ज्, त्, द्, प्, ब्, य्, and व्, if medial, are often elided :—

Sk. मुकुलः a bed Pr. मउलो M. माळ an elevated plain
Sk. सूची a needle Pr. सुई M. सुई
Sk. गजः an elephant Pr. गओ
Sk. गदा a club Pr. गआ
Sk. विपुलः large Pr. विउलं
Sk. जीव life Pr. जीअं

9. र is sometimes changed to ल :—

Sk. हरिद्रा turmeric Pr. हलद्दा M. हळद
Sk. अंगुरि a finger Pr. अंगुली M. आंगुळ
Sk. अंगार a charcoal Pr. इंगालो M. इंगळ

10. The dentals are changed to the cerebrals :—

Sk. अस्थि a bone Pr. अट्ठि M. हाड
Sk. ग्रन्थिः a knot Pr. गण्ठि M. गांठ
Sk. धक्क to shake Pr. ढक्क M. ढकलणें
Sk. दण्डः a staff Pr. डण्ड M. दांड

Note.—In the Prákrit the cerebrals have obtained great supremacy, and have frequently supplanted the other letters. "With regard to the nasal, the substitution of ण् for न् is universal."—*Bopp.*

Note.—The dental द is sometimes changed to ज or ल; as, Sk. अद्य to-day, Pr. अज्ज, M. आज; Sk. मृद् to grind, Pr. मल, M. मळणें.

11. The visarga at the end of Sanskṛit words is invariably changed to ओ; as Sk. मार्गः a way, Pr. मग्गो, माग a track.

III.—The Compound Consonants.

§ 371. The Compound Consonants are reduced to letters of the same class, according to the following rules :—

12. (*a*) क्क is substituted for the conjuncts क्य, क्र, र्क, क्ल, क्व.

क्ख for क्ष, ष्क, स्क, ष्ख, स्ख.
ग्ग for ग्य, र्ग.
त्त for त्र, त्व, र्त.
प्प for प्त, प्र, र्प, ल्प, प्ल, प्य.

13. (*b*) When a sibilant is combined with a strong letter the sibilant is changed to an aspirate of the class of the strong letter, or to some other strong letter of corresponding sound;

as Sk. कुक्षि belly, Pr. कुच्छी, M. कूस side of the body; Sk. क्षेत्र a field, Pr. छेत्त, M. शेत; Sk. पुष्कर a pond, Pr. पोक्खरों, M. पोखरण.

14. (c) Of two dissimilar strong letters, the last displaces the first:—

क्क = क्क
ब्ज = ज्ज
क्त or प्त = त्त
ग्द or ब्द = द्द
क्प or त्प = प्प

15. (d) The sibilants, combined with the weak letters, retain a place in the modified conjunct; श्न, श्य, ष्म, ष्य, श्र, श्व, ष्व, &c. = स्य.

16. (e) The weak letter in conjunction with श is sometimes changed to the anusvár, and श to स—

Sk. अश्रु a tear, Pr. अस्सुं, M. आंसू
Sk. स्पर्श a touch, Pr. फनसो, M. आफडणें

§ 372. We give below a few additional words to illustrate the above changes:—

Sanskrit.	Prákrit.	Maráṭhí.
आर्यं respectable	अज्जे	अजी, जी
अद्य to-day	अज्ज	आज
कार्यं, कर्म work	कज्ज, कम्मो	काज, काम
राज्यं kingdom	रज्ज	राज, राज्य
कर्णः an ear	कण्णो	कान
हस्तः a hand	हत्थो	हात
दधि curds	दही	दहीं
कुंभकारः a potter	कुंभारो	कुंभार
श्रेष्ठी superior, banker	सेट्ठि	शेट
शुष्क dry	सुक्ख	सुका
बहिर outside	बाहिर	बाहेर
बलीवर्दाः oxen	बइल्ला	बैल
स्तंभः a pillar	खंभो	खांब
देवालयं a temple	देऊलु	देऊळ
स्थान a place	ठाण	ठाण
हरिद्रा turmeric	हलद्दा	हळद

Sanskrit.	Prákrit.	Maráthí.
बीजं seed	बिअ	बीं, बीज
विद्युत् lightning	विज्जू	वीज
पुस्तकम् a book	पोथो	पोथी
भक्तं rice	भत्तं	भात
भगिनी a sister	बहिणि	बहीण
अंधकार: darkness	अंधआर	अंधार
आत्मा self, *nom. sing.*	आपा, अप्पा	आपा a father
आत्मानम् self, *acc. plu.*	अप्पाणं	आपण
य: who	जो	जो
वदति to speak	बोलई	बोलतो
पक्कं ripe	पिक्क	पिकलें

§ 373. Not only Sanskrit words, but the inflections also underwent changes in the Prákrit :—

Declension of the noun बुद्ध Buddha.

	Singular. Sanskrit.	*Singular.* Prákrit.	*Plural.* Sanskrit.	*Plural.* Prákrit.
1.	बुद्ध:	बुद्धो	बुद्धा:	बुद्धा or द्धे
2.	बुद्धम्	बुद्धं	बुद्धान्	बुद्धा
3.	बुद्धेन	बुद्धेण	बुद्धै:	बुद्धेहि
4.	बुद्धाय	Same as the 6th Case.	बुद्धेभ्य:	Same as the 6th Case.
5.	बुद्धात्	बुद्धादो	बुद्धेभ्य:	बुद्धाहिंतो or द्धंतो
6.	बुद्धस्य	बुद्धस्स	बुद्धानाम्	बुद्धाणं
7.	बुद्धे	बुद्धे, or बुद्धम्मि	बुद्धेषु	बुद्धेसु

Conjugation of the verb हस् to laugh.

ACTIVE CONJUGATION.

Present Tense.

	Singular. Sanskrit.	*Singular.* Prákrit.	*Plural.* Sanskrit.	*Plural.* Prákrit.
1.	हसामि	हसामि	हसाम:	हसामो-मु
2.	हससि	हससि	हसथ	हसह-स्था
3.	हसति	हसदि-इ	हसंति	हसंति

IMPERATIVE MOOD.

1.	हसानि	हसमु	हसाम	हसामो
2.	हस	हस-सु	हसत	हसह
3.	हसतु	हसदु-उ	हसंतु	हसंतु

Infinitive.

Sk. तुम्, Pr. तुं or दुं.

Participles.

Sk. त्वा, Pr. तूण or ऊण ; Sk. अंत, Pr. अंत or एंत.

Note.—The Prákrit languages bear a strong resemblance to the modern European dialects which are derived from Latin, and which have superseded it as a popular language. The Italian, which is at present spoken in the old home of Latin, is exactly similar, in respect of its derivation, to the Prákrit, and we shall give the following comparative table by way of illustration :—

Latin.	Italian.	Sanskṛit.	Prákrit.
perfectus	perfetto	muktas	mutto
dictus	detto	yuktas	jutto
fructus	frutto	bhaktas	bhatto
ruptus	rotto	uptas	utto
planctus	pianto	viklavas	vikkavo

Present Tense.

	Latin.	Italian.	Sanskṛit.	Prákrit.
1.	vendo	vendo	hasámi	hasámi
2.	vendis	vendi	hasasi	hasasi
3.	vendit	vende	hasati	hasadi
1.	vendimus	vendiamo	hasámah	hasamo
2.	venditis	vendete	hasatha	hasaha
3.	vendunt	vendono	hasanti	hasanti

§ 374. The Sanskṛit, as well as the Prákrit, contains certain words which are of a peculiar nature, and are designated देशज country-born, by the Indian grammarians, and they have descended into Maráṭhí from those languages. A few of these words (which however are not found in Sanskṛit) are the following :—

Pr. बप्प a father, M. बाप (Sk. पिता)
Pr. पोट्ट or पोट्ट a belly, M. पोट (Sk. उदरं)
Pr. छिनालिआ a harlot, M. छिनाल or शिंदळ (Sk. पुंश्चली)
Pr. खुण्ट a peg, M. खुंटा (Sk. स्तंभः)
Pr. थरत्तरेदि to tremble, M. थरथरणें (Sk. प्रकंपनं)
Pr. डुब्बंतं to sink, M. डुबणें (Sk. मज्जंतम्)

Pr. ढक्केहि to cover or shut, M. ढांकणें or झांकणें (Sk. पिधत्त)
Pr. घडाव to fabricate, M. घडणें (Sk. कारय)
Pr. कड्डमि to draw, M. ओढणें (Sk. कर्षामि)
Pr. घोट्ट gulp, M. घोटणें (Sk. पिब)
Pr. सिप्पि a shell, M. शिंपी (Sk. शुक्ति)

Note.—"The Brahmans scattered through all the different provinces of Hindustan, no doubt, adopted many of the words of the languages of the tribes among whom they resided, and introduced them into the sacred tongue."—*Stevenson.* "How could the Aryan people have spread itself over the whole of India, without adopting very much from the aboriginal population which they found there, and which had submitted to them partly in a peaceable manner, and partly under compulsion, and yet even to this day only imperfectly!" "Where peoples speaking different languages live in constant mutual intercourse, traffic or fight with one another, suffer and enjoy together, they take over much from each other without examination, and this process must have gone on in their earliest times, when their mutual relations were still of a naif character."—*Dr. H. Gundert.*

§ 375. Besides Maráṭhí, the following are the principal modern vernaculars derived from the Prákrit dialects :—*Gujaráti, Sindhi, Panjábi, Hindi, Bengalli,* and *Oriya.*

§ 376. The Prákrit, that is, the immediate source of Maráṭhí, has undergone the following changes in these languages :—

1. In Prákrit the different letters of a Sanskrit conjunct are changed to the same classes, but in Maráṭhí one of the letters of the conjunct is omitted, and its preceding vowel is lengthened :—

Sk. निद्रा sleep	Pr. निद्दा	M. नीज
Sk. दुग्धं milk	Pr. दुद्धं	M. दूध
Sk. पक्ष: a wing	Pr. पक्खो	M. पाख
Sk. हस्त: a hand	Pr. हत्थे	M. हात
Sk. सूत्रं thread	Pr. सत्तं	M. सूत
Sk. प्राघूर्ण: a guest	Pr. पाहुणो	M. पाहुणा
Sk. कोष्टं a granary	Pr. कोट्ठ	M. कोठा

2. Sometimes the compound letter is dissolved in Maráṭhí and अ, इ, or उ, is inserted :—

Sk. भक्तः a devotee Pr. भत्तो M. भगत
Sk. रक्तं blood Pr. रत्तं M. रगत
Sk. ग्रहणं an eclipse M. गिराण
Sk. लग्नं a wedding M. लगीन
Sk. वर्षं a year M. वरीस

3. In Maráṭhí the hiatus of the Prákrit is often avoided :—

Sk. खादनं eating Pr. खाअणं M. खाणें
Sk. रुदनं crying Pr. रूअणं M. रडणें
Sk. राजा a king Pr. राआ M. राव
Sk. द्विगुणं two-fold Pr. दुउणो M. दून
Sk. हृदयं a heart Pr. हिअअं M. हिय्या

4. The visarga, which in Prákrit is changed to ओ, is either dropped in Maráṭhí, or changed to आ :—

Sk. घोटकः a horse Pr. घोडओ M. घोडा
Sk. घर्मः perspiration Pr. घम्मो M. घाम
Sk. गर्भः pith Pr. गब्भो M. गाभा

Note.—In Maráthì the Prákrit ओ is retained in two pronouns, जो who (Sk. यः, Pr. जो) and तो that or he (Sk. सः).

5. The sibilants and ह, when forming the first member of a compound, or the last letter of a word, sometimes affect the initial consonant :—

Sk. पुष्पं a flower M. फूल
Sk. बाष्पं a vapour Pr. बप्फो M. वाफ
Sk. पनसः the jacktree Pr. फणसो M. फणस
Sk. महिषी a buffalo M. भैंस or ह्मैस

6. The initial vowels of the Sanskṛit prefixes are elided in Maráṭhí :—

Sk. अभ्यञ्जनं anointing M. भिजणें to be wet
Sk. अवस्थानं abode M. वठाण a room
Sk. अरघट्ट a well wheel M. रहाट
Sk. अरण्यं a forest Pr. रण्ण M. रान

§ 377. Though Maráṭhí is mainly derived from Sanskṛit through the medium of Prákṛit, there are several other languages which contribute their quota of very useful vocables to it. We shall classify below the various elements which enter into the composition of Maráṭhí.

§ 378. The component elements of Maráṭhí may be divided into *two* general classes, viz., 1st, the *Sanskṛitic*, and 2ndly, the *Non-Sanskṛitic*. These two classes are sub-divided into more particular classes in the following manner :—

1. The Sanskṛitic element is of *two* kinds, viz., the *Tatsama* (तत्सम) and the *Tadbháva* (तद्भव). The former word literally signifies "like that," *i.e.*, like the Sanskṛit, and comprehends pure Sanskṛit words ; and the latter word means "that which is derived from it," *i.e.*, Sanskṛit, and indicates words derived from Sanskṛit by a change of form.

2. The Non-Sanskṛitic element is of three kinds, and the three classes of words are of the following description :—

(1) The *Deśí* or *Deśaj*, *i.e.*, indigenous words, and they are those words which have been introduced into the language from the dialects of the aborigines.

Note.—"The Deśaj element claims almost all the words beginning with the cerebral letters, which, as initials, were probably not originally in use in the Sanskṛit, almost all the words beginning with the letter *jh.*"—*Dr. John Wilson.*

(2) The *Imitative Particles* (अनुकरणवाचक शब्द), or words, both simple and reduplicated, which have been produced by the Maráṭhas themselves, in imitation of sounds, real or imaginary. Thus, *simple* कट, imitative of a sharp sound ; the *duplicative* कटकट a brawl.

Note.—The imitative particles are so numerous in the Maráṭhí language, and the words derived from them so multiform, that it would be possible to construct a *complete form of speech exclusively of them.* And if the legitimate mode of prosecuting enquiry into the origin of old and fully developed languages is to study them in the light of the modern languages, especially of those which are actually in the process of formation, or whose process of formation can be clearly traced, shall we not seriously consider if every language may not have *originally descended from the humble imitative particles which seem to satisfy completely the wants of savages and illiterate men ?*

The action of the human mind is uniform ; men reason now as they reasoned in times past. The philosophies, dramas, histories and mythologies indicate absolute oneness of the human thought and feeling in the rudimentary or general form. And the study of the etymology of words is a powerful evidence that men conceived of objects and gave them descriptive names in most cases in exactly the same way over the whole face of the world. Why may we not suppose that men first called objects by *audible names or sounds, in imitation of sounds which they actually heard, or fancied they heard,* as is done to this day by savages and half-civilized people. "I believe," says Leibnitz, "that languages are the best mirror of the human mind, and that an exact analysis of the signification [and forms] of words would make us better acquainted than anything else with the operations of the understanding." Words, as sounds, are "statues in sound"--representations in and by sound of our notions, as pictures hewn in stone. The first conceptions formed of things—whether objects or actions—*by the sound,* actually belonging to them, or, by analogy, imagined to belong to them, gave rise to the names, *as sounds,* by which they are called.

Note.—And, indeed, if the radical forms of words in the oldest languages be closely examined, there will be found not a few words which can be traced to imitative particles, and we shall subjoin a few such radical forms from Sanskṛit :—

Sk. कास् to cough	M. खोकणें
Sk. कुट् to bend	M. कुटका
Sk. खन् to dig	M. खणणें
Sk. गद् to speak	M. equiv. गदगदणें
Sk. चम् to eat	M. चावणें
Sk. तन् to pull	M· ताणणें
Sk. त्रुट् to break	M. तुटणें
Sk. त्वर् to hurry	M. equiv. तुरतुर
Sk. दृ to tear	M. & H. डर
Sk. दह् to burn	M. दाहणें
Sk. दुल् to shake	M. डोलणें
Sk. ध्वक्ष् to destroy	M. ढकलणें
Sk. लट् to babble	M. equiv. लटलटणें
Sk. लल् to babble, to play	M. equiv. ललकारणें
Sk. लड् to put out the tongue, to play.	M. लाडका

3. *Anga-desi* words, or words borrowed from the languages of the inhabitants of Arabia, Persia, China, England, &c., settled in the country.

§ 379. These five classes of words have become a prolific source of new and multiform derivatives, swelling the Maráṭhí vocabulary to upwards of sixty thousand words, and have thus risen to the rank of Roots. We have styled them Maráṭhí Roots in this grammar.

Obs.—Maráṭhí, as regards its vocabulary, is more copious than Prákṛit, and lays claim to a more vigorous idiomatic phraseology than Sanskṛit, while its perennial source of the imitative particles, in which t fondly revels, gives it a character of vitality and picturesqueness which it is impossible to find in equal degree in any of the other living languages of the world.

§ 380. We will cite a few examples to illustrate the derivation of Maráṭhí words from what we have denominated *Maráṭhí Roots.*

Note.—The Sanskṛit, Arabic, Persian, and various other words which we have denominated *Maráṭhí Roots*, are, in their turn, derived from simpler forms or roots, which often are, chiefly as regards the Indo-Germanic languages, of a monosyllabic character. They are "the elements of speech which existed prior to the whole development of the means of grammatical distinction, before the growth of inflection, before the separation of the parts of speech."—*Whitney*. "All roots are monosyllabic; all polysyllabic roots are either reduplicated forms of the root, or prepositions grown up with them; जागृ to wake; अवधीर् to despise=अव+धीर्. A monosyllable may be composed of the simple vowel and consonant, or several consonants combined; as गा to go; स्था to stand. A single vowel can express a verbal idea; as इ to go."—*Bopp*. "By the annexation of syllables to these roots, substantives and adjectives are derived. There are, however, a few roots, feminine abstracts, which in their pure forms are *used* as words, and declined with the case-terminations; these are भी fear, युध् contest, मुद् joy."—*Bopp*.

1. Maráṭhí Roots of the Tatsama Class.

Root Sk. नट a dancer, a tribe of jugglers (Sk. root; नट् to strut).

Derivatives.

Nouns: नटबाज a swaggerer, a beau; नटबाजी swaggering; नटवा a rope-dancer; नटवी an actress, a strut; नटाई roguishness;

नटीण an actress ; नटुवा a dancer.

Adjectives : नटखट roguish ; नटवाट rascally.

Verbs : नटणें to dress finely ; नटविणें to deck out finely.

Adverbs : नटून थटून pompously.

Phrases : नटामाजी नेटकी जाया an attractive, but an unreal object ; literally, the guise of a lovely woman as assumed by a male actor.

2. Of the Tadbháva Class.

Root बोल (णें) to speak (Sk. ब्रू to speak).

Derivatives.

Nouns : बोल a word ; बोलणें speaking ; बोलवा, बोलवाय popular talk ; बोलाचाली conversation ; बोलावणें invitation ; बोली a language ; अबोला reserve.

Adjectives : बोलका eloquent ; बोलगडा loquacious ; बोलता that speaks.

Verbs : बोलणें to speak ; बोलाविणें to call.

3. Of the Deśáj Class.

(1) Root ओढ (णें) to draw (derived through the Pr. वड्ढि).

Derivatives.

Noun : ओढ a pull, a tendency ; ओढकर a hauler ; ओढकाठी the draw-pole ; ओढगस्ती straitened circumstances ; ओढण a heavy pull, a traditional custom ; ओढणबाकी the balance due carried forward; ओढणशिल्लक balance in hand brought up ; ओढणी a shawl drawn over the head and shoulders ; ओढदोरा the draw-string of a purse ; ओढश heavy draught ; ओढपट्टी the pin which confines the beam of a loom ; ओढव the inclined plane at a draw-well; ओढवण the dry bed of a mountain torrent ; ओढा a stay, a brook ; ओढाओढ a general and violent pulling and hauling ; ओढाखोडा a comprehensive term for brooks and streams ; ओढाताण or ओढाटाण a pulling about violently or rudely ; ओढामाणकी or ओढामाणक्या *f. plu.*, hanging or holding back affectedly ; ओढावण or णें a kind of a drag-carriage ; ओढाळकी, ओढाळगिरी or ओढाळी the roaming about of a bullock, that is ओढाळ ; ओढील or ळ the two ends of a female garment tied round the waist ; ओढें an act of revenge or requital of evil; ओढ्या जगन्नाथ an image of जगन्नाथ (of Puri), said to have been drawn out of the sea.

Adjective : ओढक that haggles, insists upon obstinately; ओढ-गस्त that is in straitened circumstances; ओढाळ that is ever breaking loose from the fold; ओढिस्त that is in distressed circumstances; ओढीक that draws well, embarrassed in circumstances; ओढग a gross term for a step-child.

Verb : ओढणें to pull, to hang or hold back; ओढवणें to tend impulsively; ओढविणें to stretch out (the hand, &c.) upon or towards.

Adverb : ओढून ताणून forcingly, not naturally.

Phrase : ओढून चंद्रबळ forced, far-fetched; ओढून आणणें to draw one's self up haughtily; ओढून बळका करणें to outwit one's self; वरून ओढून टाकणें to give a smattering or superficial knowledge of, &c.

(2) Root डोळा an eye (*not* derived from the Prákrit).

Derivatives.

Noun : डोळढापणें a blind for the eyes; डोळाफोडी the name of a bird; डोळू a hole; डोळूक head of a fish; डोळेझांक connivance; डोळेझांकणी a play; डोळेझांपणी a blind for the eyes (of a bullock); डोळेफोड narrow inspection; डोळेभेट the parting look, a hurried interview; डोळमोड working.

Adjective : डोळस having sight; डोळे फुटका that has lost his sight; डोळफोड that pains the eyes; डोळमिचका that blinks.

Adverb : डोळे उजेडी in the dusk of the evening; डोळ्यांदेखत or तां within one's own experience; डोळ्यांमागें in the absence of.

Phrase : डोळ्यांचा अंधार करणें to err against light.

4. Of the Class of the Imitative Particles.

Root बुळबुळ imitation of light showering.

Derivatives.

Nouns : बुळक-बुळकी a loose stool; बुळकांडी, -कांडी or -कुंडी a stream from a slit receptacle; बुळका a porpoise; बुळबुळ greasiness, drizzling; बुळबुळाट greasiness; बुळबुळी a particular plant; बुळबुळीत greasiness; बुळी a term at cards.

Adjective : बुळचा lubricous, slack; बुळबुळीत oily; बुळा impotent.

Verb : बुळकणें to slip suddenly; बुळबुळणें to crawl about; बुळ-बुळाविणें to besmear with grease.

Adverb : बुळबुळ or ळां continually dripping.

5. Of the Anya-desaj Class.

Root Ar. नाल a horse-shoe.

Derivatives.

नालकरी *m.*, नालबंद a shoer of horses; नालकी *f.*, a sort of palkhi; नालडबा *m.*, a set of horse-shoes; नालबंदी *f.*, the price for shoeing a horse; नालमेख a horse-shoe nail; नालसाहेब a familiar term for the bearer of a particular pole in the Mohurrum.

Root Pers. मिजाज temper, fastidiousness.

Derivatives.

Adjective : मिजाजी—शी, मिजाजखोर fastidious.

§ 381. The various elements which enter into the composition of Maráthí have each its peculiar use. The Imitative Particles and the Désaj words occur chiefly in the speech of the lower classes, and give their thoughts and feelings a bodily form and expression. The *Tadbhávas* are employed by the higher classes for all popular purposes, while the *Tatsamas* enter copiously into their formal and learned discourse. The *Anya-Dési* languages (the Arabic and Persian, through the Urdu) contribute a large number of valuable vocables relating to the arts and institutions of civilized life, and impart to the language into which they are incorporated, singular life and energy. When a formal discourse of a secular nature is to be sustained with courtesy and dignity, or a manly passion to be expressed with vehemence, Urdu words and phrases are freely used by the Maráthís. It is no exaggeration to say that Urdu is pre-eminently a kingly language. Its phraseology has a dignity and a majesty, and, withal, a fire and energy that no other Indian vernacular possesses. Born and cradled in the camp, it has always continued to be the language of the Court and the camp, communicating its manly force and vigour to every language it has come in contact with. The English is inspiring a new moral life into Maráthí, and contributing to it some new useful words.

Note.—"Although the stuff and backbone of these seven (modern Indian languages) languages is pure Indo-Germanic, yet we must not ignore or underrate the influence which Arabic vocables have exercised. This influence began in Sindh so early as Muhammad Kassim's conquest of that country in the early part of the eighth century." "Mohammad of Ghazni's numerous expeditions extended the knowledge of the general language of the Mussalmans to all Western India in the eleventh century, and by the middle of the thirteenth, Arabic words were heard in almost every city and town."—*Beames.*

Note.—1. When two or more synonymous words derived from different sources exist in the language, they usually *differ in meaning*. The *Tatsama* is used when a thing is spoken of in an *indefinite* way or described as *large* and *dignified* ; the *Tadbháva* and the *Dèsaj* express an idea in a particular and popular form, and the *Anya-Dèsi* (Urdu, Arabic and Persian) in a *forcible*, and not unfrequently, in an *offensive* form :—

(1) *Tat.* सर्पः a snake, *Prak.* सप्पो, *M.* साप.—The *Tadbháva* means a serpent generally, except नाग the cobra, but the *Tatsama* सर्प denotes a large and terrible reptile of the serpent tribe.

(2) *Tat.* मार्ग : a way, *Prak.* मग्गो, *M.* माग a track, trace, *Urdu* रस्ता a road.—The *Tatsama* मार्ग is confined to learned discourse, while the popular current form in the language is the Urdu रस्ता. There is, therefore, no necessity for a separate *Tadbháva* derivation from मार्ग in the sense of "a way" for common use. The *Tadbháva* माग is, consequently never used in Maráthí in that sense, but that of (1) a trace, track; (2) channel to conduct water ; and (3) a loom.

(3) *Deśaj* पागोटें a turban; Urdu पगडी.—Now while पागोटें means a turban generally, पगडी denotes a particular kind of turban, employed chiefly in phrases denoting vanity or conceit. Thus पगडी फेंकणें to cock the turban with an air, whereas पागोटें घालणें is simply to wear a turban ; so also पगडी घेणें is "to eclipse an eminent person by one's superior merit." Equivalent expressions with पागोटें are never used, and would be quite tame.

(4) *Tat.* स्वभाव disposition, *Anya-Désaj* (Persian) मिजास, (Arab.) तब्यत. The *Tatsama* is commonly used to denote temperament or disposition, and मिजास expresses fastidiousness as well as arrogance ; मि-

आव बादशहाची आणि अवलाद भडभुंजाची he has the airs of a prince, but is the offspring of a rustic (*lit.* of a grain parcher).

Obs. – It is usually Persian words, and not Arabic, which have an exaggerated or offensive meaning in Maráthi. Thus the Persian word मिजास a temper, disposition, conveys an offensive sense, while the Arabic equivalent तबियत, also occurring in the language, is quite as good as the Sanskrit स्वभाव; and in the provinces where Arabic words are used, the Sanskrit equivalents are not so common.

Obs. – Urdu (Arabic and Persian) words are, however, never used to express domestic relations or feelings ; it is chiefly the *Tadbhávas* that are so employed. Urdu words are generally used in reference to unlawful love, and they characterise the language of amorous poetry.

Note. – 2. When two *Tadbháva* synonyms somewhat *differ in* form, the less corrupted form expresses a sense analogous to the classical root than the other, and *vice versá*. Thus, for instance, देवर्षि a divine sage or Vaidik Rishi is a *Tatsama*, and देवरुषी and देवलशी are two *Tadbhávas* derived from it. देवलशी is more altered in form than देवरुषी, and the former has a more offensive sense than the latter. देवरुषी is a dealer with gods, and देवलशी a dealer with devils.

Note.—3. What is true of words is true also of the *inflections*. Some Maráthi case-endings are derived from Sanskrit inflections, and some from Maráthi words. Of the inflections derived form Sanskrit, some exist in a more, and some others in a less, corrupted from. Thus the dative स is derived from the Sanskrit स्य, while the dative ला from the Maráthi word लागीं. Further, the genitive चा, which, like the dative स, is derived from the Sanskrit स्य, is more altered in form than स : –

(1) Of the two dative terminations, the one which is more like its Sanskrit original is less definite and pointed in sense than that derived from a pure Maráthi word; तूं दिवसास or दिवसाचा (चा=स्य) ये come in the day time, but दोहोंला ये come at two o'clock.

(2) Of the two derivatives from the Sanskrit स्य, स, which is more analogous to it, is less pointed and emphatic than चा. Both स and चा are employed to denote the adverbial relation of time, but चा is used when *attention is to be specially called* to the particular circumstance of time ; तूं रात्रीचा कोठें जातोस where do you go *at night*; तूं काल रात्रीस कोठें होतास *where* were you last night ? The locative ई being immediately derived like स, from a Sanskrit inflection, agrees with स in use; तूं काल रात्रीं or रात्रीस कोठें होतास *where* were you last night ?

CHAPTER XXI.

THE PRINCIPLES OF MARÁṬHÍ DERIVATION.

§ 382—§ 431.

§ 382. All the Maráṭhí words which cannot be traced to a simpler form in the language, no matter what be the original language from which they are derived, whether Sanskṛit, Prákrit, Arabic, Persian, or English, may be denominated Maráṭhí roots. (§ 379)

§ 383. New words are formed from the Maráṭhí roots in the following *seven* ways :—

(1) By modifying the radical vowels or consonants : बांधणें to bind ; बांध a dam ; बांधा a shape ; डोळा an eye ; डोळू an eyelet or a little hole ; पडणें to fall ; पाडणें to fell ; फाटणें to tear (*intrans.*); फाडणें to tear (*trans.*)

(2) By modifying both the radical vowels and consonants : सुटणें to get loose, unloose ; सोडणें to loose.

(3) By joining letters or particles either before or after a word : तुटणें to break ; अ + तूट = अतूट unbroken ; राग anger ; राग + ईट = रागीट passionate. The particle before a word is called a prefix (उपसर्ग), and the particle after it, a suffix (प्रत्यय).

(4) By doubling the simple word : दाणे grain, दाणेदुणे grain, &c.

(5) By uniting two words to express one notion, both words retaining a place in the compound : काळें black and मांजर a cat = काळमांजर a polecat.

(6) By the union of two words so that one of the words is somewhat lost : तेल oil and पाणी water = तेलवणी ; आंबट sour and वास smell = आंबवास.

(7) By the union of two words, which, without entering into formal composition, express one simple idea : as हाताखालचा an assistant.

Note.—In formal composition the inflections indicating the relation existing between the two uniting words are dropped : राजाचा वाडा a king's house ; राजवाडा a palace ; तांबडी माती red earth ; तांबडमाती red earth. The genitive चा of राजाचा and ई of तांबडी are omitted in the compounds राजवाडा and तांबडमाती.

§ 384. The first two classes of derivatives are called (I.) Primary Derivatives; the third class, (II.) Secondary Derivatives; the fourth class, (III.) Reduplicatives; and the last three classes, (IV.) Compounds.

1. The Primary Derivatives.

§ 385. There are two principal classes of Primary Derivatives, viz., the Causals and the Potentials.

I. *The Causal Verb.*

§ 386. The causal verb indicates usually instrumental or indirect agency; मी गोविंदाला रामाकडून मारविलें I got Govind beaten by Rámá; मला तो बसवितो he causes me to sit, *i. e.*, I do not sit by my own effort. The agent does the action denoted by the causal verb through the instrumentality of another person.

§ 387. The causal verb is essentially transitive, but it may be derived from a transitive or an intransitive verb. In the above two examples मारविलें is derived from the transitive verb मारणें, and बसविलें from the intransitive verb बसणें.

§ 388. The causal verb is derived from the original verb by the addition of अव; as मार to strike + अव = मारव; त्यानें आपल्या मुलाला पंतोजीकडून मारविलें he got his son punished by the teacher.

Note.—In the Dakhan इव is substituted for अव, and the former form is now generally adopted in the imperative mood; त्याच्या कडून करीव get it done by him.

§ 389. Monosyllabic roots like खा eat thou, पी drink thou, ये come thou, as well as the roots ending in ह, like लीह write thou, take a double व; त्याकडून खाववीलें I caused it to be eaten by him; माझ्या लेकीच्या हातून रामाला एक रुपया देवविला I caused my daughter to give Rámà a rupee; त्याच्या कडून लिहवविलें I got it written by him.

Note.--The particle अव is derived from अय् or अय employed in Sanskṛit to make up the causal forms, and अय or अय् is derived either from इ to go, or from ई to wish, to demand, to pray. If derived from ई to wish, the causal form expresses "the secondary notion of the causal verbs, in which the subject completes the action, not by the deed, but by the will; thus, *e.g.* कारयामि 'I cause to make' would properly mean 'I require the making'; whether it were intended that 'any one made,' or 'any thing was made'; but if the causal character springs from a root which originally signifies 'to go,' we must observe that in Sanskṛit several verbs of motion signify also 'to make' *e. g.*, वेदयामि might properly signify, 'I make to know', मारयामि 'I kill,' 'I make to die."—*Bopp.*

Note.—This अय is changed in Prákrit either to ए or आवे, as Sk. कारयति he causes to make, Pr. कारेदि or कारावेदि; and in Maráṭhí the Sanskṛit अय is changed in correspondence with the latter Prákrit form आवे to अव; करवितो he causes to make.

Note.—Some Maráṭhí verbs assume the full form of आवे, except the final ए; बोलणें to speak, बोलावणें to call. (§ 390)

Note.—Some Maráṭhí verbs, again, simply lengthen the initial vow el of the verb, as is done in Sanskṛit before assuming the अय; चरणें to graze, चारणें to feed; Sk. कारयति, Pr. कारावेदि he causes to do.

§ 390. The Maráṭhí causal particle अव may sometimes be used, also, in the form of आव. It is only some verbs of the First Conjugation that assume आव; as फितवणें or फितावणें to seduce, from फितणें to be seduced; बोलावणें to call, from बोलणें to speak.

Note.—Some nouns and adjectives assume either अव or आव to make up verbs, and the verbs so derived are either transitive actives, or neuters :—

Noun दुःख pain; *Verb* दुखणें, दुखवणें or दुखावणें to hurt or be hurt.
Adjective आंबट sour; *Verb* आंबटवणें or आंबटावणें to make sour, or be turned sour.

When these verbs are used in the Second Conjugation, they are transitive in sense, otherwise only intransitive; माझें मन दुखवलें or दुखावलें my mind was hurt; त्वा माझें मन दुखविलें or दुखाविलें you hurt my mind. The form in आव is usually used in the Dakhan.

Note.—Some nouns, &c., assume only आव; राग anger, रागावणें to get angry; दुणा two-fold, दुणावणें to become dou bled वेडा mad, वेडावणें to become mad, or to mock.

§ 391. The causative अव is assumed by some intransitive verbs, chiefly the neuters, after they have by a change of their radical form become transitive actives; the form made up with the अव then becomes strictly causative; thus, चरणें to graze, चारणें to feed, and चारवणें to cause to feed.

§ 392. The radical changes of form which the intransitive neuter verbs undergo are of two kinds; lst, they lengthen their initial vowel, as पडणें to fall, *intransitive*; पाडणें to fell, *transitive*; and 2ndly, they both lengthen the initial vowel, as well as change a radical consonant, as फिटणें to get loose, *intransitive*; फेडणें to loose, *transitive*. We give below some Maráṭhí verbs of both these kinds :—

1. The verbs that lengthen only the initial vowel :—

Intransitive.	*Transitive.*	*Causative.*
गळणें to drop	गाळणें to strain	गाळवणें to cause to strain
चरणें to graze	चारणें to feed	चारवणें to cause to feed
टळणें to pass by	टाळणें to remove	टाळवणें to cause to remove
तरणें to float, or be saved	तारणें to save	तारवणें to cause to save
दबणें to be crushed	दाबणें to crush	दाबवणें to cause to crush
पडणें to fall	पाडणें to fell	पाडवणें to cause to fell
मरणें to die	मारणें to kill	मारवणें to cause to kill
सरणें to remove	सारणें to remove	सारवणें to cause to remove

2. The verbs that modify both the initial vowel and the radical consonant :—

Intransitive.	*Transitive.*	*Causative.*
तुटणें to break	तोडणें to break	तोडवणें to cause to break
फिटणें to get loose	फेडणें to loose	फेडवणें to cause to loose
फुटणें to break	फोडणें to break	फोडवणें to cause to break
सुटणें to get loose	सोडणें to loose	सोडवणें to cause to loose

§ 393. The grammatical construction of the causal derivatives differs according to their origin.

1. When the original verb is transitive, its subject is put in the instrumental case governed by the postposition कडून, and another subject is used with its causal form; रामा भाकर खातो Rama eats bread; Caus. मीं रामाकडून भाकर खाववितों, I cause

Rama to eat bread. In the causal sentence, रामा is put in the instrumental case governed by करून, and separated from all direct control upon the causal verb, and a foreign agent is introduced as the direct subject of the verb.

Note—In Sanskrit, also, the subject of the simple verb becomes instrumental when the verb assumes the causal form; रामो भार्यां त्यजति Rama abandons his wife; *Causal*—रामेण भार्यां त्याजयति (He) makes Rama abandon his wife.

2. When the original verb is intransitive, its subject is made the object, either accusative or dative, of its causal form, and a foreign agent is introduced as the direct subject of the causal form; as रामा निजतो Rama sleeps; Caus. तो रामाला निजवितो he causes Rama to sleep.

§ 394. In both the causal constructions *foreign direct* agency is implied, but the additional idea of *indirect* agency is necessarily implied only when the original verb is transitive, not when it is intransitive.

§ 395. The Anomalous Verbs are like the intransitives in regard to their causal construction; as रामा शिकतो Rama learns; Caus. तो रामाला शिकवितो he teaches Rama.

§ 396. The idea of indirect agency can be expressed by the causal forms of the Intransitive and Anomalous Verbs by joining an additional व to them; त्यानें रामाला रावजीकडून बसाविवलें He got Rama seated by Raoji; त्यानें रामाला हरीकडून शिकविवलें He caused Rama to be taught by Hari.

§ 397. When an additional व is joined to the causal forms of the simple transitives, they become double causatives; त्यानें त्याचें पारिपत्य त्याच्या बापाला सांगून पंतोजीकडून करविवलें he got him punished by the teacher through his father.

§ 398. The causal verbs, no matter what be their derivation, or construction, are all transitives, and can be conjugated regularly in the Second Conjugation. (Sect. 220.)

II.—*The Potential Verb.*

§ 399. The Potential Verb expresses the *ability* of the

agent to do the action denoted माझ्यानें शंभर रुपये देववत नाहींत I cannot pay one hundred rupees.

§ 400. The Potential Verb, whether transitive or intransitive, is derived from the simple verb by the insertion of व; as करणें to do; करवणें to be able to do. The व is doubled when the verbal root is monosyllabic, as देववत नाहीं I cannot give, or ends in इ, as माझ्यानें लिहववतें I can write.

Note.—The Maráṭhí Potential form in व is derived from the Sanskrit passive verb which annexes य to the root; Sk. root कृष्, Pass. कृष्यते. In Prakṛit this य is either retained, or changed to ईअ or इज्ज; Sk. पठ्यते, Pr. पढीअइ or पढिज्जइ. The य is also changed in Prakṛit to a double व, *i. e.,* व्व *vva;* as Sk. श्रूयते it is heard, Pr. सुव्वइ; Sk. हूयते it is offered, Pr. हुव्वइ. In Gujarati the य is changed to आ, and the forms made up with आ are either *Passive* or *Potential*; Pass. रामथी रावण मरायो Ravan was killed by Ram; *Potential,* तेनाथी चलाय he could walk

Note.—In the passive the object of the active voice is made the subject and put in the nominative case, and the original subject is put in the instrumental case; Act. नृपः स्तेन दंडयति the king punishes a thief; Pass. स्तेनो नृपण दंडयते a thief is punished by the king.

Note.—Besides the full passive sense indicated by the Sanskṛit passive form, it is capable of expressing the following two ideas:—

1. It has an active meaning, having the force of a reflexive verb; पुत्रं व्यजायत she bore a son.

2. It is frequently used impersonally in expressions like श्रूयताम् "let it be heard," and आस्यताम "let it be placed," instead of "hear thou," and "place thou;" so also मया ज्ञायते "it is known by me," for "I think."

Note.—Even the intransitive verb is capable of being used in Sanskrit in the passive construction when it takes the form of an impersonal verb. It agrees with "it" understood, and is put in the singular number though the agent may be dual or plural; मया स्थीयत it is staid by me, *i. e.* I stay here.

Note.—All these different peculiarities of the Sanskṛit Passive exist in the Maráṭhí Potential verb which may be either transitive or intransitive. It is *conjugated impersonally* in the Bháve Prayoga;

and its sense of possibility or potentiality (*i.e.*, *latent* activity) is the result of the reflexive character of its Sanskrit original.

§ 401. Compound Potential Verbs have been considered in the chapter on the Compound Verbs (§ 302).

II.—Secondary Derivatives.

§ 402. The Secondary Derivatives are formed by the employment of Prefixes (उपसर्ग) and Suffixes (प्रत्यय).

Prefixes.

§ 403. The Maráṭhí Prefixes are chiefly derived from two languages, the Sanskṛit and Urdu (Arabic and Persian), and are usually put before words of cognate origin. Sometimes, however, they are used with other words.

I.—*Sanskṛit Prefixes.*

§ 404. अ, अन् (Gr. *a*, Anglo-Saxon *un*) not; अपार boundless; M. अबोला reserve ; M. अचूक infallible. When a word begins with a vowel, the अन् is used ; आयास weariness, अनायास ease ; एक one, अनेक many.

अति beyond, much ; अतिक्रम passing beyond, transgression ; अतिस्नेह intimacy ; M. अतिशहाणा too wise.

अधि over ; अधिदेव a superior god ; अधिकार authority.

अनु after; अनुसरण going after, imitation ; अनुज born after ; अनुनासिक nasal.

अप badly off ; अपशकुन a bad omen.

अपि upon ; अपिधान a placing upon, a covering.

अभि towards ; अभिमुख having the face towards ; अभिधान a name.

अव down ; अवतार्य a crossing down, an incarnation ; अवकृपा displeasure ; अवज्ञा disobedience.

आ near ; आकार a form ; आग्रह entreaty.

इति so ; इत्यर्थ the sum and substance : इत्यादि et cetera.

उत् up ; उत्साह ardour ; उत्कर्ष flourishing condition.

उप next, below ; उपसर्ग a prefix ; उपनेत्र spectacles ; उपकार a favour.

कु bad ; कुकर्म a bad deed ; कुविचार a bad thought.

चिर a long time ; चिरकाल for a long time ; चिरंजीवी a daughter.

दुर्, दुस् bad ; दुर्गुण a bad quality ; दुराचार evil practices.

न not ; नास्तिक an atheist.

नाना various ; नानाविध various.

नि into, downwards ; निर्वाह conducting ; नि:पतन fallen down; निमग्न absorbed in.

नि:, निर्, निस् without ; निर्दोषी blameless ; निराकार formless.

पर another ; परजन a stranger ; M. परगांव another village.

परा back, away ; पराङ्मुख having the face turned back ; पराजय defeat.

परि round ; पर्यटन walking roundabout.

पश्चात् after ; पश्चात्ताप repentance.

पुनर् again ; पुनर्जन्म regeneration ; पुनर्विवाह a remarriage.

पृथक् separately ; पृथक्करण separation ; पृथग्विध various, manifold.

प्र before ; प्रभु the being before, a lord ; प्रधान a minister.

प्रति back, again ; प्रतिबिंब a reflected beam ; प्रत्युत्तर a reply.

बहिर् out ; बहिर्द्वार adultery.

वि apart ; वियोग disjoining, separation ; विधवा a widow.

स with ; सजीव having life ; सजाति of the same caste.

सत् good ; सत्कर्म a good action ; सज्जन a virtuous person.

सम् together with ; संगम going with, a junction ; संबंध a connection.

सह with, together with ; सहवास intercourse.

सु well ; सुरूप good-looking ; सुविचार a good thought.

स्व one's own ; स्वदेश a native country ; स्वबुद्धि one's own intellect.

स्वयं of one's self, spontaneously ; स्वयंभू self-existent ; स्वयंवर the choosing of a husband.

II.—*Urdu Prefixes.*

§ 405. कम (P.) deficient ; कमजोर weak.

गैर (A.) other ; गैरसमज a misunderstanding ; गैरखर्च expenses in an improper way.

दर, हर (H.) each ; दरमाहा every month ; दरदिवस daily.

ना (A.) not ; नापसंद or त disapproved ; नामर्द effeminate.

पेश (P.) before, a leader ; पेशवा Peshwá.

बद (P.) bad ; बदकाम a bad deed ; बदनाम *adj.* infamous.

बिन (H.) without ; बिनचूक without a mistake ; बिनहरकत without opposition.

बे (P.) without ; बेइलाज without remedy ; बेडौल shapeless, clumsy.

सर (H.) head ; सरसुभेदार the head Subhédár.

Suffixes.

§ 406. The suffixes used in Maráṭhí are more numerous than the prefixes, and are derived from various languages. They are divided into three classes, according to their origin—Sanskṛit, Maráṭhí and Urdu.

I.—*Sanskrit Suffixes.*

Abstract Nouns.

§ 407. Sanskṛit words assume the suffixes ता, त्व, and य to make up abstract nouns, and these particles are affixed to nouns as well as adjectives. The abstract nouns formed with ता are feminine, and those ending in त्व and य are neuter. When a word is modified by य, its initial vowel is displaced by a वृद्धि vowel or proper diphthong (§ 18).

मित्र (*sub.*) a friend ; मित्रता or त्व, or मैत्र्य friendship.

गुरु (*adj.*) heavy ; गुरुता or त्व, or गौरव heaviness.

दृढ (*adj.*) hard ; दृढता, दृढत्व, or दार्ढ्य hardness.

ब्राह्मण (*sub.*) a Bráhman ; ब्राह्मणता or त्व, or ब्राह्मण्य Bráhmaṇism.

Note.—The abstract nouns, derived in the above manner, are used in Maráṭhí poetry to denote an idea of plurality or multitude ; as ग्राम a town, ग्रामता a multitude of towns ; केदार a field, कैदार्य a number of fields ; thus, for instance, in the following line जनता means a multitude of people :—

प्रभुनें करुणा करुनि, प्रणता, जनता सदैव रक्षावी.—*Moropant.*

Adjectives.

§ 408. By affixing अ, इ, य, आयन, इय, adjectives are derived from nouns, to denote *pertaining* to. When affixing these particles, the following radical changes take place in the noun :—

1. The final उ, ऊ or ओ is changed to अव्.

2. The final अ, आ, इ or ई is dropped.

3. The initial double letter is dissolved, and the first consonant, if originally united with य, assumes ऐ, and if united with व, assumes औ.

4. The initial letter, if not a conjunct containing य or व, is displaced by its corresponding वृद्धि vowel.

(अ) भृगु a Rishi+अ=भार्गव a descendant of भृगु; यदु Yadu, यादव: वसिष्ठ Vasishṭha, वासिष्ठ the son of Vasishṭha ; सुमित्रा the wife of Daśaratha, सौमित्र the son of Sumitrá (Lakshman).

(इ) दशरथ king Daśaratha, दाशरथि pertaining toDaśaratha, *i.e.*, his son; कृष्ण the god Kṛishṇa, कार्ष्णि pertaining to Kṛishṇa.

(य) गर्ग the Rishi Garga+य=गार्ग्य the son of Garga ; दिति the name of a giant woman, दैत्य the offspring of Diti ; ग्राम a village, ग्राम्य belonging to a village, तालु the palate, तालव्य palatal.

(आयन) कत a Rishi, कात्य + आयन = कात्यायन the son of Kata.

(ईय) भ्रातृ a brother+ईय=भ्रात्रीय the son of a brother ; पर्वत a mountain, पर्वतीय mountainous.

(एय) गंगा the river Ganges+एय=गांगेय the son of Ganges ; विधवा a widow, वैधवेय son of a widow.

(इक) मास a month, मासिक monthly ; लोक the world, लौकिक worldly ; नौ a ship, नाविक naval.

Note.—Some words do not lengthen the initial vowel when modified by the above suffixes; पर्वत a mountain, पर्वतीय pertaining to a mountain ; त्वत् thee, त्वदीय relating to "thee"; अंत an end, अंत्य pertaining to an end; दंत a tooth, दंत्य dental.

§ 409. By joining the affixes मत् (मान), ईय, इन, लु, मय, इत, the sense of "full of or abounding" is obtained :—

इत ; लज्जा shame, लज्जित ashamed ; दुःख sorrow, दुःखित sorrowful.

इन ; मल dirt, मलिन dirty ; फल fruit, फलिन having fruit.

ईय ; वेत्र a reed or cane, वेत्रकीय abounding in reeds ; स्व self, स्व कीय one's own.

मत् (मान्) ; श्री wealth, श्रीमान् wealthy ; मत् or मान् is changed to वत् or वान् in certain nouns; as ज्ञान knowledge, ज्ञानवान् learned.

मय ; काष्ठ wood, काष्ठमय full of wood or wooden ; मांस flesh, मांसमय fleshy.

लु ; कृपा grace, कृपालु gracious ; श्रद्धा faith, श्रद्धालु having faith.

Miscellaneous Words.

§ 410. The following Sanskrit words are often employed in Maráṭhí as suffixes to form new words, such as nouns, adjectives, and participles. Strictly speaking they make up compounds. Some of these words are placed before as well as after nouns to make up new words :—

अंकित marked, restrained ; आज्ञा + अंकित = आज्ञांकित marked or lined by command, and hence subject to direction ; स्त्री a woman + अंकित = स्त्र्यंकित ruled by a wife ; क्रोधांकित, ज्ञानांकित शास्त्रांकित, धर्मांकित, &c.

अतीत past ; escaped from ; कामातीत (काम lust + अतीत freed) freed from lust ; जरातीत exempt from decay ; देहातीत disembodied ; दृश्यातीत disappeared ; वयातीत aged.

अधीन subject to, dependent upon ; स्व self + अधीन = स्वाधीन independent ; पर another + अधीन = पराधीन dependent ; लोभाधीन given to avarice, पापाधीन given to sin.

अन्वित connected with, possessed or possessing ; शर्करा sugar + अन्वित = शर्करान्वित mixed with sugar; क्रोधान्वित filled with anger ; अकर्मान्वित connected with wickedness ; दयान्वित full of kindness ; विवेकान्वित discreet.

अभिमुख having the face towards, favourable to; सूर्य the sun + अभिमुख = सूर्याभिमुख facing the sun; पूर्वाभिमुख facing the east ; अध्ययनाभिमुख favourable to study.

अर्थी that desires or seeks ; विद्या + अर्थी = विद्यार्थी a student; धनार्थी one whose aim is to get money; पुत्रार्थी wishing to have children ; मोक्षार्थी desiring to have final and eternal happiness.

अर्ह fit ; पूजन worship + अर्ह = पूजनार्ह worthy of worship or respect ; भक्षणार्ह fit to be eaten ; अध्ययनार्ह worthy of study.

आक्रांत seized by, overcome by ; चिंता anxiety + आक्रांत = चिंताक्रांत overcome by care, anxious ; क्षुधाक्रांत tormented by hunger; भयाक्रांत oppressed by fear.

आकीर्ण filled with, covered with ; जल water + आकीर्ण = जलाकीर्ण filled with water ; सैन्याकीर्ण covered or surrounded by an army.

आकुल filled with, overcome by; क्रोधाकुल inflamed with anger.

चिंताकुल distressed by anxiety; निद्राकुल overpowered by sleep ; हर्षाकुल transported with joy.

आढ्य wealthy ; धन riches + आढ्य = धनाढ्य rich in treasures, immensely rich ; विद्याढ्य rich in learning; बलाढ्य strong ; रसाढ्य, रोगाढ्य, मदाढ्य, &c.

आनुकूल्य propitiousness, favourableness ; द्रव्य wealth + आनुकूल्य द्रव्यानुकूल्य affluence, or easiness of circumstances : लोकानुकूल्य favour of the people, popularity.

आतुर excited, distressed ; तृष्णातुर distressed by thirst; लोभातुर carried away by covetousness.

आपन्न distressed, afflicted ; खेद sorrow + आपन्न = खेदापन्न afflicted with sorrow ; संशयापन्न distressed or agitated with doubt.

आरूढ mounted or ascended upon ; अनुभवारूढ experienced ; इंद्रियारूढ come under the cognizance of the senses, perceived; ज्ञानारूढ, योगारूढ &c.

आवह that brings, confers, occasions ; सुख + आवह = सुखावह producing pleasure ; संकटावह producing trouble ; दोषावह, शोकावह, &c.

उच्छेद utter rooting out or utter demolition ; धर्मोच्छेद the utter demolition of religion ; कुलोच्छेद, वनोच्छेद &c.

उत्तर after ; लोकोत्तर beyond what is common, transcendent.

उत्थ rising; अज्ञानोत्थ sprung from ignorance; ज्वरोत्थ arisen from fever.

उन्मुख having the face set towards; about to go or do; मरणोन्मुख about to die; गमनोन्मुख about to go.

कर doer; प्रकाशकर light producing; सुखकर, आनंदकर.

कामुक desirous; विद्याकामुक seeking knowledge; धनकामुक seeking riches; मोक्षकामुक seeking eternal happiness.

गत gone, past; गतधन lost riches; गतकाळ the past time; गतबुद्धि, गताभिमान; हस्तगत, अंतर्गत, &c.

ग्रस्त devoured, seized; कामग्रस्त inflamed with lust; शापग्रस्त accursed; दारिद्र्यग्रस्त, चिंताग्रस्त, &c.

घात ruining; आत्मघात self-destruction; प्राणघात destroying life, &c.

घ्न that kills or destroys; पापघ्न sin destroyer; रोगघ्न an antidote; कृतघ्न ungrateful.

चिंतक that thinks or is concerned about; शुभचिंतक a well-wisher; अनिष्टचिंतक an ill-wisher.

च्युत fallen; अधिकारच्युत fallen from authority; पदच्युत dethroned.

जित conquered or overcome; जितकाम one in whom lust is subdued; जितक्रोध one in whom anger is subdued; जितमनस्क one who possesses self-command; जितद्रव्य who has acquired treasure. When जित comes last, it has the opposite signification; कामजित one subdued by lust; क्रोधजित; स्त्रीजित vanquished by a woman.

दर्शी that sees; गुणदर्शी, सूक्ष्मदर्शी, तत्त्वदर्शी, दीर्घदर्शी, आत्मदर्शी.

नाशक that destroys; पित्तनाशक that destroys bile; वायुनाशक.

निष्ठ fixed in; मनोनिष्ठ fixed in mind, देहनिष्ठ &c.

पर strange, other; परधन another's treasure; परदेश. Also, appertaining to; ज्ञानपर appertaining to knowledge; लोकनिंदापर भाषण करूं नये we should not engage in scandalous conversation.

परायण following after, devoted to, appertaining to; ईश्वरपरायण; ह्या मनोवृत्ति ईश्वरपरायण झाल्या these feelings were devoted to God; ज्ञानपरायण.

भूत become; पात्रभूत becoming or constituting a vessel; त्रासभूत becoming a trouble; कारणभूत becoming a reason or occasion. Also, "become affected by," with the principal word modified by ई: कारणीभूत become, caused or occasioned; प्रमाणीभूत become, proved or evidenced.

रूप like or resembling; पितृरूप like a father. Also, of the very form and essence, composed of; पिशाचरूप of the form of a devil, fiendish; नररूप like a man, human.

शून्य void, destitute of; द्रव्यशून्य destitute of wealth; ज्ञानशून्य &c.

शूर bold; eminent for some qualities or works; दानशूर eminently liberal; परोपकारशूर; रणशूर; भोजनशूर; गानशूर &c.

स्थ that stands or rests; गृहस्थ one who lives comfortably in a house, hence a gentleman; मार्गस्थ a traveller; पात्रस्थ standing in a vessel.

हत struck, destroyed; हतचैतन्य deprived of life; हतज्ञान, हतशक्ति, हतश्री &c.

हर, हारक, हारी that seizes, carries off; धनहर a thief; सुखहर, पित्तहर, दुःखहर.

MARÁṬHÍ SUFFIXES.

I.—*Nouns.*

1. *Abstract Nouns.*

§ 411. Maráṭhí Abstract Nouns are derived from adjectives by affixing पण and पणा; वाईट bad, वाईटपण or-पणा badness. Those abstract nouns which end in पण are neuter, and those in पणा are masculine.

When the suffixes पण and पणा are joined to adjectives ending in आ, the आ is changed to ए; चांगला good, चांगलेपण or चांगलेपणा goodness; भला honest, भलेपण or भलेपणा honesty. चांगला is changed, also, to चांगुल in the abstract noun; चांगुलपण or -पणा.

The suffixes पण and पणा can be applied indiscriminately to every Maráṭhí adjective, and, optionally, even to Sanskṛit adjectives; as निर्दय (S.) cruel, निर्दयता, or निर्दयपण or -पणा cruelty.

Note.—The abstract noun in पण, and not in पणा, is usually declined; शहाणपण wisdom, शहाणपणाला to wisdom.

2. Nouns of Agency.

आडी, आड्या ; वाट a way, वाटाडी or वाटाड्या a guide.

आरी ; पूजा worship, पुजारी a worshipper.

ऊ ; मारणें to beat, मारू a striker ; पोटभरू.

कर, करी ; गांव a village, गांवकर or करी a villager ; खेळकर a player.

वान, वाला (S. पाल) ; गाडी a carriage, गाडीवान a coachman ; भाजीवाला a seller of vegetables.

Nouns denoting office, condition, &c.

की ; पाटील the head of a village, पाटीलकी the office of a patel.

डी ; पलंग a bedstead, पलंगडी a small bedstead.

ऊं ; बकरी a she-goat, बकरूं a kid ; वाघ a tiger, वाघरूं a tiger in contempt.

कुली ; चिंधी a rag ; चिंधकुली, चिंधुकली a small rag ; चांद (S. चंद्र) the moon, चांदकुली, चांदुकली a small cake ; भात rice, भातुकली, &c.

5. Miscellaneous Nouns.

अ ; चढणें to ascend, चढण an ascent ; दळण, पाळण, &c.

आ ; भरणें to fill, भरणा store.

अवा ; बोलणें to speak, बोलवा a report.

आई ; चढणें to attack, चढाई attacking ; लढणें to fight, लढाई a fight.

आव ; पाडणें to throw down, पाडाव overthrow ; ठरविणें, ठराव a resolution.

आवळ ; धुणें to wash, धुणावळ price for washing ; बांधणावळ.

ई ; थुंकणें to spit, थुंकी spittle ; उडी jumping ; चाळणी sieve.

ऊ ; खाणें to eat, खाऊ an eatable ; झाडणें to sweep, झाडू a broom.

ऊं ; हसणें to laugh, हसूं laughing.

ती ; वसणें to inhabit, वसती habitation.

वण ; वाढणें to be expended, वाढवण a broom.

री ; मुतणें to make water, मुतरी urinary.

II.—*Adjectives*.

1. *Denoting "of or pertaining to."*

§ 412. ई ; कोंकण Konkan, कोंकणी belonging to Konkan.

ईल ; आंत in, आंतील interior ; वर up, वरील upper.

च्या ; घर a house, घरच्या household.

ला ; तेथें there, तेथला belonging to that place.

वट ; रान a desert, रानवट belonging to a desert.

Note.—The suffix च्या, which is the genitive ending, does not inflect the noun when it is used as an adjective suffix. The ला is the corruption of ईल , and changes the final vowel, if it be any other than अ, to अ; एथें here, एथला of this place.

2. *Denoting made or acted upon.*

ईव ; बांधणें to build, बांधीव built.

पट, वट ; धुणें to wash, धुपट, धुवट washed.

3. *Denoting "full of or abounding."*

आडू ; खेळ a play, खेळाडू frolicsome.

आळू ; झोंप sleep, झोंपाळू sleepy.

कट ; मळ filth, मळकट filthy.

कर ; खोडी mischief, खोडकर mischievous.

ईट ; राग anger, रागीट angry.

ई ; लोभ covetousness, लोभी covetous.

4. *Denoting Likeness or Manner.*

कट ; पोर a child, पोरकट childish.

चट ; पाणी water, पाणचट waterish.

या ; बायको a woman, बायक्या womanish.

5. *Denoting Diminution.*

ट ; उंच high, उंचट highish.

सर ; काळा black, काळसर blackish.

सा ; लहान little, लहानसा littlish.

6. *Denoting Doing.*

का ; मार a beating, मारका given to beating.

रा ; खाजणें to itch, खाजरा itch-producing.

खाऊ ; लांच a bribe, लांचखाऊ a bribe-receiver ; मार a beating, मारखाऊ that constantly receives a beating.

भरू ; पोट the belly, पोटभरू that stuffs his belly.

III.—*Verbs.*

§ 413. A few verbs are derived in Maráṭhi from nouns and adjectives in the following manner :—

1. A great many nouns and adjectives are converted into verbs by affixing the gerundial termination णें : as दुःख pain, दुखणें to pain ; मळकट dirty, मळकटणें to get dirty.

If the noun or the adjective ends in आ, the आ is dropped before affixing णें : सपाटा, a flap, सपाटणें to despatch ; नागवा naked, नागवणें to strip ; इच्छा a desire, इच्छणें to desire.

2. Some verbs are derived from nouns and adjectives by adding आळणें : माणूस a man, माणसाळणें to become human ; वेडा mad, वेडाळणें to become mad ; पोट a belly, पोटाळणें to clasp to the belly.

Note.—Very valuable verbs are derived by adding अव or आव (§ 390).

III.—Hindustani Suffixes.

I. *Abstract Nouns.*

§ 414. आई ; भला honest, भलाई honesty ; धीट bold, धीटाई boldness.

आ, आई, ई ; गरम warm, गरमा or गरमाई or गरमी warmth.

आस ; मिठ्ठे sweet, मिठास sweetness.

ती ; कम little, कमती deficiency.

ई P. ; नेक true, good, नेकी goodness ; खुब good, खुबी goodness ; दोस्त a friend, दोस्ती friendship.

गी ; बंदा a slave, बंदगी service ; रवाना a pass, रवानगी sending off.

2. *Nouns of Agency.*

खोर P. ; हराम unjust, हरामखोर a wicked doer.

गर P. ; जीन a saddle, जिनगर a saddler.

गार P.; सिकल polishing of weapons, सिकलगार a polisher of weapons; गुन्हा an offence, गुन्हेगार an offender.

दार P.; सुभा a province, सुभेदार the head of a province.

बंद; नाल a horse-shoe, नालबंद farrier.

वान P.; बाग a garden, बागवान a gardener; मेहर a favour, मेहरबान gracious.

वार; उमेद hope, उमेदवार an expectant.

3. *Nouns denoting office, condition, &c.*

ई; सराफ a banker, सराफी money-changing.

गिरी; गुलाम a slave, गुलामगिरी slavery.

दाई; सोदा a blackguard, सोदेदाई blackguardism.

4. *Nouns denoting place or receptacle.*

जार P.; गुल a flower, गुलजार a garden.

दान or दानी; कलम a pen, कलमदानी a box for holding a pen; गुलाब a rose, गुलाबदानी a vessel for holding rose-water.

स्तान; कबर a grave, कबरस्तान a grave-yard.

आबाद P.; हैदर Hyder, हैदराबाद the city of Hyder, or of liars.

खाना; कार work, कारखाना a factory.

II.—Adjectives.

Denoting full of or abounding.

आ H.; भुक hunger, भुका hungry.

ई; बाजार a bazaar, बाजारी pertaining to a bazaar.

दार P.; इमान faith, इमानदार faithful.

मंद; अक्कल sense, अक्कलमंद sensible.

वर, आवर; जोर strength, जोरावर strong.

III.—Reduplicatives.

§ 415. The Reduplicatives are made up by doubling the original word: धोंडा a stone, duplicated form, धोंडा गिंडा stones and all other such things; भाकरी भिकरी bread, &c.

These words are formed for the purpose of intensifying the *meaning*, or making the word *more imitative*. They may be regarded as a species of the Copulative Compounds.

§ 416. The Reduplicatives are formed in various way, and we shall specify below a few of them :—

§ 417. 1 When persons or things are spoken of *comprehensively*—as comprising *many individuals* of a class—the reduplicatives are formed in the following ways :—

(1) The original word may be followed by a word of *similar sound*, but *conveying no distinct sense* ; as धोंडागिंडा, being the reduplicative form of धोंडा a stone, and conveying the sense of stones and *everything else* ; शेजारिपाजारी, खडेउडे, सोयराधायरा ओळखपाळख, भिकारीटाकारी, घरबिर, &c. Sometimes the original word comes last; अडोशीपडोशी neighbours, &c. The word पडोशी is a Hindustani word for a neighbour. English equivalents are—hurly-burly, helter-skelter, hurry-skurry, higgledy-piggledy, hugger-mugger, namby-pamby, topsy-turvy, wish-wash, tittle-tattle, chit-chat, &c.

(2) Or, the original word may be followed by a word of *similar sense*, or of both *similar sense* and *sound*.—

(*a*) Of similar general *sense* only ; आणभाष oath and language; भातभाजी rice and vegetables ; शाकभाजी, काजळकुंकूं, लांकूडफाटा, घासकाडी, मीठभाकर, हेलपाटी, शेतभात, पोरबाळ, कुणबीमाळी, &c.

(*b*) Of both similar general sense and sound ; लंगडालुळा lame and halt ; शेटसावकार bankers and traders ; अंधळापांगळा; सगासोयरा, झाडझुडूप, वईवाडा, तेलीतंबोली, श्रेणीफणी, &c. English equivalents are " wear and tear " ; " rattle and clatter " ; " racket and riot "; " rags and tatters "; " follies and foibles"; "fun and frolic" ; " toil and trouble" ; "sorrow and suffering"; " thorns and thistles " ; " pride and passion "; &c.

§ 418. Of these two general classes of the reduplicatives, those of the first class are more comprehensive than those of the second; कोणी कुणबीमाळी आले नाहींत none of the common people of the agricultural class have come ; but कोणी कुणबीबिणबी आले नाहींत means that absolutely none—neither cultivators nor *any other* people—have come.

§ 419. 2. Sometimes the noun is simply repeated, when it conveys the following senses :—

(*a*) It may denote *individuals of a group* or *class separately;* घरघर; house and house, गांवगांव, माणूसमाणूस, बायकोबायको झाडझाड, &c. मी घरघर फिरलों पण मला कोणी कांहीं दिलें नाहीं I visited every house separately, but nobody gave me anything ; माणूसमाणूस प्रकृतीनें भिन्न असतें every man is by nature different ; रामानें झाडझाड हुडकलें Rama searched every tree separately ; यांतून आंबे आंबे काढा take out every mango separately from this.

(*b*) It may separate a group of indviduals from other individuals ; तेथें बायकाबायका बसल्या होत्या the women were sitting there by themselves; भाऊभाऊ वेगळे झाले आहेत only the brothers have separated; ब्राह्मणब्राह्मण जमले होते only the Brahmans had met, not the other castes. Adjectives may be similarly employed ; जे लोक जमले आहेत त्यांत गोरा गोरा तितका इंग्रज आणि काळाकाळा तितका हबशी of the people that are assembled all those that are white are English, and those that are black are Abyssinians.

(*c*) Sometimes the reduplicative has only an *intensive* force ; मग तिला घामघाम सुटला then she perspired fearfully ; त्यानें त्याचे हालहाल केले he reduced him to extreme distress ; त्या घोड्याचा फेणफेण काढिला he tired the horse so much that it frothed terribly; त्याचे तुकडेतुकडे केले he cut him to pieces; लुगड्याच्या चिंध्याचिंध्या केल्या the dress was torn to shreds.

(*d*) It expresses measure or *standard distributively ;* त्यानें पायलीपायली तांदूळ वाटले he distributed the rice, giving a *paili* to each ; तो बोटबोट कापड चोरितो he steals cloth each time of the measure of a finger's breadth.

(*e*) The reduplicative may be *extended* indefinitely to convey an *additional* intensity of meaning; मीं घर घर घर; फिरलों ; तो देश देश देश भटकला.

राम राम राम राम व्यर्थ काय शापिलें.

In this way any other parts of speech may be reduplicated.

"वद वद वद वद रसने सांब सांब सांब सांब"

§ 420. 3. Sometimes a *letter is inserted* in the reduplicative.

(*a*) The privative vowel अ may be inserted to express a *difference* or an alternative ; पात्रापात्र worthy and unworthy ;

धर्माधर्म right and wrong ; भक्ष्याभक्ष्य fit to eat and otherwise ; योग्यायोग्य असे सर्वच आले होते all—both worthy and unworthy—had come. Sometimes the privative particle न is inserted ; अस्तिनास्ति it is or it is not ; भवतिनभवति it is or it is not—argument ; कायहो काल तुमची त्यांची भवतिनभवति चालली होती, मग पुढें काय ठरलें Well, you had an argument with him yesterday and what was decided at last ? These are purely Sanskrit formations. Marathi equivalents are होयना yes or no ; देणें घेणें, येणें जाणें, &c.

(*b*) आ is inserted to express the sense of promiscuous action carried on vigorously ; खेटराखेटर a vigorous striking with slippers among individuals united in a mass without order ; सांधासांध the joining of many things or by many persons ; बांधाबांध active and hurried packing up of many things or by many persons. The final vowel of the reduplicative may be displaced by ई ; गोळागोळी, लाथालाथी, मारामारी.

(*c*) ओं may be inserted to express the sense of *universality* ; गांवोगांव हिंडला he went to every town and village ; रस्तों ; रस्तीं takes the locative termination ईं.

(*d*) च may be inserted to denote the sense of *abundance*. जेथें तेथें घरच्घर दृष्टीस पडतें you see any amount of houses everywhere ; घे आतां पैकाच पैका take now any amount of money.

(*e*) The genitive termination चा may be introduced to express the idea of *abundance* or *completion* ; गांवचेगांव पाहावयास आलें होतें the whole village had come to see it ; त्याचें घरचेंघर बसलें his whole house was ruined ; माशांचे थव्यांचेथवे दृष्टीस पडतात shoals of fishes are to be seen ; त्या लढाईंत फौजांच्याफौजा गर्क झाल्या many armies perished in that war.

(*f*) The letter न may be inserted to express the sense of *completion* ; त्याचा पैसानपैसा चुकविला I paid every piece of his ; घरनघर ; दमडीनदमडी ; वर्षनवर्ष ; पायरीनपायरी.

(*g*) कीं is introduced in the reduplicative, the second member being a word of a similar sound to express the idea of daring, or firm resolution ; डोंचकें कीं बोचकें the head or the bundle, having the force of the English equivalent "by hook or by crook."

(h) आड is introduced to express the sense of "every other"; साल आड साल every other year; दिवस आड दिवस every other day; घर आड घर every other house; त्या कुंपणांत झाड आड झाड बाभळी आहेत every other tree in the hedge is a Babhool tree.

(i) आंत is inserted to express the following ideas:—

1. *Superior excellence*: शहरांत शहर मुंबई of all the cities Bombay is the best.

2. *Similarity*: तो पोरांत पोर आणि थोरांत थोर he is like a child among children, and an adult among adults.

3. *In addition to*; besides—indicating multiplication or succession in a series: कामांत काम सांगूं नका do not order work *on* work; दुःखांत दुःख sorrow on sorrow; खर्चांत खर्च expense on expense.

(j) The first member is put in the dative case to express *similarity*, or *equality*; माझ्या घोड्यास घोडा मिळेल तेव्हां मीं जोडीं जोडीन when I find a horse exactly like mine, I shall harness a pair; रुपयास रुपया घेईन I will take a rupee for a rupee.

(k) The demonstrative तो is inserted for *emphasizing* the *inherent nature* or *character* of the person or thing denoted by the first member; बाप तो बाप, त्याची सर कोणाला येईल who can equal one who is a real father? पुणें तें पुणें; रजपुत ते रजपुत.

§ 421. Imitative particles are reduplicated, and nouns are formed, as कट, making कटकट bother.

Reduplicative Adjectives.

§ 422. Adjectival reduplicatives are produced in the following ways:—

§ 423. I. The Adjective is *simply repeated*, or a word of *similar import* is joined to it; लाललाल or तांबडा लाल very red, *lit.* red red; त्याचा अंत जवळजवळ आला आहे his end is quite near; पांढरासफेत very white; गोडगोड दूध very sweet milk. These formations—

(1) *intensify* the sense of the original adjective.

(2) They may express *gradual progression*; तुम्ही थोडेंथोडें वाचा read a little at a time; सकाळची सावली आंखूडआंखूड होते the morning shadow becomes gradually shorter.

(3) They may express the sense of the adjective *distributively*: सर्वांना एकएक लाडू द्या give a cake to each of them.

(4) They may express the sense of *plurality* with plural nouns; पुष्कळ मुख्य मुख्य लोक आले होते many great men had come; त्या गांवांत मोठमोठीं or मोठीं मोठीं घरें आहेत there are large houses in that town; तिला चांगल्याचांगल्या भेटी आल्या she had very nice presents.

(5) They may have a distributive force, denoting individuals severally of a number; मोठमोठीं or मोठींमोठीं or मोठालीं झाडें तेवढीं तोडा, लहानालीं मात्र ठेवा cut down every large tree, but keep every small one; मोठंमोठे पेरू एकीकडे ठेवा keep every large guava separate.

These formations are employed to qualify plural nouns.

§ 424. II. A word *corresponding in sound* to the adjective is added, but the adjunct by itself conveys no distinct sense whatsoever; साधासुधा plain, simple; वाकडातिकडा crooked; आंबटचिंबट sour.

(*a*) A word of similar general *sense* and *sound* may be added; उघडाबोडका destitute; उघडानागडा wholly unclothed.

(*b*) Or a noun intensifying the sense of the adjective is joined; गोडसाखर sweet as sugar—very sweet; आंबटचिंच sour as tamarind—very sour; उघडाबंब uncovered like a pump—wholly uncovered; तिखटतिखट आग hot as fire—very hot.

The above formations express the idea of *intensity*.

§ 425. III. Adjectives of an *opposite*, or *cognate signification* are joined together to express the sense of *variety* or *comprehensiveness*; लहानमोठे पांच हजार होते there were, including the young and old, five thousand persons present; हिरवींपिवळीं, लालगुलाबी अशीं फुलें आणा being green and yellow, red and pink flowers.

Verbs.

§ 426. The Verbal Reduplicatives are made up in the following ways:—

(1) Words of a *similar sense* aro joined to make up verbal reduplicatives; आपटणेंधोपटणें, पारखणेंसुलाखणें, थकणेंभागणें. These are *intensives*—denoting the completeness and perfection of the action expressed by the original verb.

(2) Words of an *opposite signification* are joined ; खाणेंपिणें; येणें-जाणें ; बसणेंउठणें, etc. These words express comprehensiveness.

(3) Sometimes the verb is simply doubled with बी substituted for the initial syllable of the second member ; उठणेंबिठणें, बोलणेंबिलणें, वाचणेंबिचणें etc. These express the sense of comprehensiveness.

(4) Sometimes सवरणें or संवरणें may be joined to the verb ; करणेंसवरणें; जाणेंसवरणें ; लिहिणेंसवरणें, पळणेंसवरणें etc.—सवरणें intensifies the signification of the verb to which it is conjoined, or simply serves as an expletive without any special meaning.

Adverbial Reduplicatives.

§ 427. The Adverb may be simply doubled to intensify its sense ; नाडी मंदमंद चालते the pulse beats very slowly ; कित्येक प्राणी हळूहळू चालतात, कित्येक लवकर लवकर some creatures move very slowly and some very fast ; तो जवळजवळ आला he came quite close ; तो आतांआतां मजकडेस येऊं लागला आहे he has quite recently commenced to come to me.

§ 428. Sometimes some particle is inserted between the two members of the reduplicative : मधोमध quite in the middle ; खालोखाल rather below or under ; मागोमाग immediately after or behind ; तोंडोतोंड up to the mouth or brim—inserting ओ; समरासमोर or समोरासमोर face to face, front to front—inserting आ.

§ 429. The imitative particles form many adverbial reduplicatives ; कटकट denoting sharp sound ; फरफर denoting the sound of tearing or brushing along the ground ; सळसळ denoting the sound emitted by boiling liquids.

§ 430. When the nasalised आ is affixed to the reduplicative, its sense is intensified ; फरफरां, कडकडां, भरभरां etc.

§ 431. Sometimes both the numbers of the reduplicative are modified by आं or आ ; भरांभरां, भडाभडां, झरांझरां.

CHAPTER XXII.

THE PRINCIPLES OF MARATHI DERIVATION—*continued.*

IV.—Compounds.

§ 432—§ 451.

§ 432. A compound is a union of two distinct words, expressing one idea: as रण battle + भूमि a field = रणभूमि a battle-field.

§ 433. The elements which enter into composition may, or may not, retain a place in the compound. Sometimes two or more words may express one simple notion, without *formally* entering into composition. Hence there are three general classes of compounds, viz., the *Obvious*, the *Obscure*, and the *Apparent*:—

1. *Obvious Compounds*: पोळपाट a table for rolling out cakes =पोळी a cake+पाट a table.

2. *Obscure Compounds*: करपटाण the smell of singed food= करपट singed (food)+घाण smell; आंघोळ bathing=अंग body+ घोळणें to wash; देव्हारा a shrine=देव god+घर house.

3. *Apparent Compounds*: हाताचा कुशळ an expert; प्रीति करणें to love.

§ 434. None but words of cognate origin should be combined, though there are not a few compounds in Maráṭhí of long established usage, which do not follow this rule:—

वस्त्रगाळ strained through a cloth=वस्त्र S.+गाळ M.
गायमुख a cow's mouth=गाय M.+मुख S.
खरेदीपत्र a bond=खरेदी Pers.+पत्र S.
ज्यडजकचेरी a judge's office=ज्यडज Eng.+कचेरी H.

Note.—It may not be superfluous to add that valuable as composition is in expressing our thoughts with brevity and vigour, it is impossible to condemn adequately the bad taste which would impose long compounds, consisting of more than two words, upon a popular dialect, derived as it is from Sanskrit and Prakrit by a rigid process of elision. Even Sanskṛit, though it is capable of stringing together hundreds of syllables into one monstrous word, does not quietly submit to such pedantic conceit.

§ 435. The Maráṭhí compounds are either of purely Sanskṛit, or purely Maráṭhi origin. In compounds of Sanskṛit origin, two or more words may be combined, but in those derived from Maráṭhí, only two words are united :—

Sk. ब्रह्मविष्णुमहेश the Hindu Triad = ब्रह्मा + विष्णु + महेश विद्यागृह a school.

M. आईबाप father and mother ; घरधनी a householder.

§ 436. The compounds may be SUBSTANTIVES, ADJECTIVES, or ADVERBS.

1. THE SUBSTANTIVE COMPOUNDS.

§ 437. In the substantive compound, (1) two words may be put together, the former describing or determining the sense of the latter; or (2) two words may be put together which are usually united by the conjunction "and". These two classes of substantive compounds are designated *Determinative* and *Copulative* respectively :—

1. *The Determinative Compound* : गजमोजणी measuring by rule=गजानें मोजणी.

2. *The Copulative Compound* : शेलापागोटें shawl and turban= शेला आणि पागोटें.

(1) *The Determinative Compounds.*

§ 438. The qualifying or determining word in these compounds may be a *noun*, or an *adjective.*

1. When the determining word is a noun, it may indicate a *case-relation* in reference to the noun which it precedes, or it may be used *appositionally.*

2. The determining adjective may be either an adjective of *quality*, or of *number*.

Hence the determinative compounds are divided by the Sanskṛit grammarians into three classes, *viz.*, the *Tatpurush* (तत्पुरुष his man), *Karmadháraya* (कर्मधारय), and *Dvigu* (द्विगु two oxen).

§ 439. In the *Tatpurush* Compound, the first word expresses a case-relation; as चोरभय lit. thief-fear=चोरापासून भय fear arising from thieves; the case-relation existing between the two members of this compound is *ablative*. In the *Karmadhâraya*, the first word may be an adjective, or a substantive used adjectively; काळमांजर a pole-cat=काळें black+मांजर a cat; विद्याधन knowledge which is like a treasure=विद्या knowledge +धन a treasure; देवमाणूस a simple and harmless man. These compounds correspond to the English formations "blackbird," "god-man," &c. In the *Dvigu*, the first word is a numeral adjective, and the second is the noun which it qualifies; पंचपाळें a kind of a cruet consisting of five vessels=पांच five and पाळें vessel; चौपाळा a swing; पंचांग an almanac; त्रिभुवन three worlds. The English corresponding compounds are "a twelve-month," "a two-pence," "a quadruped."

§ 440. The case-relation existing between the two single words of a *Tatpurush* compound may appertain to any case, excluding the Nominative and the Vocative.

1st.—*The Accusative Tatpurush*: लांचखाऊ a bribe-receiver; ग्रंथकर्ता an author. It indicates, the *thing* which a person does.

2nd.—*The Instrumental Tatpurush*: हातचरक a mill turned by the hand; देवदत्त one given by God. It indicates the *instrument* by which a thing is done.

3rd.—*The Dative Tatpurush*: बाजारवाडा the market-house; देवयज्ञ an oblation to the gods. It indicates the *purpose* or design for which a thing is designed or done.

4th.—*The Ablative Tatpurush*: रोगदु:ख pain arising from sickness; जातिभ्रष्ट fallen from caste. It indicates the *source* from which a thing originates.

5th.—*The Genitive Tatpurush*: घरधनी a householder; विद्याभ्यास the study of the sciences. It indicates the relation of *origin* or *possession*.

6th.—*The Locative Tatpurush*: धुळाक्षरें letters in sand; पाणकोंबडा a water-fowl. It indicates the thing *in which* anything *is*, or *is done*.

Note.—In the *Tatpurush* compound the first word drops its inflection, as, for instance, in गजमोजणी=गजानें मोजणी, the instrumental नें

being dropped ; and hence it is not always easy to determine what particular case relation is implied by the first word. Thus, the word विद्यालय a school=विद्या knowledge + आलय a place, may mean a place *for* knowledge, or a place *of* knowledge, or a place obtained *by* knowledge, or a place *in* which विद्या or knowledge is communicated, &c., and it may therefore be a dative, a genitive, an instrumental or a locative *Tatpurush* compound.

Note.—The Karmadháraya may be viewed also as a *Tatpurush* ; विद्याधन may mean knowledge which is *like* a treasure, or the treasure *of* knowledge, or a treasure obtained *by* knowledge. In the last two senses, it is *Tatpurush* ; and in the first *Karmadháraya.*

Note.—In the Karmadháraya as in the Tatpurush, the first word drops its inflections ; as तांबडी red + माती earth = तांबडमाती.

Note.—In the Sanskṛit compounds introduced into Maráṭhí the first word of a *Tatpurush* or *Karmadháraya,* may come last.—*Tatpurush* : राजहंस king of the geese, instead of हंसराज ; so also नरसिंह a man like a lion, instead of सिंहनर ; पूर्वरात्र the fore part of the night ; *Karm.* राजाधम the lowest King ; भरतश्रेष्ठ the best Bharat.

(2) *The Copulative Compound.*

§ 441. The co-ordinate relation existing between two words is usually indicated by the conjunction आणि and, but when the conjunction is dropped, and the words are united, they form the copulative (or द्वंद्व) compound ; घर a house + दार a door= घरदार house and other property ; आईबाप parents.

Note.—In English the co-ordinate conjunction is *not omitted* ; " rice and curry ; " " there is *bread and butter* for the children. " In Maráṭhí sometimes a fragment of आणि " and " exists in a copulative reduplicative ; चिंधीनी चिंधी or चिंधीनचिंधी every shred of a rag.

§ 442. The reduplicative Compounds, which fall under the class of the Copulatives, are considered in detail under the Reduplicatives. (§ 415)

2. The Adjective Compound.

§ 443. When the *whole compound* is used predicatively of a subject, it is called an Adjective Compound, or बहुव्रीहि (possessing much rice) ; घोडमुख having the face of a horse ; किन्नर सर्व घोडमुख होते all the Kinnars were beings with the faces of horses.

§ 444. The *Bahuvrihi* is usually derived from a substantive compound. In fact, when a substantive compound is used adjectively or predicatively, it becomes *Bahuvrihi* ; *Karma.* कमलाक्ष eyes like a lotus ; *Bahu.* कमलाक्ष " lotus-eyed" ; ती कमलाक्ष पाहिली काय? have you seen that lotus-eyed woman ? कोंबडा द्विपाद आहे, चतुष्पद नाहीं a cock is a biped, not a quadruped ; अज्ञान ignorant ; *Tatpurush* गजानन an elephant's head ; *Bahu.* गजानन the elephant-headed.

§ 445. The *Bahuvrîhi* is usually derived in Maráṭhí from the substantive compounds, by a modification of their final vowel.

1. If the final vowel is अ, the अ is changed to ई or या in the *Bahuvrîhi* ; चतुर्मुख four faces, चतुर्मुखी four-faced ; वांकडमान्या crooked-necked = वांकडी + मान ; दुतोंडी two-tongued ; लांबनाक्या long-nosed. If the final word is of Sanskṛit origin, the अ is superseded by ई ; सुगंध fragrance, सुगंधी fragrant. Sometimes the अ may not be changed ; as घोडमुख horse-faced.

2. Sometimes the genitive termination चा is affixed to the compound ; सभाधैर्य boldness in an assembly, सभाधैर्याचा having boldness in an assembly.

3. Words of Sanskṛit derivation affix क and other particles ; पित्तमूलक causing bile ; अंडज one produced in the egg ; अंबुजसंभव produced from a lotus.

§ 446. The *Bahuvrîhi* compound *stands for the object* which it describes, and suggests it. Thus, गजानन the elephant-headed, could be used predicatively, as तो गजानन आहे he is elephant-headed, or it could stand for the person usually described or suggested by it, *i.e.*, for गणपति who is elephant-headed. Also लंबकर्ण long-eared is either an adjective, or a noun denoting an ass, the animal possessed of long ears. The English equivalents are " left-handed," " high-minded," &c.

3. The Adverbial Compound.

§ 447. In the *Avyayibháva* or Adverbial Compounds, the first word is an adverbial particle, and the second usually a substantive, the whole being used adverbially ; हरदिवस every day = हर + दिवस ; हररोज daily.

§ 448. The following elements enter into the composition of the Adverbial Compounds :—

1. *A particle and a noun :* हरदिवस daily ; यथाक्रम regularly.
2. *Two particles :* जेथें कोठें anywhere ; यथातथा so and so.
3. *A particle and an adjective :* यथायोग्य suitably.
4. *A particle and a participle :* यथायुक्त rightly.
5. *A particle and an inflected noun :* आजदिवशीं to-day; हरवेळीं every time; यथाज्ञानें according to one's knowledge.

II.—Obscure Compounds.

§ 449. There are a few compounds in Maráṭhí, both of Sanskṛit and Maráṭhí formation, which, on account of the incompleteness of some of the true words entering into their composition, cannot be easily recognized as compounds ; they appear as derivatives, and sometimes as primitives. Thus, for instance, the word पायठा a step, or the word सोनार(सोनी)a goldsmith, or गुराख्या a cowherd, looks like a derivative, and not at all like a compound, compounded of two distinct words ; but all these words are, in reality, compounds, each containing two words, the last existing in its imperfect form :—

M. उन्हाळा summer= उन्ह (S. उष्ण) hot, and काळ season.

M. हिंवाळा cold season= हिंव (S. हिम) cold, and काळ season.

M. पायठा a step= पाय a foot+ ठाय a place.

M. सोनार a goldsmith, Pr. सोण्ण+आरो, S. सुवर्ण gold+कार a maker.

M. कुंभार a potter, Pr. कुम्हारो, S. कुम्भकार.

M. चांभार a leather maker, Pr. चम्मारो, S. चर्मकार.

M. सुतार a carpenter, S. सूत्रधार.

M. कहार a palanquin bearer, S. स्कंधधार.

M. गाभार a sanctuary, Pr. गब्भारो, S. गर्भ+आगार.

M. धुपेल oil of resin =धूप resin+ तेल oil.

M. आंबसाण a sour smell=आंबट sour+घाण smell.

M. केकताड a kind of palm = केकत+ताड palm.

M. वर्साळा an extra payment = वरती above + वळणें to turn.

M. गुराख्या cowherd= गुरें cattle + राख्या keeper.

M. दुपार noon=दोन+प्रहर.

Note.—English equivalents would be daisy= day's- eye ; biscuit= *bis coctus* twice cooked ; verdict=*verum dictum*.

Note.—The numerals, especially those above ten दश, are obscure compounds. The following is a table of the numerals from one and upwards :—

Maráṭhí.	Prakrit.	Sanskṛit.
एक one	एक्क	एक
दोन two	दो	द्वि, द्वे
तीन three	तिण्णि	त्रि, त्रीणि
चार four	चत्तारि	चतुर, चत्वारि
पांच five	पञ्च	पंचन्
सहा six	छ	षष्
सात seven	सत्त	सप्तन्
आठ eight	अट्ठ	अष्ट
नव nine	णभ	नव
दहा ten	दस	दश

These are simple derivatives from Sanskṛit.

अकरा eleven	एआरह	एकादश
बारा twelve	बारह	द्वादश
तेरा thirteen	तेरह	त्रयोदश
चौदा fourteen	चउद्दह	चतुर्दश
पंधरा fifteen	पण्णरह	पंचदश
सोळा sixteen	सोलह	षोडश
सतरा seventeen	सत्तरह	सप्तदश
अठरा eighteen	अट्ठरह	अष्टादश
एकुणीस nineteen	ऊनविसई	ऊनविंशति
वीस twenty	वीसई	विंशति

These are from Sanskṛit compounds ; अकरा eleven=Pr. एआरह =Sk. एक +oneदश ten, and so on.

तीस thirty	तीसा	त्रिंशत्
चाळीस forty	चत्तालीसा	चत्वारिंशत्
पन्नास fifty	पणासा	पंचाशत्
साठ sixty	सट्ठी	षष्टि
सत्तर seventy	सत्तारी	सप्तति
ऐंशी eighty	असीइ	अशीति
नव्वद ninety	नउए	नवति
शंभर hundred	सत, सय, संभ	शत

§ 450. In the formation of the Maráṭhí obscure compounds, *i.e.*, compounds in which composition is concealed, only two words are combined, and they follow the following principles of combination :—

1. Maráṭhí words do not generally contain more than four syllables, and words in composition consequently drop or elide some of their letters ; thus, आंबट + घाण = आंबटाण sour smell.

2. When the final and the initial consonant unite, the initial is dropped, and the final assumes its vowel ; गड + ठाणा = गडाणा; गुरें + राख्या = गुराख्या a cowherd. But if the last word ends in the semi-vowel य or व, the semi-vowel is dropped, and the initial consonant retains its place.

3. When the same letter ends both the members of the compound, one of them, particularly the last, is dropped ; पाय + ठाय = पायठा a step of a ladder.

4. Sometimes the surds are changed to sonants for euphonic harmony ; प is changed to व, ट to स, or a sibilant is inserted between the surd and its preceding sonant ; thus, तेल oil + पाणी water = तेलवणी ; आंबट + घाण = आंबसाण or आंबटाण, or simply अंबटाण a sour smell.

5. When the initial letter of the second member is ह, the aspirate of the class of the final is substituted for both the uniting letters; as अंग a body + होळणें to wash = आंघोळ bathing.

III.—Apparent Compounds.

§ 451. Some Maráṭhí words together express a simple notion without entering into composition ; as हाताखालचा an assistant, आंगांत घालणें to wear, हाताचा जड close-fisted.

The Maráṭhí compound verbs belong to the class of the Apparent Compounds, for which see Chapter VII.

CHAPTER XXIII.

PERMUTATION OF LETTERS, OR THE LAWS OF SANDHI (संधि).

§ 452—§ 460.

§ 452. When two Sanskṛit words are combined, the uniting letters, *i.e.*, the final letter of the first word and the initial letter of the second undergo a change; thus, एक one + ईश्वर lord = एकेश्वर one lord, the अ and ई coalescing into ए. These changes of the letters are denominated संधि or combination, by the Sanskṛit grammarians. Since Sanskṛit is the predominant element in Maráṭhí, a knowledge of the laws of *Sandhi* is essential to the Maráṭhí student.

§ 453. The laws of *Sandhi* belong either (1) to *the union of the* vowels, or (2) to *the union of the* consonants, the former being denominated अच्संधि , and the latter हल्संधि.

I.—*The Ach Sandhi, or the Combination of the Vowels.*

§ 454. 1. When two *similar* vowels (§ 16), short or long, unite, they coalesce into their long vowel. Thus अ or आ is similar to अ or आ,and when two of these vowels unite, they are changed to आ, which is their long vowel, and so with इ, उ, &c.

अ + अ = आ ; वस्त्र + अन्न = वस्त्रान्न food and clothes.

अ + आ = आ ; धर्म +आश्रय= धर्माश्रय the support of religion.

आ + अ = आ ; गंगा + अर्पण = गंगार्पण an offering to the Ganges.

आ + आ = आ ; सीता + आज्ञा = सीताज्ञा the command of Sítá.

इ + इ = ई ; हरि + इच्छा= हरीच्छा the will of Hari.

इ + ई = ई ; मति + ईश्वर = मतीश्वर the lord of intellect.

ई + इ = ई ; करी + इंद्र = करींद्र the lord of lions.

ई + ई = ई ; नदी + ईश = नदीश the lord of rivers.

उ + उ = ऊ ; भानु + उदय = भानूदय the sun-rise.

उ + ऊ = ऊ ; धेनु + ऊरू = धेनूरू the thigh of the cow.

ऊ + उ = ऊ ;स्वयंभू+ उदय= स्वयंभूदय the appearing of the self-existent.

ऊ + ऊ = ऊ ; उरू + ऊर्जा = ऊरूर्जा careful preservative of the thigh.

ऋ + ऋ = ॠ ; मातृ + ऋद्धि = मातॄद्धि a mother's wealth.

2. When अ or आ is followed by a *dissimilar* vowel (इ, ई, उ or ऊ) they both are changed into the *improper diphthong* or गुण of the class to which the second of the uniting vowels belongs, *i.e.*, if the second uniting vowel is इ or ई, the गुण substituted is ए, and if the second uniting vowel is उ or ऊ, the गुण substituted is ओ :—

अ + इ = ए ; मुख + इंदु = मुखेंदु the face of the moon.
अ + ई = ए ; परम + ईश्वर = परमेश्वर the great lord ; God.
आ + इ = ए ; रमा + इष्ट = रमेष्ट the welfare of Ramá.
आ + ई = ए ; गंगा + ईश = गंगेश the lord of Ganga.
अ + उ = ओ; अन्न + उदक = अन्नोदक food and water.
आ + ऊ = ओ; इंद्र + ऊरू = इंद्रोरू the thigh of Indra.
आ + उ = ओ; सुता + उत्साह = सुतोत्साह the joy of a daughter.
आ + ऊ = ओ; गंगा + ऊर्मि = गंगोर्मि the wave of the Ganges.

3. When अ or आ is followed by the dissimilars ऋ, ॠ, ऌ, or ॡ, they are changed to the corresponding गुण letters अर् and अल् :—

अ + ऋ = अर् ; देव + ऋषि = देवर्षि a divine Rishi.
आ + ऋ = अर ; महा + ऋद्धि = महर्द्धि great wealth.
अ + ऌ = अल्; देव + ऌकार = देवल्कार the divine letter *li*.

4. When अ or आ is followed by a *diphthong*, whether proper or improper, the two are changed to their *proper diphthong* :—

अ + ए = ऐ ; एक + एक = एकैक each one.
आ + ए = ऐ ; महा + एकांत = महैकांत great solitude.
अ + ऐ = ऐ ; देव + ऐक्य = देवैक्य unity of God.
आ + ऐ = ऐ ; विद्या + ऐश्वर्य = विद्यैश्वर्य the glory of knowledge.

5. When a simple vowel (*i.e.*, not diphthongal), with the exception of अ or आ, is followed by a *dissimilar* vowel, whether simple or diphthongal, the former is changed to its corresponding semi-vowel, and the latter combines with it :—

इ + आ = या जाति + आधार = जात्याधार the support of caste.
इ + अ = य ; नीति + अभ्यास = नीत्यभ्यास the practice of morality.

इ + ए = ये ; प्रति + एक = प्रत्येक every one.
उ + अ = व ; लघु + अन्वय = लघ्वन्वय short connection.
उ + ऐ = वै ; विष्णु + ऐश्वर्य = विष्ण्वैश्वर्य the glory of Vishnu.
ऋ + आ = रा ; पितृ + आज्ञा = पित्राज्ञा a father's command.
ऋ + औ = रौ ; मातृ + औषध = मात्रौषध a mother's medicine.

6. When the improper diphthongs ए and ओ are followed by any other vowel, simple or diphthongal, they are changed to अय् and अव् respectively :—

ए + अ = अय् ; ने + अन = नयन the eye.
ओ + अ = अव् ; पो + अन = पवन wind.

7. When the proper diphthongs ऐ and औ are followed by any other vowel, simple or diphthongal, they are changed to आय् and आव् respectively :—

ऐ + अ = आय् ; नै + अक = नायक a leader.
औ + इ = आवि ; नौ + इक = नाविक a sailor.

§ 455. The following table will be found useful in determining the *Sandhi* change of the vowels. The *Sandhi* or union change will be found "at the junction of the perpendicular and horizontal lines ;" for instance, the change of the final vowel ई, in union with the initial vowel ए, is ए, as the horizontal line beginning at ई, and the terminating line commencing at ए, meet at the letter ये.

Final Vowels.	Initial Vowels.											
	अ	आ	इ	ई	उ	ऊ	ऋ	ॠ	ए	ऐ	ओ	औ
अ	आ	आ	ए	ए	ओ	ओ	अर्	अर्	ऐ	ऐ	औ	औ
आ	आ	आ	ए	ए	ओ	ओ	अर्	अर्	ऐ	ऐ	औ	औ
इ	य	या	ई	ई	यु	यू	यृ	यॄ	ये	यै	यो	यौ
ई	य	या	ई	ई	यु	यू	यृ	यॄ	ये	यै	यो	यौ
उ	व	वा	वि	वी	ऊ	ऊ	वृ	वॄ	वे	वै	वो	वौ
ऊ	व	वा	वि	वी	ऊ	ऊ	वृ	वॄ	वे	वै	वो	वौ
ऋ	र	रा	रि	री	रु	रू	ॠ	ॠ	रे	रै	रो	रौ
ॠ	र	रा	रि	री	रु	रू	ॠ	ॠ	रे	रै	रो	रौ
ए	अय	अया	अयि	अयी	अयु	अयू	अयृ	अयॄ	अये	अयै	अयो	अयौ
ऐ	आय	आया	आयि	आयी	आयु	आयू	आयृ	आयॄ	आये	आयै	आयो	आयौ
ओ	अव	अवा	अवि	अवी	अवु	अवू	अवृ	अवॄ	अवे	अवै	अवो	अवौ
औ	आव	आवा	आवि	आवी	आवु	आवू	आवृ	आवॄ	आवे	आवै	आवो	आवौ

II.—*The Hal Sandhi, or the Combination of Consonants.*

§ 456. When two consonants combine, they undergo either a *change of place*, or a *change of quality* and *place*. When a consonant, which is a surd, or sonant, is changed in combination to its opposite character, the change is said to be a *change of quality* : as जगत्+ईश=जगदीश Lord of the world. In this example, त्, which is a surd, is changed to its corresponding sonant द्. When a consonant of one organ or place is changed to a consonant of another organ, it is said to undergo a *change of place* : as, सत् + शास्त्र = सच् + शास्त्र = सच्शास्त्र or सच्छास्त्र the true Scriptures. In this example the letter त्, which is a dental, is changed to च्, which is a palatal.

§ 457. In combination it is only the initial letter of the second word that has the power of assimilating. It changes the final of the first word to its own character. But the final is never changed to an aspirate, though the initial letter be an aspirate : सत्+भय=सद्भय holy fear, not सध्भय.

§ 458. I.—The following are the rules in regard to the consonantal *Changes of Quality* :—

1. The final consonant, if a surd, is changed to its corresponding sonant, when the initial is a sonant :—

षट् + रिपु = षड्रिपु six enemies.
अप् + घट = अब्घट a water jar.
जगत्+ईश=जगदीश the Lord of the world.

2. The final consonant, if a sonant, is changed to a surd when the initial is a surd; thus, क्षुध्+पिपासा==क्षुत्पिपासा hunger and thirst.

Note.—The aspirate being always changed to its unaspirate in combination (§ 376), the ध of क्षुध् becomes त्, and not थ्.

§ 459. The nasals, chiefly न and म, which are sonants, may optionally change the finals to their corresponding nasals :

दिक् + नाग = दिग्नाग or दिङ्नाग a wild elephant.
षट् + मास = षड्मास or षण्मास six months.
जगत् + नाथ = जगद्नाथ or जगन्नाथ Lord of the world.
अप + नदी = अब्नदी or अम्नदी a water-river.
वाक् + मय = वाग्मय or वाङ्मय eloquent.

§ 460. The consonantal *Changes of Place* occur chiefly in regard to the *Dentals*, the *Anusvára*, and the *Visarga*.

The Dentals.

1. The dental त् (including थ्, द्, and ध्) becomes palatal before the palatals, *viz.* च्, छ्, ज्, झ्, ञ्, and श् :—

सत् + चरित्र = सच्चरित्र good conduct.
सत् + जन = सज्जन a good man.
सत् + शास्त्र = सच्शास्त्र or सच्छास्त्र true Scripture.

2. The dentals त्, थ्, &c., before the cerebrals ट्, ठ्, ड्, ढ्, and ण् (not ष्), are changed to the cerebrals, :—

सत् + टीका = सट्टीका a good commentary.
भगवत् + डमरु = भगवड्डमरु the drum of God.

The त् before ल् is changed to ल् : as उत् + लंघन = उल्लंघन breach of law.

4. The dental न् before च् and छ requires the insertion of श् ; before त् and थ् the insertion of स् ; and before ट् and ठ् the insertion of ष् :—

धावन् + छाग = धावंश्छाग a running goat.
महान् + ठक्कुर = महांष्ठक्कुर a great idol.
पतन् + तरु = पतंस्तरु a falling tree.

5. The dental न् before ल् is changed to a nasalised ल्ँ : as महान् + लाभ = महाल्ँलाभ a great gain.

The Anusvára.

§ 461. 1. The anusvára followed by a vowel is changed to म् : as, किं + अत्र = किमत्र what is there ?

2. Before the consonants it may remain unchanged ; but it is usual to change it to a nasal corresponding to the class of the letter which follows it. But it is never changed before र, श, ष, स, and ह, as these letters have no corresponding nasal letter.

The Visarga.

§ 462. The visarga, followed by a surd, is changed to the sibilant corresponding to the class of the surd ; but since the gutturals and the labials have no class-sibilants, the visarga before these surds remains unchanged :—

रजः + कण = रजःकण a particle of dust.

पूर्णः + चंद्र = पूर्णश्चंद्र the full moon.

भग्नः + ठकुर = भग्नठकुर the broken idol.

नद्याः + तीर = नद्यास्तीर the bank of a river.

नद्याः + पार = नद्याःपार the opposite side of a river.

Note.—The visarga preceded by इ or उ, before क, ख, प, फ, is changed to ष् ; as निष्काम loveless, which is compounded of निः + काम; नि : + पाप = निष्पाप sinless man ; निष्फल fruitless, दुष्कर difficult. Indeed, the words निः, दुः, बहिः, आविः, प्रादुः and चतुः followed by words beginning with क, ख, प, फ, always take ष्; thus—

निः + काम = निष्काम loveless.

निः + फल = निष्फल fruitless.

दुः + कृत्य = दुष्कृत्य a sinful act.

चतुः + कोण = चतुष्कोण a square.

2. The visarga before the sibilants either remains unchanged or is changed to the sibilants that stand before it ; as दुः + शासन = दुःशासन or दुश्शासन difficult of government ; सत्वः + षंड = सत्वःषंड or सत्वष्षंड; प्रथमः + सर्ग = प्रथमः सर्ग or प्रथमस्सर्ग the first six sections.

3. The visarga followed by a sonant, whether a vowel or a consonant, is usually changed to र्: as निः + धन = निर्धन without wealth, impoverished ; दुः + आत्मा = दुरात्मा an evil spirit. If the visarga is preceded by अ and followed by a sonant consonant, it is dropped, and the preceding अ is changed to ओ; as , मनः + रम = मनोरम pleasing ; रजः + गुण = रजोगुण the second of the three properties of the creature.

4. But if the visarga preceded by अ is followed by अ, the visarga is dropped, the preceding अ changed to ओ, and the initial अ elided. The elision is marked by the sign ऽ, called अवग्रह ; अयः + अस्त्र = अयोऽस्त्र an iron weapon.

5. If the visarga is preceded by आ and followed by any sonant (vowel or consonant), or if the visarga is preceded by any vowel except अ, the visarga is dropped.

PART III.

CHAPTER XXIV.

Syntax.

THE RULES OF CONCORDANCE.

§ 463—§ 511.

§ 463. Syntax treats of the forms discussed in the preceding parts, and the mode of combining them into *sentences.*

§ 464. A sentence is the utterance of a complete thought. A thought is a judgment in regard to the relation subsisting between two notions, one notion being affirmed, or denied of the other ; कालिदास मोठा कवि होता Kalidas was a great poet ; ह्या ग्रंथाची भाषा साधारण नाहीं the language of this book is not common.

§ 465. The relation between the notions combined in a thought or sentence is indicated by inflections. The inflections so employed are called *relational.*

§ 466. The words in a Maráṭhí sentence are usually arranged in the following order : *first* the subject, *next* the object, *then* the adverb, and *lastly,* the verb ; thus, दुष्ट पारध्यानें आमची सुंदर मैना ठार मारिली, the cruel sportsman killed our pretty jay. The subject or the object may be qualified by an adjective, which is placed immediately before it, as are the adjectives दुष्ट and सुंदर in the above sentence.

§ 467. When the verb has two objects, the accusative and dative, the accusative object is put nearest the verb : आपण एकमेकांस सुख द्यावें we should make each other happy. In this sentence सुख is the accusative, and एकमेकांस, the dative object.

Note.—The order of words is changed when a person speaks with emotion, or when any special word is to be made emphatic. The emphasized word is put as near to the beginning of the sentence as possible : संपेल कोठून ? तिचा आरंभच करायास अजून कोणास फावलें आहे ? how could it be finished ? who has yet found time even to make a commencement ? कोठें आहे तो चिमणा किनऱ्या where is the small fiddler ?

Note.—Nevertheless words are made emphatic chiefly by the tone in which they are uttered, seldom or never by any grammatical construction.

§ 468. The Maráṭhí sentences, of whatever nature, whether assertive, interrogative, imperative, or exclamatory, are constructed in a uniform way, the distinction between them being denoted simply by the *tone* of the voice :—

Assertive: माझी तरवार खोलींत आहे my sword is in the room.

Interrogative : माझी तरवार खोलींत आहे? is my sword in the room?

Imperative : माझी तरवार आण bring my sword.

Exclamatory : माझी तरवार खोलींत आहे well done, my sword is in the room!

Note.—In the interrogative sentence the interrogative particles or words may or may not be employed.

1. When the enquiry refers to the bare assertion or negation of a fact or event, the interrogative sentence is generally used without any interrogative particle : माझी तरवार खोलींत आहे ? is my sword in the room? तुम्ही त्याचे बाप आहां ? are you his father? आज पाऊस पडेल ? will it rain to-day? Optionally the interjectional particle काय what? may be put at the end of the sentence ; आपण त्याचे मामा आहां काय? are you his uncle? पाऊस पडेल काय ? will it rain ?

2. When the enquiry refers to any other particular, such as the name, place, time, manner, &c , various interrogative words are always employed to make up the interrogative sentence: आपलें नांव काय? what is your name, Sir? तूं कोठें राहतोस where do you reside? केव्हां आलास ? when did you come? हें कोणीं आणिलें who brought it?

The Verb.

§ 469. The verb implies action, and an action has an agent, and it may have also an object. (Sect. 180.)

§ 470. The Maráṭhí verbs, together with their inflections, are etymologically either *active* or *passive*, and they consequently have a tendency either to the subject or to the object : रामा खातो Rama eats ; रामानें भाकर खाल्ली Ram ate bread. The etymologically passive particle ला has an affinity to the object.

§ 471. The passive ला ceases to be attracted to the object, if the object is *inflected*—changed by a case-ending. It is then drawn neither to the subject, nor to the object, but takes a different course—it assumes the neuter singular form, which indicates indifference or neutrality. (Sect. 210.)

§ 472. The verb may therefore be constructed so as to agree with *the subject*, or *the object*, or *with neither*. Hence there are three *Constructions*—the Subjective, the Objective, and the Neuter—the कर्तरि, the कर्मणि and the भावे. (Sect. 209.)

§ 473. When the verb agrees with a noun, assuming its gender, number and person, the noun, whether the subjcet or the objcet, onght to be in an *uninflected case*. The uninflected case of the subject is the *Nominative*, and the uninflected case of the object is the *Accusative*.

§ 474. In the Subjective construction, the subject is in the *Nominative case*, and in the Objective construction, the object is in the *Accusative case*. Both these cases have uninflected forms.

§ 475. When the subject is inflected, it takes either the *Instrumental*, or the *Dative* case ; म्या केलें I did ; रामाला जाववतें Rama is able to go.

§ 476. When the object is inflected, it takes only the *Dative case* ; त्यानें चोराला धरिलें he caught the thief.

THE SUBJECT.

The Kinds of Subjects.

§ 477. THE SUBJECT MAY BE A WORD, A PHRASE, OR A SENTENCE :—

A word : नदी वाहाते the river flows.

A phrase: तिचें पारिपत्य होणें चुकलें नाहीं she did not escape punishment; मला आईबापांची आज्ञा मानणें मान्य आहे it is imperative that I should obey my parents.

A sentence : वाईट वस्त्रांवरून कोणास हंसावें हें हलक्या मनुष्याचें काम आहे it is the part of a low man to laugh at any one for his bad clothes ; तें ऐकून दुर्गीच्या मनांत आलें कीं औदार्याविषयीं आणि विश्वास ठेवण्याविषयीं नानीनें आपणाला भागू पेक्षां अधिक चांगलें म्हणावें having heard it, Durgí wished that Nání might praise her more than Bhágú for her generosity, and her readiness to confide in her.

Note.—A phrase (क्रियापदविरहित वाक्य) is a combination of words without the finite verb.

Note.—The finite verb (सावधिक or पुरुषवाचक क्रियापद) is the form of the verb limited by the gender, number and person of the subject or object.

§ 478. When a sentence is used as the subject, a demonstrative pronoun like हा this, is inserted in apposition, with or without a noun: आईचें ऐकूं नये, आणि त्या दुष्ट कुलंकिणीचें ऐकावें हें तुला कसें बरें वाटलें how could you think that you should rather listen to that wicked woman than to your mother? या द्वारांतून त्या पर्वता-कडेस जायास मार्ग आहे ही गोष्ट खरी आहे it is true that there is a way to go to the mountain through this gate.

When the demonstrative is employed by itself for this purpose, it is always in the neuter singular; but if it is used with a noun, it agrees in gender and number with that noun, as illustrated in the above sentences.

§ 479. The noun sentence might be used after the verb "to be," as a nominal predicate (§ 485) with कीं as in English; तुझी इच्छा आहे कीं यमाचे यातनेंत पडावें is it your desire that you should suffer the torments of hell? In English the noun sentence, as in the above sentence, is constructed with the impersonal phrase "is it" that, &c.

The Case of the Subject.

§ 480. THE SUBJECT OF THE VERB IS USUALLY IN THE NOMINATIVE CASE; गोविंद चांगला मुलगा आहे Govind is a good boy. हजारों लोक तेथें जमले होते thousands of people had assembled there. The subject in the *nominative*, or *uninflected* case, is called, by way of distinction, the NOMINATIVE.

§ 481. In the following instances the subject of the verb does NOT take the Nominative Case:—

1. When the *transitive verb* is used *in the past tense*, the subject is in the instrumental case; चोरांनीं त्याचें घर लुटलें the robbers plundered his house; त्यानें मला बोलाविलें he called me.

Note.—" The Sanskrit is entirely deficient in a tense intended to express the completion of an action. When the completion of an action is to be expressed, we most commonly find the action expressed changed into a passive one ; and, in fact, so that a participle which, in form and signification, corresponds to the Latin *tus*, is combined with the present of the verb substantive, or the latter is to be supplied, as, in general, the verb substantive, in Sanskṛit is omitted almost everywhere, when it possibly can be done. In the episode of the Sávitri, it should be said, ' Thou hast gone as far as thou hast to go,' when the latter words are expressed by गतं त्वया (ga tan, euphonic for gatam) gone by thee."—*Bopp*. The Maráṭhí past inflection is derived from this passive form.

2. In the *subjunctive mood* the subject is usually in the instrumental case ; आम्हीं रोज त्याच्या घरीं जावें we used to go every day to his house ; शिपायांनीं चोरांस धरून आणावें the sepoys should apprehend the thieves and bring them up.

But when the subjunctive mood expresses the *dubitative sense*, the subject is put in the nominative case ; तो आला असावा he might have come.

Note.—The Sanskṛit passive participle in तव्य from which the Maráṭhí subjunctive in आव is derived, is usually constructed with the instrumental subject, and agrees with the object ; धर्मस्त्वया कर्तव्य : right is to be done by thee. (§ 203.)

3. When the verb is potential, the subject is either in the *dative case*, or the ***instrumental, derived from the genitive***; मला or माझ्यानें चालवतें I can walk ; रामाला or रामाच्यानें हा पाण्याचा घडा उचलवला Rama could lift up this pot of water. (§ 235.)

Note.—The *potential verb* is a modification of the Sanskṛit passive form, which is frequently used in the neuter construction ; मया ज्ञायते it is known by me. (§ 400.)

4. The subject of the compound verbs may be dative, instrumental, etc.; म्या or मला गेलें पाहिजे I must go ; मला करायाचें आहे. I have to do it.

The Relation of the Nominative to the Verb.

§ 482. When the subject is in the nominative case, the verb habitually agrees with it in gender, number, and

PERSON; मीं काल त्याच्या घरीं गेलों होतों I went to his house yesterday; तूं कां घेणार नाहींस why will you not take it? तें पाहून मुलें रडूं लागलीं the children having seen that, began to cry; आह्मी गरीब आहों we are poor; आपण सगळीं मिळून त्यास वर्गणी देऊं we shall all together give him a contribution.

1. When an individual is spoken of respectfully, the noun denoting the individual is considered to be in the plural number, and the verb is accordingly put in the plural; वरून गोपाळराव खालीं आले Gopálráv came downstairs; आईसाहेब सांगतात म्हणून आपण परत जावें we should go back as the lady mother bids us; औरंगाबादेमध्यें शिवराव म्हणून कोणी एक गृहस्थ होते there was a gentleman living in Aurangabad of the name of Sivaráv.

Note.—The singular noun of dignity referring to females may be optionally put in the neuter plural; बाईसाहेब आलीं असतीं पण मध्यें विघ्न आलें the lady would have come, but was prevented; बाई, तुम्ही मोठीं सुज्ञ आहां madam, you are very considerate. The neuter gender is usually used in the Konkan in speaking of ladies of high rank, such as the wives of chiefs, kings, &c.

2. A noun of address is followed by a verb in the second person, whether or not a second personal pronoun is inserted; कां रामा, आज तूं कोणीकडे गेला होतास? well, Rámá, where did you go to-day? रेवा चल लवकर, तिकडे काय करितेस? Reva, come away soon; what are you doing there?

Note.—Persons of rank are addressed in the third person, and the verb is constructed in the third plural: रावसाहेब जसा हुकूम करितील तो करायास मीं तयार आहें, I am willing to act as your honour may bid me; कां कोठें गेल्या होत्या well, where did your ladyship go?

§ 483. The subject of the verb is sometimes omitted. It is omitted in the following instances:—

1. When the verb is अकर्तृक or *impersonal*; माझ्या पोटांत कळमळतें I feel sickish; उजाडलें it is daybreak. The verb is constructed in the Bhave construction, called the *Bháva kartṛik* in which the subject is not strictly omitted, but implied in the verb.

2. When the subject of the verb denotes indefinitely, in the conditional clause, "some one" or "somebody"; त्या वाटेनें गेलें

असतां तुमचें ओझें उतरेल असें तुम्हास कोणीं सांगितलें who told you that if you went that way yon would get rid of your load ? ओल्या जमिनीवर निजलें तर लागलेंच अंग धरतें if one sleeps on a damp ground, he is affected immediately with rheumatism. The verb is constructed in the neuter singular.

3. In the passive phrases, the subject understood being "they" ; त्यास कोश असें म्हणतात it is called a dictionary (lit. they call it a dictionary) ; असें असतां ह्या मार्गांत ही जी चिखलाची जागा ती बुजवून कां टाकीत नाहींत when such is the case, why do not they fill up this muddy place in the road ? त्या गांवांत सर्व पदार्थ तोलून विकतात all things are sold in this town by weight. (§ 305, 2.)

Note.—The English passive froms are usually expressed in the above mauner in Maráṭhí; the sentence is constructed in the ordinary way, the subject of the verb in the plural number only being omitted: या गांवांत लोक सर्व पदार्थ तोलून विकितात people sell all things in this town by weight, which in the passive form would be expressed without the subject ; as, या गांवांत सर्व पदार्थ तोलून विकितात all things are sold in this town by weight. Such idioms are found in many European languages; the indicative plural active being put impersonally for the passive verb. Thus, for instance, the following Greek sentence: τὴν ψυχήν σου ἀπαιτοῦσιν ἀπό σου *they require* thy life (thy life is required.) The English "they" is impersonal. In English the same idiom is sometimes used—*they call* him a gentleman, for "he is called a gentleman." It is also common in Hebrew.

§ 484. Sometimes the subject is not omitted, but used in the neuter singular, and the verb agrees with it in gender and number. This construction is employed in the following instances :—

1. When the agent of an act is not known, or is supposed to be unknown ; आं, कोण हाक मारितें ? eh, who is calling out to me ? तिकडे कोणी निजलें आहेसें वाटतें it appears somebody is sleeping there ; तें कोण येतें who comes there ? कोणी माणूस येतें some human being is coming.

2. When a most general statement is made ; ज्याला डोळे आहेत तें पाहील whosoever has eyes will see ; ज्याला समजेल तें शिकवील whosoever understands will teach.

3. When the humble condition of a person is described with delicacy; एथें येऊन इतका श्रम घेऊन जें भाकरीकारितां शेतें टिपतें तें गरीबच असेल बाबा surely, Sir, that person who takes so much pains to glean corn for food, must be poor. This construction would not be used in reference to the happy or honourable condition of a person; जो तुला पोषितो तो तुजपेक्षां थोर असलाच पाहिजे one who feeds you must be superior to you.

§ 485. WHEN THE SUBSTANTIVE VERB "TO BE" IS FOLLOWED BY A NOMINAL PREDICATE, IT AGREES WITH ITS SUBJECT, AND NOT WITH THE NOMINAL PREDICATE; तूं फार भली बायको आहेस you are a very honest woman; तूं मुलगा झाली असतीस तर suppose you had become a boy; तूं मला पन्नास रुपये देणें आहेस you owe me fifty Rupees.

Note.—When the verb "to be" is constructed with a noun or an adjective to make up the predicate, the noun or the adjective so united is called the *nominal predicate*, and the verb "to be" is denominated the copula or link.

Note.—The verb "to be" when used as the copula, may sometimes be omitted :—

1. It is usually omitted in the interrogative sentence constructed with the interrogative pronoun काय; तुझें नांव काय? what is your name?

2. In answer to questions like the above; माझें नांव गोपाळ my name is Gopal.

3. In emphatic sentences; तूं मूर्ख खरा you are indeed foolish.

4. In definitions; कोश म्हणजे शब्दसंग्रहाचें पुस्तक a dictionary is a book containing a collection of words.

5. In proverbial expressions; जेथें गांव तेथें महारवाडा wherever there is a village there exists a ward occupied by the Mahárs.

Note.—In negative sentences नाहीं is equivalent to न + आहे, and the verb आहे is therefore inherent in नाहीं. In the Konkan, however, आहे is added to नाहीं to make up the form of the *perfect definite* distinct from the *past*; he did not come तो आला नाहीं. *past*; he has not come तो आला नाहीं आहे, *perfect definite*.

Note.—Besides the verb to be असणें and its forms, some other verbs have a copulative force. The verb होणें to become is one of them; तो शाहाणा झाला he has become wise. The neuter passives दिसणें to look,

शोभणें to look becomingly, &c., are of the same nature; तो विद्वान् दिसतो he looks a learned man.

Two or More Nominatives.

§ 486. WHEN TWO OR MORE NOMINATIVES ARE CONNECTED BY A COPULATIVE CONJUNCTION, EXPRESSED OR UNDERSTOOD, THEY ARE USUALLY FOLLOWED BY A PLURAL VERB: वडील पोवार आणि वडील सांवत तेथेंच अवसान धरून उभे होते the elder Powar and the elder Sánvat stood even there with courage; कृष्णसेनाचे सारथि आणि घोडे मरून पडले होते the charioteers and the horses of Krishnasená were lying dead; जिकडे तिकडे गवतें आणि नाना प्रकारचीं झाडें उगवलीं होतीं everywhere various kinds of trees and grasses had sprung up. एके दिवशीं त्रिंबक आणि हरि सकाळच्या प्रहरीं गोष्टी सांगत फिरायास गेले one day Trimbak and Hari went chatting for a morning walk.

1. When the two singular nominatives denote *persons,* and are of the *same gender,* they take a plural verb: रामा आणि जगू आले आहेत Rama and Jagu have come; दुर्गा आणि सावित्री या बहिणी होत्या Durga and Sávitri were sisters.

2. But when the nominatives denoting *persons,* differ in *gender,* they, whether singular or plural, take the verb in the *neuter plural:* रमी आणि गोविंदा चोरून दौलतसिंगाकडे पाहात होतीं Ramí and Govindá were stealthily looking at Davlatsing; जानोजी साळवी व त्याची बायको कोठें गेलीं आहेत? where have Janoji the weaver and his wife gone to? In such cases, that is, when the nominatives *differ* in gender, they are often collected into one head, and a *neuter plural demonstrative* is placed *in apposition;* एके दिवशीं सदाशिवपंत व बया हीं ओटीवर बसलीं आहेत इतक्यांत शस्त्रवैद्य तेथें आला one day as Sadásivapant and Bayá sat in the verandah, a surgeon came there. Sometimes some such words as दोघें both, इत्यादि &c., are used appositionally; as धाकू आणि साळी हीं दोघें बेकार होऊन आलीं Dháku and Sáli have both come, with the loss of employment.

3. When two or more singular nominatives denote *irrational animals,* or *inanimate objects,* the verb often agrees in gender and number with the last word: आमची गाई आणि घोडा आला नाहीं our cow and horse have not come; आपल्या जमिनींत दाणा कडबा फळफळावळ उत्पन्न होते grain, fodder, fruit, &c., grow in our

fields; तर यापुढें आपणास हिंवाळा आणि उन्हाळा नाहींसा होता then we should no more have had the winter and summer.

Sometimes, however, a *plural* verb may be used with the plural of the appositional demonstrative pronoun: आमची गाई घोडा आणि बकरी हीं मेलीं our cow, horse, and goat have died. This construction is usually followed, when it is necessary to direct the attention to *each of the nominatives separately*: कारण जेथें अग्नि आणि गंधक हे प्रज्वलित आहेत अशा ठिकाणीं जाऊन पडाल for you will fall into a place which burns with fire and brimstone; धर्म, अर्थ, काम आणि मोक्ष हे पुरुषाचे धर्म होत the chief duty of man is the pursuit of religion, wealth, love, and salvation; हिचें रम्य मुख व भाषणाची हातवटी हीं हिचा थोरपणा सांगतात her pleasing face and address speak for her respectability.

4. When the subjects are of different *persons*, the verb in the plural number, agrees, *in person*, with the one in the *first* in preference to that in the second or third, and with the one in the *second* in preference to that in the third:—

1st and 2nd persons: तें तू आणि मीं यांना वांटूं that you and I shall distribute to them.

1st and 3rd persons: मिरु आणि मीं जाऊन त्याची प्रार्थना करितों Miru and I will go and entreat him; माझी बहीण आणि मीं किती सुखी आहों! how happy my sister and I are.

2nd and 3rd persons: ती आणि तू अशीं दोघें आलां होतां she and you had both come.

In such a construction the pronoun with which the verb agrees is put last. If this order is not observed an appositional demonstrative may be inserted; मीं, तूं, आणि तो असे जाऊं I, you and he shall go, or असे आपण such we, or असे आपण तिघे जाऊं such we three persons shall go, may be said.

Note.—When the subjects are connected by a *disjunctive conjunction*, the verb agrees with the nearest: तूं अथवा दुसरा कोणी आमच्या घरीं आला तर आम्हीं असें करायाचे नाहीं if you or any other person should come to our house, we would not act so.

The Object.

The Case of the Object.

§ 487. The object is either in the *Accusative* or the *Dative* case.

§ 488. When the object of the transitive verb denotes a lifeless thing, it is usually in the Accusative case; काल राघूनें लाजिरवाणें काम केलें Raghu committed a shameful act yesterday; पहिल्यानें त्यानें बर्फी खाल्ली at first he ate the sweetmeat.

§ 489. When nouns denoting inanimate objects are *emphasized*, they may take the dative case: ह्या नासक्या आंब्याला काय मीं खाऊं? What shall I eat this rotten mango? ह्या विश्वाला कसें चालवावें how should this world be managed? In Hindi the same idiom is used; उस पथरको उठाया he lifted up that stone (dative).

§ 490. When the object of a transitive verb is a *person*, it is usually put in the dative case; त्यानें रामाला हाकून दिलें he drove away Rama.

§ 491. If the person expressed by the object be represented as destitute of life, liberty, or power,—in fact, reduced to the condition of an *inanimate* thing, the object is then constructed in the accusative case; चल, मीं तुला एक राजा दाखवितों come away, I will show you a king—show something like a picture—a new strange thing; but चला आपण राजाला जाऊन पाहूं come on, we shall go and see the king. So also वाघानें दहा माणसें खाल्लीं the tiger ate ten men; एकादा चांगला गडी शोधून आणाल? Will you look out a good servant and fetch him?

Note.—Nouns denoting *irrational animals* are usually put in the dative case; मांजराला एथें आण bring the cat here; एका कावळ्यानें तुमच्या चिमणीला खाऊन टाकिलें a crow ate up your sparrow.

§ 492. The personal pronouns of the 1st and 2nd persons, which express personality most emphatically, are always used in the dative in prose, though there occur numerous exceptions in poetry; तुला कोणीं सांगितलें? Who told you? मला तुम्हींच सांगितलें you yourself told me.

Note.—Some pure transitives may take either an accusative or a dative object; and when the action of the verb affects the object quite *superficially*, the dative object is used, but when the action changes its vitality or its essential state or form, the accusative is used:

(1) त्यानें मुलाला मारिलें he struck the boy;
त्यानें मूल मारिला he killed the boy.

(2) त्यानें चोराला धरिलें he caught the thief;
त्यानें चोर धरिला he detected the thief.

(3) त्यानें गाईला बांधिलें he tied up the cow;
त्यानें गाई बांधिली he fastened the cow which had broken loose.

Note.—When the noun is separated from the action of the verb by its dative case-termination, it assumes a character of independence and dignity, but in the accusative, which is the most dependent case, it holds a position of absolute subjection.

The Relation of the Object to the Verb.

§ 493. If the subject is inflected, and the object is uninflected, then only the verb agrees with the object. The verb can never agree with the object, if the subject is uninflected रामा भाकर खातो Rama eats bread; रामानें भाकर खाल्ली Rama ate bread; रामा भाकर खाईल Rama will eat bread; रामानें भाकर खावी Rama ought to eat bread; रामाला भाकर खाल्ली पाहिजे Rama must eat bread; रामाच्यानें or रामाला भाकर खाववते Rama can eat bread.

§ 494. The verb can agree only with an uninflected or accusative object, never with an inflected or dative one; as राजानें जय मिळविला the king gained a victory; राजा रयतेला नाडितो the king robs his subjects. In the former example the verb agrees with the object, in the latter it does not agree with it.

Note.—The anomalous verbs, which are essentially reflexive, and which, therefore, usually take the subjective construction, may sometimes be used as pure transitives in the objective or neuter construction, to express *the complete subjection* of the object: ती डाव जिंकली she won the game; त्यानें सर्व गोट्या जिंकल्या he won all the marbles; कुत्रा त्याला चावला the dog bit him, but कुत्र्यानें काठी चावली the dog bit and chewed the stick.

Note.—The *reflexive* nature of the Anomalous verbs is indicated partly by their conjugation, they being always conjugated intransitively though they are transitive in sense (§ 239). In their radical Sanskṛit forms they have a reflexive force. In Sanskṛit these Anomalous verbs originally denoted that the action expressed by them was performed for the *benefit* of the agent. Sk. पचति he cooks, transitive पचते he cooks for himself, intransitive; यजति he sacrifices, यजते he sacrifices for himself. Some of the Sanskṛit reflexive verbs are the following,—च्यु, जन्, दश्, प्राप्, ब्रू, विस्मृ, हृ, &c.; and corresponding Maráṭhí derivatives for them are चुकणें to miss, जनणें to bear, डसणें to bite, पावणें to obtain, बोलणें to speak, विसरणें to forget, हरणें to take away.

Note.—"These distinctions, however, rest, in many cases, in Sanskṛit as well as Greek, on peculiar conceptions which it is difficult to analyse or realise; and in Sanskṛit as well as Greek, the right use of the Active and Middle voices is best learnt by practice. Thus नी to lead, is used as parasmaipada in such expressions as गंडं विनयति he carries off a swelling; but as atmanepada, in क्रोधं विनयते he turns away or dismisses with wrath; a subtle distinction which it is possible to appreciate when stated, but difficult to bring under any general rules."—*Max-Müller.*

Two Objects.

§ 495. THE TRANSITIVE VERB MAY TAKE TWO OR MORE OBJECTS: रावजीला सुपारी आणि नारळ दे give a betelnut and cocoanut to Rávjí.

§ 496. The transitive verb may take two or more ACCUSATIVE objects coupled by "and;" तेथें द्राक्षें आणि निंबें आणून ठेविलीं होतीं they had placed there grapes and lemons.

When the verb is constructed in the कर्मणी or objective construction, with two or more accusative objects, *it usually agrees with the last;* मुरंबा आणि कलिंगड खाल्लें तेंही दिलें नाहीं they ate jam and melon, of which they did not give me either; तिजकरितां खडेसाखर, बदामें आणि दुसऱ्या वस्तू कोण जाणें किती चोरल्या असतील I do not know how much of sugarcandy, almonds, and several other things I must have stolen for her. Like the nominatives of the verb (§ 399, 2), the objects of the verb are often collected into one head, and a demonstrative pronoun, with or without a noun, is put in apposition; आमचे

आसजन आणि प्रपंचसुखें हीं सर्व सोडून द्यावीं काय? should we abandon all our relatives and world ly comforts? तेथें द्राक्षें, चकोत्रे, लिंबें, अननस, डाळिंबें, केळीं, अंजीर, पेरू अशीं नानाप्रकारचीं फळें आधींच आपून ठेविलीं होतीं they had already placed there grapes, lemons, shaddocks, pine-apples, pomegranates, plantains, figs, guavas, and several other such kinds of fruit; त्यानें दगड, विटा आणि चुना, हीं आणिलीं he brought stones, bricks and mortar.

Note.—1. When the objects are connected by a disjunctive conjunction, the verb agrees only with the last word; तिजपासून पैसे किंवा तमाखू तुला मिळाला नाहीं, म्हणून तूं तिची टोपली अडकाविली you withheld her basket because you could not get money or tobacco from her.

§ 497. The transitive verb may take two objects in different cases—*one in the* ACCUSATIVE, and *the other* in the DATIVE case: रामजीस चार रुपये द्या give four Rupees to Rámjí. The accusative object is usually the direct (प्रत्यक्ष or मुख्य), and the dative, the indirect or personal (परोक्ष or पुरुषवाचक) object.

§ 498. That object is *direct* which is *im mediately* acted upon by the verb, and is *essential to complete its sense*; and that is *indirect* which is acted upon by the verb remotely. The indirect is called a personal object, when it denotes a person.

§ 499. It is such verbs as express the idea of *giving*, whether real or imaginary, that take two such objects—accusative and dative. The noun denoting the thing given is put in the accusative case, and the noun denoting the person to whom the thing is given is put in the dative case; रामानें सदूला आंबा दिला Rama gave a mango to Sadu; हरीनें मला एक गोष्ट सांगितली Hari told me a story; राणीला गायकवाड महाराजांनीं एक नजराणा पाठविला The Guikawad Maharaj sent a present to the Queen. Some more such verbs are मागणें to beg, शिकणें to teach, पुसणें to ask, etc. These verbs agree with the accusative object, and not the dative; त्याला त्यानें सर्व विषय शिकविले he taught him all the subjects.

Note.—The postposition पाशीं and जवळ are often idiomatically substituted for the dative termination; त्याजवळ तें सांग tell it to him; त्याजवळ दे give it to him; मजजवळ त्याला पाठविलें आहे he has been sent to me.

§ 500. When the direct object denotes an *action*, the dative supine is usually used; तो तें वाचावयास इच्छितो he wishes to read it; ती लिहावयास शिकते she learns to write. The infinitive may, also, in some cases, be used to express an action; तो येऊं पाहतो he desires to come.

§ 501. The dative supine may have its own object; तो कविता म्हणावयास शिकतो he learns to recite poetry.

§ 502. The dative supine and the present participle in तां or तांना are used as the indirect object to complete the sense of the direct object which is a noun or pronoun; as तिला लिहावयास शिकविलें they taught her to write. They taught her—what? To write लिहावयास; म्या रामाला पोहतांना पाहिलें I saw Rama swimming.

1. The *verbs of authority*, such as सांगणें to tell, शिकविणें to teach, आज्ञापिणें to command, लावणें to influence, &c., take the supine as a complement or indirect object; त्याला तें करावयास लाविलें I got him to do it. In English the infinitive is used as the complement in such cases.

2. When what a person *is actually engaged in* is to be expressed, the present participle in तां or तांना alone is used as the complement or indirect object: त्याला मारितांना म्या पाहिलें I saw him beating; तिला गातांना म्या ऐकिलें I heard her singing. The verbs पाहणें to see, ऐकणें to hear, &c., take this participial complement.

§ 503. Sometimes the transitive verb so acts upon the direct object that it produces some *change* in it, as when we say, He made the *water* wine. Such verbs are called *factitive* verbs. Some of the factitive verbs are करणें to make, म्हणणें to say or call, नेमणें to appoint, समजणें to understand or consider, मानणें to think.

§ 504. Factitive verbs take two objects—the *one* on which the verb acts, and the *other* which results from that activity. The latter is called the *factitive* object.

§ 505. In Sanskrit both the objects are accusative, as is the case in English; but in Maráṭhí one is accusative, and the other, dative; बेडकांनीं शहामृगाला राजा केलें, the frogs made the ostrich king; मीं त्याला माझा मित्र समजतों I regard him as my friend; आपणास मीं पिता मानितों I consider you to be my father. The direct object in these examples is dative, and the indirect or factitive, accusative.

§ 506. The factitive verb agrees with its direct object, and if the direct object is in the dative case, it takes the Neuter construction; त्यांनीं त्याला चाकर केलें they made him a servant.

Note.—It is certain that the verb in such constructions ought to be *singular neuter* as both the subject and the direct object are inflected.

Note.—The most satisfactory mode of determining the direct object is to convert the active into the passive verb, and the object that becomes the subject of the passive verb is the direct object. The passive of बेडकांनीं शहामृगास राजा केलें would be बेडकांकडून शहामृग राजा केला गेला the ostrich was made king by the frogs, not बेडकांकडून राजा शहामृग केला गेला.

§ 507. The construction of the factitive verb may be modified, and the verb then agrees with the factitive object; त्यांनीं राजाचा रंक केला they made a slave of the king; त्यांनीं लोखंडाचें सोनें केलें they made iron into gold. When the conversion of lifeless things is spoken of, the idiom given last is usually followed.

§ 508. The accusative noun which forms the factitive object, may be substituted by an adjective; लोकांनीं त्याला वेडें केलें the people made him mad; सुज्ञांनीं वेड्यांस शहाणें करावें the prudent ones ought to make those who are foolish wise. When an adjective is thus used as a factitive object, it agrees in gender and number with the direct object; but if the direct object is inflected, *i.e.,* is in the dative case, it is put in the neuter singular as in the above examples. The adjectives वेडें and शहाणें are neuter singular.

§ 509. When the direct object denotes a lifeless thing, it is usually put in the accusative case, and then the factitive adjective agrees with it in gender and number; त्यानें भिंत काळी केली he made the wall black.

Note.—The indirect object must be distinguished from the adverbial adjunct; त्याला येतांना म्यां ओळखिलें I made him out as he came.

The Object being a Sentence.

§ 509. THE OBJECT OF THE TRANSITIVE VERB MAY BE A SENTENCE: पण बायकोनें सांगितलें कडी काढूं नको but the wife told him not to take off the hook. The transitive verb is put in the neuter singular.

§ 510. The objective sentence may either *follow*, or *precede* the governing verb; मला वाटतें कीं मीं आतां या यातनेंतून सुटावें I think I should now get out of this torment; पैसे काय केले म्हणून गुरुजीनें पुसलें the master asked what I had done with the money.

(*a*) When the objective sentence comes *after* the governing verb, it is introduced by कीं that, expressed or understood; मग विचार करूं लागली कीं पुढें कशी गत करावी then she began to consider how she should act in future; मला वाटलें होतें कीं मीं तुजवर कृपा ठेवितों तेणेंकरून तूं माझ्या मुलीस बऱ्या गुणाची शिक्षा लाविशील I thought that since I was kind to you, you would teach my child good ways.

(*b*) But when the objective sentence comes *before* the governing verb, the demonstrative pronoun हा this, असा such, in the neuter singular, the conjunction म्हणून &c., are inserted between the objective sentence and the principal verb; आतां मीं कोणता उपाय करूं असें ती बोले then she would say, what means shall I use? मीं तुझ्या घरीं येईन म्हणून म्हणाला he said that he would come to my house; राजानें माझें घर लुटलें, माझी बायको नेली, माझीं मुलेंमाणसें बंदीखान्यांत घातलीं, आणि माझी चौघांमध्यें अगदीं अप्रतिष्ठा केली म्हणून हा बोलतो he says that the king has plundered his house, carried away his wife, imprisoned his children, and publicly disgraced him.

Note.—The objective sentence is usually governed by verbs of म्हणणें *saying*, वाटणें *thinking*, विचारणें *asking*, सांगणें *telling*, आज्ञा करणें *commanding*, ऐकणें *hearing*, समजणें *understanding*, ऐकणें *hearing*, &c.

§ 511. The objective sentence usually *reports the words of the speaker*. In Maráṭhí the words of the speaker are simply *quoted*, and introduced by such particles as कीं, or followed by such words as असें, हें, म्हणून, &c. In English a different mode of construction is followed. The Maráṭhí sentence, मी तुझे घरीं येईन म्हणून तो मला म्हणाला, lit. "he said to me, that I will come to your house," would be rendered in English thus: "he said to me that he would come to my house." We give below a few more examples :—

(Eng.)—Rághu said that he was going home, (Mar.) राघु म्हणाला कीं मी घरीं जातों, lit. Râghu said that, "I am going home."

(Eng.)—I told him that he was the man that I wished to see, (Mar.) मी त्याला सांगितलें कीं ज्या मनुष्याला पाहावाला मी इच्छितों तो तूं आहेस, lit. I told him that, "you are the man I wish to see."

(Eng.)—You asked him where you went yesterday, (Mar.) तूं त्याला विचारिलें कीं मी काल कोठें गेलों होतों, lit. you asked him that "where did I go yesterday ?"

Direct (Eng.)—I said to him, "Are you a tailor?" (Mar.) मी त्याला म्हणालों (or त्याला विचारिलें) तूं शिंपी आहेस काय; *Indirect* (Eng.) I asked him if he were a tailor.

CHAPTER XXV.

THE ATTRIBUTE.

The Adjective.

§ 512—§530.

§ 512. The adjective is used either before a noun to qualify it, or after it with the verb "to be" as a predicative ; ज्ञानी मनुष्यें मान पावतात learned men are respected ; तो फार दयाळु आहे he is very kind. In the first sentence the adjective is used attributively (गुणविशेषण), and in the last, predicatively (विधि-विशेषण).

§ 513. The adjective agrees with the noun it qualifies in gender and number ; तो चांगला आहे he is good.

§ 514. The declinable adjective is inflected to indicate its agreement in gender and number with the noun which it qualifies, but not so the indeclinable ; रामा चांगला आहे खरा पण त्याची प्रकृति सदृढ नाहीं Rama is indeed good, but not healthy ; गुरुजीनें आज त्याची मोठी तारीफ केली the teacher praised him very much to-day.

§ 515. The declinable adjective simply assumes या or ए before an inflected noun ; मग मीं हलक्या लोकांशीं बोलणार नाहीं I will not then speak with low people ; पहिल्या तडाक्यास तर मींच सांपडलों आहें I have fallen into your hands at the very outset. Of the two forms, that in या is preferable, but for the sake of variety, both forms may sometimes be used : शाळेच्या सुटीचे आरंभाचा दिवस the first day of school-holidays.

Note.—Sometimes the indeclinable adjective may be inflected for the sake of emphasis (त्यांकडे अवगणनेनें पाहातो) गरीबा बिचाऱ्या (he looks at him contemptuously) O thou poor fellow ! तूं माझ्या पूज्या मामा, तूं माझे अपराध क्षमा करशील O my worthy uncle, you will really pardon my faults ? The adjectives गरीब and पूज्य are inflected.

Note.—A singular noun of dignity being used in the plural number, the adjective qualifying it assumes plural inflections : गोपाळराव भले खरे Gopalrao is indeed honest ; हे त्या दोघां मुलांचे बाप this gentleman is the father of those two boys.

§ 516. When the adjective is used attributively to two or more nouns, it agrees with the nearest : हा चांगला आंगरखा-पागोटें, सखलाद this good coat, turban and plaid ; त्या हवेंतलीं जनावरें व पक्षी एथें आढळतात the beasts and birds of that climate are found here ; हा चांगला मुलगा आणि मुलगी मला आवडतात I like this good boy and girl.

§ 517. When the adjective is used predicatively to two or more nouns, it follows the rules of concordance given below :—

1. When both the nouns denote persons and are of the same gender, the adjective is used in the plural number : तूं आणि मीं नित्य अरण्यांत राहाणारे you and I are constant tenants of the forest. But if the subjects are of different genders, the predicative

adjective is in the neuter plural: त्याचा बाप आणि आई मोठीं भलीं आहेत his father and mother are very good people.

2. When the subjects denote inanimate objects, the predicative adjective always agrees with the last: त्याचें डोकें आणि चोंच मोठी होती its head and beak were large; ओढे जिकडे तिकडे झुळझुळ वाहात असतात, व त्यांच्या योगानें सर्व डोंगर व सखल दऱ्या हिरव्या गार दिसतात the streams flow gently here and there, and make the hills and low valleys look very green. The demonstrative pronoun हा this, may be optionally inserted in the neuter plural; त्याचें डोकें आणि चोंच हीं मोठीं आहेत.

§ 518. Sometimes two or more adjectives may qualify a noun: म्या एक उंच व जाड झाड पाहिलें I saw a tall and thick tree; जुनीं व फाटकीं पागोटीं केवळ तेथें होतीं there were only old and torn turbans there.

§ 519. When two or more adjectives are employed, the demonstrative pronoun असा such, is elegantly inserted between the adjectives and the noun they qualify: सुंदर व कुलीन असा एक तरुण तेथें अकस्मात् प्राप्त झाला a handsome and noble youth suddenly appeared on the spot; आह्मी दांडगा आणि निर्लज्ज अशा एका रावाच्या समागमें आहों we are in the company of a rude and impudent gentleman.

When the noun is inflected, the demonstrative pronoun is often inserted in this way, and then the demonstrative alone is inflected to agree with the noun, and not the adjectives, as in the second of the above examples.

§ 520. The adjective may be used as the object of a transitive verb: कोणाचें वाईट करूं नये, बरेंच करावें we should not do harm anybody, but only good.

When the declinable adjective is used by itself as the object of a transitive verb, it assumes its neuter singular form: याला खरें सांगितलें, खोटें नाहीं we told him the truth, not untruth.

§ 521. When the declinable adjective is used along with another object, either a noun or pronoun, it may be constructed in two ways:—

(*a*) When the noun or the pronoun is accusative, the adjectival object agrees with it in gender and number : तिनें कोळशानें भिंत अगदीं काळी केली she made the wall quite black with charcoal; आपलें तोंड एथून काळें कर go away from here.

(*b*) When the noun or pronoun is dative, the adjective is put in the neuter singular : वैद्यानें तिला औषध देऊन बरें केलें the doctor having given her medicine, cured her ; मी तुम्हाला शहाणें समजतों I consider you wise ; त्याला पंतोजीनें शहाणें म्हटलें the Pantoji called him wise.

Note.—The verbs करणें to do, समजणें to understand, मानणें to consider, म्हणणें to call, &c., take an adjective as the factitive or indirect object. (§ 508)

§ 522. When two or more objects are compared, with the view of stating their resemblance or difference, or the degree in which they resemble or differ, the adjective indicative of the difference or resemblance is *inflected* in certain languages, such as Sanskṛit, Zend, English, &c., but in Maráṭhi, the adjective is not so inflected, but is placed in the sentence *in a certain position*. The following is the rule of comparison :—

WHEN OBJECTS ARE COMPARED, THE ADJECTIVE IS SIMPLY PLACED AFTER THE ABLATIVE CASE OF THE NOUN WITH WHICH ANOTHER NOUN IS COMPARED : तीं नक्षत्रें सूर्यापेक्षां लहान नाहींत those stars are not smaller than the sun. In this sentence the " stars " are compared with the " sun, " and the adjective लहान small is simply placed after the ablative case सूर्यापेक्षां than the sun. The above Maráṭhi sentence may be thus translated literally ; "those stars *than the sun small* are not." The principal noun, *i. e.*, the noun with which another is compared, may be inflected by the ablative termination हून as well as by the ablative postposition पेक्षां than ; हें काम तुझ्याहून आपल्याचें काम आहे this is the doing of one older than yourself ; तेल पाण्यापेक्षां हलकें असतें oil is lighter than water.

§ 523. When it is necessary to say that a certain object possesses the quality indicated by the adjective in the *highest degree*, that is, more than all the other objects of the class, THE

PRINCIPAL NOUN DOES NOT INDICATE ONE SINGLE OBJECT, BUT THE WHOLE CLASS OR SPECIES OF THAT OBJECT : तो सर्व मुलांपेक्षां शहाणा आहे he is the wisest of all the boys, literally, " he *than all the boys* wise is."

Note.—When the comparison is only between two or more *individual* objects, the comparison is said, in English, to be of the *comparative degree*, and when the comparison is between an object or objects and *the whole class* of those objects, it is said to be of the *superlative degree*, and the two degrees together are called *degrees of comparison* (तारतम्यभाव कोटि).

Note.–The Sanskrit particles of comparison are तर and ईयस for the comparative degree, and तम and इ, for the superlative ; as पुण्य pure, पुण्यतर purer, पुण्यतम purest. Even substantives are compared in this way ; स्त्री a woman, स्त्रीतरा more of a woman ; नृ a man, नृतमः a thorough man. In Persian the particles are तर and तरीन, which in Zend the parent of Persian, are तर and तेम; बेह good, बेहतर better, and बेहतरीन best. The root of these particles of comparison is तृ to step beyond. In English तर exists in the form of *er*, and इ in that of *est;* " small," "small-*er*, " " small-*est*."

Note.—Though none of these particles are employed in Maráṭhí a few Sankṛit words expressive of the highest degree of quality are of common use in the language : उत्कृष्ट excellent, उत्तम best, धर्मिष्ठ most religious, वरिष्ठ highest, श्रेष्ठ best, प्रथम first. The Persian word बेहतर " better " is also naturalised in the language.

Note.—The superlative is sometimes made up without the superlative particles in the same way as in Maráṭhí by means of the locative case : काव्येषु नाटकं रम्यं among poetical compositions the Drama is the most pleasant. Sometimes the genitive is also used : गवां or गोषु कृष्णा बहु क्षीरा the black among the cows gives the largest quantity of milk.

§ 524. The following other methods are, also, employed for making up the forms for the superlative degree :—

1. The principal noun may be put in the locative case, governed by the postposition आंत or मध्यें, instead of in the ablative, inflected by हून or पेक्षां; हा सर्व आंब्यांत मोठा आहे this is the largest mango ; सर्वांमध्यें हाच काय तो शहाणा he is, indeed, of all men the wisest !

2. The superlative adverbs अति, अतिशय extremely, अगदीं utterly, &c., may be joined to the adjective : त्यांतला अगदीं लहान तुकडा त्यानें घेतला he took the smallest of the pieces.

3. The adjectives मोठा great and चांगला good may be joined to the adjective: त्यानें एक मोठी लांब काठी हातीं धरली he held a very long rod in his hand ; तो मोठा दुष्ट आहे he is very wicked ; तो मोठा लबाड दिसतो he looks a great liar; तो चांगला विद्वान आहे he is a very learned man; तो चांगला शहाणा आहे he is a very wise man ; आमचा देश चांगला सुपीक आहे our country is very fertile ; तूं मोठा दांडगा, निर्लज्ज आहेस you are very rude, very impudent.

4. The adjective may be doubled, or another noun or adjective of cognate signification joined to it : तो लाल लाल झाला he became very red ; or तांबडा लाल झाला, lit., he became red red ; or तो लालगुंज झाला, lit., he became red like the गुंज flower ; or तो लालभडक झाला he became of a bright, flaring red ; त्याचें तोंड काळें ठिक्कर झालें आहे his face has become very black, or coal black ; पांढरा सफेत white white, *i.e.* very white ; or पांढरा फटफटीत white as crystal, extremely white.

Note.—In the last three paragraphs the comparison is not direct.

§ 525. EQUALITY BETWEEN OBJECTS IS DENOTED BY THE USE OF THE DEMONSTRATIVES इतका and एवढा SUBSTITUTED FOR THE POSTPOSITION हून or पेक्षां; तो माझ्या इतका तरुण दिसतो he looks as young as myself ; सूर्या इतका चंद्र लांब नाहीं the moon is not so far as the sun.

Note.—एवढा denotes magnitude or quantity, and इतका, both quantity and number (171); इतके रुपये मला नकोत I do not want so many rupees ; इतका or एवढा भात so much rice.

§ 526. Similarity of qualities is indicated by the words सारिखा, समान, प्रमाणें like, &c. : तुझ्या सारिखा मीं एथें दुसऱ्याच्या धर्मावर पोट भरितों I, like you, live here on the charity of others.

§ 527. A small degree of quality is expressed by modifying the adjective by सा or सर : तो काळसर or काळासा दिसला he looked somewhat black ; or the adjective is modified by the adverbs जरा, किंचित, अमळ. &c.: तो जरा काळा आहे he is a little dark.

§ 528. When an adjective qualifies a noun, expressing the sense of *plurality*, it is usually *repeated* ; तेथें मुख्य मुख्य लोक आले

होते great men had come there; त्या गांवांत मोठ मोठीं or मोठीं मोठीं घरें आहेत there are large houses in that town; तुला पुष्कळ चांगल्या चांगल्या भेटी आल्या असतील you must have received many excellent presents. In Maráṭhí as in the other Indian vernaculars, the adjective of quality is thus usually repeated, while in English it is used singly.

Note.—By affixing ला the adjective has the same sense that it conveys in its reduplicated form: त्या गांवांत मोठमोठीं or मोठालीं घरें आहेत.

§ 529. The reduplicated adjective expresses the following *additional* senses:—

1. It expresses the sense of the adjective *distributively*: सर्वांना एक एक लाडू वाटा give a cake to each of them all; ते सर्व जेवले पण चतकोर चतकोर पोळी मात्र घेतली they all ate, but each took only a quarter of a cake.

2. It expresses *gradual progression*: तुम्ही थोडें थोडें वाचा read a little at a time; सकाळची सावली आंखूड आंखूड होते, आणि संध्याकाळची लांब लांब the shadow of the morning becomes gradually shorter and that of the evening longer.

3. It expresses *intensity*: तो लाल लाल झाला he became very red; त्याचा अंत जवळ जवळ आला आहे his end is quite near.

§ 530. Adjectives of opposite or cognate signification are combined to express the sense of *comprehensiveness*: लहान मोठे मिळून पांच हजार होते there were, including the young and old, five thousand men present; हिरवीं पिंवळीं अशीं फुलें त्याच्या हातीं होतीं he had in his hand flowers—green, yellow, &c.

§ 531. WHEN A NOUN IS JOINED TO ANOTHER NOUN TO EXPLAIN OR ILLUSTRATE IT, IT IS SAID TO BE USED IN APPOSITION, AND THE VERB AND THE ADJECTIVE AGREE WITH THE APPOSITION, AND NOT WITH THE ORIGINAL WORD: ते वेळेस रामराव, कृष्णराव, व सावित्रीबाई, दौलतरावाचीं मुलें, तेथें होतीं at that time Rámrao, Krishnarao, and Sávitribáí, the children of Davlatráv, were there; मला पुढें एक म्हातारा बावा व एक मुलगा अशीं दोन माणसें भेटलीं further on I met two persons, an old man and a boy; मुंबई बेट जेव्हां फिरंग्यांच्या स्वाधीन होतें तेव्हां तें इतकें मोठें नव्हतें the island of Bombay was not so large when it was in the possession of the Portuguese. In the last sentence मुंबई Bombay is feminine and बेट island is neuter, and the verb होतें was, the pronouns तें it, and the adverb इतकें so, and the adjective मोठें large, agree with the appositional word बेट, and not with the original word मुंबई.

Note.—1. *Titles* of persons are put after their names : भाऊ डाक्तर त्याला औषध देत असतात Dr. Bhau attends him ; नेपोलियन बादशाहाच्या पुत्रास झुलू लोकांनीं ठार मारिलें the Zulus killed the son of the Emperor Napoleon ; रामा शिपाई आला आहे the sepoy Rama has come. In English the titles are put *before* the names ; *King* Edward, *Corporal* Anderson, *Dr.* Cook ; so also titles, conferred on nativos by the English Government, precede the names : रावसाहेब विश्वनाथ नारायण आले आहेत Ráv Sáheb Vishvanáth Náráyan has come ; प्रोफेसर केरो लक्ष्मण Professor Kero Lakshman.

Note.—2. Nouns indicating *trades, professions*, &c., are put after the proper nouns : खंडू माळी झाडें लावितो the gardener Khandu is planting trees ; जानोबा शिंपी आपलें काम उत्तम जाणतो the tailor Jánobá knows his work very well.

Note.—3. The nouns denoting *countries, cities, rivers*, &c., are put after the proper names : इंग्लंड देश the country of England ; मुंबई शहर the city of Bombay ; गंगानदी the river Ganges. But in addresses and dates on letters in business documents, Government records, &c., the words denoting towns, provinces, &c., precede the proper names: शहर मुंबई एथें सुखरूप असों विशेष we are quite well in the city of Bombay, &c.; तालुके संगमेश्वर, जिल्हा रत्नागिरी the taluka of Sangameshvar, the zilla of Ratnagiri.

CHAPTER XXVI.

PRONOUNS.

1. *Personal Pronouns.*

§ 532—§ 582.

§ 532. The first person singular is usually employed in speaking of one's self : मीं तुमच्या घरीं उद्यां येईन I shall come to your house to-morrow ; बाई, तुम्ही मजकडे यां समयीं रदबदली करूं नये you must not, madam, speak to me on his behalf on this occasion. (This is said by the king to his page's mother in the Bálmitra.)

Note.—1. The editors of newspapers, representing the public, habitually use the first person plural : आम्ही ऐकतों कीं सरकारानें मामलतदारांची बदली केली आहे we hear that the Government has effected the transference of the mámlatdár. Public officials in their official character may use the plural number : आम्ही या कैद्याच्या अर्जाचा विचार करूं we shall consider the petition of this prisoner.

Note.—2. A person might, if of acknowledged dignity, use the first person plural when speaking of himself : आम्हांस असें वाटतें I think so, lit., we thinks so ; आमचें येणें होणार नाहीं I shall not be able to come.

Note.—3. When expressing displeasure at the conduct of another, children, as well as grown-up people, sometimes assume आम्ही we ; तें सर्व खरें पण आम्हाला थट्टा नाहीं सोसत, त्याला काय करावें ? it is all true, but I cannot bear jesting; what can I do to that ? आम्ही नाहीं तुजशीं बोलत जा go away, I won't speak with you.

Note.—4. A person might modestly use आपण for मीं ; आपण त्याचा विचार करूं I (lit. you and I) shall think about it.

§ 533. IN ADDRESSING A PERSON, THE SECOND PLURAL FORM IS USUALLY USED : (the king says) हें मीं थोडें दिलें, मला वाटतें कीं इतक्यांत तुमचें संकट दूर होणार नाहीं I have given this to you which is but little ; I believe it is not enough to afford you complete relief; बाई तुमच्या थोरपणा पाहून मला संतोष झाला. तुमची काय इच्छा आहे ? कोणत्या गोष्टीनें मीं तुमचें प्रिय करीन ? I am very much gratified at your goodness, madam. What are your wishes ? What can I do for your pleasure ?

1. In addressing *inferiors*, such as children, younger relatives, menials, criminals, &c., the second *singular* is used : (to the page) नाहीं, मुला, कांहीं प्रयोजन नाहीं ; तुझी आई तुजकडे येईल, तुला ती एथेंच भेटेल, अंमळ धीर धर no, there is no occasion for it ; your mother will come to you, she will meet you only here. Have patience for a moment.

Note.—1. But the children of persons of equal or superior station may be adressed in the plural number : बाबा तुम्हांला हा खाऊ पाहिजे child do you want this sweetmeat ? Servants always use the plural form.

Note.—2. Equals, friends and relatives, might use the singular number to one another, if the degree of familiarity between them admits of it.

2. BUT ALL OTHERS, OF WHATEVER STATION THEY MAY BE, SHOULD BE ADDRESSED IN THE PLURAL NUMBER. The king thus addresses the page's brother, who is an officer in the army: या राव, आंत यावें Good morning, sir; please walk in; तुमचे तीर्थरूप बहुत सज्जन आणि मोठे शूर होते your father was a man of great integrity and courage.

Note.—1. When the king is displeased with the same officer and regards him as a criminal, he uses the singular number: तुझी तरवार दलपतरावाच्या स्वाधीन कर. घाला हो याला एक महिना बंदिखान्यांत deliver your sword over to Dalpatráv. Put him in prison for a month. In the following sentence the plural pronominal form (आपण) with the honorific subjunctive is used *sarcastically*: आतां जावें राव, आपल्या बंदिखान्यांत you may go now, sir, to your prison.

Note.—2. The singular may sometimes be used instead of the plural *in excited moments of tenderness.* The king changes the plural to the singular when addressing the page's mother, being very much affected by her tender language: माझे माते, तूं मला इतका थोरपणा देऊं नको; ऊठ, उभी राहा O my mother! do not thou give me so much respect. Arise and stand up. The mother is usually addressed by the natives in the singular number, but the father, in the plural.

Note.—3. In addressing the Deity the singular number is used: देवा, तूंच केवळ माझा त्राता आहेस O God, thou only art my Saviour.

§ 534. In addressing one's own masters and persons of dignity, as well as equals who are spoken to in a formal way, the reflexive pronoun आपण is substituted for the second person plural: रावसाहेब आपला थोरपणा पाहून आम्ही आनंद पावलों sir, we are delighted at your magnanimity. With आपण in the nominative case, the verb is in the second person plural, as with तुम्ही.

A still more polite form of address would be with such honorific expressions as महाराज, राव, रावसाहेब, सरकार, &c., used in the place of आपण and तुम्ही constructed with the verb in the third person plural. This is a most *indirect*, and therefore a most respectful mode of address. Thus, (the schoolmaster, speaking to the king, says): महाराजांचा ज्यांत संतोष तें म्या करावें I should do what would please your Majesty; (the squire is thus addressed) येथें माझा उपाय नाहीं असें रावसाहेबांच्या मनांत यावें म्हणून सांगतें I will tell it to you that your honour may know that I am quite helpless in this matter; चार दिवस अधिक गेले म्हणून रावजी रागावतील I am behind the time of payment a few days, and you, sir, might therefore be annoyed.

Obs.—In English, though titles are substituted for the second personal pronoun in addressing superiors, the pronoun is not entirely dispensed with; the honorific nouns are joined to the genitive of the pronoun; as *your* excellency, *your* honour, &c. In Maráṭhí the forms of direct address are entirely rejected: म्या म्हटलें, रावजींस राग आला म्हणून त्यांनीं आमचें घोडें परत लावून दिलें I said to myself that perhaps *your* honour was annoyed and therefore you sent back the horse.

Note.—In more familiar intercourse, or in moments of strong emotion, the simple तुम्ही you might be used instead of आपण, or the honorific expressions. The page's mother, when overpowered with a sense of gratitude and affection for the king's most wonderful kindness to her and her son, thus addresses the king: तुम्हां सारखे उदार, दानिदयाळ यांचें सदा कल्याण असो म्हणून देवापाशीं प्रार्थना करीन I will ever pray to God that he may ever bless such as are like you, generous and kind to the poor. So also the old beggar when blessing the squire uses the singular number: भगवान् तुला सुखी राखो may God bless you.

Note.—In addressing persons by name, the names of males should be used with the honorific suffixes राव, रावजी, जी, पंत, बा, बाजी, &c., and the names of females with बाई, ताई, &c.; thus गोपाळराव or गोपाळरावजी कोणीकडे चाललां Gopálráv, where are you going? The form रावजी is more respectful than that in राव. The जी and बा are often assumed by those who are not Brahmans, though बा is freely applied to the names of the popular gods, as खंडोबा the god Khandobá, विठोबा the god Viṭhobá. Brahmans chiefly take पंत, unless they have studied any of the Shastras, or are officiating as priests; केरोपंत Keropant (a secular Brahman); रामशास्त्री Rám Sástri (a Brahman versed in the Sástras); महादेवभट or महादेवभटजी Mahadeva bhat (a Brahman priest).

Note.—The forms of names are sometimes modified when the honorific suffixes are used; धोंडु a man's name in its simple form, being changed to धोंडोपंत, धोंडभट, धोंडुजी धोंडोबा, धोंडशास्त्री; so also राघु, Rághú रंगू, रंगोपंत, रंगराव, राघोबा, राघूजी, रघुनाथ- रघुनाथराव, &c.

Obs.—The safest course for the Englishman to follow in this matter is the following:—An Englishman may be called by (1) his *Christian name*, or by (2) his *surname*, or by (3) his surname with Mr. prefixed, or (4) addressed as sir, &c. The Maráṭhí simple name without the honorific suffix, corresponds to the (1) *Christian name* ; the name with the honorific suffixes corresponds to the (2) *surname*, or (3) to the *surname with Mr.*; and for (4) the last form of address, the name of the person spoken to should not be repeated, but some such expressions as महाराज, राव, रावसाहेब, शेट, नानासाहेब (for नारायण), बाबासाहेब, तात्यासाहेब, अण्णासाहेब, साहेब, &c., should be substituted; रावसाहेब आपणास राग तर नाहीं आला, Sir, I hope you are not annoyed. Or the person may be called by his official title: कां मास्तर आज आगबोट येणार ? well, master (ticket-master), is the steamer expected to-day?

Note.—There are besides what are called cap-names or टोपण (a lid, cover) names, by which persons are known amongst friends, or in families. They are different from nick-names or sobriquets, in that they do not imply any contempt. On the contrary, they are terms of respect, used in familiar daily intercourse. Every person has one, and he is familiarly known by it. The following are examples:— अण्णा, आप्पा, आबा, आत्या, काका, तात्या, दाजी, दादा, नाना, बापा, बाबा बापाजी, बाबाजी, बापू, भाऊ, मामा, रावजी, राव, &c. They would be used in this way. A person inquiring for Narayanrao would ask: Is Nana at home; or, Is Nana Saheb at home? काकाजी तुम्हाला काय वाटतें Well, Kakaji, what do you think? तातोबाना सांगा कीं बापूसाहेबांनीं बोलाविलें आहे Tell Tatoba that Bapu Saheb has called him. Women have similar names, and younger members of the family must always use them. The Topan names are also denominated व्यावहारिक नांवें common names, चालतीं or वहातीं नांवें current names, प्रतिष्ठानांवें respectful names, उपचारिक नांवें courteous names, and पोषाखी नांवें dress–names.

Note.—As there are respectful names so are there nick-names, indicative of contempt: बगडे shrunken-handed, फेंगडे bow-legged, थोटे one destitute of toes or fingers, हेंदरे dirty, etc.

§ 535. In speaking respectfully of persons when present or absent, the third person plural is used: आपण त्यांस न पुसतां गेलों तर ते आपणास काय म्हणतील what would he (literally they) think of us if we went away without taking leave of him? ते ह्या पोरांच्या मुलांचे वडील आणि जसीं यांचीं मुलें तसेच तेही दयावान् आहेत that gentleman is the father of these children, and he is as kind as they are; हें वर्तमान पावारांस कळतांच त्यांनीं शत्रूकडचे सेनापति होते त्यांस लिहून पाठविलें as soon as the Powar heard of this affair, he wrote to the commander of the enemy's force.

§ 536. When the personal pronouns take inflected nouns in apposition, they usually assume their crude-forms: आम्हां कुणब्यांची काय कथा सांगावी ? what can we say about us peasants ? मज गरिबाला दान द्यावें you ought to give a gift to me, a poor man ; तुमचे सारिखीं थोर मनुष्यें आम्हां गरिबांच्या घरीं ? what, persons like you to come to the house of us poor people !

The first and second personal pronouns assume their instrumental forms, and not their crude forms, before names in the *instrumental* case: म्या गांवच्या धन्यानें त्याजपाशीं एक गोष्ट मागितली असतां त्यानें नाहीं म्हणावें ? when I, the lord of the village, asked a thing of him, should he have refused to give it to me ? तुम्हीं रावांनीं याप्रमाणें करूं नये you, gentlemen, should not act so.

Note.—When the noun is uninflected, the pronouns are also uninflected : मीं गरीब काय करूं शकतों what can I, poor man, do ?

The Indefinite Personal Pronouns.

§ 537. आपण and स्वतः are substituted for all the personal pronouns (Sect. 159); मला बाहेर ठेवून आपण खुशाल आंत गोष्टी करीत बसला he having kept me outside, sat inside talking away leisurely ; आतां आपण काय करावें ? what shall we do now? त्याची चाकरी करावी, तर स्वतःचें कोणी पहावें ? If I should serve him, then who should look after my affairs ?

§ 538. They have usually a reflexive force, and are used to emphasize the personal pronouns : मीं स्वतः तें केलें I myself did it; तुला स्वतःला दिसतें कोठें ? where can you yourself see ?

§ 539. आपण is always substituted for the personal pronouns, when they *refer to the subject of the sentence*, and not otherwise. The English sentence—"I will remain in my own house" will be in Maráṭhí, मीं आपल्या (not माझ्या) घरांत राहीन; they have gone in their own boat; ते आपल्या (not त्यांच्या) नावेंत गेले आहेत ; he has robbed himself, त्यानें आपणासच फसविलें.

§ 540. आपण is not substituted for the personal pronouns (though they may refer to the subject), *if they form a part of the subject*; thus, Rama and his wife came yesterday from Puna, रामा आणि त्याची बायको (not आपली बायको) काल पुण्याहून आलीं.

If आपली was put for त्याची, it would mean not Rama's wife but that of the person speaking. But रामा आपली बायको घेऊन काल पुण्याहून आला Rama taking his wife with him came yesterday from Puna is correct; आपली बायको घेऊन forms a distinct clause by itself, in which the pronoun is joined to the object.

§ 541. When the personal pronouns do not refer to the subject, they cannot be substituted by आपण; I will go to his village, मी त्याच्या गांवीं जाईन; you should not take my book, तूं माझें पुस्तक घेऊं नये. But "you went to your own village" would be तूं आपल्या (not तुझ्या) गांवीं गेलास.

§ 542. The reduplicative form आपआपला each his own, is distributive; ते आपआपलीं पुस्तकें घेऊन आले they came, each bringing his own books; सर्वांस आपआपलीं कृत्यें आवडतात all like their own doings.

§ 543. The form आपसांत or आपसामध्यें amongst (our-your-their) selves, is used to express mutual relation; तुम्ही आपसांत वांटून घ्या you divide it among yourselves; ते आपसांत भांडले they quarrelled among themselves.

§ 544. आपण may be substituted for आम्ही in the following special senses :—

(1) A person may speak of himself in a style of dignity, and then use either आम्ही or आपण in the plural number for himself; आपण असें समजतों our honour or majesty thinks so.

(2) It may be substituted for आम्ही we, in the sense of "I together with others"; आपण सगळा दिवस पाहिजे तें करूं we (you and I) shall do the whole day whatever we like; आपणा चौघांस आज जेवायाचें आमंत्रण आहे we four are invited to-day to dinner.

(3) A person, when speaking *modestly* to another of his intention or ability to do a certain thing, may use आपण for मी I, in the sense of "I and you",—giving thus the person addressed the pleasure of feeling that the matter under consideration cannot be performed without his assistance: आपण याचा विचार करूं I (literally "you and I") will consider it.

§ 545. आपण may be substituted for तुम्ही when a person is addressed most respectfully; आपण आज्ञा द्याल तर आपून साक्षावितों

If your honour will order me, I shall bring and show it to you. When speaking courteously to a gentleman आपण is always used, unless the honorific phrases रावसाहेब, etc., are used. (Sect. 534.)

§ 546. आपण may be substituted for the third personal pronoun, in the sense of "they" when speaking of an absent person in a reverential style ; आपण सांगतील तें करूं I shall do what his Highness or Honour will order.

§ 547. आपला is erroneously used for आपण; मीं आपल्याला (for आपणाला) भेटायास आलों होतों I have come to see your Honour.

§ 548. आपला is used often as an expletive; मीं आपला एथून उठलों तों आपला त्याच्या घरीं गेलों I just got up from here and went straight to his house.

Note.—The Hindusthani pronominal form आप self, is sometimes used ; आप सुखी जग सुखी all are well if self be well. It is, however, often used in compounds in the sense of *our*, *one's own* ; आपहस्तें by one's own hand ; आपखुशीनें of his own will ; आपढंग wilful pranks ; आपखुशानें,-खुशें-खुश,-खुक voluntarily; of one's self.

Note.—The formations आपले आपण and आपल्या आपण are adverbial, and denote "of one's accord", "of itself"; तें आपलेआपण निघालें it got out of itself ; शेवटीं कोणी हाक न मारितां तीं आपलेआपण कावरींबावरीं झालेलीं उठलीं at last before any one called out to them, they of themselves, got up quite excited.

Note.—आपआप is another adverbial form having the same sense ; तें आपआप सुटेल It will get loose of itself, spontaneously. The idea of spontaneity is expressed, also, by joining the pluperfect participle होऊन to आपण; तो आपण होऊन आला he came of his own accord. It may mean also *personally*.

3. *The Relative Pronoun.*

§ 549. The relative is used to introduce an attributive clause which describes or explains the noun, called its antecedent : जो मनुष्य आईबापांची आज्ञा मोडितो तो किती तरी हीनभाग्य आहे how unfortunate is that man who disobeys his parents. THE ANTECEDENT IS JOINED TO THE RELATIVE, AS IN THE ABOVE EXAMPLE : मनुष्य man, is joined to जो who, जो मनुष्य the man who, literally "who man."

§ 550. EVERY RELATIVE IS FOLLOWED BY THE DEMONSTRATIVE PRONOUN तो, DENOMINATED ITS CORRELATIVE (§ 165), AND THE CORRELATIVE MAY STAND BY ITSELF, OR WITH ANOTHER NOUN JOINED TO IT : तुमच्या भतारानें जे उपकार केले ते फेडायाचा योग देवानें आणिला आहे God has given me the opportunity of repaying the favours conferred upon me by your husband ; ज्या गांवांत तो रहात होता त्या गांवांतच त्याला नोकरी लागली he was employed in the very village in which he lived.

§ 551. When the antecedent is a pronoun of the first, or second person, it is joined *both* to the relative and the correlative : जो मीं बंदिशाळेंत राहाण्यास योग्य नाहीं तो मीं न्यायाधीशापुढें उभा राहायास कसा होईन ? how shall I, who am not fit to dwell in a prison, be worthy to appear before the judge ? ज्या तुला वाचतां येत नाहीं त्या तुला हें पुस्तक देऊन काय उपयोग ? of what use is it to give this book to you who cannot read ?

§ 552. When the antecedent is joined to the relative in the relative clause, as, for instance, जो माणूस the man who, or rather " what man, " the relative clause forms *one idea* with the antecedent ; but when the relative clause stands by itself, and the *antecedent precedes it*, the relative clause does not form one idea with the antecedent, but bears the relation to it of an *apposition* or *formal explanation* : आपला पूर्वज जो नामांकित संग राजा त्याच्या वंशांतील हा शेवटला पुरुष होता he was the last man of the family of our ancestor, the illustrious Sang rájá ; असलीं हीं उदार कांटे झाडें ज्यांवर तूं काल उगीच रागें भरलास तीं इतकीं उपयोगी आहेत these most generous, thorny shrubs, at which you were, without cause, annoyed yesterday, are so useful.

1. Sometimes the appositional or explanatory clause is used *before the antecedent*, and then the demonstrative असा *such*, *is inserted* between the appositional clause and the antecedent, and the correlative तो is omitted : ज्यांच्या हातीं सुवर्ण विणे आहेत असे पवित्र कुमार आपल्या दृष्टीस पडतील we shall see such holy youths as have golden harps in their hands ; ज्यांस अग्निज्वाळांत जाळून टाकिलें, ज्यांस पशूच्या तोंडीं दिलें व समुद्रांत बुडविलें असे आपल्या दृष्टीस पडतील we shall see such persons as were burnt in flames, devoured by wild beasts, and drowned in the sea. In the latter

sentence the antecedent is entirely omitted. By substituting the correlative ते for असे, the relative clause will cease to be appositional.

2. The appositional clause commencing with the relative may be used, by itself, ending with असा, and the antecedent introduced by another relative may be followed by its correlative तो, as in the ordinary construction (§ 549): ज्यांचे हातीं सुवर्ण विणे आहेत असे जे पवित्र कुमार ते अपाल्या दृष्टीस पडतील we shall meet such holy youths as hold golden harps in their hands.

3. Sometimes the antecedent with असा may complete the correlative sentence, and its relative appositional clause, introduced by कीं, may follow it : निर्लज्ज अशा एका रावाच्या समागमें आहों कीं जो आपले ठायीं नसता थोरपणा आणितो आहे आणि एकमेकांचें आगतस्वागत कसें करावें याविषयीं मूर्ख आहे we are in the company of a rude and shameless gentleman, who assumes a superiority to which he has no title, and who is deplorably ignorant of the rules of etiquette.

Note.—Sometimes the relative clause introduced by कीं has the force of the adverbial clause of purpose : याला माझ्या राज्याचा स्तंभ, विश्वासू सेवक, आणि माझ्या मुलांचा मित्र करून ठेवावा, कीं जो एकादे दिवशीं प्रसंग पडला असतां आपल्या बापाप्रमाणें राज्याच्या कल्याणार्थ प्राण खर्च करील I should make him the pillar of my kingdom, my faithful servant, and the companion of my children, that he might, like his father, offer his life for the welfare of my kingdom. When the relative clause with कीं जो is used adverbially, the antecedent is not preceded by the demonstrative असा, as is the case when the relative clause is used adjectively. In the above example the antecedent याला is not qualified by असा, while, in the example in the preceding paragraph, the antecedent रावाच्या is qualified by the demonstrative in its crude form of अशा.

4. Sometimes the relative clause may follow the clause containing the antecedent, without inserting कीं or असा. It is then used as a purely appositional or attributive clause in company with a number of other attributive phrases. The relative clause comes last, and rounds a highly rhetorical period : त्यानें माझा रथ मोडला त्यांत काय माझा तोटा झाला नाहीं? रथ सोनेरी रंगाचा, नुकता नवा केलेला, ज्याचे दोन हजार रुपये मला पडले? what, have I not suffered a great loss in that he broke my chariot—a

chariot that was gilt, that was but recently made, and which cost me two thousand rupees ? In this sentence the noun रथ is followed first by a prepositional attributive phrase, next by a participal one, and lastly by a relative clause. Again, त्याची भलाई किती, संतोषवृत्ति काय, ज्याचा सिंहासारखा पराक्रम, मेंढरासारखी गरीबी how just and contented he was in his disposition, whose valour was like the valour of a lion, and meekness like that of the lamb ! This is a most peculiar construction, and the relative clause is most elegantly used.

तिसरे दिवशीं चक्रव्यूह सुदुर्भेद्य युक्तिनें रचिला ।
जो धीर वीर हीर प्रवर प्रकरेंकरोनियां खचिला ॥

Moropant.

Note.—When the relative clause does not express the sense of an appositional or attributive clause, it should never be used after a complete sentence containing the antecedent. The relative clause is sometimes used in English in this way, but even in that language the relative has, then, the force of a *conjunction*, and is equivalent to "and who." In translating the conjunctional relative, the Maráthí demonstrative तो is substituted for the relative pronoun. There was a young woman there watching the field, *who* said, &c.; तेथें एक तरणी स्त्री शेताची राखण करीत बसली होती, ती (not जी) म्हणाली ; तिची आई बाहेरून आली, तिणें (not जिणें) नानीस पुसलें कीं दुर्गा कोठें आहे, her mother returned home, and she inquired where Durga was ; तेथें एक गुहा होती त्या गुहेंत मीं निजलों there was a cave there, *in which* I slept.

§ 553. THE RELATIVE AGREES WITH THE ANTECEDENT IN GENDER AND NUMBER : जें नुकसान व्हावयाचें तें होऊन चुकलें whatever injury was to be sustained has been borne ; जो मनुष्य आईबापांची आज्ञा मोडितो तो किती हतभाग्य तरी how miserable is that man who disobeys his parents.

§ 554. WHEN THE RELATIVE IS FOLLOWED BY SEVERAL NOUNS, IT, LIKE THE ADJECTIVE, AGREES WITH THE NOUN NEAREST IT: समजण्यास प्रयोजक जें शास्त्र, कागद, पत्र, दूत, महार इत्यादि पदार्थ तो डोळा that which is useful in imparting knowledge, as, for example, the Scriptures, a letter, a messenger, a guide, &c., is called an eye.

Sometimes, however, the relative may agree with the last word in the sentence, particularly if it be the principal one neglecting the words nearest it: ग्यायाचें जें पंचपात्री, पेला इत्यादि लहान पात्र तें उपपात्र a goblet, cup, and other small drinking vessels are called *upapátra*. The principal word stands, as it were, in opposition to all the other antecedents, in the way in which the demonstrative हा this, असा such, &c., are used. (§ 566)

§ 555. The relative may be optionally omitted: माझे पेटींत कांहीं जुनीं चिरगुटें असतील तीं मीं सगळीं शोधून काढीन I will take out whatever old dresses I may have got in my box; मुलांनीं वडील सांगतात तें निमूटपणें ऐकावें children should quietly listen to what their elders tell them. In conversation the relative is often dropped.

§ 556. The emphatic sense of the relative is expressed by repeating it, or by uniting कोणी with it: जो जो पदार्थ ती मागे तो तो or तो आम्ही तिला देऊं 'whatever thing she asked we gave her; जो कोणी विश्वास ठेवील तो तरेल he that believes shall be saved. This emphatic sense may also be expressed by the omission of the antecedent noun: ज्यांत आपलें अनहित तेंच निषेधिलें आहे whatsoever is injurious has alone been forbidden us.

4. *The Demonstrative Pronouns.*

§ 557. The demonstrative pronouns are हा this, तो that, असा such, etc.

§ 558. The pronoun हा this denotes something that is (1) *present*, or *near in place* or *time*, or (2) something just mentioned, or (3) that is just about to be mentioned; त्यांनीं जेव्हां हें ऐकिलें तेव्हां ते कुंठित झाले when they heard this they were confounded; परंतु हें लक्ष्यांत ठेवा कीं जर घरधन्याला तें अगोदर कळलें असतें तर तो निजून राहता ना but bear this in mind that if the master of the house had known it beforehand, he would not have kept sleeping.

§ 559. The pronoun तो that usually refers to a person or thing *previously mentioned*; त्यांनीं तें ऐकिलें तेव्हां त्यांना मोठा राग आला when they heard that they were very angry; त्या दिवसापासून तो बरा झाला he got better from that time.

But it is chiefly used in *opposition* to हा this, or by way of distinction, and in such cases, हा this generally refers to that which is nearer, and तो that to what is more remote; हा जावो,

आणि तो राहो let this man (who is nearer the speaker) go, and let that (who is more remote) remain.

Note.—When *this* and *that* refer to foregoing words or phrases, *this* generally refers, in English, to the latter, and *that* to the former; but in Marathi the demonstratives by themselves are not often so used, but the words themselves are repeated ; नीति आणि ज्ञान हीं दोन्ही उपयोगाचीं आहेत खरीं तरी ज्ञानापेक्षां नीति विशेष महत्त्वाची मानिली पाहिजे. Both virtue and knowledge are useful, but the former ought to be considered of greater importance than the latter. In the following verse the pronouns are, however, independently used—परि यापरीस ती थोडी :—

आर्या आर्यासि रुचे. इच्छा यावीं जशी असे गोडी।
आहे इतरा छंदीं गोडी, परि या परीस ती थोडी ॥ १ ॥

§ 560. The demonstratives हा this and तो that may be used *independently* for the nouns they refer to ; त्यानें हातांत लाडू घेऊन म्हटलें "हा घ्या तुम्हाला खायाला" he held a cake in his hand and said, "Take this for you to eat."

§ 561. The pronouns, in their masculine and feminine forms are essentially *personal*, and when they stand by themselves, *without an immediate reference* to a noun *expressly mentioned* before, they denote *a person* or human being only ; हा कोण हो who is this? ही काय करिती आहे what is this (woman) doing ? हें काय वाटेंत पडलें आहे what is this (thing) lying on the way ? अहो ती कोणी बायको आहे Oh, Sir, it is some woman.

§ 562. But when a masculine or feminine noun denoting a lifeless thing has been previously *mentioned* or declared expressly, the masculine हा or the feminine ही, used by itself, may not denote a person ; त्यानें भाकर हातांत घेऊन म्हटलें "ही घ्या आणि प्रभूच्या स्मरणासाठीं खा," then he took bread in his hand and said, "Take this, and eat it in remembrance of the Lord." If the clause—त्यानें भाकर हातांत घेऊन म्हटलें he took the bread in his hand, and said—be not *uttered in the hearing* of the people to whom the words ही घ्या etc., are addressed, the feminine domonstrative will not be used, only the neuter will be employed ; thus, (उपाध्यानें भाकर हातांत घेऊन म्हणावें,) हें घ्या आणि प्रभूच्या स्मरणासाठीं खा the priest, taking the bread in his hand should say (words not uttered before the congregation) " Take this (neut. sing.), and eat it in remembrance of the Lord."

§ 563. But in a printed narrative, a sentence like this may occur ; नंतर त्यानें खुरचीकडेस बोट करून म्हटलें, ही घ्या बसायाला then he pointed to the chair and said, Take this (fem.) for you to sit on. For, in a narrative both the noun and the demonstrative are uttered at once by the reader.

§ 564. The demonstrative असा such expresses kind; असा माणूस कोणी पाहिला नाहीं such a man no one has seen ; अशांना काय करावें what shall we do with such (women) ?

§ 565. The Demonstratives follow the Rules of Concordance given under the attributive Adjectives. (Sect. 513.)

§ 566. The demonstratives हा and असा are often used *appositionally*, and serve the following uses :—

1. हा this, is often used in apposition to the subject, when the nominal predicate defines or explains the latter : रामा हा गोपाळरावाचा मुलगा होता Rámá was the son of Gopálráv ; मुंबई हें शहर आहे Bombay is a city.

2. हा and असा are usually inserted in apposition when the verb has two or more subjects : रामा आणि गोविंदा हे मौज पाहायास गेले होते both Rámá and Govindá went to see sights ; पुढें एक म्हातारा बाबा व एक मुलगी अशीं दोन मनुष्यें भेटलीं further on I met two persons, an old man and a girl. Or they may be used when the subject is composed of two or more words : गोविंदशास्त्री लेले हे आले होते Govind Sástri Lele had come.

Note.—असा expresses kind or sort, and हा points out individuality. When the demonstrative used in apposition is followed by another noun, it agrees with the latter : हा जो परमेश्वराच्या भक्तीपासून अंतीं मोठा लाभ होतो हीच सुगति होय the happiness which we obtain at last from the worship of God that alone is salvation. अनंत ब्रह्मांडाच्या माळा, हे तो भगवंताची लिळा.

3. The appositional हा is inflected instead of the nouns for which it stands : हत्ती, घोडे आणि बैल ह्यांस चारा घाला give grass to the elephants, horses, and oxen ; रामा, हरि आणि गोपाळ ह्यांपेक्षां सखा हुषार आहे Sakhi is cleverer than Rámá, Hári, and Gopal.

4. हा is inserted in apposition when an adjective is predicated of two or more nouns : त्याचें डोकें आणि चोंच हीं मोठीं होतीं his head and beak were large ; गौरी, मथुरा आणि काशी ह्या मोठ्या शहाण्या आहेत Gavrî, Mathurà and Kàsí are very wise.

5. हा or असा is also used, in *apposition,* when a sentence, used as the subject or object of the verb, is placed before it मुली घे हें तुला न्याहारीस दिलें, असें म्हणून तो चालता झाला child, take this, I have given it to you for breakfast ; so saying, he walked away ; त्या मुलीची आई लबाड नव्हे अथवा त्या मुलीनें तुला लटकें सांगितलें नाहीं, हें तुझ्यानें कशावरून सांगवेल ? how can you say that the mother of that woman is not a liar, or that the girl has not told a falsehood ? कोणास म्हातारपणामुळें, दुखण्यामुळें किंवा दुर्दैवामुळें भीक मागणें प्राप्त होतें तें तो लक्ष्यांत आणीत नाहीं he does not consider that some are obliged to beg by old age, sickness or misfortune.

§ 567. The demonstrative used appositionally to nouns agrees with those nouns in gender and number ; बैल आणि रेडे हे मात्र तेथें होते only the oxen and the buffaloes were there. Where the nouns differ in gender, the demonstrative is used in the neuter plural; त्यानें आपलें घर, गाडी, घोडा, आणि बाग हीं विकून टाकिलीं he sold off his house, carriage, horse, and garden. If the appositional demonstrative is followed by a noun, it agrees with that noun, and not with those which precede it : त्यांनीं त्या वेळीं आपल्या बंदुकी, तरवारी, आणि ढाली अशीं हत्यारें बरोबर घेतलीं at that time they took with them such weapons as muskets, swords and shields.

§ 568. The demonstrative used appositionally to a sentence is always in the neuter singular, unless it be followed by a noun, when it agrees with that noun : जेथें कोणी आपली कृपा इच्छितो आणि ती त्यावर आपल्याच्यानें करवत नाहीं अशी गोष्ट होते, तेथें त्याचा दोष, आपला नाहीं where it so happens that a person expects a favour of us, and it is not in our power to confer it on him, there he is to blame, not we. Instead of अशी गोष्ट होते we might simply say असें होतें.

Although the demonstrative may be employed in apposition to two or more clauses, it is always in the singular number ;

त्यास तूं हांसावें आणि त्यानें तुझी खोडी काढिली म्हणजे त्वां त्यास मारावें हें काय तुला शोभतें ? does it become you that you should laugh at him, and that when he teases you you should beat him !

§ 569. When attention is required to be directed to each clause separately, the demonstrative तो that, in its neuter singular form, is placed in apposition to each clause, and the demonstrative neuter singular हें this, is placed last, in apposition to the whole sentence collectively, with or without a noun : त्यानें शरू लावितांना केंस भाजून घेतले तें, आपले दिवाणखान्यांतला आरसा फोडिला तें, गाडी मोडिली तें, हे सर्व अपराध (or हें सर्व all this) मीं त्याला क्षमा नाहीं केले ? he burnt his hair when letting off fireworks ; he broke the looking-glass that was in the parlour ? he broke the carriage ; did I not forgive him all these faults ?

§ 570. The demonstrative तो is usually substituted for the third person ; but when two persons are metioned, हा is used for the nearer, and तो for the more distant. Thus the English sentence, " let him go, and let this man remain," would be rendered तो जावो, हा राहो. In like manner, " let him go, and that man stay, " would be हा जावो, तो राहो.

As regards the rules on the employment of the demonstrative तो that, as a correlative, see the Relative Pronoun (§550).

5. *The Interrogative Pronoun.*

§ 571. The interrogative कोण refers both to persons and things, but chiefly to the former : तुझी आई कोण आहे मुली ? who is your mother, child ? त्यानें कोणाचा अपराध केला ? against whom has he committed an offence ? तुम्ही हा उद्योग करितां ह्याचा विषय कोण ? what is your object in engaging in this business ?

When the agent is unknown, the interrogative कोण is used with the *neuter singular verb* ; अं कोण हाक मारितें ? eh, who is calling out to me ?

§ 572. The form कोणता or कोणचा is employed when inquiry refers to one of a class of objects : ह्या आंब्यांतून तूं कोणता घेतोस ? which will you take of these mangoes ? कोणत्या मुलानें तुला ही गोष्ट सांगितली ? which boy told you this story ? तुम्हांला ह्या घोड्यांतून कोणचा पाहिजे ? which of these horses do you want ?

§ 573. कोणता is sometimes used for कोण emphatically ; आपल्या बाळाच्या मरणाचा आपणास विसर पडावा असें कोणत्या आईच्या मनांत येईल बरे ? what mother would wish to forget the death of her own child ?

§ 574. काय what is used in relation to things ; त्याला काय पाहिजे ? what does he want ? त्याचा उद्देश काय ? what is his object ?

§ 575. काय what has the following peculiar uses :—

1. It is used for the relative pronoun जें in the sense of "whatever"; तो काय (जें) देईल तें घेऊन ये bring whatever he may give you.

2. It is used as an exclamation of surprise at the greatness of a thing, both in reference to men and things : हा काय हो मूर्ख what a fool he is ! काय हें धैर्य what courage, this !

3. It is used also to express surprise at the *number* and *variety* of objects in a reduplicated form : मीं काय काय त्याचे गुण सांगूं ? what and how many excellencies of his shall I recount ?

4. Or it may simply express the collective sense of extent, variety, and distribution : त्यानें काय काय तुला दिलें तें मला सांग tell me what all he gave you ? The various articles may be separately enumerated, and a single काय may precede each noun ; सजगोरा काय, जोंधळा काय, गहूं काय, जो जिनस पाहिजे तो आहे there is bájrí there, jvárí, in short, every article you may wish for.

5. It may also be used as an interjectional particle of surprise or interrogation : काय, त्वा त्याला मारिलें काय ? what did you strike him ?

§ 576. It is used as a particle of interrogation : आज पाऊस पडेल काय ? will it rain to-day ?

§ 577. The interrogatives किती and केवढा, signifying how much or how many, have corresponding relative and demonstrative forms (§ 171); and a distinction is sometimes made between them in sense and use, but utterly ignored by the best of authors. किती means how many, implying number, and केवढा how much, expressing quantity and extent ; किती आंबे पाहिजेत ? how many mangoes do you want ? केवढें तेल त्वा ओतिलें ? how much oil did you pour out ?

The sense of degree is best expressed by किती ; मनुष्यांची बुद्धि किती दुर्बल व मंद आहे, व त्यांचें ज्ञान किती अल्प व अपूर्ण आहे how poor and dull is the understanding of men, and how scanty and imperfect their knowledge ! कांहीं मतें कांहीं लोकांस किती सबळ वाटतात how strong do some opinions appear to some people !

6. *The Indefinite Pronoun.*

§ 578. कोण as an indefinite pronoun signifies some one ; खालीं कोण आला आहे some one has come downstairs. When the person is quite unknown, the form कोणसा is used ; तुला कोणसा हाक मारितो आहे some one, I do not know who, is calling out to you. कोणी has the sense of any one ; कोणी आलें ह्मणजे मला सांगा tell me when any one comes. कोण एक expresses some particular person or thing, both singular and plural ; आज आपल्या एथें कोण एक मनुष्यें येणार आहेत to-day some people are going to come to our house; कोण एकानें असें म्हटलें आहे some one has said so ; a certain man has said so.

Note.—The form कोण एक has the form of the English indefinite article, and the indefinite phrase "a certain," which is often employed in that language in commencing a story : कोण एक मालोजी नांवाचा मनुष्य होता there was a certain man of the name of Málojí. The indefinite numeral एक has the same sense : एक अति दरिद्री संताजी नांवाचा मोलकरी होता there was a certain very poor man of the name of Santájí ; त्यांचें पोषण कसें होईल ह्मणून त्यास एके समयीं मोठी काळजी पडली at a certain time or *on a certain occasion,* he felt very anxious as to how he might feed them. एक may also mean "some one," "any one ;" एका वैद्याला or एकाद्या वैद्याला बोलावा call some doctor, any you may find.

Note.—The Maráṭhi noun has the force of the English article inherent in it, and the context determines whether it is definite or indefinite ; शेवटीं गांव आला हो at last we have come to *a* town, or at last we have come to *the* town (which we have been looking forward to) ; तो वाघ असावा it must be a tiger ; हा पाहा बैल आला see, here the ox comes.

§ 579. कोणता as an indefinite pronoun answers to the question put with the interrogative कोणता ? कोणता घ्यावा which one shall I take ? Answer, कोणताही घे take any you please.

§ 580. काय as an indefinite pronoun signifies that which, whatever: जो काय देईल तें घेऊन ये bring whatever he might give you.

§ 581. कांहीं some, expresses a few, or a little: कांहीं लोकांस असें वाटतें some people think so; त्यांत कांहीं तेल कांहीं पाणी होतें there was some oil and some water in it.

कांहीं has a partitive sense; त्यांतले कांहीं अंजीर व सुकेळीं मुलगी व आपण मिळून खाल्लीं he and his daughter ate some of the figs and dried plantains from it. It expresses, also, something more or less, not nothing: केवळ उपाशी जाऊं नको, कांहीं खा do not go without taking any food; eat something more or less. With the negative particle it signifies *not at all*: तुला कांहीं मिळायाचें नाहीं you shall not have anything at all.

It is used when any matter or business is spoken of indefinitely: तुम्हांपाशीं कांहीं बोलायाचें आहे I have to speak to you something. Used adverbially it expresses an indefinite degree: ईश्वरप्राप्तीचें सुख कांहीं विलक्षण आहे the happiness obtained from the possession of God is something indescribably wonderful.

The phrase कांहीं करून signifies by some means or other; आपण कांहीं करून माझी गरज पुरवावी you must by some means or other supply my want.

The pronoun कांहीं combined with एक means some few persons or things: कांहीं एक लोक असे आहेत कीं त्यांस सगळा दिवस तंबाखू खायास पाहिजे there are some people of such a nature that they must chew tobacco the whole day. With the negative particle it denotes, not even one, nothing at all; पेंढाऱ्यांनीं कांहीं एक भांडें घरांत ठेविलें नाहीं the Pendharis did dot leave a single vessel in the house; मी तुला कांहीं एक द्यावयाचा नाहीं I sha'nt give you anything at all.

कांहीं when reduplicated has a distributive force: कांहीं कांहीं शेतें बरीं आहेत; कांहीं कांहीं वाईट some fields here and there are good; some here and there are bad; हें चित्र कांहीं कांहीं अंशीं चांगलें, कांहीं कांहीं अंशीं अगदीं घाणेरडें this picture is good in some parts, in others it is very bad.

Reduplicated with वाहीं it expresses some little degree: काहीं वाहीं गूळ घेतला, काहीं वाहीं घ्यावयाचा आहे I have purchased some little jagri, some little more is yet to be bought; औषध घेतांच काहीं वाहीं दिसूं लागलें as soon as I took the medicine, some little effect began to show itself.

582. Besides the senses of एक one given under section 578, it has the following:—

1. The numeral एक is used indefinitely; तेथें एक माणूस उभा होता some one person was standing there.

2. It expresses the sense of one particularly or pre-eminently; तो एक वीर an unrivalled hero he; तो एक सोश an arrant scamp he.

3. It may denote excess or continuousness; एक रड चालली होती, there was a ceaseless wail going on.

4. It may mean one, alike or identical; तुम्ही आम्ही एक we are both one and the same.

5. It may denote other, not the same; हें औषध एक, तें एक this and that are different medicines.

6. It may mean one, unchangeable; तुम्हीं थोर, तुमचें वचन एक असावें you are great, and your word ought never to change.

CHAPTER XXVII.

THE USES OF THE CASES.

1. The Nominative Case.

(कर्तृकारक or प्रथमा.)

§ 453—§ 464.

§ 583. The Nominative is the case of the subject when the verb takes the *Kartari* construction (§ 210); माझा धाकटा भाऊ आला आहे my younger brother has come. It is also the case of the nominal predicate: या मुलाचा बाप साळवी होता the father of this boy was a weaver; तूं फार भली बायको आहेस you are a very honest woman.

2. The Accusative Case.

(कर्मकारक or द्वितीया.)

§ 584. The Accusative case expresses the direct object of the verb ; ही तुझी ठकाविद्या मीं बापास सांगेन I will tell this your trickery to father ; तुम्ही हीं पक्वान्नें फार खाऊं नका do not eat these sweetmeats much.

Note—1. The accusative object is used, also, as the internal object of the compound verb. (§ 295).

§ 585. The accusative case is employed to express the adverbial relations of (*a*) *space*, (*b*) *time*, and (*c*) *measure* :—

(*a*) रोज मीं दोन कोस चालतों I walk four miles every day.
तो दोन चार घरें हिंडला he went over to two or four houses.

(*b*) ती बारा महिने अनवाणी चालते she walks barefoot all the year round.

(*c*) त्याला दोन शेर पीठ आणि चार हात बनात द्या give him two seers of flour, and two yards of broadcloth.

दास म्हणे मना सावध असावें, दुश्चित नसावें सर्व काळ.—*Rámdás.*

सूता जा कृष्णेला, घेउनि ये भय नसे तुला लेश.—*Moropant.*

Note.—The measure of excess or inferiority, as well as the rate of measurement is indicated by the instrumental case (§ 586, 14-15).

Note.—The suffix भर is joined to the accusative of space, time and measure, to express the idea of thoroughness, fulness, etc. It may be put to the accusative either before or after it ; मूठभर रुपये दिले he gave a handful of rupees, or भरमुठ रुपये दिले he gave a handful closely stuffed and crammed.

3. The Instrumental Case.

(करणकारक or तृतीया.)

§ 586. The instrumental case principally denotes the *instrument* whereby an action is performed : as, या भयंकर शस्त्रानें याच्यानें कोणास उपद्रव करवणार नाहीं इतकें बरें so much the better that he cannot do harm to anybody with this dreadful weapon.

पथ्य नाम वीठोबाचें। आणिक वाचें नसेवी.—*Tukárám.*

§ 587. The instrumental case indicates several other relations besides that of instrumentality. The following are a few of them :—

2. *The agent,* or the subject of the verb ; तिनें मला लवकर येतें म्हणून सांगितलें she told me that she would come soon ; एकमेकांस साहित्य करावें म्हणून आपणास ईश्वरें या लोकीं पाठविलें आहे God has sent us on earth to help one another.

सत्यातें जोडावें सुज्ञें, धर्मासि पळ न सोडावें.—*Moropant.*

निष्फळ होती मेघें, स्यजिलीं आलींहि जीविका शेतें.—*Moropant.*

Note.—The subject is always in the instrumental case in certain instances. (§ 481, 1, 2).

3. *The operating cause or power :* मानाऊनें त्या लाजेनेंच जीव दिला Mánáú died from that very disgrace ; आंता माझी खात्री झाली कीं हीं कोणी मोठे कुटुंबांतील दरिद्रानें अशे दशेस आलीं आहेत I am now convinced that they belong to some respectable family, and have been reduced to this state by poverty.

सर्व कांहीं घडे संगतीच्या गुणें । साधूचीं लक्षणें साधूसंगें.—*Rámdás.*

4. *Manner :* त्यांणीं मोठे प्रीतीनें, मोठे नम्रतेनें त्यांचें आगतस्वागत केलें they received them with great affection and meekness.

पाशांतें तोडावें धीरें न कशापि पाप जोडावें.—*Moropant.*

5. *The accompanying circumstance :* त्या काळीं बारा हजार स्वारांनीं शिवाजी मुसलमानावर पडला at that time Shiváji attacked the Mahomedans with twelve thousand horsemen ; महामुद वीस हजार घोडयांनिशीं पंजाबांत शिरला Mahomed penetrated into the Panjab with twenty thousand horse. The instrumental termination often assumes the form of निशीं, as in the last example, to express this sense; शेलापागोटयानिशीं स्वयंपाक घरांत जाऊं नये, we should not go into the kitchen with our clothes on,—lit., with our scarf and turban put on.

6. *The contents of a thing* : तेथेंच त्याणें मोहरांनीं भरलेला कमरेचा कसा काढिला आणि दौलतरावांसमोर रिकामा केला only there he took out the scrip filled with *moharas*, which he had tied round his waist, and emptied it before Davlatráv.

7. *A reference, i.e.,* it is joined to nouns, adjectives, or verbs, to point out in *reference to what they are to be understood:* याची आई शरीरानें निरोगी नव्हती पण सुंदर आणि संसारकामांत मोठी दक्ष

होती his mother was not healthy in body, but she was beautiful and clever in housewifery ; हरण एका डोळ्यानें अंधळें होतें the deer was blind of one eye.

मळस्यागें झाला शरीरें निर्मळ । अंतरींचा मळ कैसा गेला.—*Tukárám.*

8. *Space, proximity, &c.*—

(*a*) *Near to, in motion :* मीं उगा वाटेनें चाललों होतों I was quietly going along the road.

प्राणी संसाराशीं आला । तितुका मृत्युपंथें गेला.—*Tukárám.*

(*b*) *Close to :* तिनें त्याला उराशीं धरिलें she held him to her bosom; तो चालला होता त्या वाटेंत दोहों बाजूंनीं कांटझाडें होतीं there were thorny trees along both sides of the road by which he went.

(*c*) *Motion from :* पुण्यासनें मीं साताऱ्यास गेलों I went from Poona to Satara.

Note.—When the नें has an ablative force equivalent to हून,ऊन from, as in the last instance, it is always written without the anuswár.

9. *Intercourse, opposition, &c. :* त्यानें त्याशीं मारामारी केली he fought with him ; लोकांशीं विनयानें, थोरपणानें चालत नाहींत ते हलके लोक those who do not behave towards others with gentleness and honour, are base.

झाला स्त्रियेचा लंपट मायबापाशीं उद्धट.—*Tukárám.*

10. *Purpose :* तथापि आमुच्या कार्योद्देशें अवश्य गेलें पाहिजे for our benefit you must of necessity go.

11. *Time :* दोन तासांनीं त्याचा प्राण गेला he died in two hours.

तपोधैर्यांचा पर्वत । चूर्ण झाला क्षणार्धें.—*Mukteswar.*

12. *Direction, authority :* मग भिमाबाईच्या विचारानें मनीं सखीची चाकरी करायास राहिली then Sakhí remained there to wait on Maní with the permission of Bhimábái ; त्याला कायद्यानें दोषी ठरविलें he was convicted by law ; त्याच्या दृष्टीनें in his sight.

13. *Comparison :* आणि त्याचे अवस्थेशीं आपली अवस्था लावून आपण मोठे मनुष्य असें मानून गर्वानें फुगतो he compares his own condition with that of the other person, and fancying that he is some great man swells with pride.

14. *The measure of excess or inferiority* in comparison : तो दोन वर्षांनीं मोठा he is older by two years.

15. *Rate of* in measurement and quantity: शेरानें विकतो, पायलीनें विक्रीत नाहीं he sells by *seers*, not by *páyalis* (bushels).

Obs.—The English student should notice the prepositions which express the different senses of the instrumental and all the other following cases. The senses of the Maráthí instrumental are expressed in English by the prepositions "by," "with," "against," "in," "according to," "along," &c. No one who would speak Maráthí idiomatically should neglect the chapters on the "Uses of the Cases."

4. The Dative Case.

(संप्रदानकारक or चतुर्थी)

§ 588. The dative primarily denotes the *person* or *thing remotely connected with an action as its object*; etymologically it signifies a *giving*, real or imaginary; तुम्हाला हे खाऊसाठीं दिले असतील this must be given to you as pocket-money; गणपतराव धाकट्यांस पुष्कळ बर्फी वाटितो आणि आपणास घेतो Ganpatráo gives much sweetmeat to the younger lads, and takes much for himself also. The dative object is usually the *indirect object*. The dative case has several other senses. It signifies—

2. *The direct object:* वडील पोवार त्याला धरितो the elder Powár holds him; मीं तुला ओळखितों, तसा बाबा तुला ओळखीत नाहीं father does not know you so well as I know you. When the object is a person, the dative is used as the direct object (§ 490).

3. *The subject with the potential verb;* आह्माला काम केल्यावांचून राहवत नाहीं we cannot do without working; तिजसारखी तुला सुकी भाकर खाववणार नाहीं you will not be able to eat dry bread as she does (§ 481, 3).

4. *The person or thing to which an action refers, chiefly with intransitive verbs:* दोघे मुलगे मोठे झाले तेव्हां राण्यास धास्ती पडली the Rání became anxious when the two boys grew up; तुम्ही आह्मांस फार भयंकर दिसतां you appear to us very dreadful.

The following are a few particulars indicated by the *dative of reference*:—

(a) The person or thing benefited or injured: औषधोपचार करून दुखणाइताला गुण आला the patient recovered by the remedies that were used; नकटीचे लग्नाला बाराशें विघ्नें there are a thousand

obstacles in the way of the marriage of a woman that has a snub nose.

(*b*) *Possession* with the verb असणें: त्याला लहान लहान सहा मुलें होतीं he had six small children.

(*c*) *The person for whom sympathy is expressed :*

कोणे कोणासी रडावें ॥ एका मागें एकीं जावें ॥

(*d*) *The thing in which a person suffers :* त्या साखरेच्या व्यापारांत तो हजार रुपयांला मेला he lost in that sugar-trade to the extent of one thousand rupees ; तेणेंकरून ते मनुष्यपणाला मुकतात they lose their manhood by it.

(*e*) *The person supplicated :* तुम्ही सर्व देवाला शरण जा go all of you for help to God.

(*f*) *Effect or consequence :* मला वाटतें कीं तूं माझी काकळूत जाणून, तसा माझे दुःखास कारण होणार नाहींस I believe you will not so cause me pain when you know my distress ; आपले नाशाला मात्र तो लढला he fought only to his ruin.

(*g*) *Definiteness, i.e.,* being used with an adjective, or a noun or a neuter verb, it *limits* its sense : जिभेला गोड sweet to the taste ; खायाला मात्र चांगले good only for food.

(*h*) *Comparison :* सीतेला जसा राम तसा तुला नळ शोभतो as Ráma suits Sita, so Nala suits you.

"श्रीकृष्ण रुक्मिणीला, श्रीकृष्णा रुक्मिणी जशी आतां ॥

दमयंतीस नळ नळा, दमयंती आयकों जनें गातां" ॥ *Moropant.*

(*i*) *Utility, office, &c. :* घे हे दोहीं हातांस दोन माझे मित्रा take these two for both hands, my friend ; तो पोरें चाकरीस ठेवित असतो he employs boys as servants.

तुवां जाऊनि तपोवना, कौशिक ऋषीच्या दर्शना.—*Mukteswar.*

5. *Compensation,* substitution : शिवीला शिवी आणि लातेला लात an abuse for an abuse, and a kick for a kick.

6. *The relation of space :*—

(*a*) *Place in or on :* त्याचे डोक्याला पागोटें होतें he had a turban on his head.

(*b*) *Motion to :* दुसरीं मुलें वाढतील आणि रोजगारास चढतील other boys would be promoted and rise to high appointments ; तो गांवाला गेला he has gone to town.

7. *Time :—*

(*a*) *Point of time* : उद्यां चोहोंला या come to-morrow at four.

(*b*) *Time indefinitely* : काल रात्रीस तूं कोठें होतास where were you last night ?

(*c*) *Extent, limit, &c.* : त्यास परत यावयास अजून दोन वर्षें आहेत it will take two years more for him to return ; दहाला दोन मिन्टें आहेत it wants two minutes to ten.

Note.—The dative ला indicates time *definitely*, and स *indefinitely*. The dative in स is never used to indicate a point or period of time, but only *indefinite* time ; तूं बरोबर दोहोंला, not दोहोंस ये come exactly at two o'clock.

5. The Ablative Case.

(अपादानकारक or पंचमी).

§ 589. (1) The ablative expresses the relation of ablation, *i.e.*, of *carrying away* or taking away ; चौथ्या दिवशीं त्रिंबकशेट गांवांहून परत आला the fourth day Trimbakshet returned from the village ; तूं दैवाचा कीं असले निर्दय पोरीचे हातून तरी सुटलास you are lucky that you have at least escaped from the hands of such a cruel girl.

Note.—The postpositions जवळ, पाशीं etc., are substituted for the dative case-endings as more courteous forms ; महाराजांजवळ नेऊन दे give it to the gentleman is more courteous than महाराजांना नेऊन दे. In English the same idiom is sometimes used ;

" Yet to the General's voice they soon obeyed.—*Milton.* "

Note.—The ablative termination हून or ऊन is affixed either *directly* to the noun, or to nouns governed by *postpositions*; गोपाळराव माडीवरून खालीं आले Gopalárav came downstairs ; मीं त्याचे तोंडून सर्व वर्तमान ऐकणार I am going to hear the whole story from his lips ; त्यानें घरांतून हांक मारिली he called out from inside the house. The English "from,"—governing an adverb, is rendered in Maráthi by ऊन ; "from above" वरून; " from here " एथून ; " from inside " आंतून.

Note.—पासून is generally used in the place of हून to denote the *sense of ablation*, expressed in English by the preposition *from* : ग्यास हा पदार्थ कोळश्यापासून उत्पन्न होतो gas is produced from coal ; त्यांत दहा हजारांपासून एक लक्षपर्यंत लोक आहेत there are from one thousand to one lac of people in it ; त्याच्या चेष्टांपासून कोणाला उपद्रव झाला नसेल no one could have suffered from his pranks ; गुरूपासून पळून जाईन असें म्हणणें to say that he would run away from the teacher. It is when *motion from a place* is expressed that हून is usually joined to nouns denoting *place* or location ; गांवाहून आला he came from town. When *motion from a person* is expressed, पासून, or जवळून is employed ; तो मजपासून गेला he went from me ; मीं त्याजवळून आलों I have come from him.

Note.—(1) Postpositions and adverbs, inflected by हून or ऊन, when expressing the sense of plurality, have a locative, and not ablative force ; घराच्या आंतून व बाहेरून सर्व दिवे टांगिले होते lights were hung both inside and outside the house ; इकडून तिकडून सर्व झाडें दिसत होतीं everywhere trees only were visible.

2. Postpositions inflected by ऊन, when governing plural nouns, convey the locative sense ; मुंबईच्या व्यापाऱ्यांनीं तारवांतून कापूस मात्र आणिला the merchants of Bombay brought only cotton in the ships ; झाडावरून पाखरें बसलीं the birds perched on the trees.

3. The postpositions, as well as adverbs, express the sense of *passage or channel*, corresponding with through ; टपालांतून आली it came by post. The instrumental नें is also used ; या दारानें जा go by the door.

(2) Another important meaning of the form हून is *than*, and it is chiefly used as a particle of *comparison* : त्या मुलीच्या मुद्रेवरूनच दिसतें कीं ती कांहीं याहून चांगली अवस्था भोगावयास उत्पन्न झाली आहे it appears from the very features of the girl that she is born to live in a somewhat better condition than this (§ 522).

6. The Genitive Case.

(संबंधकारक or षष्ठी.)

§ 590. The genitive case expresses *connection generally*, or *the relation of genus and species between two objects;* hence the genitive is usually governed by a *noun*: यांत जर माझा तिळमात्र अन्याय आहे तर चोराचे हाल ते माझे हाल if I am in the slightest degree to blame for it, then my condition shall be as distressful as that of a thief ; पण भाऊ तूं याचा परिहार कसा करितोस तें सांग but, brother, tell me how you exculpate yourself from this.

Note.—All adjectives *limit* the signification of the nouns which they qualify, or, in other words, *indicate the relation of species and genus*; adjectives and genitives consequently *agree in their uses.* Etymologically, the genitive in most languages is adjectival, and in Maráthí and several other languages it has often purely an adjectival force (§ 461, 8).

Note.—" The real power of the genitive is to express the genus or kind. If I say a bird of water, 'of the water' defines the genus to which a certain bird belongs ; it refers to the genus of water-birds. In such phrases as son of the father, or father of the son, the genitives have the same effect. They would answer the same purpose as the adjectives paternal and maternal."—*Max Müller.*

§ 591. The following are the principal relations indicated in Maráṭhí by the genitive case :—

1. *Origin, descent, family relations, &c.* : गोदावरीबाईची वडील मुलगी गंगा म्हणून होती the elder daughter of Godávaribáí was one Gangá ; बरें तूं आत्मारामाची बहीण, म्हणून त्वा त्यास प्रथम भेटावें हें नीट आहे well, you are Átmárám's sister, and it is therefore right that you should first go and see him.

Note.—The genitive denotes *descent*, even *without* the addition of a substantive : राजकुमारानें तिला विचारिलें, तूं कोणाची आहेस ? the prince asked her, whose are you ? (mark the answer) तेव्हां ती म्हणाली, चंदानो म्हणून एक रजपुताचा भेद आहे त्या जातींतील एक पुरुषाची मी मुलगी आहें ? then she said, I am the daughter of a man belonging to the Rajput tribe of Chandáno.

2. *Possession* : आनंदानें तिचे तोंडावाटे एक शब्द निघेना she could not utter a single word for joy ; या वेळेस हीं सगळीं पहिले चिठ्ठींतले मुलीचीं आहेत at this time all these belong to the girl mentioned in the first note.

Note.—The *neuter* genitive, *without the governing noun*, expresses *possession, affairs, nature* or *property*, &c. : ज्याचें त्याला द्यावें हा उत्तम पक्ष the best thing is to give to one what is his own ; ज्याचें त्याला बरें दिसतें one likes what he does, or likes his own affairs.

3. *Material :* त्र्यंबकशेटीनें आपले जवळचे पैशांचा एक चांगला तारांचा पिंजरा आणविला Trimbakshet ordered an excellent cage of wires out of his own money; तिणें कांहीं खीर आणि गव्हांची पोळी अशी तिजकडे दिली she gave her a little custard and a cake of wheat.

4. *Contents :* त्र्यंबकशेटीनें पिंजरा खालीं काढिला आणि पाहतो तीं दाण्याच्या खणांत व पाण्याच्या पेल्यांत कांहीं नाहीं Trimbakshet took down the cage, and found that there was nothing in the box of grain and the cup of water ; बरफीची बरणी कोठें आहे ती तुला ठाऊक नाहीं काय ? do not you know where the jar of sweetmeat is ?

5. *Members,* or *partition :* तुमची आवडच आहे तर एक सुपारीचें खांड द्या since you so wish it, give me a bit of betelnut ; ती रस्त्याच्या बाजूस बसली होती she was sitting by the side of the road.

Note.—The *genitive* denotes the *whole,* and the governing word the *part.*

6. *The person with reference to an emotion :* यावर माझा किती लोभ how much I loved him ? त्या गरीब मुलांचा यथेष्ट जेवतांना उत्साह पाहून तो धार्मिक वैद्य फार फार समाधान पावला the charitable physician was very much gratified when he saw the pleasure with which the poor children ate to their satisfaction.

Note.—The emotional genitive may be rendered in various ways ; thus आईबापांची प्रीति the love of parents, may express either (1) आईबापांवरली प्रीति love for parents, or (2) आईबापांतली प्रीति love borne by parents ; शत्रूचें भय the fear of an enemy may mean either (1) शत्रूपासून भय fear *from* an enemy, or (2) शत्रूच्या मनांतील भय the fear felt by an enemy.

7. *The object :* तिणें त्या कोंकराचें पालन केलें she tended that kid ; तिचा विश्वास धर believe her.

Note.—The compound verbs sometimes govern a genitive object. (§ 298, 2).

Note.—The genitive is sometimes used objectively to an *adjective* ; तो बाळहत्येचा दोषी खरा he is indeed guilty of infanticide.

8. *Quality :* अंगचें बळ bodily strength ; घरचा पैका family stock ; माझी बैलाची गाडी घेऊन मीं स्वतः तुम्हास न्यावयास येईन I will come myself with my bullock-cart to take you.

Note.—The noun, as in the above phrase अंगचें बळ, is not usually modified before assuming the genitive termination चा, when it expresses the sense of quality; घरचा household, but घराचा of the house. The first is an adjective, and the last is a genitive case; घराचा धनी the master or owner of the house, and घरचीं माणसें is the same as घरांतलीं माणसें householders, or persons living in the house; घराचे वासे rafters of the house, forming a part of the house, but घरचे वासे household rafters, in or somewhere near the house, but not forming any part of the house. Sometimes another adjective may be derived from the same root; सोन्याचे golden, or सोनेरी either golden or gilt from सोनें gold. It is usually such words as express a local relation, in some way or other, that, like the adverbs, do not inflect the root before taking the genitive चा; as आंगचा of the body, तोंडचा of the mouth, देशचा of the country, उत्तरचा of the north, &c.; other nouns terminating in अ inflect it; काम work, कामाचा (not कामचा), useful. The inflected adverbs are वरचा of above, खालचा of below, कालचा of yesterday, &c.

Note.—The genitive termination indicates the gender of the noun it qualifies; and when it inflects a third personal pronoun, a demonstrative or a relative, the pronominal genitive expresses the gender and number of the possessor, as well as of the thing possessed: त्याचा of him, तिचा, तिचे of her, &c.

Note.—The locative in ई becomes adjectival by the aid of the suffix चा; अंतरींचा internal, of the mind (§ 593, *Note*).

9. *Completion, abundance:* ह्या माशांचे थव्यांचे थवे दर वर्षास तेथून भूमध्यसमुद्रांत येतात shoals on shoals of this kind of fish come out thence every year into the Mediterranean Sea; गांवचें गांव मजा पाहावयास लोटलें होतें the whole village had come to see the fun.

10. *A change of state:* दारिद्र्याचा श्रीमंत होतो आणि श्रीमंताचा दरिद्री होतो a poor man becomes a rich man, and a rich man becomes a poor man; आज मला गुरूनें पंचतंत्रांतली गोष्ट संस्कृताची प्राकृत करायास सांगितली आहे the tutor has told me to translate a Sanskṛit story from the Panchatantra into the vernacular to-day.

11. *Adaptation* or use: ती स्नानाची जागा that is a place for bathing; तिला एकादें पांघरायाचें वस्त्रही दे give her also some wearing apparel.

§ 592. In the above instances we have shown the *connection* indicated by the genitive between *two nouns.* It has sometimes a reference to *adjectives, adverbs,* and *verbs.* Thus—

1. *The genitive with an adjective :—*

With an adjective to denote the ground or object : तो बाळहत्येचा दोषी ठरला he was convicted of infanticide.

II. *The genitive with an adverb :—*

The partitive genitive is chiefly joined to adverbs ; घराचे बाहेर बसूं नको do not sit outside the house.

Note.—The postpositions are affixed to the inflected form of the noun, or its *genitive case* : as घरावर or घराच्यावर on the house.

III. *The genitive with a verb :—*

1. *The genitive is sometimes used as both the subject and object of the verb* : आपला पक्ष खोटा आहे असें कबूल करण्याचें अद्यापि जानूच्या मनांत नव्हतें still it was not in Jánú's mind to acknowledge that his opinion was wrong ; मीं त्याचें ऐकणार नाहीं I will not hear what he may say.

Note.—The noun बोलणें saying, &c., is no doubt, understood.

Note.—The objective genitive is chiefly governed by the compound verbs, and expresses the object of some feeling ; त्याचा मला राग आला I was angry with him ; राजाचा अपमान केला they dishonoured the king (§ 296).

2. The genitive is used *adverbially to express the relation of time* : तो दिवसाचा निजतो he sleeps by day.

Note.—The genitive expresses *time more emphatically* than the dative in स: तो रोज सांजचा येई आणि तीं दोघें रात्रीचीं फार वेळ एकांतांत असत he used to come every day in the evening, and they both would be alone for a long time in the night. In this sentence the attention is directed to the *time* of their meeting, while in the following to the *place* and *not to the time* ; तूं रात्रीस बाहेर होतास, तर कोठें होतास you were out in the night, and *where* were you ?

7. The Locative.

(अधिकरणकारक or सप्तमी.)

§ 593. The Locative Case expresses the relation of place : तें त्यांच्या कानीं पडून ते तिकडेच पाहूं लागले it (the sound) having fallen *upon their* ears, they began to look only *in* that direction ; यासाठीं तो सकाळीं बाहेर निघून गेला for this reason he went out *in* the morning.

मुखीं नाम हातीं मोक्ष ॥ ऐसी साक्ष बहुतांची ॥

वेदाचा अर्थ आम्हांसीच ठावा, इतरांनीं वाहवा भार माथां—Tukaram.

Note.—The locative sometimes takes the genitive termination : तोंडींचा घांस देणें to give a mouthful out of one's own mouth.

जाणावा तो योगी सदा वीतरागी ।। अहंभाव त्यागी अंतरींचा ॥

Note.—The चा is an adjectival affix, like ला in तोंडांतला.

§ 594. The locative expresses the following other relations :—

2. *The object of the verb* : त्याच्या अंगीं लाव म्हणजे तो लबाड खरा when you convict him, then you will prove him a liar.

3. *Instrumentality* : तो तोंडीं जेवितो he eats *with* the mouth ; आंगीं केलें तें काम what is done *by* oneself is well done.

होत असे भला भल्याचे संगतीं ॥ जाय अधोगतीं दुष्टसंगें ॥ —*Tukárám.*

चंचुपुटीं मधु सुढाळी ॥ मुखीं घोपितां क्षुधाकाळीं ॥—*Mukteswar.*

देखिला त्रिभुवननाथ डोळां.—*Mukteshwar.*

4. *Purpose* : आपणची ध्यानीं बैसला आसनीं ॥ जनीं आणि वनीं देव ॥ he sat down *for* meditation, and felt God to be in the society of men and in the desert.

CHAPTER XXVIII.

POSTPOSITIONS GOVERNING CASES.

§ 595—§ 599.

§ 595. Several postpositions are used in the place of case-terminations, or joined to case-terminations to *vary* their sense : तो आंबा मजजवळ दे or मला दे give that mango to me.

1. The Instrumental Case.

(करण or तृतीया.)

§ 596. The following postpositions indicate the relation of *instrumentality* :—

1. करून expresses *simple instrumentality*, and is affixed to the instrumental case in एं: त्यानें शस्त्रें करून मारिलें he killed him with a weapon.

2. करवीं is of the same import as करून: तुला करवेंना, तर मुला-करवीं or करवें करीव if you cannot do it yourself, get it done by your child.

3. कडून has several other significations besides that of instrumentality, thus—

(*a*) *Instrumentality*: रामानें बाणेंकडून रावणास मारिलें Ráma killed Ráwan with an arrow.

(*b*) *Indirect agency*: मी त्याकडून घर बांधवीन I will cause the house to be built by him; सराफाकडून रुपये देववीन I will give you money through the shroff.

(*c*) *Channel or medium*: पर्जन्यें‌कडून सर्वांस सुख होतें all are refreshed by rain.

(*d*) *Source*: त्याकडून (or पासून or जवळून) रुपये घ्या take the money from him; तो हिंदुस्थानाकडून आला he has come from Upper Hindusthan. This is the *ablative* force of कडून.

4. जवळून has generally the *ablative* force, but as an instrumental postposition it denotes indirect *agency*: हें भांडें मजजवळून फुटलें the vessel was broken by me, *i.e.*, it broke while I had it in my hands.

5. द्वारां or द्वारें expresses *instrumentality* or *medium*: शास्त्र-द्वारां तुमचे मनाची निवृत्ति होईल your mind will be satisfied through the Scriptures.

2. The Dative Case.

(संप्रदान or चतुर्थी)

§ 597. The following postpositions indicate the *dative* relation :—

1. प्रत has two significations ; thus—

(*a*) *The object*: राजा प्रधानाप्रत बोलतो the king spoke to his minister.

(*b*) *Place*: तो गांवाप्रत गेला he has gone to the town ; ही वाट संपून आम्ही घराप्रत होऊं, तेव्हांच्या साऱ्या गोष्टी these things will be of avail when we have finished our journey and arrived at home. This postposition occurs in learned discourse.

2. जवळ expresses the *object* : as, त्याजजवळ सांग tell him ; त्याजवळ दे give it to him.

3. लागीं is generally used in poetry. It expresses—

(*a*) *The object* : किती शिकवूं तुजलागीं ॥

मनारे प्रीती धरी हरिपाईं ॥

(*b*) *Ground* or *reason* : ह्यालागीं पातला रघुवीर: for this reason Raghuvir came ; निजतनयविवाहालागीं यावें you should come for the marriage of my son.

(*c*) *Utility* or *fitness* : कागद लिहिण्याच्या लागीं आहे paper is fit for writing.

4. The *postpositions* करितां, कारणें, साठीं, स्तव, अर्थीं denote the *purpose* or *reason*. Thus, ब्राह्मणाकारणें गाय दे give a cow for the Brahman.

5. पाशीं, like जवळ, expresses the object ; त्याला or त्याजजवळ or त्यापाशीं सांग tell it to him.

6. कडे at, expresses the object ; त्याकडेस पाठीव send it to him.

3. The Ablative Case.

(अपादान or पंचमी.)

§ 598. The following are the ablative postpositions :—

1. कडून denotes the *source* : त्याकडून रुपये घ्या take money from him (*See* कडून under the instrumental case, § 596).

2. जवळून denotes—

(*a*) *The source* or *motion* from : मी त्याजजवळून आलों I have come from him.

(*b*) *Agency* : हें भांडें मजजवळून फुटलें the vessel was broken by me.

(*c*) *Proximity* : तो आमच्या गांवाजवळून गेला he went by our village.

3. पासून denotes—

(*a*) The *source,* implying (1) *origin:* ह्या झाडापासून फळ होतें this tree bears fruit ; मजपासून हें पातक घडलें I have committed this sin ; (2) *privation:* माझ्यापासून (or जवळून) दोन रुपये नेले ते त्यानें आणिले नाहींत he has not brought the two rupees he took from me.

(*b*) *Since :* त्या दिवसापासून घरीं आहें I have been at home since that day.

(*c*) *Distance from* in space ; आमच्या घरापासून दूर आहे it is far from my house.

4. पेक्षां is used to express comparison : ह्या वडील भावापेक्षां शहाणा आहे he is wiser than this elder brother. It also expresses a reason : ज्यापेक्षां आपण बोलावतां त्यापेक्षां मला येणें भाग आहे since you call me, I must come. (§ 589, 2)

5. वरून expresses:—

(*a*) *Source :* माडीवरून खालीं आला he came from upstairs.

(*b*) *Locality :* घोड्यांवरून सगळीं माणसें बसलीं all the people sat on horseback.

(*c*) *Approximation :* तो आमचे गांवावरून गेला he went by our village.

Note.—वरून differs from जवळून. Both agree in expressing *nearness*, but वरून indicates, in addition, to pass close to an object without touching it, so as to go from one side of it to another ; तो आमच्या घराजवळून गेला he went by our house (vicinity) ; तो आमच्या घरावरून गेला he went past our house.

(*d*) *Ground* or *reason :* तुला त्या शब्दावरून ओळखिलें I recognized you by your voice ; आपण सांगितल्यावरून गेलों I went in consequence of what you told me.

4. The Locative.

(अधिकरण or सप्तमी.)

§ 599. The following are the *Locative* postpositions. The postpositions आंत, मध्यें have a purely locative force ; घरामध्यें बसून काय होतें what benefit is there in staying at home ? मांडवांत नवरी आली इतक्यांत लढाईची बातमी आली the news of battle arrived as soon as the bride came into the shed.

Note.—The following idiom is worthy of notice ; **आंत** *in* is idiomatically used for **वर** *on* in such cases as **बोंटांत आंगठी** a ring *in* (for *on*) the finger : so also **पायांत जोडा** shoes *in* the feet : **आंगांत अंगरखा** a coat *in* the body ; **डोक्यांत पागोटें** a turban *in* the head, &c.

CHAPTER XXIX.

THE USES OF THE TENSES.

§ 600—650.

§ 600. The tenses have been considered as simple and compound. The simple tenses differ from the compound not only in regard to their form, but also their signification. The former express time indefinitely, the point of time at which actions happen, without regard to duration, and they are appropriately employed to indicate single acts or habits, while the latter indicate a duration or continuance of time, the time during which a thing is done.

§ 601. Hence the simple present, past and future tenses, may be denominated present indefinite, past indefinite, and future indefinite.

The Indicative Mood.

Present Tense.

The Present Indefinite.

§ 602. 1. The present indefinite indicates an act which has lately commenced, and is in a state of progression: **तूं थट्टा करितोस** you are jesting.

2. It indicates an action that is just about to commence: **चल मीं तुला कांहीं मौज दाखवितों** come, I will show you something strange ; or come I am going to show you, etc.

3. It indicates an action that will certainly happen: **उद्यां सकाळपासून तुम्हांस मोकळीक देतों** I shall give you leave to-morrow, the whole day, from morning to evening ; **जर आम्हीं राई दिली नाहीं, तर तुझा बाप आम्हांपासून रुपये पांचशें ठोकून घेतो** if we should not give him the orchard, your father will directly demand the five hundred rupees from us ; **आतां सरकार मला खचीत मारितें** now the Government will certainly execute me.

4. It expresses a general truth or maxim true at all times : जो आपल्या मुखानें आपली स्तुति करितो तो लघुत्व पावतो he who with his own mouth spreads abroad his own fame, is sure to meet with contempt.

5. It denotes an act long since past, but present at the time referred to in the discourse : भोजराजा विचारितो Bhoj Rájá asks ; देवराव त्याजवळ गेले आणि म्हणतात, मुला, तूं एथें काय करितो आहेस Devráva went to him and said, child, what are you doing here ? मिळवुनिया प्रधान चतुर ॥ विचारीं बैसले सकळ नृपवर ॥ म्हणती आम्हांसी नाटोपे नंदकुमार ॥ कैसा प्रकार करावा ॥ (*Sridhar*) having collected their ministers, all the kings sat for consultation, and said (in Maráṭhí, and say) " We cannot control the son of Nand, and we do not know what to do." This construction is usually adopted in animated and descriptive narrative.

6. It expresses a habit : मीं याचकांस लाखों रुपये सहज देतों I am in the habit of freely giving to the poor hundreds of thousands of rupees.

7. It is used in quoting from an extant author : मोरोपंत असें म्हणतात the poet Moropant says thus.

The Present Imperfect or Progressive.

§ 603. 1. It expresses that the action is in a state of progression : तो लिहीत आहे he is writing ; आम्ही तुमची वाट पाहात आहों we wait your coming.

2. It expresses an act that was in progression at a past time, when employed with a past verb : पांखरें येत आहेत जात आहेत असें त्यानें पाहिलें he saw the birds going and coming. (§ 602, 5) It is used in this way in *narratives*. (§ 511, *Note*)

3. It expresses an act that has been in continuance for an indefinite period : तूं एथें किती दिवस अनुष्ठान करीत आहेस how long have you been performing acts of devotion here ?

The Present Imperfect or Progressive Emphatic.

§ 604. The Present Imperfect Emphatic does not differ much in sense from the present imperfect tense, and is not seldom identified with it, but the following particulars are, nevertheless, important :—

1. It expresses the sense of continuance more strongly than the present imperfect: पहा मा लिहित आहें see, I am actually engaged in writing, *i.e.*, at this very moment ; मुला तूं एथें काय करितो आहेस ? child, what are you engaged in doing here ?

2. It expresses an action that has been in progress for some time, though not quite without interruption : आज दहा वर्षें तो लिहितो आहे पण अजून त्याचा ग्रंथ तयार झाला नाहीं he has been engaged in writing these ten years, but still his book is not ready. The man might not be writing at that very moment.

The Present Perfect Tense.

§ 605. The Perfect Tense implies an action perfected some time ago, but the consequences of which extend to the present time : आपण एकमेकांचें साह्य करावें, म्हणून आपणास ईश्वरें या लोकीं पाठविलें आहे God has sent us into the world that we may help each other ; त्यांसंगतीं जेवायास बहिणीनें बोलाविलें आहे my sister has invited me to dine with them.

Note.—" The Present Complete or Perfect *I have written* may perhaps seem at first to belong rather to the Past Tenses, since it speaks of the action as finished. But we must understand by present time, not merely the immediate instant, but also any portion of time reaching up to and including it. Thus the statement, " I have lived in London seven years," implies that the speaker is still living in London, and the period of time referred to reaches up to the moment of speaking."

" So, if a person says, "I *have* once *seen* a total eclipse of the sun," the sense is *once in my life;* and the circumstance is referred, as before, to a period of time still continuing and *present*."

" On the other hand, when a person says, " I *saw* a total eclipse of the sun in the year 1851," he distinctly refers the event to a period (the year 1851) altogether detached from the present and *past*.— *Dr. Smith's English Grammar.*

Obs.—In English the perfect tense is employed to denote a past action recently finished, but in Maráṭhí the past indefinite is used for it : " I have just heard the news," would be in Maráṭhí त्या आतांच वार्ता ऐकिली I just now *heard* the news. Hence a Maráṭhí would answer the question—" Have you marked him present " ? thus ; होय मांडिलें " *yes, I did mark him*," instead of " yes, *I have* marked him."

2. It has the force of the progressive present, and indicates the continuance of a state or act in present time. When the perfect tense has this sense, the transitive past participle, constructed with आहे, has the force of a passive participle, and the *intransitive* past participle has the force of a neuter intransitive (§ 186, 3., In English in such constructions the passive voice is usually employed: आई पुरली आहे तेथें जातो he goes to the place where his mother is buried; त्यांच्या तेथें गोष्टी चालल्या आहेत they are engaged there in conversation; शाकभाज्या पुष्कळ झालेल्या आहेत; जिकडे तिकडे पाणी जमलें आहे, त्यांतुन कागदांचीं तारवें करून मुलें पोंहवीत आहेत the vegetables and herbs have grown in abundance; here and there there are pools of water on which children are sailing paper boats which they have made.

The Present Habitual.

§ 606. The Present Habitual expresses the habitual condition or occupation of the agent: मासे समुद्रांत राहात असतात fishes live in the sea; तो प्रातःकाळीं देवाची प्रार्थना करीत असतो he prays regularly early in the morning.

The Present Prospective.

§ 607. 1. The Present Prospective signifies the future accomplishment of an act that has been resolved on; ते उद्यां येणार आहेत they are coming to-morrow; आपण त्याला काय देणार आहों? what are we going to give him?

2. It expresses emphatically the determination of the agent to do, or not to do, a certain action: तुला आज्ञा मिळणार नाहीं you *shall* not have permission to go; नाहीं मामा कधीं जाणार नाहीं no, uncle, I will never go. In the affirmative sentence the auxiliary verb is often omitted: पण हें शस्त्र घेऊन पुढें काय करणार? what do you mean to do further with this weapon? तुम्ही मजसमोर उभे राहाणार; होय? you will dare stand before me, will you? मी त्या पोरांचा अंमळ तमाशा करणार आहें I am determined to make a little sport of those lads; जर तूं कांहीं करणारच तर मुलींपुढें वाट्या ठेव if you are determined to do something, then place the cups before the young ladies. The omission of the auxiliary verb gives the sentence greater force.

Note.—When merely the proneness of an agent to do a certain act is to be expressed, the genitive supine is used instead of the future perfect tense : तो एखादे दिवशीं अनर्थ करावयाचा he is such a man as will some day or other do mischief.

The Present Dubitative.

The Present Dubitative expresses the probable occurrence of an event in present time ; तो आतां जेवीत असावा he might be dining now.

PAST TENSE.

The Past Indefinite.

§ 608. The Past Indefinite expresses an act which has transpired in time already passed or spent : तो मला काल म्हणाला he said to me yesterday ; त्यानें मला याच क्षणांत मारिलें he struck me just a moment ago ; तिनें मला संपूर्ण गोष्ट सांगितली she told me the whole story.

2. It is used in the first clause of a conditional sentence with जर if, expressed or understood, to indicate the possible, though most doubtful, occurrence of an event : कधीं तूं आमच्या दारावरून आलास तर मजकडे ये should you ever pass our door, come to me.

3. It expresses an action that will *certainly* and *without delay* happen in future time, on certain conditions being fulfilled : सांग कीं मीही त्यापाशीं धांवलों tell me, and I shall also run to him directly ; त्यांनीं सर्वांनीं एकमेकांवर पूर्ण विश्वास ठेवून व मनास धीर देऊन पुढें व्हावें, म्हणजे सुधारक पक्षाचा जय झाला they should with perfect confidence in each other and with courage come forward, and the success of the reformed party will be an accomplished fact; तूं पुढें जा, मीं मागून हाच आलों you go on ; I will follow immediately.

5. It is joined to a statement to emphasize it ; ह्यांत कांहीं संशय नाहीं कळलें there is no doubt about it, do you understand ? पण मीं काय बोलावयास आलें आहें तें समजलास do you know what I have come to say to you ?

6. It is used for the present tense when expressing a desire or opinion modestly : थोडी साखर पाहिजे होती I want (wanted)

a little sugar ; आज मला नवा जन्म दिलासें वाटलें I feel (felt) as if you had given me a new birth.

7. It expresses a present progressive action on the point of completion : हा पाहा आपला घोडा आला look here, our horse is coming.

8. It is used in the first clause of a conditional sentence with म्हणजे when, to indicate the certain occurrence of the dependent event ; तो आला म्हणजे मिळेल you will have it when he comes ; तुम्ही बोललां म्हणजे माझें कार्य होईल if you speak then my work will indeed be done.

The Past Imperfect or Progressive.

§ 609. The Past Imperfect refers to a past action as begun and in progress, but not finished : देवराव देशमुख एके दिवशीं आपल्या वतनवाडीची चौकशी करून परत येत होते one day Devráv Deshmukh, having inspected his estates, was returning.

3. It is used forcibly for the past prospective त्या दिवशीं मला तुडवीत होतां ते गृहस्थ आपणच नव्हे are not you the gentleman who was going to trample me down?

The Pluperfect Tense.

§ 610. 1. The pluperfect expresses an action which was past before some other specified past action : त्यांनीं तिला ताटीवर निजविलें होतें तेव्हां म्या पाहिलें just after they had placed her on the bier I saw her ; त्याची काठी बाहेर ठेविली होती ती आपण स्वतां आणून त्याचे जवळ ठेविली she brought and placed by him his walking-stick which he had left outside.

2. When an action takes place at some specified period or point of past time, and does not continue to exist to the present time, the pluperfect is employed : मीं काल पुण्यास गेलों होतों I went yesterday to Poona. But if the act should remain, the simple indefinite past, as in English, is used ; तो काल पुण्यास गेला he went to Poona yesterday (where he still remains). If he has returned, then तो काल पुण्यास गेला होता lit. he had been to Poona, is used.

3. The pluperfect is employed for the present perfect as a more modest expression : आपणापाशीं कांहीं मागायास आलों होतों I have come to ask something of you.

4. When an event does not happen as was expected, the unrealisation of the expectation is denoted by the pluperfect, but in English the past indefinite is often used ; मला वाटलें होतें कीं तूं पहिल्यानें मुलींचा सत्कार करशील ? I thought you would first pay your respects to the young ladies.

5. When the lapse of a long interval, or great indefiniteness is to be expressed, the pluperfect is used for the past indefinite ; मावशीनें माझे वाढदिवशीं ही आंगठी दिली होती my maternal aunt gave this ring to me on my birthday ; तूं कधीं आला होतास did you ever come ?

6. It may express the continuance of a state in past time ; नौका दोरीनें बळकट बांधली होती the boat was tied fast by a rope. The transitive pluperfect has the force of the past passive, and the intransitive, of the past imperfect ; तो बसला होता he was sitting.

The Past Habitual.

§ 611. 1. The Past Habitual expresses that a certain action was habitual, or usually performed in time past ; तो एकावर एक पांच सहा टोप्या डोईस घालून बाहेर निघे he would sally forth with five or six caps on his head.

2. With the negative particle ना, it expresses the unwillingness of the agent to do a certain action in past time, or the impossibility of the occurrence of an event : त्याला पुष्कळ सांगितलें पण तो जाईना I told him much, but he would not go ; नाव सोडितां येईना the boat would not come loose ; ती तिला सोनूशीं मैत्री करूं देईना she would not let her be friends with Sonú.

3. It is used to express the end or completion of the continuance of an action expressed by another verb : दुसरा आपणास देई तोंवर वाट पाहावी you ought at least to wait till some other person gives them to you ; तुझा जीव जाई तोंपर्यंत तूं दारू पिशील you will drink liquor till you die.

4. It expresses the consequence of an action : शरीरास आयास नपडे असें अंग राखितो he takes care that it may never become necessary to expose himself to any great bodily exertion ; माझा हात पुन्हा नीट होई असें औषध द्यावें please give me such medicine as will cure my hand.

5. In poetry the past habitual expresses all the tenses of the indicative mood.

The Compound Past Habitual.

§ 612. The Compound Past Habitual has the first sense of the simple past habitual, viz., that the act was habitual at some past period : हजारों लोक त्याचें भाषण ऐकावास दुरून दुरून येत असत thousands of people used to come from great distances to hear his speech.

The Incepto-Continuative.

§ 613. The Incepto-Coutinuative expresses the commencement and continuance of an act : धृतराष्ट्र बोलता झाला Dhritarásbtra began and spoke as follows. This form is used only in translations of Sanskṛit histories. The pure idiomatic expression for ordinary use is the infinitive of the verb with लागणें (§ 310, 1); तो वाचूं लागला he began to read.

The Dubitative Past.

§ 614. The Dubitative Past expresses the probable occurrence of an event in past time : तो गेला असावा he must have gone. It expresses a stronger degree of probability than the future perfect form : तुम्ही मला शिकविलें असेल पण मला आठवत नाहीं you may have taught me, but I have no recollection of it ; तुम्ही कांहीं तरी कुचेष्टा केली असावी you must have teased him some way or other ; त्यानेंच तें केलें असावें even he must have done it.

The Past Prospective.

§ 615. (1) The Past Prospective expresses that the agent had an intention in time past to do some action : मीं काल आपणाकडे येणार होतों पण शरीरांत विकृति झाल्यामुळें घरींच राहिलों I was to have called on you yesterday, but as I felt unwell, I stayed at home.

(2) It expresses that a certain act was on the point of happening in past time, but that it is uncertain whether it actually took place or not : काल त्याची चौकशी होणार होती yesterday he was to have been tried.

FUTURE TENSE.

The Future Indefinite.

§ 616. (1) The Future Indefinite expresses an act that is to occur in future time : उद्यां पाऊस पडेल it will rain to-morrow.

(2) It expresses willingness to perform a particular act : तूं ठेविशील त्याचाही सर्व प्रकारें समाचार घेईन I will also look after the one that you will keep ; मी त्याला माझा वांटा देईन I will give him my share.

Note.—In English a future act spoken of in reference to a past act takes the auxilliary " would " and not " will, " but in Maráṭhí the simple future is used : आम्ही प्रतिक्षणीं भिऊं कीं तूं आतां मरशील we were very moment afraid that you would instantly die.

2. It expresses the incumbency of a particular act in an interrogative sentence expressed in English by the auxiliary *should* : कां पळेन ? why should I run ? कां फोडील ? तो वेडा नाहीं why should he break it ? he is not mad.

3. It, with the particle च, expresses the certainty or incumbency expressed by "shall:" तो जाईल he will go ; तो जाईलच he shall go, *i.e.*, forced to go by another.

4. It expresses potentiality, physical or moral, expressed in English by the use of the word "*can*" in an interogative sentence : त्यास दांत आले नाहींत खाईल कसा ? he has got no teeth yet, how then can he eat ? दुसऱ्यास दुःखांत पाडून मीं सुखी कसा होईन ? how can I be happy by plunging another person into distress ?

It may express in like manner a past potential, expressed in English by *could* : सर्व मुलखांत पांडव कोठून असतील ? how could the sons of Pandu spread abroad over the whole country ?

5. It is used in the first clause of the conditional sentence with जर, expressed or understood, if great respect is to be expressed in the supposition : त्याला औषध द्याल तर तुमचा उपकार जन्मवर विसरणार नाहीं if you would have the goodness to give him medicine, I shall never forget your kindness as long as I live ; मुलींनो, आज्ञा द्याल तर मी क्षणभर जाऊन येतों ladies, if you will graciously permit me, I will just go and be back in a moment.

It may indicate also that the supposition, in the opinion of the speaker, is not likely to be realized : मला राज्यपदीं बसवाल तर मीं हें राज्य चालवीन if you please to seat me upon the throne, I will govern the kingdom for you.

Or it may express that the speaker is indifferent regarding the realization of the supposition: द्याल तर द्या you may give if you wish.

6. It is used to express the possibility of an event expressed in English by the auxiliary "*may*": कोणी तरी यास बरें करणारा भेटेल we may meet with some one or other who can cure him.

7. Where in English the present is used, in Maráṭhí the future is sometimes employed.

(*a*) The future is used in Maráṭhí when it is followed by an imperative: बाकीच्याचें तुझ्या मनास येईल तें कर do with the rest whatever you please; तुला आवडेल तें घे take whatever you like.

(*b*) The future is used in Maráṭhí when it is preceded by जेव्हां, when, or जर, if, expressed or understood: तुला भूक लागेल तेव्हां खायास मागतां येतें when you are hungry, you can ask for food; जर तो येईल तर तो तुला घेऊन जाईल if he comes, he will take you.

8. The Future is used where in English "would" or "should" is employed—

(*a*) When an act that at a particular past time was considered as about to happen is mentioned, the future is employed: आम्ही प्रतीक्षणीं भिऊं कीं तूं आतां मरशील we were every moment afraid that you would instantly die.

(*b*) It is used after a supposition to express what is supposed to be an impossible consequence: असा कोण दुष्ट आहे कीं दुसरा विपत्तींत पडला असतां त्यास हांसेल? who is there so wicked that he *would mock* another who has fallen into adverse circumstances?

9. It is used as a more respectful form than the imperative or the subjunctive mood for making a request: मज दीनावर दया करून आपण त्याला पाहाल? would you, sir, have pity on my miserable self, and do me the favour of coming and seeing him?

The Future Imperfect.

§ 617. (1) The Future Imperfect expresses the continuance of a particular act in the future time: उद्यां ह्या वेळेस तो प्रवास करीत असेल he will be travelling this time to-morrow; मी बारा

वाजतां तुझी वाट पहात असेन I shall be waiting for you at twelve o'clock. The verb राहणें substituted for असणें signifies the same thing : मीं तुझी वाट पाहात राहीन.

(2) It expresses also contingency, a little doubt or uncertainty as to whether the action will really take place or not : आमच्या गांवीं हा पाऊस पडत असेल most probably we have these showers in our village; तुझा बाप तुझी वाट पाहात असेल your father most probably will be expecting your return; या वेळेस मीं उद्यां पुण्यास असेन I shall most probably be at Poona this time to-morrow.

Future Inceptive.

§ 618. The Future Inceptive expresses the commencement and continuance of a future act in future time : तो चालता होईल he will begin to go away.

The Future Perfect.

§ 619. The Future Perfect expresses the completion of an act before the occurrence of another future action: तुमच्या पूर्वी मीं तेथें गेलों असेन I shall have gone there before you.

2. It may express contingency : तो गेला असेल he might have gone. It expresses possibility less emphatically than the dubitative past form in असावा : तो गेला असावा he must have gone. The probability is stronger in the latter form (§ 614).

Future Prospective.

§ 620. 1. The Future Prospective expresses that the agent will be about to do something at some future time : तुम्ही याल तेव्हां मीं लिहिणार असेन I shall be going to write when you come.

2. It expresses also contingency—that the agent may probably be about to do a certain act : तो येणार असेल he may be coming.

The Future Dubitative.

§ 621. The Future Dubitative expresses the possibility of an agent's intention to do something in future time : तो आज वाचणार असावा he must be going to read to-day.

The Conditional Mood.

Present Tense.

The Present Indefinite.

§ 622. 1. The Present Indefinite expresses an act which might have happened in past time, but which did not actually take place, as well as the consequence that would then in the speaker's view have resulted : असें जर तुला म्हणता तर तुझ्यानें त्याची थट्टा करवती ? if he had spoken to you in that manner, then could you have mocked him ? It is used in both the members of the conditional sentence : मीं तसें करितों तर तुझी माझी गांठ कशी पडती had I acted so, then how should ever you and I have fallen in with one another ?

2. It may express the supposition of the near approach of a given act, or to express a consequence that would thence, in the speaker's view, result : हा हिंवाळा न येता आणि पावसाळाच राहाता तर बरें होतें were that winter never to come, and the rainy season always to remain, it would be delightful ; तो आज येता तर तुझी भेट होती were he to come to-day, you would see him.

3. It may express a general supposition : आपण सर्वच पक्षी असतों तर आपण पाहिजे तेथें जातों were we all birds, we would go wherever we pleased.

The Present Progressive.

§ 623. The Present Progressive expresses much the same sense as the preceding, but is more particularly applicable to acts in progress at the time to which the supposition refers : असा पाऊस सर्वकाळ पडत असता तर चांगलें नसतें were rain like this to fall continually, it would not be good for us; तो जर काम करीत असता तर अनर्थ कशानें घडता had he been employed at his work, how could such an accident have happened ?

The Present Dubitative.

§ 624. 1. The Present Dubitative is used to make up a conditional clause with जर, expressed or understood, to express the probable continuance of an act of which the speaker has no knowledge : जर पाऊस पडत असला तर येऊं नको do not come if it should be raining ; मीं लिहीत नसलों तर आज मला येऊन भेट if I be not writing, then only you should come and see me. It can be used in the future as well as the present.

2. It may express that the agent may have an intention to do the act supposed, but that the speaker has no knowledge of it : तो जात असला तर तें काम त्याला सांग should he be going, then entrust the business to him.

Past Tense.

The Past Indefinite.

§ 625. The Past Indefinite expresses that an event which did not actually take place might have possibly occurred : एक दोन दिवसांपुरतें तर निघालें असतें we should have had at least enough for one or two days ; तो तेथें आला असता तर तुला त्यानें जाऊं दिलें असतें if he had come there, he would have let you go ; तें थोडक्यांत चुकलें नाहीं तर ती पडली असती it missed by a little, otherwise she would have fallen, *i.e.*, she narrowly escaped falling ; जर तुम्हीं मजकरितां इतका श्रम केला नसता तर मला मरून फार दिवस झाले असते had you not been at all that trouble for me, I should have been dead long ago.

Past Dubitative.

§ 626. The Past Dubitative expresses uncertainty respecting an action, which, if it ever occurred at all, must now be fully performed : त्यानें अशी लबाडी केली असली तर मग तो द्वाड खरा should he really have been guilty of such roguery, then truly he is a blackguard ; तो मुंबईहून आला असला तर लौकर मला सांग should he have arrived from Bombay, then let me know instantly ; तो नसला गेला तरी मीं त्याकडे जाणार though he should not have gone, still I mean to go to him. It is used in the antecedent clause of a conditional sentence.

Future Tense.

The Future Indefinite.

§ 627. The Future Indefinite expresses that a person might have intended to do a certain action, but that he did not : तो जाणार असता तर बरें होतें if he had intended to go, it would be delightful.

The Future Dubitative.

§ 628. The Future Dubitative expresses an uncertainty respecting the intention of the agent to do a certain action in future time : जर तो जाणार असला तर मला सांग should he be going, then tell me (§ 614).

THE SUBJUNCTIVE MOOD.

§ 629. 1. The Subjunctive Mood etymologically expresses the sense of obligation, and is usually so employed in Maráṭhí : ज्याचा अपराध केला असेल त्यापाशीं क्षमा मागावी you ought to beg pardon of the person you have offended ; तरवारीला आपण शोभवावें, तरवारीनें आपणाला शोभवूं नये we should be an ornament to the sword, and not the sword an ornament to us ; तुला नित्य बळी उगाच कशासाठीं द्यावा why should I then daily provide an offering for you to no purpose ?

2. It denotes fitness, or authority : त्यानें सिंहासनावर बसावें, इतरांस अधिकार नाहीं that person might sit on the throne, others have no right to sit on it.

3. It signifies a considerable degree of incumbency, and is rendered by *must* : त्यानें काय उपाशीं मरावें ? what, then, must he die of hunger ?

4. It denotes a slight degree of incumbency or propriety, which is generally marked in English by the phrase *is to* : आतां यावरून काय समजावें ? what, now, are we to understand by this ? असा अर्थ जाणावा it is to be understood in this sense.

5. It is often employed in expressing a wish, or in giving a command, as a more polite form than the imperative : रावसाहेब, कलह झाला याविषयीं आम्हांवर राग न करावा sir, please do not be displeased with us for the quarrel which has happened ; हिचा स्वीकार करावा you may accept this ; ईश्वरानें तुम्हांस शतगुणित फल द्यावें may God repay you a hundred-fold ; माझा वांटा भावां बहिणींनीं खावा let my brothers and sisters eat my portion ; आपण जावें you may go. It is far more polite to say यावें or यावें आपण you may come, than जावें, when asking a person to depart, and the phrase expresses "I shall be happy to see you some other time."

Note.—The use of the verb जातों, on the occasion of leave taking, is considered unlucky, as it suggests *death*, the final departure: येतों implies a *coming again*; आतां आम्ही येतों; कृपा असूं द्यावी I shall be going; continue to regard me with affection.

6. It is used interrogatively to express inquiry: आतां आपण काय करावें ? what shall we do now ? (lit., what is imcum bent on us to do now?

Note.—The subjunctive form denotes a certain degree of incumbency which is entirely absent from the imperative: आतां आपण काय करूं? what shall we do now ?

7. Interrogatively it is used as expressive of great surprise or emotion: क्षमा, तुम्हीही असें म्हणावें ? pardon ! you, too, should speak in that way ? This is a more polite form than the present indicative: क्षमा, तुम्हीही असें म्हणतां ? It expresses emotion, with the force of the potential verb: त्याची आतां काय दशा सांगावी ? what can we now say of his state ? आल्या घटकेपासून गणपतरावानें आमचा छळ जो मांडिला आहे तो काय सांगावा? what can we say of the annoyance which Ganpatráv has offered us from the moment we came? मुला तुला काय म्हणावें ? boy, what shall I say to you ? The speaker indicates by the subjunctive form in the last three sentences, that he is quite perplexed, and does not know what to say or do.

8. With the conjunctional particles म्हणून therefore, &c., it expresses *purpose*: पुनः तो अपराध न करावा म्हणून कानास खडा लाव press a sharp-pointed pebble to his ear, in order that he may not again commit the same fault; राजा नेमावा म्हणून सर्व पक्षी एकत्र झाले होते all the fowls had assembled, in order that they might elect a king.

9. It is used for the gerund: त्या सारिख्या मनुष्याच्या स्वाधीन अधिकार करावा हें मला ठीक दिसत नाहीं it does not seem to me to be proper to place authority in the hands of such a man; हें विश्व कसें चालवावें हें ईश्वरास चांगलें ठाऊक आहे God knows full well how to govern this world; बागांत इकडून तिकडे धांवावें लागतें I have to run hither and thither in the garden.

10. It is frequently used for the past habitual tense, and then it may be rendered into English by *would*: त्यापासून को-

फार उपद्रव नसे, त्याला फारच कंटाळा आणिला तर मात्र त्यानें पिसाळावें in general he hurt no one; only when he was excessively teased, he would become outrageous; तिनें तिला नित्य गांजावें आणि जे गुण मोठे बायकांतही विरळा ते तींत नाहींत म्हणून तीस शब्द लावावा she would constantly tease her and reproach her that she did not possess the virtues which are rarely found even in grown-up women.

11. It expresses a supposition which in the opinion of the speaker should necessarily be realized: त्यानें उद्यां यावें he should come to-morrow.

12. The subjunctive may be used in the past and future, as well as the present, tense: (past) म्या तुला गाडीवर कां घ्यावें? तुझ्या हातांत दोऱ्या कां द्याव्या why should I have taken you on the coach box? why should I have put the reins into your hands? म्याही यावें तों शरिरांत विकृति झाली I too should have come, but at the very time I became unwell. Sometimes, however, the past auxiliary might be used: त्वा सांगावें होतें you should have told me. For the future, see No. 6.

Note.—Duty is either present or future, and the simple subjunctive expresses this sense of duty when it is employed to denote present or future action: आपण गरीबास अन्न द्यावें we should give food to the poor; त्यानें उद्यां भजनालयांत जावें he should go to-morrow to the place of worship. In the past tense it expresses generally the notion of the habitual occurrence of an act, or the possibility of its occurrence, or some other non-ethical relation. When duty is spoken of in relation to the past, the compound form made up with the past tense of आहे to be, is used: त्याणें यावें होतें he should have come. The auxiliary होतें might be omitted as in the above sentence in the text: म्या तुला गाडीवर कां घ्यावें (होतें)? why should I have taken you on the coach-box? The ethical sense of obligation is usually expressed by the subjunctive with the subject in the instrumental case, otherwise it denotes that of uncertainty: तो आला नसावा he could not have come; त्वा उद्यां यावें you ought to come to-morrow.

§ 630. The negative forms of the subjunctive mood are three, viz., (1) the subjunctive with न not, prefixed, as न करावें; (2) the infinitive with नये (न not and ये it comes, literally, it does not come), as म्या येऊं नये I should not come; and (3) the present participle in तां with नये, as मला येतां कामास नये I cannot with propriety come; मला करितां नये I should not do it.

Of these three forms the first is not usually used, but the second is often used to negative the subjunctive mood in most of its senses. This form takes the subject in the instrumental case. The third form has a special sense: "it expresses an inferior degree of impropriety, especially that where the impropriety does not consist in the act itself, but in that act taken in connection with the situation of the speaker at the time"; मला हें काम करितां नये I cannot with propriety do this work. म्या करूं नये would be stronger and would convey the idea that something which was in itself improper had been asked to be done (§ 285).

Note.—The original sense of the phrase in तां with नये is that of unprofitableness or inexpediency, but what is inexpedient is often morally wrong: मला खातां नये I should not eat it, *i. e.*, I am so circumstanced that it is not expedient or advantageous for me to eat it, though there is nothing wrong if I did eat it as you desire. This is a mild and polite refusal.

§ 631. The negative form of the subjunctive mood in the infinitive mood and नये being usually used, we shall give some examples of it.

1. It expresses *the ethical sense:* आपण आईबापांची आज्ञा पाळावी we should obey our parents: corresponding negative form would be आज्ञा पाळूं नये we should not obey; गरीबीची लाज कोणी धरूं नये no one ought to be ashamed of poverty; आशा सोडूं नये we *must* not give up hope. Mark the force of the subjunctive in the last example.

2. It means a *disposition* or *habit:* त्यानें काठी उगारल्यावांचून चाकरांशीं बोलूं नये he was such a man that he could not speak to his servants without brandishing a stick over them.

3. It may express *purpose:* राजाची आज्ञा सर्वांनीं मानावी हेंच राज्याचें फळ the end for which regal power is valuable is that all should obey the king's commands: a corresponding negative construction is राज्याचें फळ हेंच कीं आज्ञा व्यर्थ होऊं नये that no wish of the king should remain unfulfilled is the end for which regal power is valuable.

4. It may express *potentiality*: कितीं लाभ झाला असतांही तृप्ति होऊं नये असा स्वभाव ज्याचा तो अतृप्त he is insatiable whose nature is such that whatever he may have gained, he can never be satisfied.

5. *The Past Subjunctive;* तुझ्या हातांत दोऱ्या कां द्याव्या why should I have put the reins into your hands? The negative form would be दोऱ्या कां न द्याव्या? why should not reins have been given? or कां न द्याव्या होत्या?

(For compound subjunctive forms, see § 312.)

The Imperative Mood.

§ 632. The following are the uses of the Imperative Mood:—

1. In the first person it has two uses: first, it is used in questions of appeal: मीं येऊं? shall I come? and, secondly, it expresses its modal sense: पाहूं बरें कोठें आहे ती let me see, then, where she is; चला माडीवर जाऊं come, let us go upstairs.

2. In the second person it expresses a command, and is a more direct form than the subjunctive. The plural form is used in addressing persons courteously: तूं आपलें काम कर do your own business; या सख्यानों come away, my friends; रामराम घे आतां good-bye to you now. The man spoken to in the last sentence, being of a very inferior station, is addressed in the singular, but the courteous ये *come* is used for जा *go*.

3. In the third person it is used to bless or to curse: ईश्वर तुमचें कल्याण करो may God bless you; भगवान् तुला सुखी राखो, आणि स्वर्गसुख देवो may God keep you happy, and give you the happiness of heaven.

In the singular form the second person is always employed in the addresses to the Deity.

§ 633. The negative imperative form is made up of नको singular and नका plural joined to the infinitive of the verb: तूं ये come thou, येऊं नको do not come; या come ye, येऊं नका do not come. It simply negatives the wish to have a certain act done: चुप बोलूं नको तूं मला कंटाळा आणिलास silence, do not say a word, you have quite disgusted me.

Note.—नको has the third plural form नकोत. In the third person नको negates पाहिजे it is wanted; बाबा मला नको father, I don't want it ; बाई इतके पेढे मला नकोत not so many sugar plums for me, madam. (§ 267.)

The Infinitive Mood.

§ 634. The infinitive is used to express an action that depends upon another, and restricts it : आम्हांस उपाशी मरूं दे let us die of hunger.

§ 635. In English the infinitive, being also the gerund, admits of various uses, but in Marathi the gerund is distinct from the infinitive and also from the Supine, and consequently its use is quite restricted. It chiefly forms the object of verbs expressing the action of the *mind* or *will*—such as इच्छिणें to wish, पाहणें to see, in the sense of to desire, शकणें to be able, देणें to give, in the sense of to allow, लागणें to affect, etc.; as तो करूं इच्छितो he desires to do it ; तो येऊं पाहतो he wishes to come; ती तें करूं शकेल she will be able to do it; मला येऊं दे allow me to come ; तो वाचूं लागला he began to read. Formerly many other verbs governed the infinitve ; त्यानें औषध घेऊं आदरिलें, he set himself to take the medicine. The infinitive may be considered as a verbal accusative.

Note.—In Vedic times the verbal noun formed from a root by the termination तु (गंतु, दातु) was regularly declined . . . In process of time only the accusative form was retained, and came to denote the sense of the dative. Hence the present Infinitive form always conveys the dative sense. In Marathi, also, it is only accusative, and in capable of being used as the subject ; and its dative form (the dative supine) expresses the dative sense of purpose.

Note.—" The Sanskrit Infinitive corresponds in Latin, to the supine in *um* (*datum* दातुं), which is properly the accusative of a verbal substantive just as in Sanskrit"—*Apte.*

Note.—In Sanskrit the verbs to desire, to be able, to know, to constrain, to begin, to get, etc., govern the infinitve in तुम्.

§ 636. The dative supine can be used in the place of the infinitive in every one of the above examples ; तो करूं or करायास इच्छितो he wishes to do it. The verb देणें to allow may take only the infinitive; मला येऊं दे, let me come ; मला वारा लिहूं देत नाहीं the wind will not let me write.

Note.—In Sanskrit also the infinitive is re-placed by the dative of the verbal noun derived from the root.

§ 637. The principal use of the infinitive in English is to express the purpose of an action; I come to bury Cæsar, not to praise him, मी सीजराला पुरायास आलों आहें, त्याची कीर्ति गायास आलों नाहीं. But this sense is expressed in Marathi by the subjunctive mood, and the dative supine.

§ 638. When the purpose of an action is expressed by a *distinct sentence* or clause, the subjunctive mood is used in Marathi, otherwise only the dative supine ; [राजा नेमावा म्हणून] सर्व पक्षी एकत्र झाले होते all the fowls had assembled in order that they might elect a king. The same may be thus expressed with a dative supine ; सर्व पक्षी [राजा नेमायास] एकत्र झाले होते all the fowls had assembled (for) to elect a king.

§ 639. When the infinitive is used as the subject of the verb in English, especially with the verb " to be ", the gerund is used in Marathi ; to laugh is natural, हसणें स्वाभाविक आहे.

The Participles.

1.—*The Present Tense.*

§ 640. The present participle has three simple, and two compound forms.

I.—(1) The form in ईत is the principal one, and is usually used to make up compound tenses : तो वाचीत आहे he is reading ; तो बोलत नाहीं he does not speak ; मी गेलों तेव्हां ती रडत होती when I went, she was crying. It expresses the *currency* of action.

(2) It is used with other verbs to define them ; तूंच स्वतः उद्योग करीत ऐस do you yourself continue the work diligently ; देवास भजत जा go on worshipping God ; तो मौज पाहात उभा राहिला he stood looking at the show ; ती तेथें हांसत बसली she sat there laughing.

Note.—When the present participle in ईत is thus adverbially used it may be optionally reduplicated if the verb which it modifies is a verb of motion or action ; ती रडत or रडतरडत आली she came weeping, but ती रडत बसली or पडली she sat down or lay down weeping ; तो वाचीत वाचीत पुढें चालला he walked on reading ; तें पोर पाहा, खात खात येतें look at that boy, he comes eating.

हंसत हंसत आनंदतनय म्हणे कवि होइल तुमच्या ॥

Ánandtanaya.

(3) With the negative particle it may express the notion of *willingness*, besides that of currency: बोलत नाहींस? won't you speak? तूं माझी आंगठी घेत नाहींस? तर तुजवर मीं रागें भरेन won't you take my ring now? then I will get angry with you; दौलतसिंग घेत नाहीं Daulatsing won't take it.

II.—(1) The participle in इतां expresses that while the action denoted by it is going on, that denoted by the verb takes place: तो चालतां चालतां खालीं पडला? he fell down while walking. The participle is usually repeated to express the sense of duration.

(2) But when the participle does not express an idea of duration or continuance, it is not repeated: बारा वाजतां या come at twelve o'clock; हाक मारितांच मीं उठलों I got up as soon as he called out to me; त्याला न कळतां मागून जाऊन उभी राहिली without their knowledge she went after them and stood there; वांकडीं तोंडें न करितां त्यांनीं औषध घेऊं आदरिलें they set themselves to take the medicine without at the same time making any wry faces.

(3) The participle is used to make up the indirect object of the transitive verb when the indirect object expresses an action in progress: त्याला खेळतां म्यां पाहिलें I saw him play.

III.—(1) The participle in इतांना expresses, like that in इतां, that while the action denoted by it is going on, another action is performed: म्या जेवितांना तुझी चिठी वाचून टाकिली I read off your note while taking my meals. It usually expresses the sense of duration.

(2) It expresses the indirect object: म्या त्याला घोड्याला मारतांना पाहिलें I saw him beating the horse.

Note.—The difference between the participles इतां and इतांना, when they express the indirect verbal object, is the same that exists between the English infinitive and the present participle, used objectively: I saw him *strike*, and I saw him *striking*.

IV.—(1) The compound participle in इत असतां expresses the *progressive* sense like the above two participial forms: आम्ही खेळत असतां तो आला he came while we were playing. It is usually employed when the agent of the participle is distinct from that of the verb, as in the above example; भोजराजा राज्य करीत असतां एका ब्राह्मणानें नवी भूमि शोधून शेत पेरिलें होतें during the reign of Bhoj Rájá, a certain Brahman having acquired a piece of waste land, sowed it with grain.

(2) With or without ही even, this participle has the force of the conjunctional particle जरी although: शिकवीत असतांही ती विद्या मनांत येऊं नये although I teach him, he cannot comprehend that science; त्याजवळून ती मागितली असतां, दिली नाहीं although I asked him for it, he did not give it to me.

V.—The participle होत असतांना has the same force and use as the preceding one in होत असतां, but it is not often employed.

II.—*The Past Tense.*

§ 640. There are three past participles in ला, लेला, and ला असतां, and one pluperfect participle in ऊन.

1. The participle in ला is used with the auxiliary verbs to make up several past tenses; असें लिहिलें आहे it is thus written.

Note.—The tenses formed with only ला sometimes take postpositions, when they end a noun sentence; तुमची चाकरी सोडिल्यावर on having left your service; तुझी आई वारल्यापासून since your mother's death. (§ 515)

Note.—When the dative termination स is used to inflect the participial ला, the sentence which ends in ला assumes a suppositive character; as, गेल्यास should he go; आल्यास should he come; श्लोक काढल्यास त्यांची परीक्षा होईल whenever he shall produce his slokas, they shall be examined. This form expresses that the probability is very small, or that the speaker is quite indifferent about the contingent act.

2. (1) The form लेला is used simply as a participial adjective; इतर भाषांतरापासून आलेल्या शब्दांतील कितीएक शब्द several words introduced from foreign sources.

(2) Sometimes it is used with the auxiliary substantive verb to make up a passive form: नौका कांठाशीं बांधलेली होती the boat was tied to the shore. The past participle may, also, be considered an adjective, used as a nominal predicate.

3. The compound form in ला with असतां, like the present participial form in असतां, is employed to form adverbial or con-

junctional clauses, like those in which the particles तेव्हां then, तर then, तरी still, occur.

(1) The form in ला असतां expresses that a past event is in some way the cause or occasion of the act mentioned in the following clause: तो खालीं आला असतां त्याची बुद्धि पुन: पूर्ववत् व्हावी whenever he came down, his disposition would become the same as before.

(2) It is used in the first clause of a conditional sentence to express a probability stronger than that denoted by ल्यास: उपाय केला असतां दुर्गुण टाकवितां येईल if means be used, it will still be possible to rid him of his bad qualities.

(3) It has the sense of the particle although: तिचा तोटा माझी सगळी संपत्ति खर्च झाली असतां भरून देऊं शकणार नाहीं though I should spend all my estate, I could not make up her loss; इतकें म्हटलें असतां तो गेला though I said so much, nevertheless he went. With this form ही even might also be used: इतकें म्हटलें असतांही तो गेला.

4. (1) The principal use of the participle in ऊन is to connect two clauses which otherwise would be joined by the conjunction आणि and; and it denotes that the act expressed by it precedes in point of time that mentioned in the succeeding clause: चार पानें उलटून पुसतो he turned over four leaves, and asked; मामापुढें जाऊन त्याच्या पायां पडेन I will go into the presence of my uncle, and on my knees beg his pardon; तीं कोंकरें पाय बांधून एकावर एक रचिलीं होतीं those lambs were piled one above another, with their feet bound. In these sentences the subject or the agent of both the acts is the same.

(2) The subject of the participle may be different from that of the verb: गाणें होऊन फार दिवस राहील after singing is over, still a good part of the day will remain; भेट होऊन वर्ष लोटलेंसें वाटतें I think a year has passed since I saw you last; त्याला मरून किती दिवस झाले? how many days is it since he died?

Note.—In these examples, the sense of the pluperfect may be expressed by postpositions joined to the past tense: गाणें होऊन फार दिवस राहील may also be गाणें झाल्यावर &c.; भेट होऊन वर्ष लोटलेंसें वाटतें, or भेट झाल्यापासून or भेट झाल्याला वर्ष लोटलेंसें वाटतें; त्याला मरून, त्याला मेल्याला, &c.

(3) It expresses the cause of the verbal act that follows: आजारी पडपडून अगदीं अशक्त झालों I have got quite feeble by constant sickness; तो ताप येऊन मेला he died of fever; तो येत असतां वाटेंत मोठा पर्जन्य पडून एक नदीस उतार होत नाहीं असें पाहिलें as he was returning, he came to a river on the road, through which, from a great fall of rain that had taken place, he saw there was no passage; मला मारून तुला काय मिळणार? what would you get by killing me?

(4) It has the force of जरी although, when ऊन inflects the verb असणें; पहा मीं जाणता असून इतका घसरलों see, what a blunder I have committed, wise man as I am; ही is often added to असून.

(5) It is used to make up the forms of some compound verbs: धुऊन टाक wash it thoroughly; त्यानें तें फेंकून दिलें he flung it away.

Note.—In the phrase जाणून आहें a substitute for मीं जाणतों I know, the participle expresses the sense of the verb intensely or forcibly: हें तर मीं जाणून आहें that I know full well.

§ 641. The future participle in णार expresses that the speaker has some knowledge of the intention on the part of the agent to do the act denoted by the participle: तो येणार आहे he is going to come. It is chiefly used to make up the forms of the compound tenses. Its form in आ is used as a verbal adjective: येणारे लोक the people who intend to come.

§ 642. It is used as a noun in the form of णार as well as णारा, and the case-inflections are often added only to the former form: बोलणारे पुष्कळ, करणारे थोडे there are many to speak, but few to act; मारणाराचे, (in the Deckan मारणाऱ्याचे) हात धरवतील, पण बोलणाराचें (बोलणाऱ्याचें) तोंड धरवत नाहीं we can hold the hands of the striker, but cannot stop the mouth of the speaker.

THE GERUND.

§ 643. 1. This expresses the simple verbal act, without any circumstances of time, mode, &c., and is substantival in use, being declined in all the cases, like a neuter noun ending in एं; as करणें doing; करण्याला for doing; करण्याचा of doing, &c. Thus, त्याचीं करणीं चांगलीं आहेत his actions are good; तिचें पारिपत्य होणें चुकलें नाहीं she did not escape punishment; मला बापाची आज्ञा मान्य करणें प्राप्त आहे it is imperative that I should obey my father.

Note.—The gerund may take its object when it is a transitive verb: तूं मला पन्नास सुपाऱ्या देणें आहेस you owe me fifty betelnuts.

Note.—The verbs are given in the dictionary in the gerundial form, and the verb is named by it; as करणें धातु the verb to do.

2. It is used for the imperative as a most indefinite form: पत्र लिहीत जाणें continue to write to us. It, being indefinite, is most respectful, and occurs frequently in the old Bakhars, as well as in letters: मग रामसिंग धीर धरणें म्हणून बोलूं लागले then they said that Ramsing should have patience; तरी तुम्ही त्या दोघांस कैद करणें you may nevertheless make them both prisoners. It is a more courteous form than even the subjunctive.

3. With the verb असणें, it expresses the sense of obligation or necessity: एक दिवस आपणास मरणें आहे one day we have to die; तूं मला पन्नास रुपये देणें आहेस you have to give me fifty repees; मग जें करणें असेल तें कर then do what you think is proper.

The Supines.

§ 644. The forms of the supines are two—dative and genitive.

§ 645. *The Dative Supine.*—The dative supine has the following special uses :—

1. The dative supine is usually used for the objective infinitive: तो तें करूं or करायास इच्छितो he wishes to do it. It is only a few verbs that take the infinitive as the object, but the supine may be used with all the verbs.

2. The dative supine is used with the personal or dative object, to complete or define its sense, especially with the verbs सांगणें to tell, आज्ञापिणें to command, शिकविणें to teach, फुसलाविणें to persuade, प्रेरणें to inspire, लावणें to employ, &c.: त्यानें त्याला लांकडें फोडायास लाविलें he employed him to hew wood; त्याला प्रार्थना करायास शिकविलें he taught him to pray; त्याला मारायास मला आज्ञापिलें he commanded me to kill him. The supines are indirect objects denoting action.

3. The dative supine is employed to express *purpose*: तुम्ही काय पाहायास गेलां what went ye out for to see? आमच्या बरोबर आमचा बाग पाहवयास चला come with me to see my garden.

4. It is used as the complement of the adjective: खायास गोड, पण पचायास कठिण It is sweet to eat, but hard to digest; तो मरायास राजी आहे he is ready to die.

Note.—The dative supine is not used as the complement of the noun, but the genitive supine: a time to weep and a time to laugh, रडायाची वेळ आणि हंसायाची वेळ; a house to let, भाड्यानें द्यायाचें घर.

The Genitive Supine.

§ 646. The genitive supine is used as the complement of a noun: means to do ill deeds वाईट कृत्यें करायाचीं साधनें; a book to read वाचायाचें पुस्तक; नेसायाचा पंचा a garment to wear. It has the force of a verbal adjective.

§ 647. It expresses, like the English infinitive with certain verbs, a kind of necessity or obligation; I have to go, मला जायाचें आहे.

§ 648. It is so used in Marathi with the verbs असणें to be, पडणें to fall &c.

(*a*) आपणाशीं मला कांहीं बोलायाचें आहे I have something to say to you; हें काय सांगायाचें आहे why need I tell you that?

(*b*) With the subject in the instrumental case, it, with the verb असणें, expresses moral obligation; म्या यावयाचें होतें I should have come; but मला यावयाचें होतें with the dative subject, as in the above paragraph, would be "I had to come."

(*c*) With the subject in the nominative case it has the force of the present prospective tense; तो येणार आहे or तो यायाचा आहे he is going to come. The latter expresses the *near* and *certain* accomplishment of the future act that has been resolved on.

(*d*) It expresses more emphatically the determination of the agent to do, or not to do, a certain action than the present prospective tense: तुला आज्ञा मिळणार नाहीं you shall not have permission to go; तुला आज्ञा मिळायाची नाहीं you shall on no account have permission to go.

(*e*) आह्मांस देशांतरीं जायाचें पडेल we shall be under the necessity of going abroad. It expresses a necessity over which the speaker has no control.

§ 649. Used by itself without असणें or पडणें to complete the sentence, the genitive supine expresses the highest degree of probability—little short of absolute certainty ; ती एखाद्या दिवशीं अनर्थ करायाची she is such a person as will one day or other surely do mischief; धोंडा कानास लागला तो तुटायाचाच, पण थोडक्यांत चुकलें the stone struck his ear, and it (the ear) was ready to break off, but the act was deficient by a little, *i.e.* the ear was within an ace of being struck off.

§ 650. The following are examples of the negative construction: तुह्मी मला जमिनींत पाहिजे तितके दिवस पुरा, तरी मी मरावयाचा नाहीं bury me in the ground as many days as you please, but I shall *never die* ; तेव्हां त्रिंबक ह्मणाला, ही गोटी एक इंचभर देखील पुढें सरकावयाची नाहीं then Trimbak said that the ball would never move forward even an inch.

Note.—The gerundial dative and genitive should not be confounded with the dative and genitive supines. The gerund is simply nominal, having the force of an abstract noun, and should be used when an action is viewed as a thing or object; but when the sense of *action* or the actual performance of a thing is predominant, the supines should be used. The gerund should never be used in the cases mentioned under the Dative and Genitive Supines. Thus, तो आज रात्रीस निजायास येणार आहे he is going to come to sleep to-night is correct, but निजण्यास येणार आहे would be wrong ; त्यांच्या खेळण्यास काय ह्मणावें what shall we call their playing? खेळायास would be wrong in this sentence; आज गायाचीं गीतें तीं कोणतीं which are the hymns to be sung to-day! But गाण्याचीं गीतें आणा bring the singing songs, or songs used in singing.

Note.—The supines are inflected forms of the infinitive, which, etymologically as well as in regard to their use, are substantival in character. They are of the nature of the gerund, abstract nouns, denoting action, but, unlike the gerund, they, in the dative case, express the sense of "a purpose." Thus, "he goes to read" would be तो वाचायास जातो, not वाचण्यास जातो ; so also "what shall I do for his reading" would be त्याच्या वाचण्यास, (not वाचायास) काय करूं ? In Sanskrit the form in तुम् is not inflected in the dative to express this sense of purpose ; व्रजति पक्तुम् he goes to cook. But even in Sanskrit it is only a few special verbs that can take the forms in तुम्. Its deficiency is made up by the aid of other forms, and by the use, like the Maráthí dative supine, of a verbal dative; व्रजति पाकाय he goes to the act of cooking.—*Max Müller*.

CHAPTER XXX.

The Particles.

THE ADVERB.

§ 651—§ 682.

§ 651. The declinable adverb agrees, in gender and number, either with the subject, or with the object of the verb: ती चांगली नाचेल she will dance well; तो गायन कसें करितो? how does he sing? असा तो पराकाष्ठेच्या क्लेशांत पडला thus he fell into very great distress. The declinable adverb is thus used—

1. When the subject is uninflected, and the verb is intransitive, the adverb agrees with the subject; ती चांगली चालते she walks well; तो मजशीं वांकडा वागतो he is opposed to me.

2. When the verb takes an uninflected object, the adverb agrees with the object, in preference to the subject; ती गायन चांगलें करिते she sings well.

3. When both the subject and object are inflected, the adverb is put in the neuter singular; त्यानें त्याला कसें मारावें how could he beat him?

4. The adverb is put in the neuter singular, also, when the subject of the intransitive verb is omitted as well as inflected; होईल कसें how will it be? त्यानें जावें तरी कसें how could he go?

5. The adverb is employed in the neuter singular, also, when the object of the transitive verb is omitted, and the verb expresses merely its general sense of action; तो कसें वाचितो how does he read! ती कसें गाते how does she sing; but तो कशी पोथी वाचितो how does he read the book!

§ 652. One adverb may modify another adverb, and then both agree in gender and number; देवानें ही गोष्ट केवढी चांगली केली आहे पाहा बरें? see how well God has ordered this matter.

§ 653. Adverbs expressing the sense of quality, or rather adjectives used adverbially, can be compared like simple adjectives; रामापेक्षां मैना चांगलें वाचिते Mainá reads better than Rámá. (§ 522.)

§ 654. In a compound sentence the relative adverb introducing the initial clause is followed by its correlative ; ती जेव्हां जेव्हां आईची रागीट मुद्रा पाही तेव्हां तेव्हां तिला भय वाटे whenever she used to see her mother in anger, she was afraid.

The relative particle may be omitted ; मीं ज्वान होतों त्या वेळीं काम करीं I used to work when I was young ; तूं सांगशील तसें आम्हीं करावें we should do as you may bid us.

§ 655. The relative adverb of time (जेव्हां) may be repeated to convey the sense of frequency, and the correlative following it is usually repeated : जेव्हां जेव्हां तिजवर दृष्टि पडे तेव्हां तेव्हां तिचे डोळे आसवांनीं भरून येत whenever her eyes fell upon her, they used to fill with tears. In the following sentence the adverb is not repeated : पण मीं त्यांकडेस जायास लागतों, तेव्हां तीं मला घालवून देतात they drive me away whenever I attempt to go to them.

§ 656. When जेव्हां is joined to केव्हां, it expresses the rare occurrence of an event, and the correlative is only once mentioned : मग जेव्हां केव्हां यमनी कांहीं सांगितलें काम जपून करीत नसे, तेव्हां त्र्यंबक शेटीनें ती मैना पुन: तेथें टांगावी sometimes when she happened not to do attentively what she was bid, then Trimbakshet used to hang the jay again in that place.

Obs.—For the meanings and uses of other adverbs, See § 348.

THE POSTPOSITION.

§ 657. The postpositions, which are capable of inflection, agree with the nouns to which they refer in gender and number : त्यासभोंवते or सभोंवताले वीस हत्ती उभे होते twenty elephants stood around him. The postpositions, in conjunction with the nouns which they inflect, form adverbial phrases, and consequently follow the same laws of concordance with the declinable adverbs. (§ 508.)

§ 658. Postpositions may inflect a whole sentence: मीं रुपये घेतल्यावांचून जाणार नाहीं I will not go without taking the rupees; त्यांची भेट झाल्यावर मीं त्यास पुसेन after I have met him, I shall ask him. The postposition inflects the verbs घेतले and भेट झाली as if they were nouns (भेट झाली + यावर). When the postpositions thus govern a sentence, the sentence ends in the past tense in ला. (§ 504, 1, *Note.*)

§ 659. The demonstrative हा this, might be inserted between the sentence and the postposition by which it is governed; रामानें रावजीस टोपी बक्षीस दिली ह्यावरून सदूला वाईट वाटलें Sadu was grieved that Rámá gave a cap to Raoji as a present. (§ 566.)

Obs.—It would be best to write the postposition and the inflected noun together: as रामापेक्षां than Rámá; घराबाहेर out of the house.

THE CONJUNCTION.

§ 660. The copulative conjunctions are आणि and व. आणि differs a little from व. The former connects opposite truths, while the latter denotes variety: तो काळा आणि हा गोरा that one is dark, and this is fair; आह्मी पृथ्वीचें आंथरूण करूं आणि आकाशाचें पांघरूण we used to make the earth our bed and the sky our covering; त्याची कृतघ्नता पाहून व आपला दुर्लौकिक आणि असले गुणानें याचें अकल्याण पाहून मला बहुत खेद वाटतो I am very much pained to think of his ingratitude, dishonour, and the ruin which he has brought upon himself by such conduct.

2. आणि has occasionally a causal force which is wanting in व, and denotes that the former member is related to the latter as the antecedent cause or rather occasion: सांप्रत मला चाकरी नाहीं आणि काय करावें तें सुचत नाहीं at present I have no employment and (consequently) I do not know what I should do.

3. आणि has another peculiar force. It indicates that the act mentioned in the first clause precedes in point of time that contained in the latter clause without exercising a causal influence: त्यानें चार पानें उलटलीं आणि पुसलें he turned over four leaves and asked. When two sentences are thus connected with each other, the verb of the first clause is changed to the pluperfect participle, and the conjunction is omitted: त्यानें चार पानें उलटून पुसलें he turned over four leaves and asked; गाणें होऊन कांहीं दिवस राहिला the singing was over, and some part of the day still remained.

4. आणि and व are both elegantly used in a sentence for the sake of variety of particles: मग यमनी मैनेस पिंजऱ्यांत घालून सगळ्या घरभर फिरून आईस व बहिणीस आणि चाकरांस हाका मारून दाखवूं लागली afterwards she put the jay in the cage and went with it all over

the house, calling out to her mother, sister, and the servants, and showing it to them.

5. आणि may be indiscriminately used, but not so व.

§ 661. The copulative conjunctions are often omitted in Maráṭhí, and the omission frequently imparts naturalness and animation to the narrative: वास्तविक पाहतां तिणें तें आईस ठकविलें नाहीं, आपणास ठकविलें. अगोदर तिच्या वृत्तीस संतोष असे; आईच्या जवळ येऊन तिला समाधान वाटे; आई बाहेरून आली असतां आनंदानें जाऊन ती तिचे गळ्यांत मिठी घाली; ती सगळी सुखोत्पत्ति तिला मग नाहींशी झाली in reality she did not deceive her mother, she deceived herself. Formerly she used to be always cheerful. She would find delight in the society of her mother, and whenever her mother went out and came home, she would gladly go forward and embrace her; but all this happiness was now lost to her; त्याणें ज्यांत आपलें हित होईल तेंच सांगितलें आहे; ज्यांत आपलें अनहित तेंच निषेधिलें आहे he has bid us do what would do us good, and forbidden what would injure us.

§ 662. On the other hand, the repetition of the conjunction arrests the attention, and rivets it on the details: मग यमनी मैनेस पिंजऱ्यांत घालून सगळ्या घरभर, आईस व बहिणीस आणि चाकरांस हाक मारून दाखवूं लागली then she put the jay in the cage, and went with it all over the house, calling out to her mother, and sisters, and the servants, and showing it to them. The particles are, however, often omitted, and the attention is drawn to the details by the tone of the voice: मग खोतजीनें दौलतरावास माडीवर नेलें, तेथें द्राक्षें, निंबें, चकोत्रे, अननस, डाळिंबें, केळीं, अंजीर, पेरू अशीं नाना प्रकारचीं फळें व गुलाब, मोगरा, जाई, शेवंती, चांपा अशीं फुलें आधींच आणून ठेविलीं होतीं then the squire took Davlatráv upstairs, where he had beforehand collected such fruits as grapes, limes, shaddocks, pine-apples, pomegranates, plantains, figs, guavas, and such flowers as the rose, the jessamine, the jasmine, the Christmas flower, and the champaca; तिणें ते समयीं आनंदांत निमग्न होऊन आईच्या तोंडाचे, गालाचे, डोळ्याचे, उराचे, हाताचे पुष्कळपणें मुके घेतले she was then so much overpowered with joy that she kissed her mother profusely on her lips, her cheeks, her eyes, her breast, and her hands.

§ 663. The disjunctive conjunctions अथवा and किंवा, or, differ a little in sense, though the difference is little attended to. अथवा has only a disjunctive force, while किंवा has the additional sense of variety: कोणीं भलीं मनुष्यें दरिद्रानें पिडून माझ्या संपत्तींतून घांसभर अन्न इच्छितात, किंवा इकडे तिकडे पडलेलीं कणसें टिपतात, त्यांस सर्वथा तुझा उपद्रव नसावा if any honest people suffering from poverty desire to get a mouthful of food, or glean stray ears of corn, you should never molest them ; जर मला त्याची प्रशंसा कर्तव्य आहे ती मीं त्यांचे समक्ष केली, तर महाराजांस मानेल ? अथवा जे त्याच्या आचरणाप्रमाणें त्यास फळ तत्काळ देऊं शकतात अशांजवळ त्याची वांकडी गोष्ट बोलवेल ? would your majesty be pleased if I praised him in your presence as he deserves, or could I say anything unfavourable of him in the presence of one who could deal with him, at once, according to his deserts ?

2. अथवा and किंवा are often elegantly used to vary particles ; तो (वहमा) खरा किंवा निमित्ताकरितां आणिला, अथवा खचितच त्याच्या मनांत असा बेत होता हें स्पष्ट समजत नाहीं whether it (the charge) was true, or a trumped up one, or he really intended doing it cannot be precisely determined.

§ 664. When the second clause of a compound sentence *limits* the signification of the first, the adversative conjunction परंतु or पण, but, is inserted: तूं अन्याय कबूल झालीस ह्मणून तुझें पारिपत्य मात्र करीत नाहीं; पण तुझा फार दिवस पश्चात्ताप पाहिल्याशिवाय मी तुला माझें दुर्गे, असें म्हणणार नाहीं because you have confessed your fault, I will simply not punish you ; but I will not call you my Durgá unless I try your penitence for many days ; माझा भाऊ रीतीनें चांगला, मनानें मोकळा, स्वभावानें उदार, पण अमळ उतावळा, धट, आणि आग्रही आहे my brother has good manners, and is of a frank and generous disposition ; but he is at the same time a little rash, forward and obstinate: शपथा वाहिल्या पण खरें नाहीं बोलला he swore, but did not speak the truth; तरी or तरीं could be substituted for पण.

Note.—The adversative sentence in which the second clause limits the first, could be converted into a conditional sentence, denoting concession : जरी माझा भाऊ रीतीनें चांगला, मनानें मोकळा, &c., तरी तसाच अमळ उतावळा, &c., आहे although my brother is of good habits, &c., still he is at the same time a little rash, &c. The conditional is preferable when the opposition is pointed.

§ 665. When the second clause *contradicts* the first, the whole sentence is constructed in two ways :—

1. When the first clause is positive, *i.e.*, does not contain a negative particle, and the second clause is negative, the two clauses are simply put together, without the insertion of an adversative particle : तिनें आपणास फसविलें, आईस नाहीं she deceived herself, not her mother; अशी गोष्ट होते तेथें त्यांचा दोष, आपला नाहीं in a thing like this, it is their fault, not ours.

2. When the first clause contains a negative particle and the second is affirmative, the adversative particles may or may not be inserted : विष खाल्यानें मनुष्य वाचणार नाहीं, मरेल (or तर मरेल) by eating poison, man will not live, but die. The adversative तर then is only used, never परंतु or पण nevertheless.

3. When two opposite clauses are joined simply to indicate variety, and not contradiction, the copulative conjunction आणि and, in the sense of No. 1, is used : मुलगा अशक्त आणि मुलगी सुदृढ आहे the boy is weak, and the girl is strong.

§ 666. When more than two adversative clauses are united in one sentence, both पण but, and आणि and, in its oppositional character, are employed to connect the clauses : लोक तसें करितात तें मींहि जाणतों, पण वासूची मला अजून एक वाईट चेष्टा आढळली नाहीं, आणि आत्मारामानें नाहीं तरी सहस्रावधि केल्या असतील I am fully aware that people do so, but I have not met with a single fault in Vású, whereas Átmárám must be, at least, guilty of a thousand. In this sentence the second clause limits the first, and the third negatives the second ; hence पण very naturally comes between the first two clauses, and आणि between the second and the last.

When, however, the second clause negatives the first and the third limits the second, there is no particle inserted between the first and the second clause, while पण is inserted before the third : खोतजीचीं भांडीं सोन्यारुप्याचीं नव्हतीं, तांब्यापितळेचींच होतीं, पण स्वच्छ लकलकीत होतीं the plates and dishes of the farmer were not of gold and silver, but only of brass and copper, nevertheless they were clean and bright. तरी still, would be preferable to पण.

§ 667. In regard to the causative sentences, when the primary design of the speaker is to mention the cause, the clause containing the cause is put first, and the causal particle म्हणून is affixed to it : तेथील घरें सुकीं, आणि राहण्याच्या सोईचीं आहेत म्हणून अशीं उत्तम शहरें फार थोडीं असतील since the houses there are dry, clean, and commodious, there must be very few such excellent cities. But when the speaker does not wish to state the cause first, the clause containing the fact to be accounted for is placed first, and the causal clause beginning with कांकीं, कारण कीं, कीं, &c., follows it : तिच्या बोलण्याप्रमाणें झालें, कांकीं जे पांचहजार कुमकेस आले होते ते परत गेले it happened as she had said, for the five thousand that had come to his aid went back ; आईचा शब्द ऐकून तिला कांप सुटावा, कीं कोण जाणें तिच्या तोंडांतून काय अक्षरें निघतील whenever she heard the voice of her mother she used to tremble, for she did not know what her mother might have to say to her.

§ 668. In causative sentences expressive of purpose, the sentence expressing purpose is put before the other clause, with म्हणून at the end of the former ; but when the clause denoting purpose is placed last, it is preceded by the particle कीं : तो अपशकुन दूर करावा म्हणून राणी साहेबांनीं तत्क्षणीं एक बंदूक घेऊन कावळ्यास ठार मारिलें in order to remove the bad omen, the queen at once took a gun and killed the crow ; तिचे पिंजऱ्यावर नित्य हिरवा पाला लावी, कीं तिला उन्हाचा उपद्रव होऊं न पावे she used to put green leaves over the cage, in order that it might not suffer from the sun. When purpose is to be emphasized, the clause containing it is put first.

§ 669. The conditional particles जर and तर are employed in purely conditional or supposititive sentences : जर तूं त्याकडे नित्य गेलीस तर तुला त्याचे दुर्गुण लागतील if you always went to him, you would contract his vices ; तूं माझें सांगितलें ऐकशील तर आजच हरीकडे जा if you care to listen to me, then go this very day to Hari. The relative conditional particle जर might be optionally omitted as in the last example.

§ 670. Instead of the conjunctional particles जर and तर, the participial forms त्यास and असतां are sometimes employed.

The form in ल्यास is used when the act mentioned in the conditional clause is least important, or is least likely to occur: आमच्या गांवीं आल्यास मला भेट should you ever happen to come to our town, come and see me. The future indicative with जर may be used for this form: मला राज्यपदीं बसवाल (or बसविल्यास) should you ever seat me upon the throne. The form in असतां is more emphatic than that in ल्यास, but still it implies that what is mentioned in the consequent is more important than that which is stated in the conditional clause: मीं त्यांकडे गेलों असतां ते मला पुनः चाकरीस ठेवितील should I go to him again, he will restore me to my place in his service. When, however, the conditional clause is to be made emphatic, the past indicative with जर, expressed or understood, is employed: हें मामास कळलें तर काय म्हणेल should my maternal uncle learn this, what would he say? तूं मागें कोण्याजवळ होतास त्यांच्या हातचें अनुपत्र आणिलें तर तुला ठेवीन if you should bring a certificate from the gentleman whom you served before, I will keep you.

Note.—The past indicative denotes an act that is done and past, and about the occurrence of which there is no uncertainty or doubt whatsoever, and therefore it is fixed and real, and hence the force which it has in a conditional clause.

Note.—The forms expressing great uncertainty are considered most respectful in Maráṭhí, and are consequently employod when persons are addressed courteously: तुला कोणी पाहूं नये असें तुझ्या मनांत असल्यास मी तुला तशीच जागा देईन if you shoud perhaps desire that nobody should see you, I shall give you a suitable place; महाराजांची आज्ञा झाल्यास कळवीन should your majesty command, I shall inform you; आज्ञा घाल तर मीं क्षणभर जाऊन येतों if you will have the goodness to give me permission, I shall go and return in a moment.

§ 671. The past indicative, with जर or जरी, being the most emphatic conditional form, is always employed when the action contained in the conditional clause is more important than its result: पोरा जर तूं येथून हाललास तर खबरदार now, boy, take care if you stir hence; तिचा तोटा माझी सगळी संपत्ती खर्च केली तरी भरून देऊं शकणार नाहीं though I should spend all my estate, I could not make up her loss. जर or जरी is always expressed when the conditional clause is most emphatic.

Hence when a person speaks of himself with modesty, he uses the past tense in the conditional clause; the past tense, being an emphatic form, imposes a high degree of obligation on him: जर मला त्याची प्रशंसा कर्त्तव्य आहे ती मीं त्याच्या समक्ष केली तर महाराजांस मानेल? if I praised him before his face, as I might in justice be expected to do, then would your majesty be pleased? It would be rude to use this form in reference to a person of superior station.

§ 672. When an event is certain or of frequent occurrence, and the performance of another act depends upon it, the past tense is used followed by म्हणजे instead of तर: मामा बाहेर गेला म्हणजे तुला भेटतों when uncle goes out, I will even then meet you; तो आला म्हणजे मला सांग tell me as soon as he comes; हा मुलगा मुलांच्या मंडळींत गेला म्हणजे तीं यास हांकून देतात आणि फिरून आलास तर मारूं म्हणून म्हणतात whenever this boy goes into the company of other boys, they drive him away, and say, "we will beat you if you shall come back again."

Note.—The past indicative sometimes denotes an event which is *least* likely to happen in future time: कधीं तूं आमच्या दारावरून आलास तर मजकडे ये should you ever pass our door, come to me. The past indicative here denotes an event which is not dependent upon the *will* of the person of whom it is affirmed, and therefore most contingent.

Note.—Instead of the past tense, the imperative might be used: हा बैल रहाटाखालीं धरा (धरला) म्हणजे चांगला होईल put the ox to the water-wheel, and he will then improve.

§ 673. When an event has actually taken place, and there is no doubt in the speaker's mind about it, the present and the past tense of आहे are used to make up the verbal forms: तो जर चोर नाहीं (of which you have no doubt) तर त्यास भय नाहीं if he is not a thief, then he has nothing to fear; जर ते आले होते तर मला भेटले असतील if they had come they must have seen me; एथें जर तो आहे, तर तो तुझे दृष्टीस पडेल if he is here, then you will see him

§ 674. When the speaker does not question the occurrence of an event, but simply wants to express that he has no knowledge about it, then असला is substituted for आहे: तो द्वीपांतरीं गेला

असला तरी तेथून आणीन: though he should have gone to another continent, I will fetch him thence; त्यांना गुरूनें जावयास रजा दिली असली तर should the teacher have given them leave, what then? ते जात असले तर येऊं नको should he be going, then do not come; तूं लिहिणार असलास तर मीं लिहिणार नाहीं should you be going to write, I shall not write; जर तो एथेंच कोठें असला तर should he be in some place just here, then?

§ 675. When we wish to express that the event might have been different from that which has actually happened, the conditional mood is used: अधिकी पैशाची गरज लागती तर मीं सगळें विकलें असतें had I needed more money, I would have sold the whole; त्याला क्षमा केली असती तर रामाला इतका खेद होताना if you had pardoned him, then Rámá would not have been so much grieved. This is the most common use of the Maráṭhí conditional mood.

§ 676. When the things supposed are very shortly to happen, the conditional is used: जर तो जाता तर मीहि जातों if he were going then I would go also (Present tense).

§ 677. When the conditional clause denotes a concession, the particles जरी and तरी are used: इतकें जरी सांगितलें तरी त्यानें ऐकिलें नाहीं although I told him so much, he did not listen; देवराव अश्रु टाकीत आहेत तथापि ते तें ऐकून हंसले although Devráv was shedding tears, still he smiled when he heard that. असतां or असतांहि might be substituted for the conditional particles; इतकें म्हटलें असतां तो गेला though I said so much, still he went away.

The Interjection.

§ 678. The interjection होय, yes, requires a word of explation. In answering a question, the verb employed in the question is repeated with or without होय yes. If a man was asked if his work was completed, he would be asked काम झालें have you done your work (literally, is the work done)? He would answer, होय झालें yes, it is done, or simply झालें it is done; never only होय yes.

§ 679. But since होय is a form of the verb होणें to become, and, as a verb, is used in the sense of आहे, is (§ 224), it can naturally be used by itself when the question is put with the verb आहे to be. Thus, the question तुम्ही कुणबी आहां ? are you Kunbis ? might be answered simply by होय yes, or with the whole question repeated in a different tone, as होय, कुणबी आहों yes, we are Kunbis.

§ 680. The negative answer is given in the same way as the affirmative : तुला भूक लागली are you hungry ? Answer : नाहीं लागली or लागली नाहीं I am not hungry. So also, तूं गेला होतास did you go ? नाहीं गेलों I did not go ; तूं ब्राह्मण आहेस are you a Brahman? नाहीं no ; or नाहीं, मीं ब्राह्मण नाहीं no, I am not a Brahman; or नाहीं, मीं शिंपी आहें no, I am a tailor.

§ 681. The above information is only in reference to questions of *information*. The mode of answering questions of permission or entreaty is somewhat different. In the affirmative answer the principal verb of the question is simply repeated, or repeated with the interjection होय yes, or बरें well: मीं येऊं shall I come ? या, or होय या, or बरें या come ; or yes, come ; or well, come ; त्यानें तें पुस्तक वाचावें should he read that book ? होय वाचावें yes, he should read it, or खुशाल वाचावें he may freely read it.

§ 682. The negative answer is given with the negative verb नको or नये: तूं वाचूं नको do not thou read it ; तुम्ही येऊं नका don't come, (pl ural) ; त्यानें येऊं नये he should not come. These are the negative forms of the imperative and subjunctive moods. When नको is used as the negative form of पाहिजे (§ 266), it can be used in the answer simply by itself : तुला आंबा पाहिजे ? do you want a mango ? नको, or मला नको I don't want it, or मला आंबा नको, केळें पाहिजे I don't want a mango, but a plantain.

CHAPTER XXXI.

Prosody.

THE PRINCIPLES OF VERSIFICATION.

§ 683—§ 694.

§ 683. The laws of Maráthí versification are based chiefly upon *quantity*, *syllabification*, *rhyme*, and *accent*.

Note.—The rules of Maráthi versification are principally derived from Sanskrit.

§ 684. QUANTITY (मात्रा) indicates the *time taken in pronouncing an* (अक्षर) or syllable; SYLLABIFICATION (अक्षरपंक्ति) refers to the number of the syllables which compose a verse or a part of it; RHYME (यमक) is the *correspondence of sound in the terminating sounds* of two or more members of a verse; and ACCENT (यति । विराम) marks the sections into which a verse is divided.

§ 685. Quantity is reckoned by *mátrás* or moments, and each *short vowel* is supposed to be uttered in one moment, and hence it is equal to *one mátrá*. *A long vowel* takes twice as much time as is required to pronounce a short vowel, and is, therefore, equal in quantity to *two mátrás*. The diphthongs are included in the long vowels.

The length or quantity of the vowel is indicated by two signs, the macron or a transverse line (—) put on the top of a syllable to denote *two mátrás*, and the crescent (⌣) to denote *one mátrá*; thus कँ = 1 mátrá; बा=2 mátrás; बाॅप = 3 mátrás; वासा = 4 mátrás; मुॅखँ = 2 mátrás.

§ 686. There are some vowels which, though short, become long *by position*. They are these:—(1) a short vowel *with an anuswár over it*; (2) a short vowel, *followed by a visarga*; (3) a short vowel, *followed by a double consonant*; and (4) a short vowel (occasionally) *at the end of a verse*. Thus कुंकुम; दुःख; छिन्न; 'तेव्हां फुगवील कीं रमा गालें."

Note.—When the letter with an anuswár over it, or that followed by a double letter, is *not pronounced forcibly*, it does not become long; as जॅांव; रंवॅत; वॅन्या, तुॅक्षी, ऊॅभ्या.

§ 687. Rhyme forms an essential element of Maráthi versification, and the following verse is an example of it:—

जय जगदीशा ॥ दुरित विनाशा.
हर भव पाशा ॥ अधिक न आशा.

Note.—The terminating syllables of all the four members of the verse sound alike. The terminating letters must be of the *same organ*.

§ 688. Syllabification is essential to *some* kinds of versification, such as *slokas,* &c. In the following verse all the members correspond in the *number of their syllables,* although they do not all rhyme with each other :—

धांव मुकुंदा ॥ दुष्ट विमर्दा ॥ = 5 + 5 syllables.
धांव रमेशा ॥ दुःख विनाशा ॥ = 5 + 5 ,,

§ 689. A combination of the syllables, either according to their *number*, or their *length* (quantity) forms a गण or foot. When the syllables are combined according to their *number*, they make what may be called a *syllabic* foot, and when they are combined according to their *length*, they make a *non-syllabic* foot.

§ 690. A syllabic foot is composed of three अक्षर or syllables, and the three syllables may or may not *vary* in length; thus नमन is a syllabic foot.

Note.—The syllables composing a syllabic foot may be thus arranged according to their quantity :—

यमाचा = ⏑ - - ; राधिका = - ⏑ - ; ताराप = - - ⏑ ; नमन = ⏑ ⏑ ⏑ ; भास्कर = - ⏑ ⏑ ; जनास ⏑ - ⏑ ; समरा ⏑ ⏑ - ; मानावा - - -.
Thus there are *eight* classes of the syllabic feet, each of which is named by the *initial* letter of the above words. Thus य denotes the foot यमाचा or ⏑ - - ; र denotes the foot राधिका - ⏑ -, and so on.

§ 691. A non-syllabic foot, which is measured by the *length* of the syllables which compose it, consists of *four mátrás,* as जँ नाँ सँ = 4.

Note.—The non-syllabic feet are divided into *five* classes, according to the *position* and *quantity* of the syllables of which they consist. Thus, मेघा=4; सँविताँ=4 ; जँ नाँ सँ=4 ; भाँ जँ नँ=4 ; नँ वँ रँ सँ =4. The classes are named by the *initial* letters of these words. Thus, म denotes मेघा - - ; स denotes सँविताँ or ⏑ ⏑ -, and so on.

§ 692. The feet make a पाद or चरण a distich, and a verse consists of two or more distichs. Thus :—

द्रव्य मिळावें याकरितां । कां हलक्यांना आर्जवतां ॥
काय नव्हे हो तो धनवान् । ईशरमेच्या जो भगवान् ॥

Note.—In this verse there are four distichs, and each distich contains nine syllables, *i.e.* three syllabic feet, and fourteen mátrás, *i.e.* three and a half non-syllabic feet. The half-letters are not reckoned.

Note.—Each distich is usually marked off by *two perpendicular lines*, put at the end of it. Thus :—

लसे सळीं रुंद निरुंद काल्वे । गळोनि तेथें मकरंद काल्वे ॥
परागधी सांद्र तयांत रंगती । फुलांसवें भृंगतती तरंगती ॥

§ 693. The distichs are arranged into lines called अर्धे or halves. Thus :—

व्यापी निश्चल सत्ता । नाहीं ज्यास नियत्ता ॥
जा त्याला धरा चित्ता । तो नाशील चिंता ॥

§ 694. The accent marks off a section of the verse *where there is a slight pause made in reading or singing.* Thus :—

धांव मुकंदा दुष्ट विमर्दा ॥ धांव रमेशा दुःख विनाशा ॥
फार विपत्ती फारच भीती ॥ यांस हरावें सत्वर यावें ॥

Note.—The accent falls here on every fifth syllable.

☞ *Note.*—A *distich* is a division of the verses according to the *sense* as well as the *arrangement of the feet*, while the accent does not mark off *clauses*; it simply indicates the *place* where a pause should be made *in reading*. The syllable on which the accent falls ought to finish the *word*.

CHAPTER XXXII.

THE VARIETIES OF MARATHI VERSIFICATION.

§ 695—§ 706.

§ 695. The Maráthí poetry is divided into several classes, the principal of which are the *Áryás*, the *Ślokas*, the *Padas*, the *Sákís*, the *Dindís*, the *Ovís*, and the *Abhangs*.

The Áryá (आर्या).

§ 696. The Áryá verse is *wholly* reckoned by the *quantity* of its syllables. It consists of *four* distichs and *two lines.*

§ 697. In the arrangement of the feet care must be taken to have the *sixth foot*, in each line, to be *either* ज (⏑ – ⏑.) or न (⏑ ⏑ ⏑,), and to avoid the ज foot in every *odd* position. *i.e.* it should not be placed *first* or *third* or *fifth* or *seventh* in the line

1 2 3 4 5 6 7
तरला ययाति राजा, दर्शन होतांच संत रायाचें 30 ॥ No.
1 2 3 4 5 6 7
मवर्णन ष्वि सुवर्ान, करि गटचट कटक अंतरायाचें ॥

§ 698. The Áryás are sub-divided into *four* classes, viz., the Áryá proper, the Gíti (गीति), the Upagíti (उपगीति), the Udgiti (उद्गीति), and the Áryá-gíti (आर्या गीति).

The Aryá proper consists in all of 57 *mátrás*, 12 in the first and third, 18 in the second, and 15 in the fourth distich.

नूतनें पल्लवें कुंटला = १२ - अँसला तँरुं आणिला प्रियें नेंला - 18.
लॅवंकरें चाखोयाला = १२ = तोडोर्शी गँजें पँहा नेंला = ॥ 15.

The Gíti and the other metres differ from it only in the construction of the second and fourth distichs (§ 545).

The Gíti has 18 *mátrás* in every second and fourth distich, and the *whole* number of its *mátrás* amounts to 60 ; in the *Upagíti*, the second and fourth distichs contain 15 *mátrás* each; the *Udgíti* has 15 *mátrás* in the second and 18 in the fourth distichs; and the *Ar'yá-gíti* has 20 *mátrás* in each of the two distichs. The following is an example of the Arya-gíti :—

मी प्रिय करिन सकळवा; =12 m. आहे कीं व्रज अहो असाध्वस कळवा ॥ 20
निवसा घरिं घोरानीं, = 12 रात्रिं फिरावें शिवेच्छु न रिघो रानीं ॥ 20

The Śloka (श्लोक)

§ 699. The Śloka verse is determined by the *number of its syllables*. Its varieties are too many to be enumerated here.

It is usually composed of *four distichs*; and the distichs correspond to each other in the *number of their syllables*. The first two and the last two distichs rhyme with each other; sometimes, however, all the four rhyme. The accent forms an *essential* element of this verse, which falls in each distich on the same syllable. The distichs of a *śloka* may be composed of from one to any number of syllables, and may take any variety of feet. The following are a few specimens of *Ślokas* :—

(1)

धांव रमेशा॥ दुःख विनाशा॥
धांव मुकुंदा॥ दुष्ट विमर्दा॥

Note.—The distichs are composed of five syllables each, and rhyme by pairs.

(2)

दीन प्रेमा ये तूं रामा॥ सौख्यारामा हृद्विश्रामा॥
अंतःसद्मा नष्टच्छद्मा॥ संपद्धामा दे मत्कामा॥

Note.—The distichs are composed of eight syllables, and the accent falls upon every fourth syllable.

(3)

प्रगटलासि तूं नंदगोकुळीं॥ म्हणुनि इंदिरावास या स्थळीं॥
सकळही सुखी या व्रजीं हरी॥ विरहदुःखिता गोपसुंदरी॥

Note.—The distichs are composed of eleven syllables each.

(4)

अंगानें सरल तसाच तो मनानें॥ कालानें चल न तसाच तो धनानें॥
विद्येनें सरस तसाच तो मतीनें॥ उन्नीनें चतुर तसाच तो कृतीनें॥

Note.—The distichs are composed of 13 syllables each ; and the accent falls upon the *third* and the *tenth* syllables.

(5)

राम रघूत्तम कामरिपुप्रिय लोक शोकहर या परि भावें॥
दाशरथे तुज होउनियां पदिं लीन दीन जन बंधुसि गावें॥
आमरणस्मृति हेच असो वय याच साच सुपथांत सरावें॥
दे वरदा वर या शरणा प्रति पाप ताप जळधीस तरावें—

Note.—Each distich contains 23 syllables, and the accent falls upon the 6th, 6th, 6th, and 5th syllables.

The Padas (पद).

§ 700. The Pada is a stanza, composed of several lines, called *kaḍvens*, the first line of which is *repeated* at the end of each of the following lines, as a chorus or ध्रुवपद. The chorus may or may not correspond to the other lines in *quantity*.

A *kaḍven* is divided into two distichs, generally of unequal lengths, and is reckoned by the length of its syllables. When the *pada* is sung, the first distich of the *dhrupada* is *twice* repeated. Thus—

> आम्ही नमुं त्याला (नमुं त्याला) ॥ उपाधि नाहीं ज्याला ॥ ध्रु॰ ॥
> संशय उरला नाहीं ॥ अवघा ब्रह्मचि झाला पाहीं ॥ १ ॥ आम्ही॰ ॥
> स्वयंभु मुळचा आहे ॥ द्वैतपणासी गिळोनि राहे ॥ २ ॥ आम्ही॰ ॥
> समूळ भवचें हरलें ॥ पूर्ण निर्गुण जयासि कळलें ॥ ३ ॥ आम्ही॰ ॥
> रंगनाथ गुरुपायीं ॥ ज्याचा निश्चय दुसरा नाहीं ॥ ४ ॥ आम्ही ॰ ॥

Note.—Each line contains 28 *mátrás*; the first distich contains 12, and the second 16.

The Sákí (साकी).

§ 701. The *sáki* is a verse of *two lines*, and each line has seven feet or twenty-eight *mátrás*. The accent generally falls at the *end of the fourth foot* or the sixteenth *mátrá*. The last syllable of the lines is always long. Thus—

> दुग्ध पूर नसतां निजरूपी क्षीरसिंधु तो जैसा ॥
> वसंत आला नाहीं तरि तो उद्यानभाग जैसा ॥

Note.—The accent falls upon the 16 mátrá. The lines rhyme.

The Diṇḍí (दिंडी).

§ 702. The Diṇḍí is a verse of either two or four distichs, which correspond in the *sound* of their terminating syllables. Each distich has 19 *mátrás*, and the accent falls upon the ninth. The *mátrás* should be arranged thus :—

1st, A foot of *three mátrás, i. e.*–⏑, or ⏑–, or ⏑⏑⏑
2nd, A foot of *six mátrás, i. e.*– – –, or ⏑⏑⏑⏑⏑⏑,
or a combination of the short and long mátrás.
3rdly, A foot of *three mátrás* (as the first).
4thly, Ditto.
5thly, and lastly, A foot of *two long mátrás, i. e.*– –.

(I.) A Diṇḍí; composed of two distichs:—

कथा बोलूं हे मधुर सुधाधारा। होय शृंगारा करुण रसा थारा ॥ १ ॥
निषध राजा नळ नामधेय होता। वीरसेनाचा तनय महाहोता ॥ २ ॥

(II.) A Dindi; composed of four distichs;—

चौगुणीनें जरि पूर्ण शीतभानू। नळा ऐसा तरि कळानिधी मानूं ॥
प्रतापाचा जो न मालवे भानू। तया सारीखा कोण दुजा वानूं ॥

The Ovi (ओवी).

§ 703. This verse is determined *neither by the quantity nor the number* of its syllables. It is composed of *four distichs*, the first three of which rhyme with each other, while the last does not. It does not differ much, in construction, from prose, and is employed in the composition of narrative poems. Thus—

(1)

जें शक्तिचक्राचीं वेगळ ॥ जें ज्ञप्ति चिन्मात्र केवळ ॥
तें निजानंद निर्मळ ॥ परब्रह्म ॥ *Mukundaráya.*

(2)

जो सर्वां भूतांचे ठायीं ॥ द्वेषातें नेणेचि कांहीं ॥
आप पर जया नाहीं ॥ चैतन्य जैसें ॥ *Dnyándeva.*

(3)

कूर्परप्रहार लत्ताप्रहार ॥ मुष्टिप्रहार मस्तकप्रहार ॥
मोजोनि मारिती शतसहस्र ॥ उसणें घे घे म्हणोनी ॥ *Mukteswar.*

The Abhang (अभंग).

§ 704. The *Abhang* verse has two or four distichs, and each distich contains a *certain number of syllables.* Sometimes two short syllables are put for one long one.

§ 705. When the Abhang verse consists of *four distichs*, the first three have six syllables each, and the fourth has four. Thus,

काय वाणूं आतां ॥ न पुरे हीं वाणी ॥ मस्तक चरणीं ॥ ठेवीयला ॥ १ ॥
थोरींव सांडीली ॥ आपुली परिसें ॥ धन्य केलें कैसें ॥ लोखंडासी ॥२ ॥
जगाच्या कल्याणा ॥ संतांच्या विभूति ॥ देह कष्टविती ॥ उपकारें ॥ ३ ॥

Tukárám.

Note.—The second and third distichs rhyme with each other.

§ 706. When an Abhang is composed of two distichs, both the distichs have eight syllables; sometimes, however, the first stanza has six syllables. Both the distichs rhyme with each other. Thus—

जरी व्हावा तुज देव ॥ तरी सुलभ उपाव ॥
करीं मस्तक ठेंगणा ॥ लागें संतांच्या चरणा ॥   *Tukáram.*

There are various other classes of Abhangs, for which and other versifications the students should consult the *Navanita.*

CHAPTER XXXIII.

PECULIAR POETICAL FORMS.

§ 707—§ 718.

§ 707. Nouns and verbs, as well as some other parts of speech, assume peculiar forms in poetry, and sometimes the mode of constructing sentences also differs from that usually followed in prose. The following observations may, therefore, be found useful by the student of Maráthi poetry.

Nouns.

§ 708. The nouns ending in अ may optionally assume the final उ or ओ; ईश्वर God, or ईश्वरु; भाव faith, भावो. Thus,

आंदोळला गिरि कैलासु, ढळला वैकुंठींचा कळसु.—*Muktes'war.*
दुर्जेपर्णाचा भावो, आम्हा नाहीं ठावो, सर्वां देवदेवो आंकारला-*Dnyánadev.*

§ 709. We shall give below the noun ईश्वर Lord, declined in all the cases:—

Nom. ईश्वरु
Instr. ईश्वरें, ईश्वरेशीं-हिं-न. (एं sing., ईं plu.)
Dat. ईश्वरा, ईश्वरालागीं-लागुनि-तें-प्रत-सि, सी or शी.
Abl. ईश्वरापासुनि, पासुनियां-हुनि, हुनियां-पासाव.
Gen. ईश्वराचा-चेनि-चिया.
Loc. ईश्वरीं,-आं.

§ 710. The या and ई, employed to make up the crude-forms, are sometimes changed to इया and इये respectively:—

स्वगाडिबांस (for स्वगडयांस) वदे वचनामृता.—*Waman.*

राजे सोडविलियाविषीं (for सोडविल्याविषीं) आम्हांसि सहसा नाहीं आणें. *Mukteswar.*

आता ते करवि ते बुद्धिवेचा (for बुद्धिचा) लोप.—*Tukárám.*

Sometimes या is changed to ए :—

बोळावणेसाठीं पांडुरंग धरा कंठीं.—*Tukárám.*

उन्हाळेनीं न तापे, हिमवंतीं न कांपे.—*Dnyánadev.*

ADJECTIVES.

§ 711. The Adjectives are sometimes put in the same case with the noun which they qualify :

शल्य करावें भावें न असावें मानसें उदासीनें.—*Moropant.*

§ 712. Adjectives ending in अ are sometimes inflected like the adjectives in आ :—

हें सोंग सारीलें या रूपें अनंतें, पुढें ही बहु तें करणें आहे.—*Tukárám.*

§ 713. The adjectives are freely compared, as in Sanskṛit, with the particles of comparison (§ 520, § *Note*):—

बलवत्तर विधि ऐतो, थोराला थोरल्याचि तापातें.—*Moropant.*

त्रिभुवन पुज्यतम प्रभु सत्याचि हें, किंच तो असे ज्याही.—*Moropant.*

PRONOUNS.

§ 714. The personal pronouns assume various forms in poetry—

Nom.	मी I	तूं Thou	Plural
Acc.	मी	तूं	
Instr.		तुवा, त्वां, तां	
Dat.	मज, मातें, मस,	तुज, तूतें	आम्हांतें
Abl.			
Gen.	माझारी, माजा	तुजा	

तूं and मी are used in the accusative · मुनिनीं तूं चित्ती धरिलास.

§ 715. The domonstrative feminine pronouns ही and ती, and the relative जी, assume the forms हे, ते, and जे respectively; and the crude-forms ज्या and त्या, become जया and तया.

ज्ञानाविण जे जे कळा, ते ते आणाची भवकळा.—*Rámdas*
काय बापू आतां न पुरे हे वाणी, मस्तक चरणीं ठेवीतसें.—*Tukárám.*
म्हणे हरी प्रेहनि ने अवातें, मी कां निवारं सकळा तवातें.—*Waman*

§ 716. The forms असा, जसा, तसा, and कसा are optionally changed to ऐसा, जैसा, तैसा and कैसा. कोण who, is changed to कवण.

राजा म्हणे कवण तूं, कोणाचा पुत्र, कावगे वससि.—*Waman.*

The crude-form कशा of काय what? is changed to कासया.

कासया, गा, मज घातलें ह्यान्वा, नाहीं तुझा प्रेमा नित्य नवा.—*Tukárám*

The word इतर occurs in the forms एर and एरू—

तोची कृपानिधी वारील सांकडें, येर ते बापुडे काय रंक.—*Tukárám.*
येरू प्रवेशोनी सदनीं, म्हणे पारिसें, हो, याज्ञसेनी.—*Mukteswar.*

Note.—Sometimes pure Sanskrit forms are used; for instance, मम for माझा mine, तव for तुझा thine.

THE VERB.

§ 717. The past habitual forms are usually employed for all the forms of conjugation, present, past, and future:—

	1st Conjugation.			*2nd Conjugation.*		
1.	मीं	उठें sing.	आम्हीं उठूं plu.	मी	करीं,	आम्हीं करूं
2.	तूं	उठस	तुम्ही उठा	तूं	करीस,	तुम्ही करा
3.	तो, ती, तें उठे		ते, त्या, तीं, उठती	तो, ती, तें करी,		ते, त्या, तीं करिती

Imperative.

तूं उठि — तूं करि

Pluperfect Participle.

उठोन, उठोनि, उठुनि, उठु or उठोनियां; करोनि, करुनि, करोनियां.

Note.—The gerund is usually employed for the imperative or the subjunctive:—

आयुष्याच्या साधनें सच्चिदानंदपदवी घेणें (घ्यावी).—*Tukárám.*

Note.—Sometimes the second singular and third indicative plural forms assume सि and ति respectively; करिसि, करिताति.

Note.—Sometimes the root is put for the third person singular:—

शिष्याची जो न घे (घेई) सेवा.—*Tukárám.*

Note.—In the past second person plural लांत and लेत are sometimes substituted for लां:—

त्यांसि ह्मणे सुरपति वा ऐसा कां संकटांत आलांत. —
यमधर्म ह्मणे तया दोघींयांसीं कांरे केशवासि मुकलेति.—

Note.—Some verbs assume peculiar forms in the past tense:

पातली for पावली (Sk. प्राप्ता, प्राप्) went
हासिंनला for हांसला laughed.
धाविन्नला for धांवला ran.
खादिला for खाल्ला ate.
काढियलें for काढिलें took out.

Note.—The future terminations in ए and ई are indiscriminately used.

तुज राखेल (for राखील) कोण.—*Eknath.*
पूर्ण ब्रह्म सनातन, मी पाहेन डोळेभरी.—*Sridhar.*

Note.—As the base of the second conjugation is made up with ई, so in poetry the base of the first conjugation is formed by ए:—

तूं कैसी रमतां ह्मणेसि पळ तु दोघां ऋषी शापिति.—*Vitthal.*
निजेला मूर्च्छेनें भुजगपाति तो मृत्युशयनीं.—*Waman.*

§ 718. Passive forms made up with इज or इजे (Sk. य) are used often in poetry, both actively and passively. They are thus conjugated:—

PRESENT TENSE.

Kartari Construction.

	Singular.	*Plural.*
1.	मीं करिजेतों *m.*,-तें *f.*,-तें *n.*	आह्मी करिजेतों
2.	तूं करिजेतोस *m.*,-तीस *f.*-तेंस *n.*	तुम्ही करिजेतां
3.	तो, ती, तें करिजेतो *m.*,-ती *f.*,-तें *n.*	ते, त्या तीं करिजेतात

Bháve Construction.

	Singular	Plural	
1.	म्या	आह्मीं	करिजेतें
2.	त्वा	तुम्हीं	
3.	त्यानें, तिनें	त्यांनीं	

PAST TENSE.

Karmani Construction.

	Singular	Plural	
1.	म्या	आह्मीं	करिजेला-ली-लें,-ले ल्या-लीं
2.	त्वा	तुह्मीं	
1.	त्यानें, तिनें, त्यानें	त्यांनीं	

FUTURE TENSE.

Bhâve Construction.

3. म्या आम्हीं
2. त्वा तुम्हीं
3. त्यानें, तिनें, त्यानें, त्यांनीं

(all with) करिजेल

Imperative Mood.

त्वा or तुम्हीं करिजे, कीजे

Past Participle.

करिजेला-ली-लें *sing.* -ले-ल्या-लीं *plu.*

Note.—नाहीं is changed to नोहे; नव्हे, or नोव्हे is substituted for न + हो.

APPENDIX.

Note A.

1. Modi Characters.

1. The Modí letters are thus written and pronounced :—

Vowels.

𑘀 *a*, 𑘁 *á*, 𑘂 *i*, 𑘄 *u*, 𑘊 *e*, 𑘋 *ai*, 𑘌 *o*, 𑘍 *au*, 𑘀𑘽 *am*, 𑘀𑘾 *ah*

Consonants.

𑘎 *ka*	𑘚 *ḍa*	𑘦 *ma*
𑘏 *kha*	𑘛 *ḍha*	𑘧 *ya*
𑘐 *ga*	𑘜 *ṇa*	𑘨 *ra*
𑘑 *gha*	𑘝 *ta*	𑘩 *la*
𑘒 *ṅa*	𑘞 *tha*	𑘪 *va*
𑘓 *cha*	𑘟 *da*	𑘫 *śa*
𑘔 *chha*	𑘠 *dha*	𑘬 *sha*
𑘕 *ja*	𑘡 *na*	𑘭 *sa*
𑘖 *jha*	𑘢 *pa*	𑘮 *ha*
𑘗 *ña*	𑘣 *pha*	𑘯 *ḷa*
𑘘 *ṭa*	𑘤 *ba*	𑘎𑘿𑘬 *ksha*
𑘙 *ṭha*	𑘥 *bha*	𑘕𑘿𑘗 *dnya*

2. The following are three Modí *Bárákhaḍis*, or modes of syllabification :—

ka	*ká*	*ki*	*kí*	*ku*	*kú*	*ké*	*kai*	*ko*	*kau*	*kam*	*kah.*
𑘎	𑘎𑘰	𑘎𑘱	𑘎𑘲	𑘎𑘳	𑘎𑘴	𑘎𑘹	𑘎𑘺	𑘎𑘻	𑘎𑘼	𑘎𑘽	𑘎𑘾

ga	*gá*	*gi*	*gí*	*gu*	*gú*	*ge*	*gai*	*go*	*gau*	*gam*	*gah.*
𑘐	𑘐𑘰	𑘐𑘱	𑘐𑘲	𑘐𑘳	𑘐𑘴	𑘐𑘹	𑘐𑘺	𑘐𑘻	𑘐𑘼	𑘐𑘽	𑘐𑘾

ṭa	*ṭá*	*ṭi*	*ṭí*	*ṭu*	*ṭú*	*ṭe*	*ṭai*	*ṭo*	*ṭau*	*ṭam*	*ṭah.*
𑘘	𑘘𑘰	𑘘𑘱	𑘘𑘲	𑘘𑘳	𑘘𑘴	𑘘𑘹	𑘘𑘺	𑘘𑘻	𑘘𑘼	𑘘𑘽	𑘘𑘾

Note B.

Parsing.

(1) रावजी रोज येतो Rávjí comes every day.

रावजी is a porper noun of the 1st declension, (but declined irregularly,) 3rd singular masculine, and in the nominative case, being nominative to येतो.

रोज is an adverb modifying येतो.

येतो is an irregular intransitive verb of the 1st conjugation, present indicative, the 3rd singular masculine, and being in agreement with the nominative, is in the subjective construction.

(2) त्वा यावें you should come.

त्वा is a personal pronoun, 2nd singular, and in the instrumental case of agency, being nominative to यावें.

यावें is an irregular intransitive verb of the 1st conjugation, present subjective, the 3rd singular neuter, and is in the neuter construction, as it does not agree with its nominative त्वा.

(3) राघोबा पुस्तक वाचितो Rághobá reads a book.

राघोबा is a proper noun of the 1st declension, (but declined irregularly,) 3rd singular masculine, and in the nominative case, being nominative to वाचितो.

पुस्तक is a common noun of the 2nd declension, 3rd singular neuter, and in the accusative case, governed by वाचितो.

वाचितो is a regular transitive verb of the 2nd conjugation, 3rd singular masculine, present indicative, and, being in agreement with its nominative राघोबा, is in the subjective construction.

(4) तिनें आंबा कापिला she cut the mango.

तिनें is a personal pronoun, 3rd singular feminine, and is in the intrumental case of agency, being nominative to कापिला.

आंबा is a common noun of the 1st declension, the 3rd singular masculine, and is in the accusative case, governed by कापिला.

कापिला is a regular transitive verb of the 2nd conjugation, 3rd singular masculine, of the past indicative, and, agreeing with its object, is in the objective construction.

(5) त्या लेंकराला मारूं नको do not beat that child.

त्या is a demonstrative pronoun in the crude form, joined to लेंकराला.

लेंकराला is a common noun of the 3rd declension (but irregularly declined), the 3rd singular masculine, and is in the dative case, being the direct object to मारूं नको.

मारूं नको is a regular transitive verb of the negative form, 2nd singular of the present imperative, and, agreeing with the nominative तूं thou understood, is in the subjective construction.

(6) मला यमनीनें सोडिलें Yamani unloosed me.

मला is a personal pronoun, 1st singular masculine, and is in the dative case, being direct object to सोडिलें.

यमनीनें is a proper noun of the 1st declension, of the 3rd singular feminine, of the instrumental case of agency, and is nominative to सोडिलें.

सोडिलें is a regular transitive verb of the 2nd conjugation, the past indicative, 3rd singular, and being in the neuter construction, is of the neuter gender, and does not agree either with the subject or the object.

(7) ती त्याला हांक मारितांच तो उठेल he will arise as soon as she calls out to him.

ती is a personal pronoun, being nominative absolute by reason of the following participle मारितां.

त्याला is a personal pronoun, and is in the dative case, being object to हांक मारणें.

हांक मारतां is the present participle of the compound verb हांक मारणें, being joined to ती.

च is an adverb, modifying हांक मारितां.

तो is a personal pronoun, third person singular, nominative case, nominative to उठेल.

उठेल is a regular intransitive verb of the 1st conjugation, of the future indicative, the 3rd singular masculine, and, agreeing with the nominative तो, is in the subjective construction.

(8) मला जाववतें I can go.

मला is a personal pronoun, 1st singular masculine, in the dative case, and is nominative to जाववतें.

जाववतें is a potential intransitive verb of the 1st conjugation, the present indicative, 3rd singular neuter, and, being in the neuter construction, does not agree with its nominative मला.

(9) त्याला गेलें पाहिजे he must go.

त्याला is a dative nominative to गेलें पाहिजे.

गेलें पाहिजे is a compound obligational verb of the present tense, and being in the neuter construction, does not agree with the nominative.

NOTICES OF THE GRAMMAR.

Opinions on the First Edition.

"Of all the Sanskritic languages of Hindustan, Maráṭhí is the most difficult, on account of the variety of its grammatical forms, its idiomatic phraseology, and the richness of its vocabulary. We should, therefore, naturally expect a grammarian to have endeavoured to simplify as much as possible the introduction to the grammar of that language, and to present to the student only its most essential and characteristic features. In this respect we have always considered Stevenson's Grammar, which has for many years been the principal guide to Maráṭhí, as a signal failure, and we should only account for the fact of its having gone through four editions from the analogy of the Eton Latin Grammar, and similar mediæval institutions, which have sturdily kept their ground in the face of infinitely superior works by Madvig and others . . . A far more ambitious grammar than the elementary book just noticed [Mr. Bellairs' Grammar] has, simultaneously with it, appeared at Bombay, under the title 'The Student's Manual of Maráṭhí Grammar.' Characterised by the same lucidity as the former, but arranged on a more comprehensive plan, it shows on every page that its anonymous author has sought to apply in it the method followed in the most recent investigations on Comparative Grammar. Though intended for practical purposes only, it is calculated to prove of great service also to the scientific inquirer into the character of the language of which it treats."—*Trübner's Literary Record.*

"We have much pleasure in directing the attention of students of Maráṭhí to a new grammar of the language, published by a Native scholar. It supplies a desideratum long felt by European students of Maráṭhí, who have hitherto had no other book for their guidance than the work of Dr. Stevenson. The Manual has higher claims than that of being an elementary treatise on Maráṭhí Grammar. It is the most scientific and critical grammar of an Indian vernacular we have seen, and throws much light on the origin of the vocables, inflections, and various other points relating to the structure of Maráṭhí and other cognate languages. The book is mainly designed for those preparing for Matriculation, for whom it appears to be well-suited."—*The Times of India.*

"Upon the whole we think the Manual is well-fitted for introduction as a text-book into the High Schools."—*The Bombay Educational Record.*

"I repeat that I think it is creditable to the author, and I have no doubt that it will be found useful both to advanced Native students and to European students of Maráṭhí."—*Major Thomas Candy, Maráṭhí Translator to the Government Educational Department.*

"I am glad to find that Mr. Navalkar is about to publish a revised and improved edition of his excellent Maráṭhí Grammar, which has already found much acceptance in Western India and elsewhere. I have no doubt that the new edition of his work will prove a valuable acquisition both to those commencing the study of Maráṭhí, and to those who already make free use of that language. The junction of both parts of the work in one volume is a convenient arrangement."—*Rev. Dr. Wilson, D.D.*

Opinions on the Second Edition.

"For those who wish to master Maráṭhí this book will be simply invaluable, and it ought to be in the hands of every student who intends to Matriculate in this hitherto much neglected language."—*The Times of India.*

"The Student's Maráṭhí Grammar ought to be welcomed as an important contribution to the educational literature of the time. This is the work of a highly educated mind and one which takes special delight in linguistic research. We cordially recommend this book, and hope that it may find a wide acceptance among the students of the language, both European and Native."—*The Bombay Gazette.*

"I have gone over the greater portion of the book with great interest. It is a systematic work on Grammar. It is a good help to the teacher, who will find in it much useful information on every department of the Maráṭhí language."—*V. S. Apte, Esq., M.A., Principal of the Fergusson College, Poona.*

"I have seen enough of it (the Maráṭhí Grammar) to be able to congratulate you honestly on the good use you have made of the Science of Language in giving life to the mere art of Language. This is the only way to make the study of any grammar, not only more attractive, but really refreshing and invigorating."—*Prof. Max Müller.*

BY THE SAME AUTHOR.

AN INTRODUCTION TO MARATHI GRAMMAR,

Being an abridgment of the larger Grammar.

"It is a philosophical and withal a simple statement of the principles and idioms of Maráṭhí speech and writing, well-fitted to help foreigners who wish to know Maráṭhí philosophically and correctly."—*An American Scholar.*

"It is a marvel of condensation, and it is simplicity itself. But its special value to my mind is in the large number of peculiar and irregular idioms which are collected in its pages."—*A Scottish Scholar.*

"An Introduction to Maráṭhí Grammar has been sanctioned for use in the High Schools."—*The Director of Public Instruction, Bombay.*